YEATS'S ICONO

Yeats's Iconography

by

F.A.C. WILSON

METHUEN & CO LTD
11 NEW FETTER LANE EC 4

*First published 1960
by Victor Gollancz Ltd
First published in this series 1969
© 1960 by F. A. C. Wilson
Printed and bound in Great Britain
by Butler & Tanner Ltd, Frome and London
SBN 416 29890 7*

This book is sold subject to the condition that it shall not, by way of trade or otherwise, be lent, re-sold, hired-out, or otherwise circulated without the publisher's prior consent in any form of binding or cover other than that in which it is published and without a similar condition including this condition being imposed upon the subsequent purchaser.

For
KATHLEEN RAINE
and
THOMAS RICE HENN

Thunder has done its worst among its twigs,
Where the great crest yet blackens, never pruned,
But in its heart, alway
Ready to push new verdurous boughs, whene'er
The rotten saplings near it fall and leave it air,
Is all antiquity and no decay.
Rich, though rejected by the forest-pigs,
Its fruit, beneath whose rough, concealing rind
They that will break it find
Heart-succouring savour of each several meat,
And kernell'd drink of brain-renewing power,
With bitter condiment and sour,
And sweet economy of sweet,
And odours that remind
Of haunts of childhood and a different day.

—*Coventry Patmore 'Arbor Vitae'*

CONTENTS

page

Author's Note — 9

PART ONE

Chapter One: Introductory — 13

PART TWO

Chapter Two: *At The Hawk's Well* — 27
Chapter Three: *The Only Jealousy Of Emer* — 73
Chapter Four: *The Cat And The Moon* — 128
Chapter Five: *Calvary* — 163
Chapter Six: *The Dreaming Of The Bones* — 204
Appendix to Part Two — 241

PART THREE

Chapter Seven: Twelve Related Poems — 247
Appendix to Part Three — 304

Notes — 307
Select Bibliography — 333
Index — 341

AUTHOR'S NOTE

THIS STUDY IS a sequel to my *W. B. Yeats And Tradition*, and the Yeats scholar may like to take all my work in conjunction; but I have tried to make it possible for the two books to be read independently. My introduction is a defence of the critical method used for both works.

I want to begin my text with acknowledgment to Kathleen Raine and T. R. Henn, both for the many invaluable suggestions I have had from them and for the benefit I have obtained from their own writings. I expect I have been more influenced by *The Lonely Tower* than by any other Yeats criticism, and I owe a good deal as well to the sections on Yeats in *The Apple And The Spectroscope* and *The Harvest Of Tragedy*. I have also been enormously helped by Kathleen Raine's book on Blake (soon to appear), and I think I should say something here of the importance of this book in my field; of its importance in its own field it is not my place to speak. What Kathleen Raine has done for Yeats scholarship is to present a view of Blake which comes very close indeed to Yeats's own view of him; and any scholar who wants to know how Yeats read the poet to whom he owed the most has to master, and probably always will have to master, the learned arguments in her book.

I am also most grateful to Mrs. Yeats for information and advice, for allowing me to read certain manuscripts, and for her kindness and hospitality to me. Mrs. Yeats felt, and I agree with her, that Yeats would not have wanted quoted the rough drafts he made of the nameless, unfinished play referred to here as *The Bridegroom*; but I am indebted to her for letting me publish a synopsis of the plot as Appendix I.

Both Cambridge University and the University of Queensland have encouraged me with financial help; and I am indebted to Mr. F. Le P. Warner for much help with my notes.

Most of my terms were defined in *Yeats And Tradition* and I will not rehearse them here. One term that needs comment is *participation mystique*, which I do not use in the pejorative sense of some Jungian writers, but as far as possible without 'loaded' meaning of any kind.

F. A. C. WILSON,
August 15th, 1959.

PART ONE

INTRODUCTORY

CHAPTER ONE

INTRODUCTORY

I

THE AIM OF this book is to interpret what Yeats meant by the symbolism of five of his plays, *Four Plays For Dancers* and *The Cat And The Moon*; also by that of a number of related lyrics. I should stress, once and for all, that I am concerned primarily with what the symbols meant for the poet himself; Yeats of course hoped that the 'words on the page' would work for him, and he also believed in a collective unconscious which would operate to suggest his archetypal meanings to all readers; but it can of course be maintained that communication fails. I myself doubt whether this ever happens; but I cannot prove this statement in a book not concerned with technique; and this is why I define my field as I have done. What Yeats believed his plays and poems to mean is a valid field for scholarship; and the meaning he attached is certainly the archetypal meaning, which is therefore my main preoccupation.

My previous book, *Yeats And Tradition*, explains Yeats's motivation in writing an archetypal poetry, and I must refer the reader to this for a detailed *résumé* of his theories of poetry and drama. Briefly, he thought that any symbol which at some time or other in the world's history had been a part of religion would retain for ever, through Anima Mundi, a peculiar depth and power of communication. Not every poem he wrote is fully symbolic, of course, but his great symbols will tend to derive from one or other of world religions and (since Yeats was a heterodox religious thinker) they tend to derive from Kabbalism, alchemy, Neoplatonism and the religions of the East, from Swedenborg and Boehme, at least as often as from the Christian tradition. Yeats himself saw no disparity between his several conventions: like Jung, he believed there were close symbolic correspondences between world religions, as would be natural if all emanated from the mind in contact with absolute truth; if, as he supposed, all creeds despite differences of dogma were basically at one. Even within a single poem, then, Yeats will juxtapose symbols coined from several distinct faiths, and he will do so always with absolute fidelity to their original religious significance, which will be for him the significance laid down in the metaphysical commentaries he enjoyed reading. Because we know that Yeats would not deviate from his 'traditional' meanings, and because we know what his authorities were, it is not hard to deduce the intentional meaning of any of his works.

We know that Yeats would not so deviate because, in the first place, he tells us so himself; and also because he assumes a similar fidelity in interpreting the work of other 'traditional' poets. In his three volume work on Blake, he invariably takes for granted that Blake used his symbols eclectically and with a sense of responsibility to tradition (the tradition having become a part of his own experience): the wolf symbol will have the significance it carries in alchemy, symbolism of the eyes its Neoplatonic connotation.[1] In his two essays on Shelley he works on similar principles, generally with recourse to the Platonic symbolic system. He applies the same method to other poets and painters; to the Platonist Botticelli, for instance; while his belief that the archetypal meaning enforces itself inevitably and as a natural process makes him use his technique even on so half-conscious a symbolist as William Morris. All this may seem unpleasantly 'mathematical' to the modern literary critic (my own view is that the method is entirely justifiable, and I think Bowra has shown how deeply religious and also how eclectic the symbolist poet tends to be)[2] but it is nevertheless Yeats's own habitual technique of interpretation and in using it on himself I am proceeding as he proceeded with others and thus by a means that surely has his sanction. It surely hardly matters whether my method is 'academically respectable' when it is one my author prefers; aside from the fact that Yeats may have known more than the academics of the nature of poetry, the student of the intentional meaning has a duty to follow his lead.

I think I am using the technique which will show us what Yeats meant by his poems at the time he wrote them; and I would like to insist on this last phrase. It has been maintained that the poet in the act of creation intends no 'meaning' but simply to express sequences of images flowing up from his subconscious; and this seems to me an unsafe generalisation, bound up with the rather prevalent hope that all poets may be made to seem primitives. Some poets surely are more self-conscious craftsmen than others, and Yeats, as his laborious revisions show, was one of the most highly conscious craftsmen in our language. At least by the time he began to revise, he knew very well what effects a poem needed to achieve, and the finished poems are directed towards achieving them. Or if this is not conceded, at least it must be admitted that Yeats passionately sought after the archetypal connotations of his symbols before (sometimes immediately before) he began to coin them; so that consciously or subconsciously, the archetypes will affect the words on the page; if we do not like to think of the poet manipulating his symbols to given ends, we are left to suppose that, towards the same ends, his symbols manipulated *him*. But I should prefer to concentrate on my first proposition: if we think of Yeats as a highly sophisticated, highly conscious, symbolist, we shall be most likely to understand why he revised so methodically, and why he gave his finished works the inflections they have.

II

The bulk of this book is concerned with *Five Plays For Dancers*,* dance-plays modelled on the fifteenth-century Noh theatre. Yeats founded on the Japanese theatre after a protracted search and because he could find no model nearer home for the archetypally symbolic dramas he wanted to write: for a detailed account of the parent form a reader might use my previous book or Hiro Ishibashi's thesis on the subject.[3] In this sequel I shall have to take some, at least, of this information for granted, since I want to use the present preface to investigate an extremely vexed problem of another kind: how far the symbolic meaning of the plays is relevant to their effect as theatre.

My previous book to some extent broke fresh ground and its findings were comparatively unsupported;† but several critics have been before me in my present field. Bjersby[4] has anticipated my overall reading of *Emer*, though not, perhaps I may say, penetrating to point of detail; several critics have grasped Yeats's general intentions in *Calvary*; and a paragraph in Miner gives me support for a central thesis in my *The Dreaming Of The Bones*.[5] Becker remarks that there is definite symbolic intention in *The Cat And The Moon*, though he thinks the symbolism too private and remote to repay scrutiny.[6] Only *At The Hawk's Well* has been seen as comparatively straightforward work, and only here does Yeats's preface give no hint to the symbolic inflection; but the play follows immediately upon his resolution to write plays as heavily symbolic as 'Blake in the mood of *Thel*';[7] and we have further to accept the probability of an interior symbolism to explain why Yeats chose to bracket *At The Hawk's Well*

* I.e. *Four Plays For Dancers*, plus *The Cat And The Moon*.
† Save, of course, by Virginia Moore in her valuable book *The Unicorn*, to which I should like to acknowledge a copious debt over the whole of my research.

with three other plays of such a nature. (In the end, as my chapter on the poems will show, we have to take this play as fully symbolic because it is the projection of an image-cluster with which Yeats had been experimenting, in full awareness of the archetypal meaning, for years.) I hope, then, that I may presume some measure of justification for my readings, and go straight to the question of how far the readings are relevant to stage performance.

Yeats, even when (as here) he wrote for a drawing-room audience of 'initiates', did not expect them to come immediately, or primarily, on his esoteric symbolism. One's immediate reaction is of course at the level of pure narrative, and I think he would have been satisfied with a response at that or at any level of suggestion above, provided this response was in conformity with the archetypal reading; including, and culminating in, a response to the total 'traditional' pattern. After several hearings, I think he hoped, the listener equipped to do so might discover his inmost intention; it might disclose itself in the theatre, or when the aesthetic experience was resumed in privacy; and his urbane prefaces generally contain hints (plain statement would have destroyed the 'opacity' he strove for; he always needed to make a play a mystery) which are designed to help towards such an evaluation. Sometimes, no doubt, looking in retrospect at a play and pleased to see what had been done at the level of pure narrative, Yeats would deprecate his symbolist intentions; but for the full truth regarding his attitude to his work we need probably to look at a passage in *Essays* 1931-6, which ought I think to become a crux in Yeats criticism.[8] There, he says that our reaction to a work with symbolic potentiality tends to be curiously ambiguous; the mind's surface receives it as pure narrative (at what he calls the level of the 'child') while, at the same time and without the least sense of contradiction, a deeper level of the mind takes pleasure in the archetypal connotations and pattern (what he calls the 'sage's' reading). In what follows, I take this statement as definitive, and I hope a reader will allow for that strange fission of the mind that takes place in the presence of symbolic art; if I say little of the plays as *theatre*, of the surface pattern and significance, this is not that I am unaware of these things but because they are less than immediately relevant. One cannot write two books at once, and the first student of Yeats's ultimate symbolic intentions ought to be single-minded.

Symbols suggest and do not state, and the commentator is between a Scylla and a Charybdis: he can write obliquely and indirectly at the cost of seeming vague (this surely is the fate that overtakés some of

Yeats's own prefaces like that to *Fighting The Waves*) or he can write overtly and definitively and run the risk of being called crudely dogmatic. No commentary is of much use which fails ultimately to communicate and I have therefore chosen the latter alternative: no doubt I am often improperly precise. Yet the sphere of suggestion of an archetypal symbol can be directly presented: this is the *raison d'être* of much Jungian writing and I doubt whether I am more of a precisian than Jung. Perhaps what I can best do here is define what I take to be the function of my commentary, which is certainly not presented in pedantry, or in an authoritarian spirit, or as a substitute for the reader's own sensibility and finesse. I would like it to be read, then put aside; and after an interval of some weeks the plays and poems might be returned to in independence of it. In this way Yeats's shaping sources might be assimilated, in the normal passage of time, into the reader's own personal memory, so that he can re-enter upon the aesthetic experience with an awareness of the informing archetypes, but not with an awareness which overshadows or is intrusive. It is of course in the reader's own discretion, but I should be sorry if my essays were applied more directly than this.

III

A study of the intentional meaning tends, as has rightly been said of my previous work, to become a study of the intellectual sub-structure of a play or a poem; an examination of the ideological soil out of which it has flowered. Because I am less anxious to make these essays easy than to make them honest, I sometimes digress into the philosophical background of my texts, even where only a part of the underlying metaphysics is projected into a given work. One wants to provide a full insight into the intellectual sub-structure, and if one says only what is of the first relevance, Yeats's basic religious ideas are likely to seem eccentric in being private and idiosyncratic, which is something they generally are not. (They may be eccentric without being idiosyncratic, if we are brash enough to write off Buddhism and Hinduism and Neoplatonism as eccentric ideologies, but they certainly send down roots into culture and anthropology and do not survive vicariously as private fantasies.) I have, I think, as much right to include data of secondary relevance as the commentators on Shakespeare to present material tangential, but importantly tangential, to his own plays. I conceive of myself sometimes as providing the annotations to Yeats's work, writing in the marginalia.

My research soon convinced me that each of *Five Plays For Dancers* embodies a certain aspect of Yeats's metaphysics: *At The Hawk's Well* the religion of the Self (subjectivity); *Emer* reincarnation; *The Cat And The Moon* the cyclic process of history; *Calvary* objectivity; *The Dreaming Of The Bones* the life after death. It seems of the first scholarly importance to demonstrate that Yeats's 'system' had evolved, in so much detail, so long before *A Vision* came out: and also to demonstrate *why* it evolved on the lines it did. But, unless one is to begin with a preliminary study of the philosophy in isolation, which in divorce from the poetry would be a crabbed undertaking (and would have the disadvantage of separating precept from practice so as to be largely confusing), one has to present Yeats's ideas in some sort of sequence: they cannot be all taken together, and are perhaps best considered as they become 'tangentially relevant' to a given play. The sequence I choose is therefore conditioned by what I think the best order for study of the plays themselves, and if there is overlapping, even if the essays sometimes become hard work for the reader, this I believe to be the necessary limitation of a necessary procedure. Elaborate thoroughness, even reiteration, are sometimes necessities of scholarship; I would rather be tediously informative than dynamically virile where virility would be of little help. When the plays have been examined I take up with twelve related poems (in fact many more are considered incidentally) and this is because my reading of the poems seems to me to underline and confirm my reading of the plays. If the reader is not convinced by part two of this book alone, there is still hope that he may be convinced by the supplementary data; and if I hold back some crucial evidence until my last chapter, this is largely so as to provide documentation where it can most easily be inserted, and so as not to stretch out the early essays to disproportionate length. The structure of the book is a circle and the ideal reader, when he has finished the last chapter, might even care to read the first sections again.

My first book says something of Yeats's metaphysical system, and (if these essays are to stand independently) they are bound to contain a certain amount of repetitious matter; but generally speaking I think my arguments are new. I have not written before of Yeats's theories of reincarnation and physical beauty and have written only superficially of his theory of subjective and objective man. Much remains to be said of his theory of history as well, and this subject I resume in my *The Cat And The Moon*, where I may seem to rest too much weight on a slight structure. Yet *The Cat And The Moon is* about history, and one has to know all the minutiae of Yeats's theory to appreciate his ingenious but extremely remote symbolism; the trouble is that the re-creation of his theory needs undue *space*, and it might seem that I am insisting on the symbolic element (here subsidiary) at the expense of the simple narrative (here perhaps the play's chief virtue). I have tried to compensate for this by giving more space than elsewhere to analysis at the surface level; but the reader's best safeguard is to use the essay as I have suggested: to read it, let it lie dormant, then go back to the play with a will to experience it on its two distinct planes.

What, when all is said, is the virtue of a study of a poet's ideology? I do not imagine that poetry is morality, the mere communication of metaphysical or kindred ideas (though I do think that some Yeats critics tend to equate poetry and sensuousness, to make reading his verse almost a sub-erotic experience, by concentrating at all costs on the surface sheen). Poetry I suppose among other of its functions teaches 'what it feels like' to believe certain things, and to receive this communication it is necessary not only to have a vague sense that belief is going on, but to know what is being believed. John Crowe Ransom has spoken of the 'special gravity' of Yeats's verse,[9] our perception even of such a poem as 'The Three Bushes' (for all its apparent levity), that it is concerned with and arises from 'heart-mysteries'; and our response to that sense of profundity is in part a desire for exploration; we want to possess the poem wholly, to make it, as a totality, so far as possible part of ourselves. Sometimes, no doubt, the exploration of a text may disappoint us, and then we know that what seemed to be profound was not so, or not for us; but Yeats has many plays and poems where the result is very different, and it is arguable that these are his greatest works. *At The Hawk's Well* surely grows in stature as the symbolism is understood, and so (even if we do not believe as Yeats does) will the opening chorus of *Emer*. In such contexts, Yeats is not to be thought of as a mere stylist, whose perfect surface might perhaps pall with time; he is the true symbolist, using style and substance to attack our intelligence, emotion and senses equally, which is what symbolism aims to do.

IV

Yeats's poetry has the profundity it has because of the habits of thought to which he was given, not in spite of them: this is my cardinal conclusion after five years of study. These ideas gave rise to these emotions, and these emotions served as the dynamic of his verse: the poetry itself is testimony to the dignity, for the temperament equipped to receive them, of alchemy, the Kabbala, Neoplatonism and the other heterodox sources which Yeats used. Because charlatans have exploited them, these religions are now inseparably linked with charlatanry, but that Yeats's greatest symbolic poems use them with great purity I have very little doubt. He believed easily (and there is no especial virtue in believing only with difficulty); he believed particularly easily in whatever contributed to his intuitive perception of 'human dignity'; and for this reason he was naturally drawn to the 'subjective' faiths with their exaltation of the Self, rather than to an orthodox Christianity which deprecated the values of the personality and relied on salvation from without. He had intimate knowledge of most of the religions he used: as the member of a Rosicrucian order he had not much to learn of alchemy; he became a translator of the Upanishads; the years after 1914 saw him engrossed in the study of Neoplatonism, especially of the Platonic symbology; his position is exposed (if at all) only as a Kabbalist, where he was satisfied with Mathers's translation and did not read deeply beyond. Wherever they become relevant, his authorities are reconstructed in what follows, and they are reconstructed in a spirit of sympathy; though I neither hope nor want to 'convince' an unsympathetic reader or to 'vindicate' any kind of cause. I am not writing a history of Yeats's tradition, to demonstrate that all religions *are* one or that there is in fact a subjective convention of symbolism and belief extending from ancient Egypt through Neoplatonism and alchemy to heterodox religious circles at the present time; what matters here is simply that Yeats believed these things, and we know this because he says so himself. Nor am I much moved by the fact that some of Yeats's sources are 'academically disreputable', that Hermes Trismegistus, for instance, was not an ancient Egyptian; whatever criticism of this kind is urged, he was good enough for Milton and Blake as well as Yeats; and if we want to know why these poets found his writings so valuable, we have only to read for ourselves to find out.

These are necessary disclaimers, but I do not want to avoid positive statement; I said in my last book that I am frankly sympathetic to Yeats's metaphysical position, and it may help to say here what I find most valuable in his thought. I have written in my main text of Yeats's conception of heaven, and his charity and *awaré* (gentle sympathy) here is a great achievement; but the main advance he made on other religious thinkers of the period lies clearly in his theory of the Self. Now that poetry and theology are almost totally divorced, this statement is difficult to amplify in short space; but one has only to read

Sherrard,[10] for example, to see how totally and how injuriously religious thought at the turn of the century had attached itself to the concept of an externalised God. The pendulum is now swinging, and modern theology has begun to reassert the godhead within us, noetic intelligence and much else; but the fact remains that Yeats, almost alone, perceived this truth for himself fifty years before the professional metaphysicians, and defended his isolated position with consummate integrity all his life. He further postulated two polar religious temperaments, one of which found it hard to conceive of God other than objectively (i.e. as a being external to ourselves), and one wonders whether in this he is not still in advance of modern thought. It would be easier to dismiss him as mistaken, but Schuon's most recently englished book proposes two polar 'affective' and 'intellective' temperaments, which correspond in many salient respects with Yeats's 'objective' and 'subjective' types.[11] Yeats may have gone too far in supposing that essential Christianity is an objective religion, but it is fair to say that the historical development of Christianity has been towards objectivity, and with this reservation I think his theory of extroverted and introverted worship is considerable, and may indeed be altogether in the right.

When we come to Yeats's theory of reincarnation we are on rather different ground, for we have at once to dispense with all prejudices of ultimate right and wrong. As Yeats says himself,[12] one type of temperament will always be moved by such beliefs, while another will prefer the Christian theory of the soul: 'eternity expresses itself through contradiction'.[13] His own shaping ideas are those of half the human race; he grew up in the 'nineties, and this in the one decade of modern English social history when there was an intellectual climate favourable to their reception;[14] and he persevered beyond the mere silliness of the cliques to a personal religion of great integrity. The sincerity and stature of his mature faith are best seen from certain key poems, from the end of 'Mohini Chatterjee' and the beginning of *Emer*; just as the 'tough reasonableness' that underlies his theory of history is felt strongest (unless I am much mistaken) from 'Meditations In Time Of Civil War' and 'Nineteen Hundred and Nineteen'. Yeats's theory of history has equally, of course, a root in Eastern religion; and the most that can fairly be urged against either of these two doctrines is that they contain an admixture of merely personal fantasy; this coexists with, and to some extent weakens, the serious traditional element. Thus, as Philip Sherrard once remarked to me, some of the *detail* in 'Dove Or Swan' is eminently speculative and arbitrary;[15] while we may wish

Yeats had not found room among the rebirths for Robert Artisson and the Lorelei.[16] Yet Yeats says himself that all this 'is in one sense symbol'; that the nearest he could hope to come to the divine pattern was to present a pattern perhaps analogous to the real; and I think Eastern religion would welcome his theories as analogies. And it was of course poetically desirable that he should have elaborated his system as he did; most theories of the divine pattern remain so abstract as to be unusable in art, and Yeats benefits greatly by pulling his down to the realms of the definite and concrete.

It is fashionable to say of Yeats that he did not believe in his own theories, and to try to prove this by showing that he sometimes shifted his ground. There are of course minor discrepancies—there was a stage when he felt reservations as to the ultimate efficacy of subjective religion, which doubts he later outgrew; in the middle period he uses the word 'Asiatic' as a commendation, while in his last years he uses it in a quite different and pejorative sense. But the so-called major fluctuations—between 'Byzantium', for instance, with its rejection of the sensual, and 'A Dialogue Of Self And Soul', with its acceptance of the experiential world, are hardly evidence of any kind. The traditional philosophies teach that, in time, we are between the paired opposites, the yin and the yang, and that the wise man learns to accommodate himself to their contrary tensions; these vacillations are therefore adjustments to the currents of life itself. One's attitude towards the fact of living will vary from day to day, but this does not imply that one's belief in the heavenly world must be ambivalent; the most that can be said, is that the ambition for personal escape will be more or less pressing at different times.

Some reviewers have demanded from me a lengthy preface on Yeats's metaphysics, but I think this is all that needs to be said. We can hardly yet hope to pass final judgment on his system, simply because of the first modest necessity to find out what his poems and statements mean. But I should at least gloss the objection that the remoteness of Yeats's authorities makes his poetry invincibly obscure, and that this in turn somehow makes him inferior to other modern poets. Yeats knew much more of comparative religion than Eliot, but their poetry is often based on almost identical sources, and I have amused myself, here and there in the pages that follow, by pointing this out.

V

My first book was criticised when it came out, and it may be useful to write a few words of it here; also perhaps to say something of my two books as a unity, and what I imagine they have achieved.

One weakness of *Yeats And Tradition*, as I see it, lay in a disharmonious preface (it did not seek safety in the phrase 'intentional meaning'); and for this I have now tried to compensate by re-defining my field. Several errors in the exegesis have also been brought home to me—these are discussed in Appendix II below—but generally speaking the readings that were reached are readings by which I would abide. My two books between them thus give my interpretations of all Yeats's dance-plays on the Noh model; indeed of all his mature dramas save *The Words Upon The Windowpane*, where I have nothing to add to his own preface and what Miner has already said.[17] In the sphere of the lyric, my method is to use key poems to illuminate Yeats's symbology (so that one lyric may shed light on several lyrics beyond): thus my first book investigates such symbols as sphere and zodiac, harlot and beggar, island, tower and cave, while the present essays persevere through the major sequence, dealing with shell and fountain, sea* and statue, bird and beast. I would therefore say that this book completes an enterprise, both in dramatic criticism, and in the investigation of dominant image-clusters in Yeats's verse.

What remains is to acknowledge my title, which I owe to a suggestion by R. P. Blackmur.[18] Yeats was, I would say, frequently an iconographer in that he illustrated a conviction or theory by means of images: this fact holds good of the plays, where the whole action often constitutes a single dramatic 'image' of archetypal and sometimes even of didactic† scope. My job is to study the iconographic aspect of certain plays and poems; a purpose proposed in all modesty and in awareness that they have other aspects; with the reiteration of which saving clause perhaps I may approach the texts.

---

* The sea of Anima Mundi, that is; I had already written of Yeats's alternative symbol, the sea of life. The two usages are of course in correspondence with one another: the sea is Yeats's emblem for the tide of becoming as opposed to pure being: it stands for 'everything that is not God'.

† Donald Davie has said that Yeats's verse is as didactic as Wordsworth's, to which I would add that such scenes as the climax of *Emer* (which teaches man's incapacity for the discipline of Platonic love) are didactic in the urbanest and least depressing sense.

PART TWO

PLAYS

'I always feel that my work is not drama but the ritual of a lost faith.'—*Letters to Sturge Moore.*

CHAPTER TWO

AT THE HAWK'S WELL

I

At The Hawk's Well was the first play in our literature ever to be written on the Japanese Noh formula, and Yeats had therefore to use all the space at his disposal to explain his new technique. His notes to the play, and his other dramatic criticism of the period, are preoccupied with first principles: with the origins of Yeats's form, the product of an age of faith, an essentially religious drama devised for the entertainment of the Japanese aristocracy; with the nature of the Noh synthesis, a blend of drama, music, choric song, dance and traditional symbolism; and with the ultimate intentions of the plays, which he saw as combining visual beauty, archetypal symbolic communication and metaphysical suggestion to convey spiritual truth. Yeats had of course to give space to this preliminary matter: he had to make clear the theory behind his chorus, who combined this function with that of musicians and also prepared the stage; and the Noh stagecraft itself, where movement and gesture are stylised and all stage properties kept simple and symbolic, was also unfamiliar and had to be carefully explained. But this preoccupation with first principles, however necessary, was in one sense unfortunate, for it exists to the exclusion of all comment on the symbolism of the play.

In general, Yeats approved of the prose commentary; it was the last of three bulwarks between his dance-plays and obscurity. His first protection lay in the nature of his audiences; they would come by invitation, since the plays were for the drawing-room; and he meant to invite only people versed in 'the traditional language of passion', who would have prior knowledge of the myths and symbols he planned to use.[1] In such circumstances he could be as eclectic and allusive as the Noh playwrights themselves, or as the courtly and visionary poets of Dante's Florence, of whom he was sometimes reminded as he read the Japanese plays.[2] If his meaning was not consciously taken, the collective unconscious might operate to suggest it; and if both these hopes failed him he meant to fall back on notes: these 'need not be so long as those Dante wrote for several poems in the Convito'.[3] Notes do indeed exist for all the dance-plays save the first: there, perhaps he thought his symbolism explicit; or more likely (since his argument is a peculiarly personal one) he did not think worthwhile the private disclosures that might be involved. Forty years of misunderstanding show that the explanation he withheld is sadly lacked, and it is largely the function of this essay to provide it.

Before we investigate Yeats's symbolic meaning itself, it will be useful to say something of the formal pattern by which he hoped to convey it. Almost all Yeats's dance-plays conform to that *genre* of the Noh theatre known as the 'Noh of ghosts', the most difficult as it is the most aesthetically beautiful of the Japanese modes, and though he simplified here and there, Yeats followed the strict Noh rules with considerable fidelity. They had produced great art in fifteenth-century Japan, and might consequently be relied on in twentieth-century Dublin. The Japanese rules, as Yeats notes, did not merely require that a play shall begin *in medias res* and present the audience with a single action defined in archetypal sharpness; beyond this, they required that the action itself should conform to a certain highly stylised pattern. 'He to whom the adventures happen', to quote *The Cutting Of An Agate*, shall be 'a traveller, commonly from some distant place'; and the adventure itself shall be 'the meeting with ghost, god or goddess, at some holy place or much legended tomb'.[4] Thus in Yeats's plays also: *The Dreaming Of The Bones* is based on the wanderings of a young Irish revolutionary who finds refuge at the haunted abbey of Corcomroe; *The Cat And The Moon* on the adventures of two maimed beggars, who conjure up a saint's ghost[5] at the celebrated holy well of the Burren. Yeats followed this law of the Noh, for all its apparent arbitrariness, because he understood that it was applied to confer an archetypal status upon the characters: the wandering beggar, in the Sino-Japanese tradition, is a symbol for humanity generally, and his journey is the image of life itself, while the 'holy place' to which the journey leads serves the plays as a convenient symbol for the point of intersection of the human and divine worlds. The Waki or traveller is thus in a sense Everyman, and the adventure which befalls him often expands to universal significance.[6]

If we now look at the plot of *At The Hawk's Well*, it will be seen to be shaped in deference to these same laws. Cuchulain, the Waki of the play, travels across the sea to a holy well, where he meets a destitute Old Man: they wait for the well to be filled with miraculous holy water, but the machinations of a goddess distract them at the crucial moment. Here we have the wanderer, and, in the person of the Old Man, the beggar also, while the chorus reinforces the metaphor of the journey, comparing man's life to a 'cloud' driven through the sky by the 'salt sea-wind' of his malignant destiny. Shifting the symbol, Yeats also compares the heart of man to the wind itself:

> 'O wind, O salt wind, O sea wind!'
> Cries the heart, 'it is time to sleep;
> Why wander and nothing to find?
> Better grow old and sleep.'

Yeats's holy well serves as the point of juncture of the natural and supernatural worlds, and it is in his character as Everyman, or more precisely as the type of subjective young manhood, that Cuchulain is led to its brink. As we shall see, the symbolic adventure which befalls him is perfectly archetypal, and of crucial importance to every human soul.

The Noh theory goes on to prescribe fixed laws for the adventure itself, which must be made dramatically exciting by some miraculous, supernatural happening, of a kind that will be perfectly intelligible to the audience, and which will serve to draw down god, goddess or ghost into the world of time. Yeats founds *At The Hawk's Well* on just such an incident: there is a woman guardian to the well, and the goddess of the locality possesses herself of this woman's body and distracts Cuchulain from the well-water by playing upon his sexual desire. When Yeats founds himself upon supernatural possession in this way, he does so in the belief that it is a universal superstition, and it is interesting to see what traditions he had in mind. In the first place, he had behind him the Noh plays themselves, where possession either by god or ghost is a common theme: in *Sotoba Komachi*,[7] for instance, the ghost of a rejected suitor possesses himself of Komachi's body and goads her to madness in return for her callousness while he lived. Yeats himself quotes Greek religion as another of his sources, and he knew the elaborate passage on the subject in Plutarch's *Morals*:[8] the gods, Plutarch says, consummate their desire for mortals by possessing a human body and in this form manifesting to the person they love; they cannot consummate their love in their own persons, for the mortal body and the divine body of air will not combine. This belief Yeats found also in Indian religious legend, as he points out in *A Vision*: the novice, 'tortured by his passion' for some goddess, may pray to her to descend and have sexual intercourse with him, and the goddess may avail herself of the body of a temple courtesan to do so.[9] When

Fand possesses a human body to seduce Cuchulain from the well, Yeats is consequently interpreting a typical Noh situation through the religious folk-lore of the world.

The Japanese influence on Yeats's dance-play extends beyond the surface narrative; I am sure that it also conditions the emotional climate of the verse. *At The Hawk's Well* is remarkable for a peculiar bitterness, and the atmosphere is one of consummate disillusion: the spiritual world is regarded with disaffection, and the phenomenal world with a certain settled distaste. In a sense, of course, all this has an autobiographical explanation, and the play reflects Yeats's sexual and spiritual unhappiness at the time he wrote: the well, after all, is in one sense a receptacle symbol, and the watcher at the well, never rewarded, is the symbol of *amor courtois* and of sexual despair. But if the final failure of Yeats's love for Maud Gonne informs his play with a current of personal feeling, what I should call the philosophy of its disillusion, the nature of the precise response he made to his personal misfortunes, may indicate a Buddhistic influence upon his thought. We know that Yeats was occupied with Buddhism at this period, for his poem 'The Double Vision Of Michael Robartes' concerns itself with the Buddha's motionless 'contemplation' under his green tree, when he 'so wrought upon a moment' and 'so stretched it out' that he seemed to have 'overthrown time'; an obscure passage to which I shall return. The same poem presents the Buddha, though in a rather disillusioned spirit, as the central type of what Yeats called 'subjective' religious discipline:

> That other's moonlit eyeballs never moved
> Being fixed on all things loved, all things unloved,
> Yet little peace he had
> For those that love are sad.[10]

The tenor of Yeats's dance-play, where 'all things loved, all things unloved' are subjected to a parallel dispassionate scrutiny, where action is seen as evil and resignation as the sole good, may reflect a temporary preoccupation with Zen Buddhism or some kindred form. If Yeats reviewed his past life in such a light, and wanted to pursue his speculations in verse, he could have found no better model for the dramatic application of Buddhist theory than the Noh plays themselves.

Not all the Noh plays are informed by Buddhism, for the more primitive are purely Shintoist, but there are several which fall into the class I have in mind. The religious discipline which informs these plays is not an easy faith. *Sotoba Komachi*, for instance, begins with a terrible chorus where we are told that the whole nature of man's life, unless it is redeemed by the religion of the Self, is Maya, illusion, and it is implied that our natural pity, in watching the action that follows, must be tempered by the recognition of this fact: then we are shown the old woman Komachi, once a beautiful and vicious poetess, now a demented beggar in the throes of her remorse. At the end of the play the ghost which has possessed her is exorcised, and for this, or for the power and generosity of the religious discipline that has redeemed her, we are expected to feel joy; but as we watch Komachi's sufferings themselves, the emotion required of us is something less than compassion. This deliberate withholding of pity, which requires of the audience, sometimes, a sentiment that has been called 'emotion of winter', Yeats could have met with in other, parallel works; and I am sure that we are to receive his own play in a similar spirit. There is a very real sense in which we ought *not* to sympathise with Cuchulain, or with the old man; the dramatic fiction is that playwright and audience have learned a self-discipline which they have not; and the play is on one plane a sober representation of human folly, presented less for our pity than to be coldly assessed for what it is.

Beyond the direct influence of the Japanese plays themselves, we must consider the influence on Yeats's verse and thought of the traditional Noh masks, themselves the product of a kindred asceticism and integrity. The effect of these masks is to isolate, with chill distinction and an entire absence of superfluous emotion, the salient characteristics of manhood and womanhood, youth and age.[11] They are intended in the first place, to enforce an atmosphere of sculptural 'stillness' and to impose the author's visual conception of his characters upon the actors; they are worn also because of the impossibility of the actors wearing greasepaint, which they cannot do since the audience are so near the stage. Beyond their technical function, however, their aesthetic beauty is very great, and Yeats, who had seen several, may have caught from them an emotion and presently reproduced it in his verse. There is even the possibility that he visualised his characters in sculptural terms, or that some of his speeches are designed to provide work for the sculptor's tool. Thus the following speeches are made to isolate salient characteristics of youth and age:

> Young Man: My luck is strong,
> It will not leave me waiting, nor will they
> That dance among the stones put me asleep;
> If I grow drowsy I can pierce my foot.

> Old Man: No, do not pierce it, for the foot is tender
> It feels pain much. But find your sail again,
> And leave the well to me, for it belongs
> To all that's old and withered.

Another speech, spoken when Cuchulain seems to be about to drink from the well, completes our visual image of the Old Man:

> Old Man: That shivering is the sign. O get you gone,
> At any moment now I shall hear it bubble.
> If you are good you will leave it. I am old,
> And if I do not drink it now, will never;
> I have been watching all my life and maybe
> Only a little cupful will bubble up.

The least we can say is that Yeats's imagination caught fire from the Noh masks, and that this largely accounts for the elaborate stylisation of his characters.

Because Yeats understood that they were the product of long and essentially religious meditation, he spoke of the 'philosophical virility' of the Noh masks, and this habit of religious speculation persists at all levels of the Japanese plays. *At The Hawk's Well*, which is superficially the representation of an Irish heroic myth and really the (universalised) statement of Yeats's own gathering despair, owes them a last debt in this respect. The Noh is nothing if not metaphysical, Shintoist and Buddhist theory serving to direct and maintain the plot: thus *Nishikigi* centres on the doctrine of *karma* and *Sotoba Komachi* on the Buddhist philosophy of redemption, while *Motomezuka* is concerned with the nature of the purgatorial state.[12] Such is Yeats's justification for basing his own play on religious dogma; for using it, as I am going to show he does, to embody his philosophy of the Self. That is to say, since the religion of the Self was Yeats's own faith, he uses the play as a symbolic representation of the sufferings attendant upon man's adoption of that philosophy, as Yeats himself had experienced them, or as Cuchulain, Everyman, will experience them also. This is the explanation of what critics have often noted, an intricacy in his argument which no merely sexual interpretation can explain, as it is also of the soured pessimism of the play's general tone.

It is worth adding a note on the extent to which the Noh sanctioned Yeats in making his play so devious. There were traditionally two ways in which the Japanese plays could be represented: with concentration on the heroic legend on which a play would be founded, and on the surface spectacle (this was called the 'Noh of the eye and ear'); or with concentration on interior values (this was called the 'Noh of the mind').[13] Yeats therefore had precedent for his own two planes of communication; for writing simultaneously on the levels of 'child' and 'sage'. Sometimes the lengths to which he takes his symbolic method go beyond accepted Noh practice, but they are, as I have said elsewhere,[14] no more than the development to a logical conclusion of a principle inherent in his models themselves. And I should add that no reader familiar with the 'heterodox tradition' in symbolism will have difficulty with the esoteric interpretation of *At The Hawk's Well*; he has only, as the play opens, to ask himself the question: what is the traditional meaning of the journey to the magic well? There is only one answer to this question, as I shall presently prove.

At The Hawk's Well is concerned with the theory of the Self, and it is a profoundly disillusioned and pessimistic play, but this is not to say that the religion of the Self is disillusioned or pessimistic. It is in fact, and I should perhaps end this section on such a note, the religion of love and of delight. Some Noh plays (not all) may insist on the vision of the phenomenal world as Maya, and on the ephemeral and worthless nature of all human joy, and Yeats may have been conditioned by circumstances to accept this form of Buddhism— 'hatred of life' as he later stigmatised it[15]—while he wrote: but it is merely the negative side of his 'subjective' philosophy. The Upanishads, and also the heterodox European sects on which he relied, present us with a vision of life in the highest sense optimistic and joyous, while the system of Tantra, which had such a profound influence on Yeats's maturer thoughts,[16] interprets the Buddhist faith itself in such a way. The effect of all this on the present essay is a certain ambiguity. Yeats's archetypal image itself, rightly interpreted, communicates something approaching despair, but the philosophy we must reconstruct in order to explain it has a very different orientation. With this in mind, we may turn to a study of Yeats's Celtic sources, but the dichotomy is very real, and I shall return to it.

II

In order to make *At The Hawk's Well* the fully archetypal statement that it is, Yeats had to alter and augment the Irish legend on which his play centres. The Celtic scholars have ridiculed him for so doing, but he was, one feels, entirely justified. The nature of primitive myth, as

Yeats thought and as Jungian psychology also supposes, is to be fully archetypal: the apparently half-savage stories contain the first intuitive statements of universal spiritual truth. In the course of time, as the story is handed down through the oral tradition, the meaning typically becomes distorted—the legend of Niall, for instance, has had a most inadequate allegorical meaning attached to it—and the poet of Yeats's stamp, who combines several parallel myths to create his symbolic 'image', sees himself merely as reshaping them into their original archetypal form. Yeats obviously intended precisely this, for I shall prove that he saw his Celtic legends of Connla and Slieve Gullian as the primitive counterparts of the well-and-fountain myths of medieval alchemy; as intuitive statements, that is, of truths which the medieval writers more thoroughly understood. Jungian psychology has spent much time on these myths, and has concluded that they have precisely the significance that Yeats supposed, so that he can hardly be condemned out of hand for taking them in the sense he did.

If we begin from a study of Yeats's Celtic myths in their own right, and postpone to another section the question of their ulterior meaning, he will be seen to have drawn upon a variety of sources. In the first place, we have the story of Cuchulain's fight with the hawk. On his way from the sea-shore to the well, a bird flies down and attacks him, and Cuchulain fights it with sword and (I think Yeats means) sling:

> I had to draw my sword to drive it off,
> And after that it flew from rock to rock.
> I pelted it with stones, a good half-hour,
> And just before I had turned the big rock there
> And seen this place, it seemed to vanish away.
> Could I but find a means to bring it down,
> I'd hood it.

This hawk is in fact Fand, the goddess of the locality, trying to prevent Cuchulain from approaching her sacred well, and the whole incident is reminiscent of the Irish legend of Cuchulain and the two yoked white birds. I will quote his own prose version of the legend,[17] which begins with Cuchulain and the court ladies taking their ease outside the palace; it is almost Samhain, the Irish equivalent of Allhallows, and the supernatural world is therefore near. A 'flock of wild birds' alights on the waters, and Cuchulain shoots them idly one by one and presents them to the court women. But Eithne Inguba, his mistress, is left without a bird, and Cuchulain promises to shoot for her whatever next may come:

> Presently there come two birds who are linked together with a chain of gold and singing soft music that went near to put sleep on the whole gathering. Cuchulain goes in their pursuit, though Eithne and his charioteer try to dissuade him, believing them enchanted. Twice he casts a stone from his sling and misses, and then he throws his spear but merely pierces the wing of one bird. Thereupon the birds dive and he goes away in great vexation, and he lies upon the ground and goes to sleep, and while he sleeps two women come to him and put him under enchantment.

The interpretation of this symbolism would be as follows. The two yoked birds are the goddesses Fand and Liban, Fand's sister; when Cuchulain pierces the one bird with his spear, the meaning is[18] that his physical beauty wounds Fand with desire; and Fand and Liban then materialise in human form and put him under enchantment so that the goddess may consummate her love. Yeats's play very much alters and reshapes the myth, but we have the detail of his pursuit of the hawk, which Yeats makes him resume after the act of possession at the well. During this pursuit Fand and Cuchulain begin a relationship which ends, in *The Only Jealousy Of Emer*, with the goddess offering him her love.

Yeats changes the white bird to a hawk in deference to the general atmosphere of his play; the hawk would suggest a mingled aristocracy and savagery, and he had traditional sanction for his image as early as Egyptian mythology, where the goddess Isis materialises before Osiris in such a form.* In the play, the hawk-goddess possesses the guardian of the well, who begins her erotic dance, and this triple association of the well, the guardian, and sexual eroticism suggests the assimilation of another, quite distinct myth. In this story,[19] Niall and his brothers go in search of well water, but their path is blocked by the guardian of the well:

> The fashion of the hag is this: blacker than coal every joint and segment of her is, from crown to ground; comparable to a wild horse's tail the grey wiry mass of hair that pierced her scalp's upper

---

* There is also the story, which may or may not be canonical, that some of the detail of the play came to him when he saw the Japanese dancer Michio Ito dancing in mimesis of a hawk. Michio Ito later danced in *At The Hawk's Well*.

surface . . . blackened and smoke-bleared eyes she had; nose awry and wide nostrils. . . . The beldame's whole appearance in fact was disgusting.

The guardian of the Hawk's Well is similarly repulsive in appearance, though Yeats's description of her is made to blend with the atmosphere of muted bitterness which characterises his play:

Old Man: Why don't you speak to me? Why don't you say:
          'Are you not weary gathering those sticks?
          Are not your fingers cold?' You have not one word
          While yesterday you spoke three times. You said:
          'The well is full of hazel leaves'. You said:
          'The wind is from the west'. And after that:
          'If there is rain it's likely there'll be mud.'
          Today you are as stupid as a fish,
          No worse, worse, being less lively and as dumb.
          Your eyes are dazed and heavy.

There is a strong sexual undercurrent to the original myth. Niall's brother Fergus is the first to greet the guardian, and he is appalled by her physical appearance, to which his first words refer:

'That's the way it is, is it?', said the lad, and 'that's the very way', she answered. 'Is it guarding the well thou art?', he asked, and she said 'it is'. 'Dost thou license me to take away some water?' 'I do', she consented, 'yet only so that I have one kiss on my cheek.'

But Fergus and Niall's other brothers cannot bring themselves to touch the old woman, and so they cannot come to the well. Finally, as Cuchulain tries to do with Yeats's guardian, Niall gives her his sexual love; after which, though here we part company with Yeats's dance-play, she turns into a 'queenly' young girl and gives him water, her affection, and even 'royal rule'.

A legend which Yeats knew from Curtin's *Myths And Folklore Of Ireland* and which may also be remembered in his play is the story of the Prince of the Lonesome Isle.[20] It tells how the Prince sets out for the miraculous well of Tubber Tintye, and arrives at a sinister and deserted castle; in a chamber a woman of fabulous loveliness is sleeping, and 'at the foot of the couch was Tubber Tintye itself—the well of fire'.

'Upon my word', said the prince, 'I'll rest here a while'. And he went up on the couch and never left it for six days and nights.

Here again we have the archetypal situation of the hero making love to the guardian of the well; though in this story, as in the myth of Niall, the prince meets with good fortune, and finally rides away with the water of 'golden fire'.

If we cannot yet be certain why Yeats inverts his Irish myths, at least we can show that the imagery his dance-play uses has roots in his own early verse and prose. His description of the possessed guardian obviously derives from that of the porter in 'The Old Age Of Queen Maeve' (one of his several early poems about possession), and since the porter scene there possibly owes something to 'The Eve Of St. Agnes', this may enable us to relate his dance-play to one unexpected source.[21] Later in the play the possessed guardian dances, and Cuchulain pursues her into the rocks, only to find that she has disappeared from sight. All this, and much else in the play, seems to me to recall Yeats's early story *Dhoya*.[22] This story, it will later be useful to have noted, begins with a reminiscence of the Buddha's vigil under the Bo-tree, after which we are shown Dhoya, Yeats's slave hero, offering sacrifice to the full moon. There is no well, but instead we have a great lake, and on a cliff overlooking the lake Dhoya begins his pagan ritual. As in *At The Hawk's Well*, he starts by lighting a fire.

He turned to the moon, then hurriedly gathered a pile of leaves and branches, and making a fire cast thereon wild strawberries and the fruit of the quicken tree.

After a night spent in meditation above the fire, a supernatural being descends to Dhoya, and in a manner which recalls Fand's seduction of Cuchulain:

Suddenly a voice in the surrounding darkness called him softly by name. . . . It seemed to rise from the air, just beneath the verge of the precipice. Holding by a hazel bush he leaned out and for a moment it seemed to him the form of a beautiful woman floated before him.

Then behind him in the forest said the voice 'Dhoya, my beloved'.

He rushed in pursuit; something white was moving before him. He stretched out his hand; it was only a mass of white campion trembling in the morning breeze.

Dhoya later meets this goddess again, but once more she is taken from him by magic. The story seems beyond doubt to have had a shaping influence on the later dance-play; fire-ritual and solitary contemplation, lake or well, the descent of a goddess, vain pursuit and sexual loss, came to be concepts associated in Yeats's mind.

If we now turn from this subject to Yeats's well-symbolism itself, we shall see where he found the imagery which is not in the early story. The waters of Yeats's well confer the benefits of immortality and, as the penultimate chorus shows, of wisdom also: both of these, with such gifts as prescience and everlasting youth, are traditionally the property of Irish magic wells. The myth Yeats had primarily in mind was, I think, that of Slieve Gullian: the well there was guarded by 'goddesses' and, as in Yeats's play, they were determined that no human being should come near it:

Thither Finn approached once; but the Goddesses who guarded it, arose, and in their helplessness and confusion dashed from the palms of their hands the water of the well against him. From what fell on his lips the hero acquired the gift of prescience.[23]

Another similar myth is that of Connla's well, at whose margin there grew 'a hazel tree bearing nuts of bright crimson, which would endow with all knowledge those that might eat of them'.[24] This well again was defended from human eyes, and when Sinan attempted to pluck the berries of the sacred hazel, the spirit of the fountain itself rose against her and swept her down to the sea.[25] Yeats, I think, certainly remembers this myth in his poem, for it had the strongest personal associations for him. In 1895, when he and other members of the Golden Dawn were practising contemplation, a mental image materialised for several of those present, and it proved (we are told) to be the landscape of Connla:

In the midst of the hills we found ourselves before an ancient well. Leaning over the well on our left grew a mountain-ash tree laden with red berries.[26]

For some of the participants, the wellside showed itself in two alternating aspects, being at one moment wintry and arid, and changing as they watched to a verdant and fertile summer scene. I imagine that this is remembered in the two aspects of Yeats's own Hawk's Well, and that the dream-image fused with the detail I have taken from *Dhoya* to make the landscape of his play.

When Yeats received the mental image of Connla, the prose passage in which he records his vision explicitly interprets well and tree according to the Kabbalistic and alchemical connotations for those symbols, and this is indicative of the level at which he took his Irish myths. We cannot suppose that he thought of the legends of Connla and Slieve Gullian in any merely literal sense. He had several authorities for relating them to the medieval occult tradition: Rhys, in his book *Celtic Heathendom*, suggests an association of the sacred hazel and the Kabbalistic tree of life,[27] and George Russell wrote an essay to connect the Irish sacred wells with the alchemical 'fountains of youth'.[28] A poem by AE called 'Connla's Well' is also relevant here; Yeats liked it well enough to refashion his Irish anthology (for whose first edition it appeared too late) to find room for it, and it will illustrate the direction in which his own mind moved. AE's poem is of cosmic scope, for he says that his symbolic well and tree overshadow the world. Wherever we may be, the berries of the sacred hazel fall towards us in the purple of sunset:

> . . . when the sun sets dimmed in eve and purple fills the air,
> I think the sacred hazel tree is dropping berries there
> From starry fruitage waved aloft where Connla's well o'erflows
> For sure the immortal waters run through every wind that blows.
>
> I think when night towers up aloft and shakes the trembling dew,
> How every high and lonely thought that thrills my spirit through
> Is but a shining berry dropped down through the purple air;
> And from the magic tree of life the fruit falls everywhere.

I shall postpone to my next section the examination of Yeats's traditional sources, but it will not take long to explain AE's relatively simple poem. He identifies his 'sacred hazel tree', bearing its 'starry fruitage', with the Kabbalistic tree of life, which is the symbol of *unitum mundum* (the reconciled opposites) or of the ecstasy of true spirituality; the tree of life traditionally grows from the human heart into the skies and overshadows the whole world, and, as the poem suggests, bears the sun, moon and stars for fruit.

Yeats himself often refers to the same complex of symbols, as in 'Vacillation':

> From man's blood-sodden heart are sprung
> Those branches of the night and day
> Where the gaudy moon is hung.

In AE's poem, the divine influence is seen falling, like berries from the heaven-tree, everywhere into the world. His image of the 'immortal waters' which 'run through every wind that blows' is alchemical, for in alchemy the symbol of *aqua vitae* would signify the consoling care of the Holy Spirit, disseminated into everything that lives; thus Yeats in turn speaks of 'the Holy Spirit jetting through all the desires, hopes and aspirations of the body like an intellectual fountain'. Such, then, were the associations AE had for the image of Connla's well, and Yeats, who knew so much more of the tradition, will not have ranged less widely.

Yeats moved very far from the legend of Cuchulain in the course of constructing his 'image', but the wheel comes full circle at the end of his dance-play. There, we are returned to the cycle of the Red Branch, but to a legend quite different from that of Cuchulain and Fand.[29] After his betrothal to Emer, the Irish myth takes Cuchulain to Scotland, where he is apprenticed to Scathach, a woman of supernatural powers, who teaches him the use of all kinds of weapon and the art of war. Scathach sends Cuchulain to make war on her behalf against Aoife, queen of a neighbouring tribe; Cuchulain defeats Aoife, makes love to her on the battlefield, and begets on her a son. Years later, of course, he is deceived by 'witchcraft' into killing this son in single combat on Baile's strand, and *At The Hawk's Well* alludes systematically to this myth, as when the old man tells Cuchulain that 'all who have gazed' on Fand's 'unmoistened eyes' are cursed:

> That curse may be
> Never to win a woman's love and keep it;
> Or always to mix hatred in the love;
> Or it may be that she will kill your children,
> That you will find them, their throats torn and bloody,
> Or you will be so maddened that you kill them
> With your own hand.

After Fand's seizure of the guardian's body, there is further reference to Aoife:

The musicians cry 'Aoife, Aoife' and strike gong . . .
Young Man: What are those cries?
What is that sound that runs along the hill?
Who are they that beat a sword upon a shield?
Old Man: She has roused up the fierce women of the hills,
Aoife, and all her troop, to take your life.

By this device Yeats telescopes his two myths, for the suggestion is that Cuchulain defeats Aoife, and begets his son upon her, 'between two thorn-trees' on the hill behind the Hawk's Well.

Such is the extent of Yeats's indebtedness to Irish myth, and perhaps I should conclude this survey with a comment on his method. He puts his material to two quite distinct uses: there are those borrowings, from the story of Niall or that of Finn's attempt on the sacred well, which are used to complete and make fully archetypal the basal story of Cuchulain at the lakeside distracted by the yoked white birds; and there are also the allusions to Scathach and Aoife, meant to connect *At The Hawk's Well* with the other plays in Yeats's own Cuchulain cycle. Borrowings of the former kind, for reasons I have begun to indicate, I take as fully justified, but the attempt to insert the present play into a cycle already nearing completion, and which was begun when Yeats had not even hit upon his theme, is surely less defensible. There is, or so it seems to me, no such thing as a Cuchulain cycle among Yeats's plays, and I think Bjersby's study (valuable though it is) a piece of false emphasis; these plays, planned independently, do not cohere in any essential respect, and Yeats's attempt to interrelate them is largely wasted ingenuity. The one dramatic cycle Yeats wrote is *Four Plays For Dancers*, whose coherence will be demonstrated.

III

At The Hawk's Well is either, like AE's poem given, founded on the alchemical image of the well or fountain of life, or it is not archetypal at all, since there is no other traditional connotation for the well symbol. I am sure that it is based on that image, and that Yeats has remodelled the Celtic legend of Cuchulain and Fand, adding to it detail from the Niall and other legends, simply in order to obtain a narrative structure fully in correspondence with that of the medieval stories which are his real sources. We have therefore to make at this stage a lengthy digression from his own text, both to discover the general structure of the original or motivating myth on which he bases himself, and (if we are to do full justice to his play) to examine the philosophy behind that myth, which is profound.

The philosophy of the alchemical fountain myth, if we may take this first, is the philosophy of the Self; and this at once suggests that we are on the right lines, since it is known fact that Yeats was occupied with the theory of the Self when he wrote his play. His own version of that theory is to be found in *A Vision*, but he had clearly formulated it some years earlier, for it is glanced at in the notes to *Four Plays For Dancers*, and is central to the poem 'A Prayer For My Daughter':

> All hatred driven hence
> The soul recovers radical innocence
> And learns at last that it is self-delighting,
> Self-appeasing, self-affrighting,
> And that its own sweet will is Heaven's will.

Yeats's own version of the theory is briefly as follows. There are two main psychological types, which he speaks of as the 'subjective' and 'objective' temperaments. An orthodox Christian serves as a good example of the 'objective' temperament: he tends to regard his own personality as imperfect or even valueless; to depend upon salvation by means of an external Saviour-God; and to seek union with that God by means of mortification, self-denial, and other expiatory rites. The subjective, on the other hand, is by nature aware that he carries God always within him and that his own personality is boundless, infinitely resourceful and in fact divine; he seeks for salvation by cultivating his own Self or higher personality; and, having no need to abase himself before an external victim-saviour, tends always to worship God through joy.* Each of these two temperaments Yeats allows absolute virtue, in that either discipline may lead to mystical union in one of its forms; he sees his two types as interacting throughout recorded history, and assigns all human personality to one or the other mould.

The origins of Yeats's theory are discussed in *W. B. Yeats And Tradition*,[30] and I have there pointed out that Yeats obtained his two psychological types largely by contrasting the religious disciplines of East and West. In all that he has concluded he has the support of contemporary

---

* There is, of course, a real sense in which the subjective will cultivate austerity—I discuss it in my later essay on 'Demon And Beast'—but I ought to record my personal belief that Yeats often underestimated the importance of austerity in religious self-discipline. He did not always do so: 'Meru' is a poem concerned with subjective austerity: and there I think he is writing under the corrective influence of the preface to Evans-Wentz's *Milarepa*.

Jungian psychology, which presents us with the same types, uses the same terms 'subjective' and 'objective', and concludes that the discipline of the Self is at least as psychologically valuable as that of objective Europe. Like Yeats, Jung arrives at his conclusions by balancing the convictions of Christian man against those of Buddhistic and Brahmanistic philosophy. He has in mind the Christian concept of salvation through 'grace' (the 'grace' of an external, paternal deity) when he writes that:

> The Western attitude, with its emphasis on the object, tends to fix the ideal Christ in its outward aspect and thus to rob it of its mysterious relation to the inner man.[31]

And he has in mind the Indian theory of the *Purusha*, by which the Self at the core of each individual personality is seen as identical with God, when he goes on to say that:

> The eastern attitude (more particularly the Indian) is the other way about: everything, highest and lowest, is in the (transcendental) subject. Accordingly, the significance of the Atman, the Self, is heightened beyond all bounds. But with western man the value of the Self falls to zero: hence the universal depreciation of the soul in the west.[32]

In Yeats's own version of the theory of the Self, the Indian doctrine of the *Purusha* plays a similar prominent part. We are told that the Hindu ascetic has only to be able to say and know 'I am Brahma', or to identify his own personality, in all its understood purity, with Godhead, to escape from the wheel of becoming and attain to total mystical union.[33] The poem 'He And She' takes this argument a stage further, substituting for the ascetic's cry 'I am Brahma' the proud 'I am I':

> All creation shivers
> With that sweet cry.

The meaning here is that the 'I' itself is divine: the worshipper has only to comprehend the infinite resources of his own personality to comprehend God. For, as Yeats's translation of the Upanishads puts it, deity 'is your own Self, the immortal; the controller; nothing else matters'.[34]

For all the importance of this Indian element in Yeats's thought, we should not forget that his theory of the Self has subsidiary roots in European tradition. In Europe, the subjective worshipper has generally been regarded with suspicion—though this was not the case in ancient Greece—and the concept of divine Selfhood has been largely the province of the heterodox, persecuted sects, as of Kabbalism, alchemy, and Rosicrucianism. These were, of course, the sects to which Yeats himself subscribed (he was for years a practising Rosicrucian); his psychological theories thus inevitably contain an admixture of alchemical and other dogma, and it is with this influence that the student of *At The Hawk's Well* needs centrally to concern himself. That the theory of the Self put forward by heterodox European mysticism is perfectly in correspondence with the Oriental has been demonstrated by Jung himself, and this even though the two were, in all probability, independently evolved.

For the alchemist or Rosicrucian, the cultivation of the Self involved a long and arduous discipline. The self is not, of course, to be confused with the ego, though the ego is in a sense the germinal or potential Self; one might say that the Self is attained by means of the redemption of the ego, and by excising from it all that is unworthy in its composition. Thus the ego is, in the first place, grossly impure, and all the four faculties, as they are contained within the ego, are impure also. With this in mind, Yeats's review of the Rosicrucian play *Axel* speaks of the necessity of 'the fourfold renunciation, of the cloister, of the active life of the world, of the labouring life of the intellect, of the passionate life of love'.[35] All the four faculties, precisely because they need sublimation and because they are disharmoniously arranged within the psyche, begin by being dubious quantities, and one should not cultivate any at the expense of any other (in the sense in which nineteenth-century Christianity cultivated the spirit), but should endeavour instead to complete the alchemical *opus*; to purify all the aspects of the psyche, and to bring its constituents into that perfect harmony which may precipitate discovery of the universal Self, the deity immanent in all things. Yeats usually speaks of the harmonised psyche in Dantesque terminology, calling it Unity of Being; this spiritual equilibrium, he felt, was an end in itself, and all humanity needed to achieve it, whether one meant to proceed beyond it into the visionary world or no. It was, however, a *sine qua non* of the religious life, and the subjective mystic could not begin to approach his goal unless it was achieved.

So far, and with exceptions which will be obvious, the subjective discipline is not very different from the orthodox discipline of regeneration: the main distinction, at least as Yeats saw it, is that the subjective remakes his psyche largely by his own exertions, while the Christian is much more dependent on external 'grace'. The extent to which the subjective relies upon the strength of his own personality will be seen from the alchemical practice of *contemplatio*. When the process of reintegrating the four faculties (known to the alchemists as *perfectio*) is complete, the harmonised psyche is employed upon contemplation, a process in which any object ('image') is used for meditation, and serves to lead the devotee by gradual stages into the world of spiritual truth. Suddenly, as of its own accord, the image reveals unexpected spiritual significance, just as (to quote a familiar modern example) the bird does for Blake when it is perceived as 'an immense world of delight closed by our senses five'.[36] Here is a description of the alchemical discipline:

> Without any active participation of the part of the individual in meditation, the image before him discloses its own meaning. This is the 'comprehension' (Innewerden) that is so different from ordinary 'understanding' (Begreifen) and with this the first stage of the contemplative condition is reached, in which the individual suddenly faces a revelation of fundamental truths. It is a spiritual condition that Suso formulates into rules of meditation as profound as they are simple: 'The setting of the senses is the rising of truth' and 'If any man cannot grasp the matter, he is to remain perfectly still, and the matter will grasp him'.[37]

And the German scholar I am quoting goes on to point out that all scientific or aesthetic discovery requires a similar discipline:

> The spiritual attitude described here has nothing to do with mystagogy—'mysticism'. On the contrary, it is the foundation of all thinking that is sane and in harmony with nature, the very kind of thinking that Goethe meant when he spoke of denkendes Anschauen ('intellectual intuition'), anschauende Urteilskraft ('intuitive judgment'), exakte sinnliche Phantasie ('exact sensual imagination').[38]

When the inward eye has thus penetrated to essences, seen 'into the heart of things', the spiritual world becomes accessible, and the mystic union of the individual Purusha and the universal Self (known in alchemy as *libertas*, or as drinking from the Fountain of Life) may be achieved.

So much for the three stages of the subjective discipline, and we may now turn from the philosophy of Yeats's religion to its central, shaping myth. The entire process of regeneration was symbolically represented as a journey, and Yeats knew the pattern of the journey from several sources; I do not know precisely which of these served as the ultimate model for *At The Hawk's Well*, and shall therefore juxtapose several in the paragraphs which follow. A purely alchemical source for the journey to the Self (useful because it gives us esoteric readings for all the symbols) is *The Marriage Of Christian Rosencrux*, a document of central importance for Yeats's Order of the Golden Dawn.[39] Since the symbolism of East and West here corresponds, we must consider also the myth of the Buddha, which I shall show to be an exact counterpart to the alchemical text cited. And here I should add that Jungian psychology regards the story of Niall, as also that of the Prince of the Lonesome Isle, as primitive and unconscious statements of the regeneration myth; they are in fact classic texts in this respect. I shall therefore refer to these stories also in my reconstruction of the symbolism.

More important than any of these legends, though I believe each of them contributed something to *At The Hawk's Well*, is the myth of the Holy Grail. Well, grail, and the images of the fountain and elixir of life are identical in symbolism, as Yeats himself remarks. We know from Yeats's unpublished autobiography *The Speckled Bird*,[40] where the grail legend is allowed very great importance in his developing thought, that he knew the esoteric interpretation enforced on it, that he took the story as a parable of the stages of the religious life, and that he even thought of founding a religious order centring upon the grail mysteries. Beyond Malory and Sebastian Evans, Yeats knew the more heavily and consciously symbolic grail epic of Wolfram von Eschenbach, for he had read the poem in Jessie Weston's translation:[41] we may take it that he knew also her prose commentary, and perhaps her later study *From Ritual To Romance*,[42] but we do not have to presume this knowledge to show that his interpretation and hers will have been identical. When Jessie Weston explains the grail symbols as the legacy of a subjective, non-Christian faith, adapted to the end of orthodoxy by a series of Christian writers, she tells us that she derives her interpretation from the heterodox mystics of the 'nineties:[43] it is clear that she means by this the circles in which Yeats habitually moved, and she may even have obtained information from the poet himself. We should never suppose that Yeats knew less of the traditional symbols than the professional scholars of his day: the truth, as my last book may have shown, is that he generally knew far more. He did not, however, explain directly all he knew, preferring to write as an initiate for initiates; he does not directly explain his reading of the grail symbols, but we may take them in Weston's sense in full confidence that this is his own. With the grail legends, I shall quote from Yeats's own story *Red Hanrahan*, a simple account of the quest for the cauldron of the Dagda, which is the Celtic Grail.*[44]

Whatever the archetype used to denote the Self, be it well, grail, elixir or cauldron, the journey to regeneration takes always the same form. I shall use Jungian terms for the several stages. First comes the Call to Adventure, by which the hero is first made aware of the inadequacy of his past life, after which he must undergo a *katabasis* or initiation: this may take the form of an extended journey through a desert or Waste Land, or a perilous voyage across unknown seas, or even (since the initiatory stage is terrible) of a descent into hell. The hero is typically rescued through the Meeting with the Virgin, who will represent, at the esoteric level, the lost half of his soul. Yeats knew this symbolism both from Plato's myth of the androgyne and from such alchemical writers as Boehme, and it is often referred to in his verse, as in 'Among School Children' and 'A Man Young And Old'.[45] The marriage of hero and virgin represents the reintegration of the personality—in Yeatsian terms the union of Self and Anti-Self—and the Virgin then normally leads her lover to the well-grail, from which he will drink the waters of life, or achieve spiritual vision. The myth usually ends with the return of the hero to the world, so that he may communicate to others the spiritual wisdom he has acquired.

We may now consider the symbolism in more detail, beginning with the call to adventure, which begins the quest. The motivating factor is often a chance heard remark or the most trivial incident, but its effect is always to cause dissatisfaction with the home surroundings or known world. Thus in *The Marriage Of Christian Rosencrux*, a simple stroke of good fortune enables Christian to escape from his dungeon (symbolising the grossness of a merely material existence) and precipitates him upon his travels; thus the hero of so many medieval stories begins from some description, heard in laboratory or tavern, of the chymical

---

* It is remarkable that in *Red Hanrahan*, as in *At The Hawk's Well*, the grail adventure begins with the 'whirling of a fire-stick'. Since *Dhoya* also begins with fire-ritual, we have in fact an elaborate set of correspondences in this respect.

Eldorado, the fountain of youth; and King Arthur's quest for the grail, as Malory tells the story, starts from his accidental meeting with the 'questying beast'. In the earlier versions of the grail legend, as Weston notes, the adventure sometimes starts with the meeting with the dead knight on the bier: he is the symbol of the 'buried self', the God-like faculties in the individual psyche which have atrophied through long neglect, and which the pilgrim to the grail of the Self has to resuscitate. And indeed, even in such a story as Yeats's *Red Hanrahan*, where an incident over a casual game of cards is enough to precipitate the adventure, the symbolic meaning is always of a sudden intuitive prompting leading towards the spiritual life, and which, once experienced, can never be denied:

> Whether small or great, and no matter what the stage or grade of life, the call rings up the curtain, always, on a mystery of transfiguration, a rite, or moment, of spiritual passage, which, when complete amounts to a dying and a new birth.[46]

In the legend of Gautama, a variant form of the myth we need to keep in mind, the theme is stated in simple and concrete terms. Disturbed by the 'four signs', the future Buddha becomes dissatisfied with life in his father's palace, and sets out to find the Way by travel in the unknown world.

The adventure on which the hero embarks now commonly leads him into terrifying desert country. Thus Christian, in the alchemical legend, travels through a sombre nocturnal landscape; the Grail hero rides through the Waste Land; in the Irish legend of the cauldron of Hades—which Celtic scholars even in Yeats's youth understood as the counterpart of the grail—the journey leads through hell itself. As Jessie Weston points out, the crossing of the Waste Land is a period of spiritual trial, and its purpose is to bring about the death of the unpurified ego; the most terrible sufferings may be necessary to the hero before he can achieve this, and it is not surprising that the symbolism of hell should be used. The hero has to renounce the defensive mechanism of his first personality and descend (as Jungian scholars would say) into the darkness of the unconscious mind, in the terrible anonymity of that womb to suffer new birth.

> In order to arrive at what you are not,
> You must go through the way in which you are not.[47]

Thus the Buddha spends long years in the raiment of a beggar, and finally dies a symbolic death in a monastery at the edge of the world.

The third stage of the journey begins from the Meeting with the Virgin. Thus Hanrahan, in Yeats's own story, meets the Virgin in the grail castle, and the Prince of the Lonesome Isle the woman asleep beside the well; thus the Buddha achieves liberation only after his meeting with the girl Sujata, and the grail hero characteristically succeeds after his marriage, celebrated in perfect celibacy, with a pure maiden. At one level, of course, much of this has a sexual significance, for the subjective philosophies concede (as Christianity so often will not) that pure sexual love may be of service to the religious life and may precipitate the reintegration of the personality. Where this is the meaning, as in the unconscious symbolism of the Niall myth, the virgin may first manifest in her terrible or forbidding aspect, and only gradually be transfigured into the perfect *imago* the adventurer seeks. Unconscious pressures, that is, compel us to see woman as the great enemy and antagonist, and a protracted struggle may be necessary before this aspect of her nature can be transcended, and be replaced by the higher image of the pure bride. Thus the grail hero, in any version of the story, will be beset by hags and nightmarish projections of the terrible woman, corrupt images which have to be outfaced.

Beyond the sexual significance of the Virgin, however (and here the grail myth begins to proliferate, and to communicate on several planes), there is the traditional connotation of the lost half of man's soul. This certainly is the meaning in the alchemical myth, where Christian comes to the castle of the Virgin, sails in a boat at her direction to the Tower of Olympus (where he procures the divine elixir), and is finally to be thought of as marrying her; as this was a shaping myth of Yeats's Rosicrucian order we may be sure that the esoteric interpretation was not lost on him.[48] He knew it also from the most beautiful passage in all Boehme, and I will illustrate the full meaning from this text. Boehme saw in man's mind a dichotomy which he symbolises by a 'chaste virgin, the spirit breathed into him by God' and 'a youth, the (corrupt and unregenerate) spirit inherited from the world'; this Lucifer-like youth, the fallen human ego, must always seek reunion with the symbol of his own lost purity. Thus the youth is shown kneeling before the 'transcendental Virgin':

> Thou art my dearest bride, my Paradise and rosary, let me into thy Paradise, let me enjoy thy fair love.[49]

But the union is commonly refused:

> The Virgin: Hearken, my beast: I am greater than thou, and when thou wert about to be, then was I thy overseer. My essences are from the root of eternity. But thou art of the world, and perishest. But I live eternally.... I will then no more take thee for my beast. I will have no more thy four elements. Death devours thee. But I flourish with my new body out of thee, as a flower out of its root.[50]

Boehme's symbolism here is from the tradition of alchemy, where the youth (the 'seed of the red lion') and the young queen (the 'white lily') combine in mystical marriage for the elixir of life to be won. 'Thus body and soul, substance and spirit, universe and godhead once more become one, and the perfect human being is born anew, he who deifies the body and embodies deity.'[51] The way to the well becomes clear.

We now have to consider the significance of the well to which the virgin leads the hero, the grail which Amfortas's virgins carry in. The significance of the myth is now complex and, as Jessie Weston learned from heterodox circles in the 'nineties and as the Jungian writer Joseph Campbell has written a book to prove, it is necessary to interpret on several planes, for the hero is now, in traditional terminology, 'Master of the Three Worlds'.[52] In one sense (and I have shown that Yeats's play can be taken at such a level) the meaning is sexual: led by instinctive promptings, and after a period of deprivation in the Waste Land, the hero has encompassed the perfect marriage and all the delight which it can bring. At another level the well is an image of the integrated personality, achieved by the union of self and anti-self. And thirdly, the drinking of the well-water may symbolise the *participation mystique*, the alignment of the personality to the intellectual essences, *aqua vitae*, the waters of the Edenic world. The Master of the Three Worlds will have learned the key to the mystery of life in all three senses, for in the subjective tradition all things proceed by analogy, and the exoteric and esoteric meanings are in fact one.

One should add a paragraph on the nature of the *participation mystique* (the state of *contemplatio* and *libertas* to which the Buddha attained under his green tree), interpreting this term as a subjective would understand it. Since all things proceed by analogy, Campbell begins from the parallel of ideal sexual love, which would be for the subjective a mystical or quasi-mystical experience:

According to this mysticism of sexual love, the ultimate experience of love is a realisation that beneath the illusion of two-ness dwells identity: 'each is both'. This realisation can expand into a discovery that beneath the multitudinous individualities of the whole surrounding universe—human, animal, vegetable, even mineral—dwells identity. . . . The man or woman knowing this experience is possessed of what Schopenhauer called 'the science of beauty everywhere'.[53]

And what is possible in the lowest of the three worlds is possible also on the plane of the integrated personality. He who has this will sense that AE's 'immortal waters' do indeed flow through 'every wind that blows':

The research for physical immortality proceeds from a misunderstanding of the traditional teaching. On the contrary, the basic problem is to enlarge the pupil of the eye, so that the body with its attendant personality will no longer obstruct the view. Immortality [sc. the sense of the immortal essence of all created things] is then experienced as a present fact: 'It is here! It is here!'*[54]

Thus Blake spoke of having the good fortune 'to live always in Eden'. And Campbell goes on to interpret Buddhist and Taoist landscapes (such paintings as Yeats describes in 'Lapis Lazuli') as the trophies of those who have attained to 'present immortality':

Those who know, not only that the Everlasting lives in them, but that what they, and all things, really are is the Everlasting, dwell in the groves of the wish-fulfilling trees, drink the brew of immortality, and listen everywhere to the unheard music of eternal concord. These are the immortals. The Taoist landscape paintings of China and Japan depict supremely the heavenliness of this terrestrial state. The four benevolent animals, the phoenix, the unicorn, the tortoise and the dragon, dwell amidst the willow gardens, the bamboos and the plums, and amid the mist of sacred mountains, close to the honored spheres. Sages, with craggy bodies but spirits eternally young, meditate among those peaks, or ride curious symbolic animals across immortal tides, or converse delightfully over tea-cups to the flute of Lan Ts'ai-ho.[55]

* The last words here quote a maxim of Tantric Buddhism.

Such discipline may indeed serve to bring man 'close to the honored spheres', though we should recognise, as Campbell does, that it is a stage in mystical experience merely and not an ultimate goal. 'The stage of Narcissus looking into the pool, of the Buddha sitting contemplative under the tree' is, he says, 'a requisite step but not the end'.[56] The integrated personality makes possible fragmentary perception of spiritual truth, but further asceticism, further discipline, is needed for total mystical union.

Even when the mystical marriage has been achieved, the adventure is not at an end: the myth typically concludes with the Return to the World. Thus the Prince of the Lonesome Isle takes back his magic well-water to heal the Queen of Erin, the Amfortas of the story; the Celtic heroes bring back the holy cauldron from Hades to the world of time; the knight wins the Grail, not for himself alone, but so that the ruined land may become green. The meaning breaks surface most cleanly with the myth of Gautama, where the Buddha experiences total enlightenment at the break of day, doubts whether his message could be communicated, but is persuaded by the God Brahma to return and become 'teacher of Gods and men'. With this the adventure comes full circle, and the final lesson is brought home: even when he has completed this loneliest of human adventures, the adept owes a duty to the world of time.

So much for the basal structure of the regeneration myth, perhaps the central of all archetypal narratives. I do not know if it is yet apparent that Yeats's dance-play is the story of an inhibited grail adventure, as the story of *Red Hanrahan* is also, but it would be easy to prove the contention from the detail now at our disposal. Before we do so, however, it will be best to say something of a further complication: a version of the myth which has never, until now, been critically considered as a religious document at all, but which Yeats knew to be one, and which conditioned him to prefer the well symbolism he uses to the more orthodox and unambiguous image of the grail. We shall understand his play the better for having examined it.

IV

The version of the grail myth I have in mind, and to which I attach so much importance, is William Morris's story *The Well At The World's End*, a book which Yeats read again and again. The difficult essay on Morris in *Ideas Of Good And Evil*[57] is centrally concerned with the romance, and indicates how deeply Yeats felt for narrative and symbolism; it became, I think, the formulation of the grail legend which meant most to him, and overshadowed all earlier formulations in his mind. Morris was perhaps not temperamentally equipped for the strenuousness of total symbolism, and there are long stretches of undesigning narrative in his book; but there is also a strain of conscious symbolic intention, together with functional medieval imagery whose origin Yeats is at pains to point out. Even without all this, of course, his romance could still be read on the level of the legend of Niall, as an unconscious projection of the archetypal grail myth. It was certainly taken as such a myth in heterodox circles during the 'nineties, when Eva Gore-Booth, for instance, used its symbolism for several poems, interpreting in each case in a highly esoteric sense;[58] and Yeats took it precisely as she did, and adopted well and tree symbols in a manner which recalls her own.

Like all stories of the pilgrimage to the Self, *The Well At The World's End* begins with the Call to Adventure, and continues with the *katabasis*, or journey through the Waste Land. Ralph is Morris's hero, and the Call to Adventure comes to him in the typical form of a chance-heard rumour. He runs away from home to travel the world, and his first impulsion to the grail-quest comes with a keepsake he is given soon after setting out:

> 'Gossip, wear this about thy neck, and let no man take it from thee, and I think it will be salvation to thee in peril, and good luck to thee; so that it shall be to thee as if thou hadst drunk of the WELL AT THE WORLD'S END.'
>
> 'What is that water?' said Ralph, 'and how may I find it?' 'I know not rightly,' she said, 'but if a body might come by it, I hear say that it saveth from weariness and wounding and sickness; and it winneth love from all, and maybe life everlasting.'[59]

So Ralph sets out to find the Well, and suffers much privation in the lands through which he rides: he fights savage knights who attack him without warning, passes through brutalised townships for which the gallows-tree is a fit symbol, falls in love, to see his lover killed before his eyes. During this time, he hears many rumours of the Well, that a girl may be a man's guide to it, or even in a sense be it; and yet that its significance is not sexual merely but (if I may say as much) visionary:

> In the WELL AT THE WORLD'S END is no evil, but only the

Quenching of Sorrow and Clearing of the Eyes that they may behold.[60]

And for all that we have been told that the Well confers the gift of immortality, he learns also that 'it may not keep any man alive for ever'.[61] Here we have more than a suggestion of the theme of 'present immortality', which is so important in Yeats's own thought.

I will not retail Ralph's adventures in any detail, since they are not relevant to Yeats's text. Eventually he meets a young girl named Ursula, who has been kept as the prisoner of a vicious knight and lady, and whose escape is recounted in one of those gentle but virile scenes which Morris does so well.[62] This is the meeting with the virgin, and, if Morris intends it primarily in a naturalistic sense, it also helps Ralph to a 'reintegration of the soul' and makes possible the fulfilment of his quest. So also when Ursula escapes from a life of degradation, a reader sympathetic to Jungian thought might understand an image of man's changing view of woman, as he dispenses with her terrible in favour of her virginal aspect.★ Ursula brings Ralph to the Well at the World's End, but first she has to prevent him from drinking from a pool heavy with venom, above which a 'dry tree' grows. The symbol, I think, owes something to medieval sources; any alchemical writer would have told Morris that the Tree of the Knowledge of Good and Evil is built by men themselves. Here is Morris's own description:

> Leafless was that tree: its bole upheld but some fifty of great limbs and, as they looked on it, they doubted whether it were not made by men's hands rather than grown up out of the earth.[63]

And then at last Ursula and Ralph come to the edge of the sea and to a 'low green toft with a square stone set atop to it', and they drink, sobbing, in an ecstasy of joy. I will quote the passage which follows, for it may serve to isolate the qualities which attracted Yeats to the romance. The lovers drink:

> And therewithal a sweet weariness began to steal over them, though there was speech between them for a while, and Ralph said, 'How is it with thee, beloved?'

★ I would not say this if there were not strong reasons for doing so: the image of the virgin escaping from slavery (sometimes slavery to a terrible old woman) occurs with compulsive frequency in Morris's romances; and in accounting for this, Freudians and Jungians are likely to be at one.

AT THE HAWK'S WELL

'O well indeed,' she said.

Quoth he: 'And how tasteth to thee the water of the well?' Slowly she spake and sleepily: 'it tasteth good, and as if thy love were blended with it.'

And she smiled in his face; but he said: 'one thing I wonder over: how shall we wot if we have drunk aright? For whereas if we were sick, or old and failing, or ill-liking, and were now presently healed of this, then should we know it for sure—but now, though as I look on thee, I behold thee the fairest of all women, and on thy face is no token of toil and travail; and though the heartache of loneliness and captivity, and the shame of Utterbol, has left no mark upon thee—yet hast thou not always been sweet to my eyes, and as sweet as might be? And how then?——' But he broke off and looked at her and she smiled upon the love in his eyes, and his head fell back and he slept with a calm and smiling face. And she leaned over him to kiss his face, but even therewith her own eyes closed and she laid her head upon his breast and slept as peacefully as he.[64]

I do not know if this short extract can bring home the virtues of Morris's prose, which has for me, beneath all the archaisms, a persistent and compelling integrity. The well at which the lovers achieve oneness stands for nothing sentimental or exotic; it stands for the ultimate good to be had of human life; and the style is proportionate to the subject.

When Ralph and Ursula have drunk from the well, they return to a dedicated life in his native country. It has already been explained to them that they must do this:

For ye of the world beyond the mountains are stronger and more god-like than we (the gnomes) . . . and ye wear away your lives desiring that which ye may scarce get; and yet set your hearts on high things, desiring to be masters of the very gods. Therefore ye know sickness and sorrow, and oft ye die before your time, so that ye must depart and leave undone things which ye were born to do; which to all men is grievous. And because of this ye desire healing and thriving, whether good come of it, or ill. Therefore ye do but right to seek to the WELL AT THE WORLD'S END, that ye may the better accomplish that which behoveth you, and that ye may serve your fellows and deliver them from the thralldom of those that be strong and unwise and unkind, of whom we have heard strange tales.[65]

With this we are brought to the central argument of the story, and of all versions of the grail legend: that the elixir is not to be sought for its own sake. The end of the adventure is service, and Morris's intention is to show, under cover of his archaic symbolism, how man may arrive at the spiritual calm and fulfilment which will enable him to live purposively in the world.

So much can be said of the archetypal pattern of *The Well At The World's End*, and it remains to show that Yeats interpreted Morris's story in the way I have myself done. The proof of this lies in the essay in *Ideas Of Good And Evil*, which also provides the key to several problems arising from his interest in the romance. Central among these is the fact that he should have preferred it above all other versions of the grail myth: Morris's story, for all its beauty, is pre-eminently a secular statement of an essentially religious theme, and one would hardly have expected a visionary of Yeats's stamp to see more in it than, say, in Wagner's *Parsifal*, which he must also have known. The reasons for his preference are complex, and a paragraph of biography will be needed to explain them, after which we may confirm our findings from a study of his Morris essay. This in turn will lead us to the heart of his own play.

Yeats's attitude to Morris is qualified by personal idiosyncrasy, and by certain reservations (reflected in *At The Hawk's Well*) with which he approached the theory of the Self. Though he believed implicitly in the philosophy of the Three Worlds, he did not believe that the poet could afford to travel too far into the unknown. The discovery of the Divine Selfhood might be the ultimate spiritual goal of humanity, and it was certainly the province of the saint to attain this union, but Yeats did not believe that the artist had a similar duty:

> We (the creative artists) are only permitted to desire life, and all the rest should be our complaints or our praise of that exacting mistress, who can awake our lips with her sweet kisses.[66]

The poet especially had to be content with the middle course: he had to know enough of the life of the spirit to satisfy natural craving, but he had also to avoid the full rigour of mystical discipline, which could only inhibit his creative faculty:

> We must find some place upon the Tree of Life high enough for the forked branches to keep it safe, and low enough to be out of the little wind-tossed boughs and twigs.[67]

I think Yeats was all his life disinclined to strive for spiritual ultimates*
and preferred patiently to accept reincarnation after reincarnation,
until in some future rebirth he should have acquired all the *karma*
necessary to mystical union, and the Universal Self could be discovered naturally and without labour and pain.

If we understand Yeats's position with regard to the mystical life,
the meaning of his essay on Morris becomes apparent, and can be
summarised as follows. Yeats felt that Morris was an artist like himself,
content with the 'middle way', and the antithesis of such part-sympathisers with the visionary world as Verhaeren, Mallarmé and Maeterlinck, and even more so of such romantic subjectives as Shelley and
Rossetti. They rejected material happiness and sought, by spiritual
struggle, to encompass the full mystical vision, but Morris was satisfied
with the celebration of life, or more precisely to be a master of the
mystery of the Self in the two lower of its three aspects, the level of the
integrated personality and the sexual plane. Like his Ralph and Ursula,
he had made the pilgrimage to the well, but he did not, as Shelley,
Rossetti and the 'early Christians' had done, strive to penetrate beyond
Unity of Being to an 'unearthly paradise'; he was content with the
inferior, or as Yeats says 'heathen' attributes of the grail. One cannot
stress too strongly how exalted and noble even this discipline, as Yeats
saw it, made Morris: he had achieved union with the transcendental
virgin and drunk the miraculous water; he had fulfilled his own
personality and learned present immortality, pure contemplation, all
gifts that life can offer save that of total mystical union. And so Yeats
writes of him, in some of the most beautiful passages of his prose, that
he was reverenced by all who knew him, and in that simple manner in
which we love 'radical innocence', which is the property of the discovered Self:

> No man I have known was so well-loved; you saw him producing
> everywhere organisation and beauty, seeming, almost in the same
> moment, helpless and triumphant; and people loved him as children
> are loved.[68]

Yeats describes Morris's pure self-contemplation in terms which at
least connect it with that of Gautama, as also with that of the Amadan,

---

* This does not mean that he did not strive for spiritual progress: he coveted a place on
the Tree of Life that would be 'high enough'. I think his central problem was to convince
himself that *all* concerted striving for the ultimate vision was not in a sense objective (self-immolating). He did eventually conquer his doubts here, as we see from his subjective saint
Ribh.

the Irish 'fool of faery', who is conventionally represented as gazing in an enchanted cup. We notice that the four faculties are in perfect equipoise, the 'body' harmonising with the intellect:

> A reproduction of his portrait by Watts hangs over my mantelpiece. . . . Its grave wide-open eyes, like the eyes of some dreaming beast, remind me of the open eyes of Titian's Ariosto, while the broad vigorous body suggests a mind that has no need of the intellect to remain sane, though it give itself to every fantasy: the dreamer of the Middle Ages. It is 'the fool of faery, wide and wild as a hill', the resolute European image that yet half remembers Buddha's motionless meditation.[69]

He goes on to explain how Morris had conquered the merely 'egotistical', as the pilgrim to the well-grail must always do, and arrived at the sense of his identity with all created things: he dealt always in universals, 'those powerful emotions which resemble the more, the more powerful they are, everybody's emotion'.[70] This quality seemed to Yeats the central virtue of his art; it was something 'that neither I nor any man, racked by doubt and enquiry, can achieve and that yet, if once achieved, might seem to man and woman . . . their very soul'.[71] Because of this especially Yeats reverenced Morris's work, and spoke of him as 'among the greatest of those that prepare the last reconciliation, when the cross shall blossom with roses'.[72]

Yeats's interpretation of *The Well At The World's End* follows from his attitude to Morris himself. It centres upon the symbols of the two wells: the one poisoned, and overlooked by the dry tree, from which Ursula prevents Ralph from drinking, and the other at the world's end, from which he receives the gift of fulfilment. Yeats felt that Morris, whether intuitively or systematically, had expressed his own spiritual position with this imagery, and I imagine there can be very little doubt that this is the case. The first well, poisonous to Ralph and to Morris himself, Yeats takes as the symbol of what I shall call the higher self, by which I mean the life of uncompromising religious experience: and the full well from which he chooses to drink is read as the symbol of the *lower self*, the same image in its lower or 'natural' aspects:

> [Shelley, Rossetti and] the early Christians were of the kin of the wilderness and the dry tree, and they saw an unearthly paradise, but he was of the kin of the [full] well and of the green tree, and he saw an earthly paradise.[73]

AT THE HAWK'S WELL

Elsewhere, Yeats makes the same point in directer language, which we are now able to follow:

> He wrote indeed of nothing but of the Quest of the Grail, but it was the heathen Grail that gave every man his own food, and not the Grail of Malory and Wagner.[74]

Yeats does not go on to interpret the whole narrative, but I think I have indicated the lines on which he would have done so.

We now know all we need for proper exegesis of Yeats's play, but I will add a paragraph on Yeats's later use of Morris's imagery, which he now converts to his own ends. He uses always the image of the full well for Unity of Being, or for the lower self; while the dry well, which fills only with difficulty, is by analogy the symbol of complete mystical union.* Thus in *Autobiographies*, he speaks of man's mind, when Unity of Being is achieved, as 'a dark well, no surface, depth only', and uses the symbol of 'Narcissus and his pool'.[75] He speaks of Titian as an artist who has attained to Unity of Being, and we remember that he has compared Morris to Titian's Ariosto: the men of Titian's paintings, he says, seem to gaze into the full 'well' of the Self, 'like great hawks at rest', and 'whatever thought broods in the dark eyes' has 'drawn its life' from the sitter's 'whole body'.[76] In these words we have of course the central complex of images employed in *At The Hawk's Well*, and there can be no doubt either of their significance or of Yeats's ultimate source. We are justified, as I shall now proceed to do, in interpreting from Morris and the great grail tradition.

V

At The Hawk's Well is a play of consummate spiritual disillusion, and its theme is that the search for the higher self is inevitably doomed to failure. Yeats did not of course consistently believe that this was the case, but he had persuaded himself of it at the time he wrote his play, since this was a period of spiritual distress and tension. His early religious disciplines had been those of the Golden Dawn, and he tells us, using a symbolism parallel to that of his dance-play, how in middle life he had come to regard the techniques of meditation he then learned as objective (externalising) and impure. They did not suffice even for the limited spiritual knowledge that was his goal:

---

* Less narrowly defined, the dry well traditionally symbolises any ambition inimical to human happiness, any unattainable goal, spiritual or sexual: so also sometimes in Yeats.

> I was seeking something unchanged and unmixed and always outside myself, a stone or elixir that was always outside my reach and . . . I myself was the fleeting thing that held out my hand.[77]

Yeats wrote several poems to illustrate his dilemma, the nearest of which to his dance-play is 'The Empty Cup'. A 'crazy man'—Yeats is thinking of the Amadan, the fool of Irish faery, always represented as holding an overflowing vessel[78]—may find the grail without effort, since in Yeats's system the mad stand always close to the values of the spiritual world,[79] but his madness will prevent him from taking advantage of it. The normal man, on the other hand, can discover the grail only with great difficulty, and never in its replenished state:

> October last I found it too,
> But found it dry as bone,
> And for that reason am I crazed
> And my sleep is gone.

In the poem, as in Yeats's play, there is a sexual significance together with the mystical, in the form of a bitter comment on the unfairness with which love distributes its rewards. Yeats's disillusion at this time was operative on all levels, and it must have seemed to him that his personal grail would never be replenished, his hopes, whether sexual or spiritual, never be fulfilled. The draft version of the play makes this very clear:

> Accursed the life of man, what he hopes for never comes.
> Between passion and emptiness, what he hopes for never comes.

The version Yeats published asks bitterly whether anything in life is worth the hard pain of birth, and this gives us an index to the mood in which it was composed.

The landscape of Yeats's play is used to reinforce its bitter tenor. It is significant on two planes: both of the sufferings which *amor courtois* brings to the lover, and, on the level at which Yeats primarily wants us to read, of the inimical nature of the spiritual life (of which *amor courtois* would have seemed to Yeats a special form). Dry tree and dry well are images of the dark night of the soul:

> I call to the eye of the mind
> A well long choked up and dry
> And boughs long stripped by the wind.

This rocky locality is of course the Waste Land of the grail legends, the emblem of man's spiritual lack, which can only become green when the hero has fulfilled his quest. Thus Yeats juxtaposes at once the image of Cuchulain, climbing the symbolic hill of spiritual endeavour, for this is the hero by whom the adventure is to be achieved. The same verse introduces us to him[80]

> ... Pallor of an ivory face,
> Its lofty dissolute air,
> A man climbing up to a place
> The salt sea wind has swept bare.

With this it is at once clear that Yeats's 'dissolute' hero is a Gawaine and no Parzival, and the implication, for any initiate among the audience, will be that the quest must necessarily end in failure; the whole pattern of the play follows inevitably from its first lines. The chorus is used to reinforce this suggestion:

> First Musician: The boughs of the hazel shake,
> The sun goes down in the west.
> Second Musician: The heart would be always awake,
> The heart would turn to its rest.

The heart of man is torn always between opposite desires, and it is not in Cuchulain's nature to attain to that state of perfect contemplation by which the grail can be achieved.

If we may henceforth take the sexual meaning as self-evident, and concentrate on the religious aspect of Yeats's theme, it will be clear that his symbolism is precisely that of Morris's romance. Cuchulain can obtain 'immortality' by drinking from the dry well of the higher self to which he has come; he can do so by sitting in motionless meditation at its edge, since at certain moments it is miraculously filled, though it may be that 'only a little cupful will bubble up'. The form of immortality meant here is clearly that on which I have quoted Joseph Campbell, and this can be demonstrated from two salient statements in Yeats's prose: that physical indestructibility is not worth the having, 'no better than our other desires',[81] and that true immortality is 'the full and entire possession of oneself for one single moment'.[82] The latter of these statements, twice postulated in passages written near the date of Yeats's dance-play, is clearly a quotation from *Axel*,[83] and we have therefore to interpret from that Rosicrucian text. Villiers meant precisely what I have shown that all subjectives will believe, that nothing is needed for man's salvation but the perfect balance of his sublimated faculties; if we can bring heart, mind, soul and senses into equilibrium, even momentarily, we can (granted only the self-discipline which can make permanent what would otherwise be a fleeting, fragmentary perception) recognise the divinity in our own personality, and so prepare ourselves for union with the transcendental world. Thus Blake, for example, teaches that every 'pulsation of the artery' leads us directly into 'eternity' if we can take advantage of it, and that every inch of the created world is visionary also:

> For every space smaller than a globule of man's blood
> Is visionary and is created by the Hammer of Los.
> And every space larger than a globule of man's blood opens
> Into Eternity, of which this vegetable earth is but a shadow.[84]

Thus Yeats describes the Buddha 'stretching out' a moment by contemplation until 'time' is 'overthrown',[85] and in another poem, using a stone and tree imagery identical with that of *At The Hawk's Well*, records a fleeting, fragmentary perception which he himself experienced, though he could not prolong it:

> For one throb of the artery,
> While on that old grey stone I sat
> Under the old wind-broken tree,
> I knew that One is animate,
> Mankind inanimate fantasy.

All that Cuchulain need do, then, is to seize the moment: to meditate 'like some great hawk at rest' over the 'dark well' of his own mind, until the perfect harmony of his personality is attained, and 'present immortality' manifests in the form of the life-giving elixir. The suggestion is, however, that the human heart is by nature so disorientated that the discipline can never be fulfilled.

When Cuchulain comes to the desolate landscape of the dry well, he finds an Old Man already at the well's edge, and Yeats uses the contrast of their characters to enforce some of his bitterest arguments.

Cuchulain himself has set out, like Morris's Ralph, on no more than a chance-heard rumour; he has crossed the sea without difficulty, which is to say that no period of initiation has been needed to equip him for his task. The 'night voyage across the sea' (as Frobenius calls it) is a traditional symbolic variant for the *descensus Averni*, the extinction of the first personality to which the mystic must submit. Cuchulain, however, insolently tells how his own crossing has seemed 'charmed':

> A rumour has led me,
> A story told over the wine towards dawn.
> I rose from table, found a boat, spread sail,
> And with a lucky wind under the sail
> Crossed waves that have seemed charmed, and found this shore.

The Old Man, as against this, has been waiting all his life beside the well, undergoing an endless period of initiation, suffering torments from cold, snaring the birds for food and eating grass, yet the well, which fills at once for Cuchulain, has never filled for him:

> Old Man: Why should that hollow place fill up for you,
> That will not fill for me? I have lain in wait
> For more than fifty years, to find it empty,
> Or but to find the stupid wind of the sea
> Drive round the perishable leaves.

Beneath the detail of Yeats's argument here lies a terrible spiritual malaise. It is not true, he centrally tells us, that all personalities are equally susceptible of the religious life: spiritual fulfilment, like all else, is dependent upon a mere accident of the personality. One man, Cuchulain, whose position in Yeats's cycle of personality is at the hero's crescent and thus at the stage where the visionary state may be achieved without labour, may hear of the Self for the first time 'over the wine' and discover it for himself without difficulty and indeed without any real sense of the importance of the undertaking; another may spend all his life in the desolation of the Waste Land, but for all his asceticism arrive no nearer to his goal. Recovered innocence, sanctity, acquired humility, are of no importance to the quest: one finds the grail, or does not find it, simply by those talents which are given at birth. In all this argument, which is the more terrible for being so dispassionately stated, Yeats's sympathies are obviously with the Old Man. Cuchulain is cast in the mould of William Morris, for whom (Yeats tells us) the conquest of the personality was easy; but his companion is in the mould of Yeats himself, 'racked by doubt and enquiry', for whom the elixir seemed always out of reach.

Cuchulain, arriving at the well, has already completed an essential part of his pilgrimage, for the natural subjectivity with which he is endowed has brought him directly to the goal he seeks. He has had no need to jettison his first personality, but can proceed directly to the Meeting with the Virgin, the union of self and anti-self. We should therefore expect to find the Virgin at the well-side, as she is beside the cauldron in the slightly different symbolism of Hanrahan's visit to the grail castle; there he climbs the symbolic hill much as Cuchulain does in this play, to find her sitting surrounded by the whetstone, sword and spear which are traditional grail accessories. The woman who waits for Cuchulain is of a very different kind, though the great stone on which she sits and the long rake which she holds might conceivably be taken as ironic distortions of the grail emblems of spear and whetstone. There is bitter metaphysical comment in Yeats's inversion of his own earlier imagery:

> The guardian of the well is sitting
> Upon the old grey stone at its side,
> Worn out from raking its dry bed,
> Worn out from gathering up the leaves;
> Her heavy eyes
> Know nothing, or but look upon stone.
> The wind that blows out of the sea
> Turns over the heaped-up leaves at her side;
> They rustle and diminish.

The transcendental virgin, then, does not exist, or if she does man cannot come at her: instead of the image of perfection we seek, our pilgrimage leads us only to its absolute negation, the limp creature under the dry tree. Yeats's dry tree itself confirms the barrenness of the search, for it is the Kabbalistic Tree of Life, seen in its negative or forbidding aspect: it is referred to explicitly as a hazel, since Yeats took the hazel as the Celtic equivalent for the Jewish symbol. In the branches of the 'withered hazel' the sea-wind, symbol of man's harsh and implacable destiny, blows without intermission.

In these unpromising circumstances Cuchulain and the Old Man begin their meditation, only for each to be distracted in his own way. The Old Man, if we may take him first, is visited by a magical sleep, as has happened to him several times before at moments when the well has filled:

> The accursed shadows have deluded me,
> The stones are dark and yet the well is empty.
> The water flowed and emptied while I slept.

This incident brings us very close to the grail legends, where the adventurer is often stigmatised in this way: Gawaine, for example, penetrates the castle of the Fisher King, only to be plunged into deep trance at the moment when the grail passes before him. In the Irish legends paralleling the myth, such magical inhibition is also common, and in Yeats's early story Hanrahan is cheated of his vision by a sudden supernaturally induced lassitude of the same kind. He recovers to find himself on the bare hillside and virgin, castle, grail and its attendant symbols, have all disappeared. The meaning in each of these cases is the same, and it is of course that the sleeper is rejected as undeserving.[86] Yeats's Old Man has not failed in his mystical discipline, but the discipline has repudiated him.

Cuchulain, however, is not rejected as undeserving, and his failure to drink of the miraculous water can be blamed on no cause outside himself. Together with the pessimism that is his central theme, one function of Yeats's argument is certainly to show us the strength of the subjective personality: thus Cuchulain is perfectly confident that the good fortune which has made him what he is will not desert him during his vigil at the well:

> My luck is strong,
> It will not leave me waiting, nor will they
> That dance among the stones put me asleep.

And it does indeed happen that, despite Cuchulain's having had no initiatory period to 'make his soul', and even though he has not been fortified by the meeting with the transcendental virgin, the water begins to flow as soon as he arrives. For the pure subjective, as Yeats saw the type, contains within his first personality all that is necessary to his salvation, and the three stages of the alchemical discipline, *perfectio*, *contemplatio* and *libertas*, follow for him in simple and unbroken sequence. And yet, as the proverb says, 'the setting of the senses is the rising of truth', and if one of man's four faculties asserts itself against the others, his meditation must be broken.* This happens with Cuchulain, and the implication is that it is inevitably the fate of all who cultivate the mystical life. The drafts of the play make it clear that Fand, the 'mountain witch', has as many disguises as there are men, and that the 'dancers' who symbolise the presences of the spiritual world mock humanity at every turn.

We cannot perhaps fully understand the significance of Yeats's climax without the analogy of the myth of Gautama, which here becomes strikingly relevant. There are references to the Buddha in *Dhoya*, in Yeats's study of Morris, and in that image in 'The Double Vision Of Michael Robartes' which describes his making 'a moment' eternal by contemplation, so that we have every right to see parallelism here also. When the future Buddha begins his motionless meditation under the Green Tree, the legend has him tempted by Mara, God of love and death: the God makes three attempts to break his concentration, and these compare closely with the successive machinations of Fand. As Fand does, the God first materialises in his own person, and attacks Gautama with every weapon at his command; then he sends down his three daughters, Desire, Pining and Lust, and finally calls up his army, who pelt the future Buddha with mountain crags. When all these devices have failed, Mara capitulates to his adversary, who then passes through the successive stages of emancipation and experiences total enlightenment at the break of day. Cuchulain, however, is defeated at every turn: he does indeed fight off Fand when she attacks him in person (as a hawk), but he is distracted both by desire for the possessed guardian and, at the end of the play, by his determination to do battle with the army the Goddess sends against him, the 'women of the hills'. The Old Man implores him not to leave the well, but Cuchulain is adamant:

> I will face them!
> He comes! Cuchulain, son of Sualtim, comes!

Thus Cuchulain is overcome by each of the passions of love and war, and the contrast with the Eastern legend becomes obvious. The discipline of the Self, I think Yeats implied, demands superhuman potentialities, which we may look for in the future Buddha, but have no right to expect of merely natural man.

* The hawk-symbol in Yeats's poetry is often associated with abstraction, the dissociation of the faculties (as in 'Meditations In Time Of Civil War'). The hawk in his play, as I have tried to suggest, has several meanings, but this is one way in which we might take it.

Yeats himself came to read into his play a further significance of a slightly different kind (though it corroborates the reading I have given), for he thought of it in later life as illustrative of his philosophy of the hero. When Yeats speaks of this type in *A Vision*[87] he has spiritual heroism in mind; Nietzsche, and indeed all the other subjective philosophers of the world, serve as representative examples. Because the hero finds it easy to achieve Unity of Being, Yeats says that his proper task is to align himself to 'the overflowing fountain of personal life' within him; he must then 'deliver' his personality, by 'philosophic intellect', from 'all that is topical or temporary', after which he will announce a philosophy 'marble-pure—the logical expression of a mind alone with the object of its desire'. But though the hero's true function is to make himself 'a cup that remembers but its own fullness', he has to struggle against 'sensuality, ambition, curiosity in all its species':

> The nature of the hero is conscious of the most extreme degree of deception, and is wrought to a frenzy of desire for truth of self. The man is pursued by a series of accidents which ... drive him into all sorts of ambitions alien to his nature ... and these ambitions he defends by some kind of superficial intellectual action, the pamphlet, the violent speech, the sword of the swashbuckler.[88]

Read in the calmer climate of *A Vision* Yeats's disillusioned play thus becomes a symbolic representation of the (avoidable) downfall of the hero. Cuchulain should, and it is there suggested *could*, earn deliverance from the wheel of becoming by participation in the higher self, after which he should offer his spiritual history to the world; instead, he condemns himself to a career of violent and meaningless action, and this is responsible for the developing tragedy of his life. Taken in this way, *At The Hawk's Well* supplies the psychological data for Yeats's whole Cuchulain cycle, though I do not think he intended quite this at the time it was composed. So far from assuming that the hero can and must fulfil his adventure, the play allows Cuchulain no chance to achieve the grail: where *A Vision* blames the adventurer, in the drama it is the adventure itself that is condemned.

Eccentric as it may make *At The Hawk's Well* in the canon of Yeats's work, there is no doubt that such is its central argument. The spiritual life is stigmatised as inhuman, and Yeats drives home his interpretation through the closing songs. As Cuchulain's quest reaches its climax of failure, the chorus turn away from the action altogether, and they do so with the gesture of one who is appalled by the atmosphere in which it has been played out. There is no indication of pity, but merely a suggestion of air not fit to breathe:

> Chorus: Come to me, human faces,
> Familiar memories:
> I have found hateful eyes
> Among the desolate places.
> Unfaltering, unmoistened eyes.
>
> Folly alone I cherish,
> I choose it for my share
> Being but a mouthful of air,
> I am content to perish;
> I am but a mouthful of sweet air.
>
> O lamentable shadows,
> Obscurity of strife!
> I choose a pleasant life
> Among indolent meadows.
> Wisdom must live a bitter life.

The argument of these lines is used to make Yeats's point, that 'wisdom is the property of the dead' and that humanity should accept its own frailty and renounce the bitter struggle for spiritual knowledge; but the emotional effect is even more conclusive than the intellectual. Yeats builds up a powerful effect by such key words as 'hateful' 'desolate' 'lamentable' 'obscurity', and by the horrifying image of Fand's dry unwinking eyes, which the moisture of generation has never touched. The spiritual life is thus made to seem almost physically repellent, a suggestion which Yeats reinforces by the rhythm and phrasing of his lyric, Japanese alike in its resignation and good sense.

The chorus from which I have quoted marks a breaking point of tension, for Yeats has accumulated his oppressive atmosphere from speech to speech throughout the play. He has done so dispassionately and entirely without comment, and by this means the tension has been greatly heightened, so that the audience is certain to respond to the appeal to natural emotion when it comes. One does not know what to admire most in the technique on which Yeats builds: the long, functionally monotonous descriptions of dry well and dry tree with which he begins; the muted bitterness of the Old Man's speeches to the Guardian; or those unforgettable single strokes by which the characters are sculpted: 'If I grow drowsy I can pierce my foot'; 'If you are good you will leave it'. Yeats achieves his effect, sometimes, by adopting the most primitive of techniques, depending on simple question and answer, or on a sentence-construction almost frightening in its crude force. How much ugliness, in what follows, is communicated by the simple accentuation of the words 'hole' and 'get':

> He has made a little heap of leaves:
> He lays the dry sticks on the leaves,
> And, shivering with cold, he has taken up
> The fire-stick and socket from its hole.
> He whirls it round to get a flame;
> And now the dry sticks take the fire,
> And now the fire leaps up and shines
> Upon the hazels and the empty well.

Into this landscape of suffering and despair Yeats sends his dissolute Gawaine, and every inflection of language shows what the outcome must be. The grail is lost even in the monosyllables used to describe it.

VI

At The Hawk's Well is the *Ash Wednesday* of Yeats's poetry. The imagery used to describe the quest itself is precisely what Eliot draws upon for the last section of *The Waste Land*, but *The Waste Land* is a poem of hope and spiritual ambition, and it was not until eight years after its composition that Eliot had reached the stage in experience reflected by Yeats's play:

Because I do not hope to know again
The infirm glory of the positive hour
Because I do not think
Because I know I shall not know
The one veritable transitory power
Because I cannot drink
There, where trees flower, and springs flow, for there is nothing
  again . . .[89]

This gives us of course the exact imagery and argument of *At The Hawk's Well*, tree, spring, and the sense of spiritual destitution, and the overall similarities are in fact astonishingly close: Eliot goes on to explain how he has reached the 'middle way' in the religious life which is the limit of his capacity, describing his initiation and spiritual death at the hands of the three symbolic 'white leopards'; his resuscitation after the meeting with the Lady 'in the white gown' who is the 'spirit of the fountain' and thus at one level of meaning the transcendental virgin; and his journey up the winding stair of intellectual beauty and spiritual knowledge, which took him no further than the third flight. Yeats reached a parallel plane of visionary understanding, though he did so by an opposite religious discipline, substituting faith in the Self for Eliot's absolute dependence, reflected in *Ash Wednesday*, on an external guiding power: like Eliot, he climbed 'beyond hope and despair' until distracted by what his play images as sexual desire. Here, for comparison with the climax of *At The Hawk's Well*, is the image Eliot uses for his own defection:

> Blown hair is sweet, brown hair over the mouth blown,
> Lilac and brown hair;
> Distraction, music of the flute, stops and steps of the mind over the third stair.[90]

The one distinction, apart from the fact that Yeats's narrative makes little of the initiatory period and *katabasis*, is that Eliot speaks of having fragmentary glimpses of a plane of mystical reality higher than that of his third stair; but this does not necessarily testify to the superiority of the Christian discipline. As I have said already, the bitterness of Yeats's dance-play indicates no more than a temporary sense of failure, and he found it possible in later life to recommence the ascent. Even while he was writing *Four Plays For Dancers* there is evidence in the confident argument of *Calvary* that he began to take fresh hope; and later, in 'A Dialogue Of Self And Soul', we are returned to the image of the basin of man's mind, in which the miraculous water of present immortality now effortlessly overflows.

At The Hawk's Well and *The Only Jealousy Of Emer* are in fact the only plays Yeats wrote in his period of total disillusion, and after this he fluctuated between confident spiritual endeavour and the determination not to make progress in the religious life at the expense of his art. In 1916, however, the collapse of his private life made the *participation mystique* appear an unthinkable ambition, and it is interesting to note that Morris's discipline of the 'lower self' or fully integrated personality is the alternative on which Yeats fell back. Here is the passage in which he describes how Morris's women make the renunciation of 'ecstasy' or spiritual ambition, and explains how they choose instead a contented identification of the rhythm of their lives and that of the passing days and seasons; an identification which is the fruit of true personality:

> They do not seek in love that ecstasy which Shelley's nightingale called death, but rather a gentle self-surrender that would lose half its sweetness if it lost the savour of coming days. They are good housewives; they sit often at the embroidery frame, have the wisdom of flocks and herds, and are above all fruitful mothers. It seems at times as if their love was less a passion for one man out of the world than submission to the hazard of destiny and the hope of motherhood and the innocent desire of the body. They accept changes and chances of life as gladly as they accept spring and summer and autumn and winter, and because they have sat under the shadow of the Green Tree and drunk the Waters of Abundance out of their hollow hands, the barren blossoms do not seem to them the most beautiful.[91]

There is fulfilment in all this, of course, for Morris's women have mastered the two lower of the three planes of life, but it is nevertheless a spiritual discipline and they have learned to accept their limitations. Yeats's own play insists that there is no discipline, save theirs, on which humanity can safely build, as noticeably in the chorus recited at the moment of Cuchulain's spiritual failure:

> Chorus: He has lost what may not be found
> Till men heap his burial mound
> And all the history ends.
> He might have lived at his ease,
> An old dog's head on his knees
> Among his children and friends.

If we allow for the harshness of tone which characterises Yeats's whole play, it will be clear that what is here opposed to the religious life is precisely that lower fulfilment which is had of the well of natural abundance. 'Folly alone I cherish', Yeats's chorus go on—a phrase in which the life of spiritual wisdom is repudiated as alien—and they propose instead that 'pleasant life' among 'indolent meadows' which Morris's characters see as the *summum bonum*.

The final chorus of Yeats's play stands even closer to his essay on Morris. What he there calls 'the barren blossoms' are themselves made to speak, and they mock their own celebrant:

> 'The man that I praise'
> Cries out the empty well
> 'Lives out all his days
> Where a hand on the bell
> Can call the milch cows
> To the comfortable door of his house.
> Who but an idiot would praise
> Dry stones in a well?
>
> 'The man that I praise'
> Cries out the leafless tree
> 'Has married and stays
> By an old hearth, and he
> On naught has set store
> But children and dogs on the floor.
> Who but an idiot would praise
> A withered tree?

Here we are returned to the detail of the prose passage I have quoted: Yeats's idealised old man and woman might be Morris's hero and heroine aged by twenty years. They have the same 'wisdom in flocks and herds', the same 'innocent joy' in parenthood, and they are shown in the same 'submission to the hazard of destiny'; so that, consciously or subconsciously, I think Yeats has in mind what he had written in 1902. The style of his play is spare and disillusioned even when he is writing of his *summum bonum*, and it may be that it did not seem to him as he wrote a 'finish worthy of the start' of the grail adventure. But it was all that life had, or seemed to have, to offer, and he therefore contrives to balance acceptance and implicit bitterness. Here again one thinks of *Ash Wednesday*:

> Teach us to care and not to care.
> Teach us to sit still.[92]

The tone in which Eliot concludes his poem is not substantially different.

CHAPTER THREE

THE ONLY JEALOUSY OF EMER

I

At The Hawk's Well was no more than a first experiment, but it solved most of Yeats's initial problems in creating an indigenous form of Noh theatre. He discovered simply by writing it the correct ratio of dialogue to choric song—a matter to which he had given much careful consideration[1]—and he learned how to construct his 'image', balancing narrative, music, dancing and metaphysical suggestion so as to achieve that archetypal communication that was his aim. His success served merely as the incentive to set himself fresh problems, and *The Only Jealousy Of Emer*, the next of his plays to be conceived if not the next to be finished, is as adventurous a piece of work as its precursor. Whatever seemed least well done in the earlier experiment would now take first place in his interests, so that the two are compensatory rather than identical achievements, and indeed survive as in some ways opposite statements of what can be learned from a Japanese play.

At The Hawk's Well, I think, stands furthest removed from the Japanese at the level of folk-lore; it is not really, as the Noh dramas often were, grounded in the primitive superstitions of the country people. The central story is certainly taken from pagan heroic legend, but a first hearing makes it clear that the significance does not end there, and we sense that Yeats's symbolism is studied 'in a learned school'. This is well shown from the verses in which the chorus set the scene, for which there are multiple symbolic associations: Gawaine on his quest for the grail, man completing the ascent of Abiegnos, the purgatorial mountain, William Morris's dry well and dry tree; none of which have any connection at all with the Irish peasant imagination:

> I call to the eye of the mind
> A well long choked up and dry
> And boughs long stripped by the wind,
> And I call to the mind's eye

> Pallor of an ivory face,
> Its lofty dissolute air,
> A man climbing up to a place
> The salt sea wind has swept bare.

Emer is quite opposite in this respect, as in some others: there is no symbolism of any kind in the words with which the chorus set the scene. They are merely darkly atmospheric, as one could wish in a play to be based on the most sinister of primitive myths:

> I call before the eyes a roof
> With cross-beams darkened by smoke.
> A fisher's net hangs from a beam,
> A long oar lies against the wall.
> I call up a poor fisher's house.

With these words Yeats must have felt that he had bought his full dramatic freedom, for he had written in *Discoveries* that this kind of primitive atmosphere was the one he most desired. In the course of one of his spirited attacks on Ibsen, who is blamed for making a play turn on 'a quarrel over the purity of the water in some Norwegian spa', and for conducting this scene in language that is 'that of the newspapers' 'words I have used when talking of the rates',[2] Yeats questions whether there is any room for naturalism in the serious theatre. All great plays, he says, have something of the appearance of 'an old wives' tale'; the dramatist takes some 'wild parable' for the sake of associations it arouses 'in the depth of his mind', and, 'scornful of the outer world', concentrates on his fantastic narrative and on his inner vision.[3] *Emer*, at the surface level, is nothing if not an 'old wives' tale', and it differs from *At The Hawk's Well* in that it is a totally satisfying achievement on this simplest of planes, so that we can if we wish take it as a 'wild parable' and nothing more.

When the setting has been described and the chorus have sung their introductory song, the curtain is drawn back on one of the most barbaric of tableaux conceivable. Cuchulain has been drowned, or perhaps thrown into a 'cataleptic trance', after his celebrated fight against the sea: his body is propped on a bed in the 'poor fisher's house'; and Emer, presently joined by Eithne, is sitting by the bed. At its foot crouches Cuchulain's ghost, dressed in grave-clothes, drawn back after death by the 'longing' and 'cries' of those who have loved him, and invisible and inaudible to the watchers though present to the audience. In this way Yeats entrenches himself in the primitivity he requires, and the developing dialogue, as Emer speculates whether some changeling may not have been put into Cuchulain's place, takes us even further into the realms of aboriginal superstition:

> It may be
> An image has been put into his place,
> A sea-borne log bewitched into his likeness
> Or some stark horseman grown too old to ride
> Among the troops of Manannan, son of the sea,
> Now that his joints are stiff.

This is an allusion to the Celtic superstition of 'the touch', or divine substitution, and Yeats has borrowed his imagery from the folk-compendium by Lady Wilde:

> The evil influence of the fairy glance does not kill, but it throws the object into a death-like trance, in which the real body is carried off to some fairy mansion, while a log of wood, or some ugly deformed creature, is left in its place, clothed with the shadow of the stolen form.[4]

In fact, Cuchulain has been 'given the touch' by Fand, the woman of the Sidhe who declares her love for him in *At The Hawk's Well*; she spirits his soul from his body as he falls senseless after fighting the sea. The 'ugly, deformed creature' of tradition is then substituted, and her waves carry his body to the fisherman's door.[5]

Yeats's letters show that he planned to make great play with this concept of divine substitution, as he does with the concept of possession in *At The Hawk's Well*. Cuchulain wears the heroic, and the changeling a 'distorted', mask; the plot requires a double change of mask as the changeling takes possession of and leaves the hero's body; and, with characteristic exaggeration, Yeats says he wrote his whole play for the sake of this device:

> *The Only Jealousy Of Emer* was written to find what dramatic effect could be got out of a mask, changed while the player remains on the stage to suggest a change of personality.[6]

Another letter speculates on the nature of the being to be substituted, and Yeats makes a number of dark suggestions; all of them, we may notice, in conformity with the plots of certain Noh plays:

> I want to follow *The Hawk's Well* with a play on *The Only Jealousy Of Emer*, but I cannot think who should be the changeling put in Cuchulain's place when he is taken to the other world. There would be two masks, changed upon the stage. Who should it be: Cuchulain's grandfather, or some god or devil or woman?[7]

In fact, when Eithne compels the changeling to declare himself, he turns out to be Bricriu of the withered arm, pagan divinity and traditional 'maker of discord'. Eithne conjures Bricriu by means of a kiss, and Yeats goes deeply into esoteric doctrine in thus asserting the power of the kiss against the touch At the same time, he establishes one of those simple antitheses from which his plays obtain their interior logic: Eithne's kisses of life have their own magical property, and in this way serve to set off Fand's 'Kiss Of Death'.

Out of his settled malevolence, Bricriu touches Emer's eyes so that she can see her husband's ghost: he does this because he knows that the gift will bring her little good. Emer's second sight shows her Cuchulain in the arms of Fand, who has crossed the sea in her chariot to regain possession of his soul and to carry him away for ever to the Country-Under-Wave. Yeats presents his goddess wearing a costume of great opulence and a golden or bronze mask, and the words given to describe her are of considerable ambiguity; they obviously connect with his highly mystical poem *The Phases Of The Moon*, though there is no compulsion on an audience to see more in them than folk-lore:

> Emer: I know her sort.
> They find our men asleep, weary with war,
> Lap them in cloudy hair or kiss their lips.
> Our men awake in ignorance of it all,
> But when we take them in our arms at night
> We cannot break their solitude.

Cuchulain and the goddess now make love in a scene of steadily growing aesthetic beauty, but Emer is told by the malignant Bricriu that there is one way in which she can rescue the man she loves. This, in deference once more to peasant superstition, is by sacrificing the thing she holds dearest in the world; for it is well known of the Sidhe that (though they do not wish to) they have to release their captives in the face of such substitute-gifts:

> The fisher, when some knowledgeable man
> Restores to him his wife or son or daughter
> Knows he must lose a boat or net, or it may be
> The cow that gives his children milk, and some
> Have offered their own lives.

So Emer renounces the chance that she will ever again be 'the apple of Cuchulain's eye', Fand vanishes at once, and, just as the hero is in the process of repossessing his now inanimate body, Eithne returns to the room. She completes the restoration, as before, with a kiss:

> Eithne: Come to me, my beloved, it is I,
>   I, Eithne Inguba. Look, he is there,
>   He has come back and moved upon the bed
>   And it is I that won him from the sea,
>   That brought him back to life.

Thus Cuchulain, awakening, thinks Eithne responsible for his rescue and falls into her arms; and with this irony, and with a strange and difficult final chorus, the play ends.

So much for the play at the simplest, exoteric level, where it is one of the wildest of all Yeats's conceptions, as it is one of the most variously beautiful. Its variety is stabilised by the perfection of his form, for *Emer*, alternating as it does between the poles of quiet aesthetic beauty (what Yeats calls 'stillness') and melodrama, is structurally one of the most flawless of his dramas. It begins from calm with the fragile opening lyric 'white shell, white wing', and this delicacy persists, for a little, into the main text. The vignette of Eithne's first entrance has a strange, subdued power:

> She stands a moment in the open door.
> Behind the open door, the bitter sea,
> The shining, bitter sea is crying out.

Then, as the atmosphere grows more sinister and the group round the bed unfolds, there are those strong lines by which Yeats hammers into our imaginations the world of Celtic myth. The imagery here is archaic, but there is modernity in the rhythms, and the verse has, as much as anything in Yeats, 'the prior virtues of good prose':

> It may be ...
> A sea-borne log bewitched into his likeness
> Or some stark horseman grown too old to ride
> Among the troops of Manannan, son of the sea,
> Now that his joints are stiff.

And even in the more conversational sections the sinewy thews of good prose remain; in Emer's bitter 'we're but two women fighting with the sea'; in the line spoken of the dead, 'It is hard to make them hear among their darkness'; or in the thrilling dispute over the corpse that leads up to the first melodramatic climax:

> I felt some evil thing that dried my heart
> When my lips touched it ...
>   ... look at that arm,
> That arm is withered to the very socket.

Then, as the centrepiece of the play, there are the octosyllabics of the meeting between Cuchulain and Fand. Much of the writing here is of a studied opulence:

> Who is it stands before me there,
> Shedding such light from limb and hair
> As when the moon, complete at last,
> With every labouring crescent past,
> And lonely with extreme delight,
> Flings out upon the fifteenth night?

But there is also the dynamic of a tough—almost a cynical—reasonableness:

> Cuchulain: O Emer, Emer, there we stand,
> Side by side and hand in hand
> Tread the threshold of the house
> As when our parents married us.
> Fand: Being among the dead you love her
> That valued every slut above her
> While you still lived.

> Cuchulain: O, my lost Emer!
> Fand: And there is not a loose-tongued schemer
> But could draw you, if not dead,
> From her table and her bed . . .

Next comes the second histrionic climax, Emer's renunciation, followed by Cuchulain's terse and terrifying summary of the action 'I have been in some strange place and am afraid'; and, finally, by a return to stasis with the final chorus of the 'statue of solitude', where 'stillness' and melodrama coexist. But the melodrama has now been sublimated, purified into great art:

> He that has loved the best
> May turn from a statue
> His too human breast

In this way *Emer* follows what seems to me the characteristic course of symbolist poetry: from calm, through violent emotion, to the discovery of a cold, hard image in which emotion and a sense of stasis can be joined. Thus 'Sailing To Byzantium' moves through a world of fluid imagery to the stasis of the last stanza with its metal bird; or (after an extensive peregrination) Yeats's late lyric 'The Statues' rights itself on the heroic image of Cuchulain, and can end on the formal invective of the final verse.[8]

Having praised *Emer* as I have done, I ought to say something of the prose revision of the play which Yeats called *Fighting The Waves*, and which he himself came to prefer. It was written as a concession to the public theatre, when Antheil had composed his music and masks had been made which Yeats admired. *Emer*, we should remember, was intended for drawing-room performance only:

> Somebody put it [the unrevised play] on a public stage in Holland, and Hildo van Krop made his powerful masks. Because the dramatist who can collaborate with a great sculptor is lucky, I rewrote the play, not only to fit it for such a stage, but to free it from abstraction and confusion . . . in prose which I have tried to make very simple.[9]

The prose of *Fighting The Waves* is of that almost naïve kind which Yeats uses again in *The Resurrection* and his unpublished play *The Bridegroom*; its simplicity is joined to genuine epical breadth; and there are none of those spurious biblical cadences that disfigure, say *The Brook Kerith*, if I may contrast his old antagonist, George Moore. Here for example is part of the opening chorus, the words the musicians speak when we first see Cuchulain's lifeless body lying on the bed:

> It is that famous man Cuchulain, the best man with any sort of weapon, the best man to gain the love of a woman; his wife Queen Emer is at his side; there is no one with her, for she has sent everyone away, but yonder at the door someone stands and hesitates, wishes to come into the room but is afraid to do so; it is young Eithne Inguba, Cuchulain's mistress. Behind her, through the open door, the stormy sea. At the foot of the bed dressed in grave-clothes, the ghost of Cuchulain is kneeling.

The end of this passage may not measure up to Yeats's verse, but I would rather have the beginning than the hectic rhythms used in *Emer*:

> A man lies dead or swooning,
> That amorous man,
> That amorous, violent man, renowned Cuchulain,
> Queen Emer at his side.
> At her own bidding all the rest are gone
> But now one comes on hesitating feet,
> Young Eithne Inguba, Cuchulain's mistress.
> She stands a moment in the open door.
> Behind the open door, the bitter sea,
> The shining, bitter sea, is crying out.

Another of the successes of the prose is the description of Cuchulain's fight with the sea.

> I think he loved her (Aoife) as no man ever loved, for when he heard the name of the man he had killed, and the name of that man's mother, he went out of his senses utterly. He ran into the sea and with shield before him and sword in hand he fought the deathless sea.

To parallel *Emer* here is to see how very similar the two plays are, but the verse is inferior in that it is orotund:

> And thereupon, knowing what man he had killed,
> And being mad with sorrow, he ran out
> And after, to his middle in the foam,
> With shield before him and with sword in hand
> He fought the deathless sea.

There is, furthermore, together with some rather stilted love-poetry at least one really bad speech·in *Emer*, where Yeats's enthusiasm for the least interesting kind of Elizabethan supernaturalism seems to run away with him. Emer is asked whether Cuchúlain has really been drowned.

> Emer: Cuchulain is not dead.
> The very heavens when that day's at hand,
> So that his death may not lack ceremony
> Will throw out fires, and the earth grow red with blood...
> [etc.]

Fighting The Waves substitutes for all this the very simple and dignified statement 'the fishermen think him dead, it was they that put the grave-clothes on him'. Or finally, one might quote the words given to Eithne at the end of the prose play, for which there is no exact parallel in the earlier version.* Emer has made her renunciation; unaware of this, Cuchulain's young mistress comes into the room and makes one last effort to recall his spirit; and Cuchulain returns:

> Eithne: Cuchulain, Cuchulain! Remember our last meeting. We lay all night among the sandhills; dawn came; we heard he crying of the birds upon the shore. Come to me, beloved.

If we know Yeats's mind well enough, we shall see here a reminiscence of a favourite passage in the *Iliad*, and one which he probably draws on for his own dramatic tableau. Much as Fand rescues Cuchulain's body after his fight with the waves, Aphrodite spirits Paris away from certain death on the battlefield, and deposits him safely on his bed in Troy. Helen comes to persude her lover back to consciousness, just as

---

* The *imagery* (and thus the allusion) does occur there, but not at the climax of the play: it is placed earlier, in the middle of a long passage of rather laboured love-poetry. Even in *Fighting The Waves*, the simplicity of this particular speech may be slightly artificial and over-sophisticated; but my adjective 'Homeric' above is approximate, of course, and does not imply consistent perfection.

Eithne comes to Cuchulain; and when Paris eventually speaks to her, his first words are of love:

> Come let us go to bed together and be happy in our love. Never has such desire overwhelmed me, not even in the beginning, when I carried you off from lovely Lacedaemon in my sea-going ships and we spent the night on the isle of Cranae in each other's arms.[10]

The lines in *Fighting The Waves*, then, are a true index to what I can only call the Homeric spirit of Yeats's prose, and he is perhaps the only modern writer to whom these words could be applied.

Fighting The Waves could not really be called a better play than *Emer*, and I hope my last paragraph does not suggest this; it is a play of music, spectacle and dances rather than of the written word, and dances and spectacle, though they may constitute fine art, are not literature. There are in fact as many as three dances to *Emer*'s one: there is the panorama at the beginning, symbolic of Cuchulain's fight with the sea; a central dance to image his seduction by Fand; and one before the final chorus, called 'Fand mourns among the waves' 'a dance which symbolises, like water in the fortune-telling books, bitterness'.[11] We lose most, clearly, in the central episode of the seduction-scene: this dance is there in the verse-play as in the prose, but in the latter it is left to communicate in its own right and Yeats dispenses with all that dialogue in octosyllabics which is one of the best things in *Emer*. He clearly suppresses it for fear that it might prove too cryptic for a public audience; there are other such suppressions (I use the word in preference to eliminations); and the success of *Fighting The Waves*, in consequence, is operatic rather than dramatic. We ought clearly to think of it as an exoteric play with *Emer* as its esoteric counterpart; of the one as an attempt at the 'Noh of the eye and ear'; and of the other as an attempt at the more inward 'Noh of the mind'. In its own *genre*, for all this, combining as it does a lavish visual beauty and a gravely dignified libretto, the prose play is unique.

I have said that *Fighting The Waves* is an achievement at the exoteric level, as it had to be to be fitted to the public stage, but this does not mean that ulterior significance has been kept out of it. One does not have to work hard to unearth the reminiscence of Homer mentioned, and there are many other borrowings both from occult theory and Yeats's tradition, of which I will instance the commentary (not present in the verse-play) on Eithne's 'Kiss of life'. Emer explains to her how a kiss may recall the dead from beyond the grave, or force an evil spirit to manifest, and she draws an elaborate analogy with the rituals of ceremonial magic. In magic, the adoration of an 'image' made of precious stone or metal may call down the god or spirit to whom the image is consecrated; thus the touch of Eithne's lips may recall Cuchulain's ghost:

> Emer (*pointing to Cuchulain's corpse*): Then kiss that image: these things are a great mystery, and maybe his mouth will feel the pressure of your mouth upon that image. Is it not thus that we approach the gods?*

There is more of this kind in *Fighting The Waves*, and much more of greater consequence as well, and when Yeats says that he has purged the play of 'abstraction and confusion', he means simply that he has forced most of his allusions beneath the surface. On the surface of *Emer*, there are symbols that point to his theories of beauty, reincarnation and Platonic love, which are the themes with which the play is concerned; Yeats is able to combine this symbolism with his folk-lore (as he is at pains to explain) simply because there is no disparity between the two, the learned symbologies of religion having grown up out of folk-lore. That these hidden themes persist in the prose-version is apparent from Yeats's preface, which he fills with allusions to Germistus Pletho and the philosophy of Samkara; to his theory of opposites and his belief in Anima Mundi; to whatever authorities he thought would help an interested reader to get beyond the pyrotechnics of a stage performance to his ultimate meaning. The preface to *Fighting The Waves*, in fact, supplies most of the data on which we must rely for an investigation of the earlier verse-play, and as such, prolix and difficult as it is, the student of *Emer* should be grateful for it.

II

One way of beginning the research for Yeats's esoteric meaning is to investigate the sources from which he took his plot. If I can show what I have shown of *At The Hawk's Well*, that he distorted and telescoped ancient legends, I shall be in a fair way to showing that he did so for similar reasons: to recover a totally archetypal image on which he could confer symbolic dimension.

* This is one of the several links between the play and Yeats's lyric 'Among School Children', where a similar logic is just beneath the surface, as in the line 'Both nuns and mothers worship images'. Is not this a (carefully veiled) attempt to read magical significance into the rituals of the Catholic Church?

The sources of *Emer* are more complex than those of its precursor, for Yeats drew both on Gaelic myth and on the Noh play *Hagoromo*. If Hiro Ishibashi is right,[12] he drew on the Noh play *Awoi No Uye* also, for Fand's ornate mask as well as for the image coined in an earlier lyric:

> Put off that mask of burning gold
> With emerald eyes.*

Hagoromo is a more definite source than this, though the story is not really similar: it tells how a Tennin (angel, or minor deity) loses her 'magic cloak', which a fisherman finds hanging on a tree. He refuses to return it unless she will dance for him and the play, which is one of the most beautiful of Noh plays, centres upon the ritual of her dance. The resemblance to *Emer* lies in the fact that the Tennin is a moon-goddess: she is goddess of the fifteenth night, the night of 'perfect fulfilment'; and her dance, which is 'a dance of pleasure', is the dance of the full moon:

> And now she, whose beauty is as the young moon,
> Shines on us in the sky of midnight
> The fifteenth night,
> With the beam of perfect fulfilment.[13]

She dances among her attendant nymphs, for 'there are heavenly nymphs, Amaotome, one for each night of the month'; in the play fifteen of these nymphs wear the white and fifteen the black dominoes. Pound's translation makes much of this detail, explaining that the dance is symbolical 'of the daily changes of the moon'. He quotes a familiar parallel in Dante:

> ... Quale ne' plenilunii sereni
> Trivia ride tra le ninfe eterne
> Che dipingono il ciel per tutti i seni

... As on clear nights of full moon Trivia [Diana] smiles among the eternal nymphs that deck the sky through all its depths.[14]

---

* Yeats knew *Awoi No Uye* in Pound's rather scrappy and inaccurate part-translation. He had read among Fenollosa's manuscripts the description of the ornate mask and costume worn by the Hannya (supernatural character), who further resembles Fand in that she travels between earth and heaven in a 'carriage'. *Hagoromo* (a play to which Pound continues to refer in his *Cantos*) was known to Yeats from his and later also Waley's translation; and is prominently quoted in Yeats's own *Visions And Beliefs*.

We cannot tell what Yeats will have made of all this, but the symbolism in *Emer*, where Fand dances before Cuchulain, connects closely with that of the Noh play:

> Cuchulain: Who is it stands before me there
> Shedding such light from limb and hair
> As when the moon, complete at last,
> With every labouring crescent past,
> And lonely with extreme delight
> Flings out upon the fifteenth night?

In *Fighting The Waves* there is the additional dance where Fand dances among her waves, who can be shown to symbolise her attendant nymphs.[15]

There are other points of similarity between the plays: *Hagoromo*, for example, has a fisherman as *Waki*, and this may have encouraged Yeats to site his own play in a fisherman's hut. More important, however, is the exact correspondence in bird and sea symbolism, for Yeats uses his images in a peculiarly Japanese sense. His first chorus shows a 'white bird', symbolising the soul, flying over the 'sea of eternity' or of the post-mortem condition, on its journey from heaven to the dry land of its reincarnation upon earth. Precisely the same symbolism occurs in a beautiful passage in the Noh play where the Tennin laments her lost cloak, without which she cannot remember the 'road' from earth to heaven. Looking out over a seascape overhung by cloud, she envies the 'wind', even the 'colour of breath' that flies up over that sea towards heaven; and she also envies the 'birds' (in Japanese tradition the souls of the dead) who preserve a sure memory of the road, 'going' to heaven or 'returning' from heaven to reincarnation, as they cross and recross above the 'waves' of the post-mortem state:

> Tennin: I have lost the knowledge of the road. Strange, a strange sorrow.
> Chorus: Enviable the colour of breath, wonder of clouds that fade along the sky that was our accustomed dwelling. Hearing the sky-bird, accustomed and well accustomed, hearing the voices grow fewer and fewer, the wild geese fewer and fewer, upon the highways of air, how deep her longing to return. Plover and seagull are on the waves in the offing. Do they go or do they return? She reaches out for the very blowing of the spring wind against heaven.[16]

None of the detail here could seem strange to Yeats: the bird he had known all his life as an emblem for the soul in most branches of folklore and tradition,[17] and wild geese flying offshore make a Celtic as much as a Japanese image for the departing dead; we may compare the description of the 'grey wing's path' at the end of his own play *The Green Helmet*. But the total panorama with its highly conscious symbolism was something new and striking, and the first chorus of *Emer* would hardly have been possible without the sophisticated Japanese source.

Yeats's enthusiasm for *Hagoromo* may have helped him with his symbolism, but his main plot he took from Irish myth. He uses, in fact, a continuation of the same legend on which he had based *At The Hawk's Well*, so that the two are in the fullest sense sister plays. Cuchulain, it will be remembered, once went out at Samhain to shoot birds as presents for the court ladies of Emain Macha, and Eithne Inguba sent him back to a certain lakeside to obtain one for her; Fand and her sister, in the shape of two yoked white birds, flew above him, and he shot at and winged one of them, which Yeats takes to mean that his physical beauty 'wounded' Fand with love. Yeats himself retells the continuation of the story,[18] where Cuchulain afterwards falls into a trance: Fand and her sister then materialise in human shape, as two women carrying green rods. They give him alternate strokes with these rods, by which is implied that they 'give him the touch', for in Yeats's words, 'in the Connacht stories the enchantment begins with a stroke, or with a touch from some person of fairy, and it is so the women deal with him'. The 'men of Ulster' then find Cuchulain's inert body and carry him 'to a house and to a bed', where he lies 'until the next November comes round'. Meanwhile his spirit is in fairyland where 'a king of the other world' (Labraid) needs his 'help in a war'; in exchange for this he is offered 'the love of Fand the wife of the sea-god Manannan'. At the end of a year Emer recovers her husband but (at least as Yeats understands the story) in a much more primitive way than in the dance-play. Here is his own paraphrase of the Gaelic original:

> She [Emer] and her women go armed with knives to the yew-tree upon Baile's strand where he [Cuchulain] had appointed a meeting with Fand, and outface Fand and drive her away.[19]

Fand accepts her discomfiture as final defeat, and promises not to see Cuchulain again.

Yeats's study of the myth in *Visions And Beliefs* is highly relevant to his play; one imagines that it grew up out of these paragraphs. He first retells the story, on the lines I have indicated, and then continues with a long note on the symbolism:

> We have here certainly a story of trance and the soul leaving the body, but probably it has passed through the minds of story-tellers who have forgotten the original meaning. There is no mention of anyone taking Cuchulain's place, but Professor Rhys in his reconstruction of the original story of 'Cuchulain and the beetle of forgetfulness' makes the prince who summons him to the adventure take his place in the court of Ulster.[20]

The theory of divine substitution was not, Yeats goes on to say, peculiar to Irish folk-lore; it was met with in all the mythologies of the world. He parallels the medieval legend of the nun possessed by the Virgin Mary, who took her place on earth, as also the story of Pwyll and Arawyn in the *Mabinogion*. Pwyll, king of Dyved, goes to the court of the dead in the ghost-king Arawyn's stead, and Arawyn substitutes for him on the Welsh throne. Yeats also compares the Norse myth of 'a false Odin that took the true Odin's place when the sun of summer became the wintry sun'.[21] In all these stories, Yeats goes on to say, the man is taken for the sake of his physical strength, for 'strength comes from among men and wisdom from among Gods who are but shadows';[22] a thought he later translated into verse, in 'Blood And The Moon':

> For wisdom is the property of the dead,
> A something incompatible with life, and power
> A property of the living.

His essay thus provided Yeats both with the material for a fruitful metaphysical speculation and with the subject for a future play. He had related the story of Cuchulain and Fand to a hypothetical original, and his drama is less concerned with the legend as we have it than with the Ur-legend or conjectural parent-myth.

Together with the changes that follow from my last paragraph, Yeats breaks with the canonical story in two salient respects. In the first place, he transposes in time what is essentially a narrative of Cuchulain's early manhood, making it take place after he has killed his son by Aoife, an incident on which he had already based the play

On Baile's Strand. In his remorse for his son's death, Cuchulain fights the sea'; and Yeats makes him wade out, his eyes always fixed on some distant object, until he falls into a trance; after this his soul is snatched from his body and the evil spirit Bricriu substituted. Yeats made this picturesque alteration for two reasons; partly (as I can only hope to confirm later) because it much enhances his symbolism and interior logic to have a hero in late middle-age; and partly in deference to the argument of *At The Hawk's Well*, because he had there put a curse on Cuchulain, and wanted to keep Fand and his hero apart till the curse could have translated itself into fact:

> That curse may be
> Never to win a woman's love and keep it;
> Or always to mix hatred in the love;
> Or it may be that she will kill your children,
> That you will find them, their throats torn and bloody,
> Or you will be so maddened that you kill them
> With your own hand.

This curse works itself out when Cuchulain does in fact kill his son, and, when Fand reappears to him, he awakes to the divine logic of events:

> Cuchulain: I know you now, for long ago
> I met you on a cloudy hill,
> Beside old thorn trees and a well.
> A woman danced and a hawk flew,
> I held out arms and hands; but you
> That now seem friendly, fled away,
> Half woman and half bird of prey.

Yeats's other departure from orthodox myth is at the end of his play, when Emer has to renounce Cuchulain's love for ever before his spirit can be retrieved. This change is at first difficult to account for, since the spirit of the myth is not in fact so primitive as Yeats would have us suppose. His prose essay hardly does justice to his original, which reads as follows:

'It is certain', said Emer, 'that I will not refuse this woman if you follow her. But all the same, everything red is beautiful, everything new is fair, everything commonplace is bitter, everything we are without is much thought of, everything we know is little thought

THE ONLY JEALOUSY OF EMER

of, till all knowledge is known. And O, Cuchulain', she said, 'I was at one time in esteem with you and I would be so again, if it were pleasing to you.'

Cuchulain says: 'by my word now . . . you are pleasing to me, and will be pleasing as long as I live'.

'Let me be given up', said Fand. 'It is better for me to be given up', said Emer. 'Not so', said Fand, 'it is I that will be given up in the end, and it is I that have been in danger of it all this time. . . . O Emer, the man is yours and well may you wear him, for you are worthy; what my arm cannot reach, that at least I may wish well to.'[23]

This is dignified and moving, and much less theatrical than the last-minute renunciation made by Yeats's own heroine, but there are two major reasons why he should have arranged his own climax differently and in the way he did. I might, first, extend the argument of my last section to say that melodrama is a virtue in the symbolist drama: where a play alternates between violence and 'stillness', it may well be a strength to have 'good theatre', rather than some subtler form of *dénouement*, at the former pole. And, second, the change was in any case necessary to Yeats's esoteric purpose: the Gaelic is simple narrative, while the most tremendous symbolic potentialities stem from the substitute-climax that he provides.

These, then, are Yeats's narrative sources, and he brought to them a number of personal associations which must have exercised a compulsive influence on his play. The descriptions of his moon-goddess, for example, are very striking, but she will seem less of a fortuitous creation if we remember that he had meditated this image for years. Yeats's interest in Fand dates back, I think, to the dreams of his early manhood, dreams which he studied closely, dividing them into the 'naturalistic' and 'visionary' categories as any occultist might do.* In one dream which seemed to have definite visionary significance, Yeats saw a woman remarkable for the 'miraculous mildness of her face'; and he half-seriously told himself that she was a purified spirit, one of those visitants which medieval occultism calls 'the Children of the Moon':

---

* Or as Eliot might: compare the lines in *Ash Wednesday*:

> Redeem
> The unread vision in the higher dream
> While jewelled unicorns draw by the gilded hearse.

All mystics believe in the 'higher dream'.

There are no such faces now. It was beautiful, as few faces are beautiful, but it had neither, one would think, the light that is in desire or hope or in fear or in speculation.[24]

And together with this impassivity, the face seemed to Yeats suffused with an elegiac sadness: 'it was peaceful like the faces of animals, or like the mute pools at evening, so peaceful that it was a little sad'.[25] I do not think it fanciful to see in this prose a first sketch of the serene 'idol' (and, ultimately, tragic heroine), who is Fand.

Whether or no Yeats continued, as he grew up, to attach visionary significance to his dream, there is every likelihood that he used so vivid an image for an early story. He had not, before *At The Hawk's Well*, used the legend of Fand herself to any extent, but he had drawn on a similar legend, where a goddess is enamoured of a human being, in his story of Red Hanrahan and Cloona of the Wave.[26] Here, Hanrahan calls up Cloona, 'a power of the air', by magic; she appears as a woman of precisely that serenity of feature which Yeats associated with his 'Children Of The Moon'; and she tells Hanrahan that he has always loved her:

You have always loved me better than your own soul, and you have sought me everywhere and in everything, though without knowing what you sought, and now I have come to you and taken on mortality.

And Cloona has loved Hanrahan in her turn 'from the night I saw you lying on the Grey Rath and saw you turning from side to side'; but, as Cuchulain was later to do with Fand, the man humiliates her and rejects her love.

>He that has loved the best
>May turn from a statue
>His too human breast.

This story seems to me doubly significant; it shows how the image of Yeats's early dream lingered in his imagination; and it also shows how he first evolved the situation on which his dance-play was to be built. Each of the plays I shall treat of in this book originates in an image or a story which Yeats conceived in early life; he needed to hibernate, if one may use the word, over an emotion, and his early stories are revived, after many years, as the basis for his mature art. *Emer*, restating as it does the theme of the mortal who loves, is loved by, and yet rejects a goddess, is no exception to this rule.

As well as his own early prose, Yeats had behind him when he wrote *Emer* William Larminie's powerful if unpolished 'Fand'. This seems to me to be one of the most spectacular achievements in Anglo-Irish nineteenth-century literature, though it has not yet been given its due; we shall now never know why Yeats did not include extracts in his own anthology of Irish poetry, but I feel sure that he had it in mind when he wrote his dance-play.[27] Larminie makes use of a moon-symbolism identical with his own—Fand is not in fact a moon-spirit in Celtic tradition—but the thrust and dynamic impact of his free verse are the qualities that will most have appealed to Yeats. He will have excused for their sake the crudities in Larminie's technique:

> Fand: Come to the summer of my beauty, come.
> Leave thou the cold pale spring;
> Winter is in its heart;
> And born of chill, to chill will it return:
> But I am summer eternal
> That have not ripened, being perfect ever,
> And shall not thence decline.
>
> *
>
> I am the moon, that having ne'er been crescent
> From fulness ne'er can wane:
> Vainly thou shalt not search for me in heaven,
> But over thee the river of my beauty
> Shall roll in floods, unstinted and unceasing,
> Shedding delight and bliss upon thy being,
> As the full moon pours light upon the sea.
>
> *
>
> Come to me, come, Cuhoolin!
> Open wide have I flung to thee
> The gates of the golden land, whose air giveth
>   life that dies not!
> Feelest thou not upon thy cheek the breezes
> Fanning thy flame of mortal to divine?
> Feelest thou not that its bliss floweth round thee,
>   soft as the waters,

> Into thy soul's mid-core, to the likeness of gods
> transforming?
> Surely into thy being already the glow divine hath
> enter'd.
> Never could'st thou endure the dull sad world again,
> The cold dark world of men and death;
> Turn from it, once and for ever
> And choose thou immortality and Fand.

If I conclude this survey of Yeats's sources with Larminie's violent poem, it is because of the importance I think it assumed in the development of his own interior 'image'. I know of no version of the myth so close in temper as this to Yeats's dance-play, nor any in which Fand is presented more nearly as he would have had her speak.

III

The right approach to Yeats's esoteric meaning is by way of his own notes, and these make it clear that he has leaned heavily upon Italian Renaissance Neoplatonism, of which he clearly knew much more than his critics have supposed. His wife had read Pico della Mirandola,[28] and though Yeats himself is modest about his knowledge of that philosopher, he acquired much that Pico could have taught him from the slightly later English Platonism of Henry More. One of his own Italian sources was Castiglione's *The Courtier*, and he says that he has drawn upon it in his text:

> I have filled *The Only Jealousy Of Emer* with my convictions about the nature and history of woman's beauty. Much that I have written might be a commentary upon Castiglione's saying that the physical beauty of woman is the spoil or monument of the victory of the soul, for physical beauty, only possible to subjective natures, is described as a result of emotional toil in past lives.[29]

The Platonism Castiglione learned from the schools of Pico and Gemistus Pletho is in fact important over the whole range of Yeats's poetry, and he is not writing idly in the famous lines in 'The Tower':

> I have prepared my peace
> *With learned Italian things*
> And the proud stones of Greece.

THE ONLY JEALOUSY OF EMER

What centrally Yeats learned from Italy was the logic of his theory of reincarnation, and of this *Emer* is perhaps his fullest statement.*

Before we go into the Italian theories, I ought to explain briefly why Yeats was predisposed to believe in them, for he had of course come to certain very similar conclusions before he took them into account. As he suggests in the note just quoted, they tend to follow naturally from the Platonic response to 'woman's beauty'. Either physical beauty has a spiritual significance or it has not; if it has (and neither Yeats nor any Platonist could doubt this for a moment) then it must be in some sense a manifestation of soul. The Italians were bound to conclude that it was such a manifestation—we have to remember their prior belief that the soul pre-existed the body—and it was easy to go on to credit the soul with certain shaping powers, which it exercised when it descended to the body between conception and birth. That the soul did descend in this way Yeats believed literally, and he had a clear image to show him how the descent was accomplished; he had read of the process in one of the finest passages in Blake, where Milton accepts the duty of reincarnation and enters his 'human shadow', leaving his 'heavenly body' and 'real immortal Self' behind in heaven:

As when a man dreams he reflects not that his body sleeps
Else he would wake, so seemed he entering his Shadow: but
With him the Spirits of the Seven Angels of the Presence
Entering, they gave him still perceptions of his Sleeping Body †
Which now arose and walked with them in Eden, as an Eighth
Image Divine tho' darkened and tho' walking as one walks
In sleep, and the Seven comforted and supported him.

*

Like as a Polypus that vegetates beneath the deep
They saw his Shadow vegetated underneath the Couch
Of Death; for when he enter'd into his Shadow, Himself,
His real and immortal Self, was, as appear'd to those
Who dwell in immortality, as One sleeping on a couch
Of gold, and those in immortality gave forth their Emanations
Like Females of sweet beauty to guard round him and to feed
His lips with food of Eden in his cold and dim repose:
But to himself he seem'd a wanderer lost in dreary night.[30]

* There is also another (and quite different) plane on which *Emer* could be called a Swedenborgian play; but discussion of this will be postponed till Chapter Six.
† i.e. the heavenly, or as Yeats sometimes calls it, the 'clarified body'. The Angels of the Presence undergo a similar parturition: their emanations accompany the man descending.

In the last resort a passage like this is either nonsense or it is simple vision, and Yeats had from very early manhood accepted it as the literal revealed truth. When he went to the Renaissance, then, he was seeking corroboration, and a clarification of the process by which the soul's work of 'shaping its vehicle' was carried out. For though Blake speaks contemptuously of the body here, he does not do so always; it is equally a 'Garden of Delight' built by the 'sons of Los' and 'Enitharmon's daughters': 'the human form divine', holy because it is a manifestation of soul.

In making M. Peter Bembo say that 'beautie is the true monument or spoile of the victorye of the soule . . . if the bodye, where she dwelleth, be not of so vile a matter, that she cannot imprint on it her propertye',[31] Castiglione clearly offered the needed corroboration; and he did so in the conventional language of the philosophy of his day. It was believed that matter was plastic; that a pure soul worked on it to construct a pure 'receptacle' or physical body; but that an impure soul could only very imperfectly do this. I will quote from Nesca Robb's *Neoplatonism Of The Italian Renaissance*:

> It was common belief among the Neoplatonists that the soul, descending from its Vehiculum Coeleste, formed a body for itself, and infused into that body the likeness of itself. Yet [this was an escape route and Yeats did not avail himself of it] matter is so variously disposed that two persons of like temperament may be totally unlike to outward view, the matter from which the one had to form his body having been more tractable than that of the other.[32]

There are many allusions to this theory in Italian Renaissance poetry, as for example in Michelangelo:

> L'immortal forma al tuo carcer terreno
> Com'angel venne.

The immortal form came like an angel to your earthly prison [having been borne down, Nesca Robb's commentary tells us, by the soul in its descent].[33]

A little later, it reached our own country with the writing of the Cambridge Platonists, and Yeats himself gives Henry More as an authority for his belief that 'the soul has a plastic power and can mould the body to any shape it will by an act of imagination'.[34] For this reason, as Castiglione says, 'the outward beautie is a true sign of the inward goodness', or in Yeats's own words 'Renaissance platonism cherished the beauty of the soul and the beauty of the body with an equal affection'.³⁵

Henry More was not centrally concerned with reincarnation and so was not able to take Yeats beyond first principles, but the Italians made much of that normal Platonic belief and adapted it to their theory with much ingenuity. The soul as they sometimes saw it progressed by a series of rebirths from primitive beginnings to a condition of great spirituality, and these changes in its metaphysical state would be reflected in its physical 'receptacle'. Michelangelo, for instance, applies this theory in his sonnets;* he thinks of the soul as reincarnating towards a goal of intellectual beauty 'con miglior sorte e con piu strema cura'; and he saw it as a law of nature that, when that zenith had been reached, a period of decline, or spiritual exhaustion, must begin. Thus he writes, of the cyclic process he envisaged, in a sonnet to his lover:

> Natura . . .
> S'al sommo errando di bellezza è giunta
> Nel tuo divino, è vecchia, e de'perire.

If now in your divine face the absolute of beauty has been attained, nature is exhausted and has reached the moment of decay.³⁶

Michelangelo illustrates his theory from the analogy of his chosen art, where the sculptor begins from immaturity, progresses slowly until he reaches his full stature as a craftsman, and afterwards deteriorates; and his argument here is perfectly traditional. All the world's great theories of reincarnation, unless confused by the idea of evolution, are founded on similar cyclic parallels; with the cycle of man's life from birth to death, or with that of the seasons, or with that of a single day. When Yeats chooses a cyclic analogy for his own theory—the moon's circuit from 'new' to 'full' 'and after that the crumbling of the moon' —he has therefore every justification.

Between incarnations, then, the soul models the body for its next rebirth, which in turn will reflect the changes in its spiritual condition; and it remains to explain by what precise means this is done. For Yeats, as for any Platonist, the soul between incarnations becomes a part of Anima Mundi; the wisdom and emotion of the dead, that is to say, is collected into an enormous reservoir of experience, with which the minds of the living may momentarily come in contact. Thus he speaks of 'a memory independent of individual memories' which

* Cf. Nesca Robb, p. 251.

nevertheless enrich it 'with their images and thought' and speaks of Anima Mundi as connected with the personal unconscious, with which it is united 'at crises of emotion'. Yeats first read of Anima Mundi in Paracelsus and Indian religion,[37] and found what he read there confirmed by Henry More; he might also have found corroboration in modern Jungian psychology, whose kindred theory of the collective unconscious is built up from similar sources. Modern psychology would also support him in his belief that Anima Mundi is the source of animal instinct; that an ancestral memory teaches the birds to build their nests, is 'master-mason to the martens building about Church walls',[38] and in the same way 'shapes the elaborate shell of the mollusc and the child in the womb'.[39] The group mind of the dead thus conditions the general principles of physical growth; a belief which, as Kathleen Raine points out, comes very close to that independently evolved by Blake.[40] In his poetry the matrix of generation is 'the womb of Enitharmon' (here perhaps a symbol for the collective unconscious) and 'the daughters of Enitharmon', the inhabitants of Anima Mundi, weave on their 'looms' the bodies of those awaiting rebirth, while their souls stand shivering on the banks of 'the river of time and space':

> The daughters of Enitharmon weave the ovarium and the integument
> In soft silk, drawn from their own bowels in lascivious delight,
> With songs of sweetest cadence to the turning spindle and reel
> Lulling the weeping spectres.[41]

In such a way 'the breeding womb' of Anima Mundi forms 'the heart and brain'—

> buds with life and forms the bones
> The little heart, the liver, and the red blood in its labyrinths[42]

—but to this doctrine Yeats adds the rider proposed by Italian Neoplatonism. The individual soul, leaving Anima Mundi for the world, also participates in the act, and imparts its stock of spiritual beauty to the body 'by an act of imagination'.*

Emer, as I have said, has roots both in Renaissance scholarship and

---

* Blake's source for his image of Enitharmon's daughters is Plato's myth of Er, where there are the same looms, the same spinning women, the same 'river of space'; but the argument of Plato comes nearer to Yeats's own thought. The spinning women manufacture the physical 'garments', but the individual souls also take part in the act, determining by an act of 'choice' the exact likeness in which they will be reborn.

in the Irish peasant imagination, and every symbol used has to have validity on both these planes. The symbol Yeats uses for Anima Mundi is the *sea*, and that this is in conformity with the unconscious usages of folk-lore there can be no doubt. In Celtic, as in Norse and Greek mythology, the land is surrounded by the 'world-ocean', which represents in all three cultures the country of the dead. In Homer, we have the 'ocean-stream' and Cimmerian darkness through which Odysseus must voyage on his journey to Hades; in Norse myth the world-encircling sea giving on the frosty land of giants, Utgard, which separates the earth from the territory of the gods; and in Irish legend the Kingdom of Manannan and his spirit-horsemen, which is the road of many pilgrims to the Isles of the Blessed. Yeats had drawn on this symbolism before for his play *The Green Helmet*, where the heroes go to the foreshore to keep tryst with a ghost:

Laegaire: Does anything stir on the sea?
 Conall: Not even a fish or a gull . . .
  I can see for a mile or two, now that the moon's at the full,
  And we have nothing to fear that has not come up with the tide.

On another plane, of course, the land in all primitive mythologies represents consciousness, and the sea, with its fairyland phantasmagoria and deeper strata of primitive terrors, is a clear image for the subconscious mind, but Yeats, believing as he did that Anima Mundi manifests through the personal unconscious, will have welcomed this extension of meaning. He will also have welcomed the correspondences in Japanese myth, which I have noticed in my paragraphs on *Hagoromo*.

For reasons which I shall later show to be quite compelling Yeats was also determined that his symbolism should be in conformity with the more artificial symbologies of religion, and here he ran into immediate difficulties. In the Platonic tradition, the normal image for Anima Mundi is the *garden*, where the archetypes or ideas of all created things grow as flowers and where the soul, between incarnations, takes its ease; a symbolism which enters our literature with Spenser's Garden of Adonis and round which Shelley wrote his 'The Sensitive Plant'. Yeats found, however, that Italian Neoplatonism used the sea and the garden as interchangeable symbols, and (remarking that Jungian psychology thought similarly) he is at pains to record the fact in the preface to *Fighting The Waves*:

> Gemistus Pletho not only substituted the sea for Adam and Eve [made it, that is, his matrix from which all life sprang and his symbol for the original world-parents] but, according to a friend learned in the Renaissance, made it symbolise the garden's round or first original, 'that concrete universal for which all philosophy is seeking'.[43]

Yeats therefore himself uses sea and garden as interchangeable symbols; as in the following beautiful passage, where he is describing how the creative artist's thought develops by means of contact with the collective unconscious:

> I think of Anima Mundi as a great pool or garden where [a thought proliferates] like a great waterplant or fragrantly branches in the air.[44]

He also lists for himself a number of literary precedents:

> Our daily thought is certainly but the line of foam at the edge of a vast luminous sea; Henry More's Anima Mundi, Wordsworth's 'immortal sea that brought us hither' and near whose edge the children sport; and in that sea [have been] some who swam or sailed, explorers who perhaps knew all its shores.[45]

Henry More does indeed represent the post-mortem condition as 'a vast Ocean of life, full of enlivening Balsame';[46] and Yeats remarks elsewhere that the symbolism of Wordsworth's Immortality Ode is precisely that of Indian tradition.[47] With so much authority behind him, Yeats could write confidently of his play to Olivia Shakespear: 'I thought of the sea as Eternity, and they all upon its edge'.[48]

Yeats's sea-symbolism enters *Emer* with the first chorus of the play, where the soul carrying its freight of spiritual beauty (the phrasing of Yeats's first line is simple metonymy) is shown returning to the world over the sea of the post-mortem condition. The symbolism of the 'white bird' echoes the 'plover' and 'seagull' imagery of *Hagoromo*, as also perhaps the traditional symbolism of the Kabbala, where the soul after death flies as a bird to the Garden of Beatitude, and takes there its rightful place at the apex of the tree of life.[49] Or at least this imagery brings to mind Yeats's lyric 'At Algeciras', which stands in the very closest relation to *Emer* and which we have to allow symbolic dimension since Yeats himself calls it 'a meditation upon death':

> The heron-billed pale cattle-birds
> That feed on some foul parasite
> Of the Moroccan flocks and herds
> Cross the narrow straits to light
> In the rich midnight of the garden trees
> Till the dawn break upon those mingled seas.

These lines are on one plane a naturalistic evening landscape, but they are also a diagrammatic exposition of Yeats's theory of reincarnation. The soul, we are to understand, has been 'tethered' in life to the 'dying animal' of the body as the cattle-bird is to its animal host, but leaves its host at 'midnight' (the symbolic moment of death) and crosses the sea of Anima Mundi to the garden of beatitude. At dawn, the moment of rebirth, it leaves that Kabbalistic garden, and returns across the 'mingled seas' where the tides of life and death meet, to be reincarnated into the living world.

The dance-play takes up this argument at the moment of daybreak, which in Yeats's traditional language is the moment of birth. The soul is imaged crossing Anima Mundi to the dry land of consciousness, and we are shown it thrown up at the sea's edge, like some wounded bird, by a sudden storm; that convulsion of the Great Memory which precipitates its rebirth into the world. All this Yeats expresses by a deceptively simple simile:

> A woman's beauty is like a white
> Frail bird, like a white sea-bird alone
> At daybreak after stormy night
> Between two furrows upon the ploughed land:
> A sudden storm, and it was thrown
> Between dark furrows upon the ploughed land.

Life, then, is presented as the shipwreck of the soul's spiritual progress, but before alighting between those 'two furrows' which symbolise its successive incarnations, the soul has flown far on its quest for the spirituality that is its goal. It has used its flight over the night sea to meditate on its experience of the beautiful—all that it may have acquired in its past lifetime—and by this process it has gained greatly in spiritual stature. All that it has acquired will be converted into physical loveliness when it is joined to the body in its next rebirth, as Yeats uses the lines which follow to explain. They describe the soul, between incarnations, 'in toils of measurement' to create its future body, and remind us that beauty for Yeats (as we know from his poem 'The Statues') was a matter of mathematical proportioning:

> How many centuries spent
> The sedentary soul
> In toils of measurement
> Beyond eagle or mole,
> Beyond hearing or seeing
> Or Archimedes' guess,
> To raise into being
> That loveliness?

In its 'many centuries' of purgatory and beatitude the soul has 'measured' both the height and the depth of beauty; it has meditated upon all its memories both of exalted spirituality and of that other beauty which is sexual and kinetic; all that the 'eagle' in it has known, all that the 'mole'. Yeats refers to the motto of one of Blake's descriptions of the pre-natal state, *The Book Of Thel*, where the symbols have this meaning.

The second verse of the song reinforces the meaning by shifting the metaphor: woman's beauty is presented under the alternative image of the 'shell'. This is a traditional image for an archetypal 'idea'; one thinks again of 'At Algeciras', where an identical shell-symbolism recurs and can be traced back to Tagore and Indian religion;[50] perhaps of Landor's shells in *Gebir*, which 'remember their august abodes/And murmur as the ocean murmurs there';[51] and beyond all this, of course, of the classical archetype of Aphrodite arising on her shell from an equally symbolic sea. Yeats will have thought especially of the Botticelli painting, to which (since Botticelli was a Platonist) he may well have attached all the values of Italian Renaissance symbolism, in constructing his own image for the emergent Venus:

> A strange, unserviceable thing,
> A fragile, exquisite, pale shell
> That the vast troubled waters bring
> To the loud sands before day has broken.
> The storm arose and suddenly fell
> Amid the dark before day had broken.

Here again we are presented with the sea of Anima Mundi—its 'vast waters' troubled as the souls expiate their past lives during the condition of the Dreaming Back—and with the 'storm' of that spiritual convulsion which Yeats thought must precede even a single soul's rebirth. And now he goes on to divert his argument into channels we could not have expected, but which follow naturally enough from his guiding quotation from Castiglione, who not only speaks of beauty as the 'monument' to spirituality, but uses also the militaristic word 'spoil'. Greek and Renaissance sculpture had taught Yeats to see an athleticism in beauty, a spareness and economy of line even in the loveliness of women, which he could not account for as the fruit of gentle spirituality alone; and he had already said as much in his poem 'The Phases Of The Moon'. There, he suggests that all the turbulent action of past incarnations is remembered in woman's beauty. The arrogance which, equally with virtue and goodness, is a constituent of loveliness may derive from past rebirths when, like Moses, the beloved led the Children of Israel out of Egypt, or, like Moses's slavedriver, was the agent of a savage discipline.* The strange lines in question may derive from a memory of Michelangelo's 'Moses', which was a favourite work of art:[52]

> ... those we loved got their long fingers
> From death and wounds, or on Sinai's top
> Or from some bloody whip in their own hands.

In the same way, his dance-play has the soul relive in memory the discipline and heroic fortitude of battles in which it has fought during incarnations long past:

> What death? What discipline?
> What bonds no man could unbind
> Being imagined within
> The labyrinths of the mind,
> What pursuing or fleeing
> What wounds, what bloody press,
> Dragged into being
> That loveliness.

This sudden shift of feeling completes the lyric aesthetically as it does logically, the unexpected conjunction of imagery of 'bloodshed' and 'pale shell' giving it great kinetic force.

Yeats's chorus is in itself, I suppose, great poetry, but it is also

---

* We have to remember that, in most of the world's theories of reincarnation, the soul may change its sex from rebirth to rebirth.

eminently functional; it foreshadows the atmosphere against which the action is to be played out. When the significance of Yeats's sea-symbolism has in this way been established, what I will call the more primitive aspect of that symbolism is introduced, in the narrative of Cuchulain's fight with the waves. I will quote, once again, from the prose version he preferred:

> I think he loved her (Aoife) as no man ever loved, for when he heard the name of the man he had killed, and the name of that man's mother, he went out of his senses utterly: he ran into the sea, and with shield before him and sword in hand he fought the deathless sea.

This, we should now be able to see, symbolises an act of spiritual rebellion; maddened by the cruel destiny that has betrayed him, Cuchulain takes up arms against the whole of Anima Mundi, against his daemons and guardian angels, against God himself and the whole metaphysical world. That this is the proper interpretation we may gauge from a late lyric,[53] in which Yeats regrets his failure to turn the symbolism to proper account in his play *On Baile's Strand*:

> And when the Fool and Blind Man stole the bread
> Cuchulain fought the ungovernable sea.
> Heart-mysteries there; and yet when all is said
> It was the dream itself enchanted me. . . .
> Players and painted stage took all my love
> And not those things which they were emblems of.

In old age, we may feel that Yeats had a personal connotation for his image which runs parallel to the archetypal, and both of them perhaps obtain in this lyric about Maud Gonne. When she rejected him and chose any 'fool' or 'blind man' as a lover, he, like his own Cuchulain, had rebelled against the whole spiritual universe; against all its cruel laws.

Cuchulain's body is retrieved from the waves; or rather, the powers of the supernatural world have conveyed it, lifeless and possessed, to the door of the 'poor fisher's house':

> . . . The waves washed his senseless image up
> And laid it at this door.

The door, in fact, is 'open' on the stormy sea as Emer sits beside the bed, a lovely and evocative piece of stagecraft which Yeats had used previously in *The Green Helmet*, where the spirit of Red Man also emerges from that misty symbolic ocean. In both contexts the suggestion is of the nearness of occult powers: all natural barriers are to be down, and there is to be free passage between the living and the dead. As we watch, Eithne appears imaged in that doorway, while the chorus repeat a fragment of the 'white wing' chorus: she is the type of feminine beauty, and the suggestion of the Venus-motif, as she stands with the sea at her back, is to remind us of her divine origin. Then she and Emer perform the weird ceremony of summoning Cuchulain's ghost, 'we're but two women struggling with the sea'; and the more primitive aspect of the symbolism is again re-established: they are indeed two lonely figures as they contend against all the powers of the occult. The ritual develops to the climax of Bricriu's manifestation, and it is pointed by many allusions to the nearness of the dead:

> Emer: Cry out his name . . . no, not yet, for first
> I'll cover up his face to hide the sea
> And throw new logs upon the hearth and stir
> The half-burnt logs until they break in flame.
> Old Manannan's unbridled horses come
> Out of the sea, and on their backs his horsemen;
> But all the enchantments of the dreaming foam
> Dread the hearth-fire.

In this way the sea of primitive superstition becomes a dominant image, and its subtle menace is felt, intangible but near at hand, throughout the play. Finally, at the climax, Fand in her chariot makes an entrance that outdazzles that of Eithne, and the Platonic aspect of the symbolism is once more suggested: she is the true Aphrodite, 'that great queen that rose out of the spray', and she eclipses Eithne as heavenly beauty must always eclipse the merely human.

I have shown Yeats, in his preface, at pains to stress the Renaissance connotations for the sea, and it should now be obvious why he does so. His symbolism is Florentine as much as it is Gaelic; as in *A Prayer For My Daughter*, he conjoins, without any sense of discrepancy, the 'murderous innocence' of the Galway coastline and the waves which give birth to Botticelli's Venus. Yeats does this because he is confident of the essential identity of all myth: that Aphrodite and Vulcan are in every way identical with Fand and the Irish sea-god,[54] who is also (we learn from the later 'Three Songs To The One Burden') the god and ancestor of tinkers:

His ranting and his roaring
Best please a wandering man.*

He is able to achieve the identification, which might well have proved harder in practice than in theory, by a simple process of omission: there is no overt mention in his text of his Platonic intentions, a device for which his notes more than compensate. Yet, at the archetypal level at which we take the play, the associations he wishes us to make do indeed suggest themselves; for all mythologies *are* one, as Yeats all his life believed, and as the cohesion and imaginative power of his play sufficiently testifies.

IV

Fand stands for heavenly beauty because her symbol is the full moon, an emblem which is given her in the first place at the level of nature-myth, but also serves to relate her to the fifteenth of Yeats's 'lunar phases': to the fifteenth rebirth. Not only she, but each of Yeats's characters is allotted to a particular rebirth in this way, and their psychology is that he associates with their respective incarnations. We need at this point to know something of the psychology of the play (which is the only one in English literature where the characters' incarnations determine their temperaments); and for completeness' sake I will first outline Yeats's theory of rebirth and then relate his personae to it.

I have already said that Yeats, like Michelangelo, adopts a cyclic (rather than a progressive) theory of reincarnation. Thus the soul in its first rebirths is savage, primitive and inept; it relies upon instinct, is 'summoned' only to physical or sexual adventure, and is 'always happy like a bird or a beast'. It grows towards a central series of rebirths, which bring it to 'completeness': to 'heroism' and then to spiritual understanding and the religion of the Self. This central phase is the period of greatest physical beauty, the body bearing the impress of the spiritual maturity that is achieved, but since the soul is now preoccupied with itself, it tends to be unstable and irrational in its relations with the exterior world. When the zenith of beauty and self-centredness has been reached, a process of spiritual decay begins ('natura è vecchia, e de'perire'); self-knowledge diminishes and the soul begins to be preoccupied with 'the world'. If it now has a religion, this will be of the inferior 'objective' kind. The last rebirths of all are a

* Lady Gregory, as well as Yeats, identifies Manannan and Hephaestos.

phase of psychological disorientation; the 'objective' saint is 'placed' in this phase, partly because Yeats thought of him as a disorientated personality, and partly because the poet's natural generosity made him wish to believe that even an inferior type of religious intuition may end in a moment of sanctity. If the disintegrating soul cannot avail itself of this moment of sanctity, perfect itself and achieve final liberation from the time-world through holiness, the suggestion is that the whole cycle has to be lived through again.[55]

Yeats's system so far seems to me perfectly defensible in its traditionalism; and the moon-symbolism by which he describes the soul's 'phases' is equally defensible, as I have tried already to show. The moon's four crescents are used as emblems for the soul's four major states: the first, broadening crescent for its primitive and intuitive beginnings; the second, rounding towards the full, for its incarnations of maturity and self-knowledge; the third crescent, 'the crumbling of the moon', for the early objective rebirths, when it turns towards the world; and the last, narrowing towards 'the dark', for the ultimate phases of decay. Where Yeats goes beyond the stablest of his authorities is in a piece of embroidery that is relevant to *Emer*: there are rebirths of maximal and minimal potentiality, the fifteenth ('full moon') and the twenty-ninth (the moon's absolute dark); and in these Yeats imagines the soul incarnating as a supernatural being, a nature-spirit, only to be restored with its next rebirth to the world of time. At the fifteenth rebirth it becomes a beautiful and at the twenty-ninth a deformed spirit, though in both these shapes it may seem to man to be *evil*, as living a life alien to ourselves.

Yeats did not give precise sources for his theory until relatively late in life, but in *Essays 1931-6* he points out his debt to the Upanishads. His own incarnations divide into two sub-cycles, in one of which the religion of the Self is possible while in the other the soul has inferior spiritual perceptivity; and he discerns a similar systematisation, together with a similar moon-symbolism, in Indian religion:

> Here and there in the Upanishads [Yeats no doubt has principally in mind the Brihadaranyaka-Upanishad, round which he wrote the end of his poem 'All Soul's Night]' mention is made of the moon's bright fortnight and of the dark fortnight of the moon's decline. He that moves towards the full moon may, if wise, go to the gods. [This means, as the context makes quite clear, earn final liberation from the time-world by the discovery of the Self.] Upon the other hand, those that move towards the dark of the moon, if they are

pious, as the crowd is pious; if they offer the right sacrifices, pray at the right Temples, can go to the blessed ghosts: find what peace can be found between death and birth. The Upanishads denied any final escape for these.[56]

Yeats associates the two forms of escape here mentioned with states of the soul called in Indian religion Sushupti and Turiya. Turiya means 'waking vision' and implies the perfect mystical marriage, while Sushupti means 'dreamless sleep'.

> The bright fortnight's escape is Turiya and in the dark fortnight, the ascetic . . . may, though unworthy of Turiya, find Sushupti an absorption in God, as if the soul were his food or fuel.[57]

Yeats's interpretation of the Brihadaranyaka-Upanishad is an intuitional, but I would say an eminently defensible one, and his theory has thus a broad traditional base. He departs from his authority in two main aspects: by decorating his theory with nature-spirits (which I have deprecated precisely because it *is* a departure); and by allowing the 'objective saint' the possibility of escape when the Upanishads would not do so; a piece of natural tolerance with which we may sympathise.

As well as his Indian sources, Yeats speaks of an astrological theory of 'the Mansions of the Moon', and Henn has pointed out that this theory is mentioned by Chaucer's Franklin.[58] A more elaborate account is that Yeats had studied in Cornelius Agrippa[59] and, since Agrippa claims that the theory is from Indian tradition, Yeats may well have discerned a faint echo of the wisdom of the Upanishads in what he read. In the astrological convention the moon, impregnated by the light of the stars, serves as a matrix-symbol (it is itself the regent of merely physical growth, and the stars inseminate it with spiritual influence); and this makes it a peculiarly apt emblem for the cycles of rebirth. Yeats exploits such iconography thoroughly: a moon-star antithesis often serves him (as at the end of *Emer*) to discriminate between merely carnal beauty and spiritual perfectibility; while the moon is of course his consistent symbol for the universal matrix:

> Crazed through much child-bearing
> The moon is staggering in the sky.[60]

Though Agrippa's is not (or not explicitly) a theory of reincarnation, he also clearly influences Yeats's arrangement of his 'four crescents' of personality. We learn from Agrippa that the moon passes through four temperamental phases, being sanguine, choleric, melancholy and phlegmatic in turn; and that the 'four humours' of mankind are a microcosm of these changes.[61] Yeats arranges the humours on his own Great Wheel precisely as Agrippa directs: the soul in its early phases being sanguine, then 'choleric' in the 'hero's crescent', when it is 'at war in its own being'; later it subsides into objective melancholia and finally into settled darkness.

All Yeats's theories bristle with authorities, and contributory influences here can be found both in Greek philosophy and in nineteenth-century poetry. It is simplest to leave to a later chapter his debt to Heraclitus and Philolaus, but his literary sources can easily enough be noticed here. Blake, much as he did, saw two 'paths' before the soul, the superior leading direct 'through Beulah to Eden', the inferior taking it on a more desolate circuit: 'through the aerial Void and all the Churches'.[62] Yeats probably took this as a definition of two subcycles of human reincarnation, subjective and objective, though it should be noted that Blake did not concede the possibility of escape through objective holiness: his objectives have to live through 'all the Churches' (which may here be a Blakean term for 'phases of rebirth').*
Shelley also may have contributed something, especially to Yeats's scathing denunciations of the objective type:

> the noisy set
> Of bankers, schoolmasters and clergymen
> The martyrs call the world.

These lines from 'Adam's Curse' have been related to a famous passage in *Epipsychidion*, where Shelley denounces the 'code of modern morals' and the 'slaves' of the 'great sect' of Christian conformism;[63] and though so precise an attribution may seem questionable, Yeats's attacks on the bourgeoisie are certainly in the general spirit of the romantic age. It is natural that he should have interpreted his very ancient theory from the point of view of his own period.

Each of the characters in *Emer* is allotted to a particular rebirth, three of them falling into late subjective incarnations while two are objectives. There is a very real connection with that section of *A Vision* which characterises Yeats's phasal types, and it seems as though he had

---

* Kathleen Raine has no doubt that Blake accepted reincarnation, and Rudd has already related his 'twenty-seven churches' and Yeats's twenty-eight phasal rebirths.

at least planned it when he wrote his play. In *A Vision*, of course, twenty-eight incarnations are noted (one for each of the moon's changes) and the *detail* of the characterisation is purely personal fantasy, reflecting Yeats's own preoccupations and the preoccupations of his 'tragic generation'. The underlying dogmas, for all this, are traditional, and this basis of two sub-cycles, one tending towards beauty and self-knowledge but also towards temperamental instability, the other tending towards objectivity, worldliness and disintegration, should always be kept in mind.

Cuchulain, to take him first, I have already shown to belong to the twelfth incarnation, which is the 'heroic' phase. Nietzsche, it will be remembered, is Yeats's representative of the type, whose concern ought to be with 'subjective philosophy' but who is 'fragmentary and violent', 'swashbuckling' and intransigent, and who tends to be betrayed 'by a series of accidents' into a way of life at variance with his real nature. All this describes well enough the hero of *At The Hawk's Well* and the series of accidents which lead him to kill his own son, and Yeats's further remarks[64] have an obvious bearing on the present play. The man born into this phase is essentially a sensitive, and assumes his 'lonely imperturbable proud mask', which seems to others so 'marble-pure', in simple self-protection; he is in reality 'overwhelmed with the sense of his own weakness' in precisely the manner of Cuchulain before Fand:

> I am not
> The young and passionate man I was
> And though that brilliant light surpass
> All crescent forms, my memories
> Weigh down my hands, abash my eyes.

Sexually, we are told that man in this rebirth gives himself to an image, an ideal of feminine beauty, rather than to an individual woman; and though he may take many lovers, his inherent spirituality will condition him to pursue this ideal all his life. Such of course is once again Cuchulain's position before Fand, for the goddess tells him that she is that absolute of beauty he has always been seeking; she uses much the same words as Cloona uses to Hanrahan in the early story, which can now be seen in its full relevance:

Cloona: You have always loved me better than your own soul, and you have sought me everywhere and in everything, though without knowing what you sought.

Yeats's further remarks on the 'sexual image' the hero pursues might almost be a description of Fand:

> The sexual image is drawn as with a diamond, tinted those pale colours sculptors sometimes put upon a statue.

In the lyric of 'pale colours' with which the play ends, Fand is presented as 'a statue of solitude': the comparison could hardly be closer.

Eithne Inguba belongs to the fourteenth incarnation, for we are told in the play that she 'lacks a day' of being 'complete'.[65] The first words spoken of her by the Musicians as she walks like an Aphrodite through the open door, the 'bitter sea' behind her, give her the attributes of dreaminess and instability:

> White shell, white wing,
> I will not choose for my friend
> A frail unserviceable thing
> That drifts and dreams, and but knows
> That waters are without end
> And that wind blows.

The fourteenth, which is a phase of beautiful women, is indeed the incarnation of self-centredness and instability, in which 'responsibility is renounced' and 'all is reverie . . . intellectual curiosity is at its weakest'.[66] Woman in the phase has 'an exaggerated sensuousness, though little sexual passion; like Eithne before Cuchulain in his 'cataleptic trance', she experiences 'terror' 'a vague beating of the wings' before 'death and stillness'; and Yeats goes on to describe her in the following terms, which may explain why Cuchulain's mistress, throughout his cycle of plays, is made so curiously colourless and evasive a personality (as also why he uses the *Iliad* to connect Eithne and Helen):

> Helen is in this phase, and she comes before the mind's eye elaborating a delicate personal discipline . . . while seeming an image of softness and quiet, she draws perpetually upon glass with a diamond. . . . For all the languor of her movements, and her indifference to the acts of others, her mind is never at peace. She will wander much alone as if she consciously meditated her masterpiece that shall be at the full moon [i.e. the even greater beauty and introspection she will have at her next rebirth], yet unseen by human eye, and when she returns to her house she will look upon her household with timid

eyes, as though she knew that all powers of self-protection have been taken away. . . .

Yeats's further description of this phase tells us that it is characterised by fluctuating moods, in which docility may alternate with 'frenzy' or even a secret vice: for woman is now the victim of every sensual folly:

> She may be seen, after lovely indifference, with flushed cheeks casting her money on the gaming table . . . one thinks too [for the precise type of beauty to be associated] of the women of Burne-Jones . . . and as we see before the mind's eye those pure faces gathered at the sleep of Arthur, or crowded upon the Golden Stair, we wonder if they too would not have filled us with surprise, or dismay, because of some craze, or passion for mere excitement or slavery to a drug.

This may explain why (in lines which contain an ironic echo of his earlier shell-imagery) Yeats characterises Eithne as convinced of her own worthlessness:

> Women like me, the violent hour once over
> Are thrown into some corner like old nutshells.

She is an ineffectual and even unsympathetic figure, and quite undeserving of the love Cuchulain feels for her; but she is also the type of human beauty at its nearest to the divine, an image of the absolute, and so it is inevitable that his love should be given.

Fand's symbol is the 'full moon' of 'perfect fulfilment', to quote the passage from *Hagoromo* on which Yeats depends, and to which he will have attached one does not know what mystique. She belongs, consequently, to the fifteenth, supernatural incarnation, when 'the body possesses the greatest possible physical beauty', being indeed 'that body which the soul will permanently inhabit, the clarified body'; when 'all effort has ceased', 'the mind is completely absorbed in being'; but there are 'terrible dreams' 'fear of solitude' and the most absolute need for human companionship.[67] At the *exoteric level* of the play, and as long as we remember that this is not the only level at which it communicates, we shall be right in associating her with such apparitions as the Sirens and the Lorelei; she is the 'terrible woman' of folk-lore,* pre-

---

* Cuchulain is at war in his own being, Eithne is unreliable, Fand seems to stagnate in callousness; Yeats's play shows us the apathy and dissociation to which subjectives are

sented by means of her Irish archetype. The Irish folk-mind, of course, is possessed by the connection between beauty and supernatural evil: the fairies and the Sidhe combine a fabulous physical pulchritude with a settled malignance. They are utterly self-absorbed, stealing from man at random what they need, the harvest, human brides and bridegrooms, even babies from their cradles, and, because of this cold self-interest, they are to be abhorred:

> When the moon's full these creatures of the full
> Are met on the waste hills by countrymen
> Who shudder and hurry by.[68]

In this way Yeats introduces into *Emer* the most fanciful detail of his 'phasal theory', as he does also the concept of the 'Kiss Of Death': the idea that a spirit can 'complete itself' by the assimilation of a human soul, which is of course universal in folk-lore and as common in India and Tibet as in the West. Thus Fand tells Cuchulain that his kiss will bring her freedom from all the cycles of rebirth; without it, she would have to progress through the objective incarnations:

> When your mouth and my mouth meet
> All my round shall be complete
> Imagining all its circles run.

But with this we should remember that there is another level at which Fand becomes a pure symbol, and that there none of these details taken from folk-lore apply in any way. On the plane of interior symbolism, she is the personification of heavenly beauty, which we may call the divine Aphrodite or by any name we choose, and on this plane all her attributes have symbolic significance, her loneliness, apparent evil, even her Kiss of Death; as I shall presently demonstrate.

Emer herself is the most difficult of Yeats's characters to relate to phase, but she is definitely in an objective rebirth, for she is the 'honest wife' of the catalogue in 'The Phases Of The Moon':

> Reformer, merchant, statesman, learned man
> Dutiful husband, honest wife by turn,
> Cradle upon cradle, and all in flight and all
> Deformed.

prone. It is a pity, from the point of view of rationalising his theory, that *Emer* does not treat of the dignity and spiritual endowment which are also constituents of the subjective Temperament: but these virtues will make themselves felt from my next chapter.

These are of course the rebirths where the incarnating spirit, 'in flight' from the values of the Self, chooses instead to live for humanity or, as in Emer's case, for a single man:

> It would be the world's servant, and as it serves,
> Choosing whatever task's most difficult
> Among things not impossible, it takes
> Upon the body and upon the soul
> The coarseness of the drudge.

For such a morality Yeats had of course little use, precisely because it seemed to him to stifle the individuality; and Emer, then, is in one of the 'inferior' rebirths of the Upanishads, 'pious as the crowd is pious'. *A Vision* does not relate the 'honest wife' to any precise phase, but perhaps we should think of Emer as in the twenty-second rebirth, which is the phase of 'immolation' 'called that of the victim'.[69]

Bricriu, finally, is a discarnate spirit in nature quite opposite to Fand, in the ultimate objective phase as she is in the ultimate subjective. *A Vision*[70] describes such spirits born 'at the dark of the moon' as 'indifferent to good and evil, to truth and falsehood', 'deformed' and 'automatic', their acts not 'immoral' or 'stupid' only because 'there is no-one there that can be judged'; and there is an even more frightening description in 'The Double Vision Of Michael Robartes', where they are spoken of as 'abstract' and 'dead beyond our death'!

> Constrained, arraigned, baffled, bent and unbent
> By these wire-jointed jaws and limbs of wood,
> Themselves obedient
> Knowing not evil and good.

Bricriu, with his total insensitivity to the pain his acts may cause, his distorted face and arm withered to the socket, is thus as good an example of this phase as Robert Artisson, the familiar invoked by the Kilkenny witches, who is described in 'Nineteen Hundred And Nineteen':

> Thereupon
> There lurches past, his great eyes without thought,
> Under the shadow of stupid, straw-pale locks,
> That insolent fiend Robert Artisson.

A Vision also tells us that these spirits of phase one 'take whatever shape, accept whatever image is imprinted upon them, transact whatever purpose is imposed upon them, and are indeed the instruments of supernatural manifestation, being the final link between the living and more powerful beings'. This explains clearly enough why Bricriu should be the changeling to take Cuchulain's place.

Bricriu is clearly in every sense the complement and antithesis of Fand, and there should be a level at which he, like her, is pure symbol. He is referred to as the 'maker of discord'; there is discussion, in the notes, of the 'theory of opposites';[71] and I think he is meant as a symbol of the 'unresolved antinomies' whose operations govern the play. Each of the characters clearly has to run a course 'between extremities'; they are 'caught between the pull' of the yin and yang, 'the dark moon and the full'.[72] Thus Cuchulain vacillates between his subjective passion for the absolute and his sense of honour and duty; Emer between her 'objective' love and the necessity of renunciation; for each of us the opposites, which cannot be transcended in the time-world, pick out some pain appropriate to our position on the great wheel. And even Fand is trapped between the antinomies, which manifest in the mingled attraction and revulsion which Cuchulain must feel for her; for absolute beauty, divine manifestation though it may be, presents an inimical and forbidding face to man while he is in time. Thus the little group on the foreshore are all equally the victims of a dilemma; and there is no way out, for the traditional 'middle course' is a delusion; there is only the possibility of choice, which is in the end a choice between sufferings. Bricriu, the bringer of the opposites like the Greek Ate, projects tensions into their lives which are to be thought of as irresoluble, and it is Yeats's insistence on this harsh moral that makes *Emer* such a bitter play.

V

The full force of Yeats's symbolism appears from his climactic scene, where Fand dances before Cuchulain and tries to win his love. All the esoteric detail that has gone before has led up to this: the characters have been placed in their respective rebirths, and Cuchulain has been shown as a man necessarily, by virtue of his incarnation, in love with the ideal; now he is confronted with his ideal 'image', and the whole symbolic *point* of the action will be in what happens next. What happens is that the man turns away from his ideal, and he does so of his own volition; for, at the level at which we must now take the argument, Emer is no more than the voice of his own conscience returning him from the heaven of Fand's beauty to the material world. This is beyond doubt a proper interpretation, for, as we shall see, Yeats wrote the final chorus to make clear that Cuchulain represents any man and his rejection of Fand a renunciation that every man must of necessity make. The scene of Fand's humiliation, then, is meant as the particular statement of a universal law, and the whole narrative has to be taken at such a level.

One interpretation of Yeats's symbolism is that which modern psychology would enforce; it is not the interpretation Yeats wants of us, but I had better mention it here, if only because it defines the issues at stake. The Jungian psychologist[73] would probably see *Emer* and *At The Hawk's Well* as two private myths on the one subject, both of them concerned with the *katabasis* and man's search for the integrated Self.* In *Emer*, the detail of Cuchulain's inert body floating on the waves makes a perfect symbol for the *katabasis* (the 'night journey across the sea'); and the confrontation with Fand, as much as that with the Guardian in Yeats's previous play, can be read as symbolic of the meeting with the transcendental virgin. As the Jungian would see it, the transcendental virgin ought to manifest as virtuous and chaste (or if she appears first as terrible—if woman is first envisaged in her dark and destructive aspect—this way of thinking ought presently to be supplanted); she ought finally to be seen as the Lady is seen in *Ash Wednesday*:

> Because of the goodness of this Lady
> And because of her loveliness, and because
> She honours the Virgin in meditation,
> We shine with brightness.

Where, as in Yeats, the pure image obstinately refuses to supplant the dark and false, the inference might very well be of some psychological tension in the poet preventing him from achieving the lower Self or

* We have to remember that the Jungian would accept the traditional interpretation of the hero-myth: that given in section three of my previous chapter. *Emer* and *At The Hawk's Well* correspond, at this level, in the following respects. Cuchulain at the mercy of the waves = the old man's long vigil by the well = the jettisoning of the first personality and the transit of the waste land. His meeting with Fand = his meeting with the Guardian, or with the 'terrible woman' or 'dark anima'. His failure to convert this into a morally beneficent image = his failure to integrate his personality. His return to Emer = his turning away from the well = the abandonment of the grail quest.

I ought to stress too that the climax of *Emer* is a *private* myth, in which Yeats accommodates received legend to his own psychological necessities. I have shown how he alters and reshapes the Gaelic original.

Nevertheless, I personally would reject the Jungian dogmas here proposed in favour of the Yeatsian dogmas which follow, and perhaps I ought to make this clear.

integrated personality: some dangerous fixation on beauty divorced from virtue and 'natural kindness', some preoccupation with a view of woman as *inimical*, perhaps an algolagnic streak. One can imagine much detail from Yeats's life and art being presented to support this view of him, rather as has been done by Frank Kermode.[74]

It is possible, on the other hand, to take *Emer* less as an illustration of Jung's theory of the dark anima than as an attempt to rebut it: to counter the psychology which underlies it with a quite opposite psychology of Yeats's own. The central situation, that is, is certainly about man's meeting with 'the Goddess as Temptress' (to use a technical Jungian term), but Yeats and Jung assess that situation in different ways. Cuchulain, for instance, sees Fand both as an 'idol' and a 'statue', and where this is the case we may think of a statue he admired and described elsewhere,[75] Rodin's *The Eternal Idol*, where the girl looks down with indifferent eyes on the young man kissing her 'a little below the breast': that callous indifference, and the potential cruelty behind it, would make Jung read the archetype as evil, but they would not have that effect on Yeats. He tells us of the Rodin that 'woman's beauty', even in total divorce from conventional virtue, is a manifestation of the divine, the contemplation of that beauty a legitimate form of mystical experience: man's meeting with the 'terrible woman', beauty engrossed in that self-absorption which men call evil, will not seem to Yeats to lead him away from 'integration' and the visionary world but to bring him closer to it. One thinks here of one of the loveliest passages in *A Vision*:

> A certain Byzantine bishop ... said upon seeing a singer of Antioch: 'I looked long upon her beauty, knowing that I would behold it on the day of Judgment, and I wept to remember that I had taken less care of my soul than she of her body', but when in the Arabian Nights Harun Al Rashid looked at the singer Heart's Miracle, and on the instant loved her, he covered her head with a little silk veil to show that her beauty 'had already retreated into the mystery of our faith'. The bishop saw a beauty that would be sanctified, but the Caliph that which was its own sanctity.[76]

Yeats would, I think, have placed Jung with his objective Byzantine bishop, and have dismissed his whole theory as unphilosophical. He certainly felt with Harun Al Rashid: physical beauty was its own justification, in itself an image of sanctity: its study an occupation for the saint.

In taking his theory of beauty to the extreme he does, Yeats has of course every precedent in his subjective philosophy. Plato, in the Symposium, teaches that the love of physical beauty (even in divorce from virtue) is a state of the soul, and a step towards the attainment of the absolute: the chief difference between his theory and Yeats's is that he finds necessary certain intermediary states of disinterest and self-knowledge. The Renaissance was less cautious: Castiglione, in M. Peter Bembo's speech already quoted, not only speaks of the spirituality of the body in its own right, but says that it requires worship; and to Michelangelo this belief was of course axiomatic. All his commentators have understood that Michelangelo was in love with

> That great nobleness,
> That great despising, of the mind,
> In which the beautiful is as the felt heat
> Of the fire of the eternal.[77]

Yeats himself refers to Michelangelo's theory of the 'profane perfection of mankind' in a famous poem, and his prose cites other similar theories in Arabian philosophy, 'the love-stories of Arabia and those of the crusades' and the mystical poets of 'Arabian Spain, Sicily and Provence'.[78]

In Yeats's play, Fand and Cuchulain meet in a scene of gathering bitterness, but the harshness of Cuchulain's speeches ought not to make us respond harshly to Fand ourselves: she personifies absolute beauty, and the first chorus exists to remind us of the devotion she deserves. We are of course to believe her promises that she means the man 'no evil'; when she says that after the Kiss of Death he will be her creature, but she will take him with her to heaven, where 'time shall seem to stay his course' and 'nothing but beauty can remain'. At the symbolic level, this means of course that the lover of beauty, if he will dedicate himself to his 'idol', can by this means alone attain to mystical experience in the condition of absolute spirituality, where all time is eternally present. The Kiss of Death will take him there, and so it is not really to be thought of as vicious; it (and Fand herself) may seem so from the point of view of the time-world, but this is because absolute beauty, as a religion, makes absolute demands. Cuchulain, we must remember, is by incarnation peculiarly fitted to respond to these demands, to die to mundane reality, and it is not therefore mere flattery when Fand says that he is 'born' to be her lover.

THE ONLY JEALOUSY OF EMER

> What could make you fit to wive
> With flesh and blood, being born to live
> Where no-one speaks of broken troth
> For all have washed out of their eyes
> Wind-blown dirt of their memories
> To improve their sight?

These lines may seem cold and aggressive, for heavenly beauty is the antagonist of all temporal values and desires the destruction of the natural man; but on the metaphysical level Cuchulain is being offered his peace.

We see this better if we understand the full meaning of Fand's words, which are of course affirmative of what Yeats supposed to be the real nature of heavenly freedom. We must clearly associate them with his belief that free love between the sexes will be normal in the heavenly world, a morality that first enters his poetry with 'The Collar Bone Of A Hare', where Yeats describes a voyage across the sea of Anima Mundi to the Isles of the Blessed, and describes how the inhabitants of paradise mock at 'the old bitter world where they marry in churches', and 'pay but a kiss for a kiss'. Yeats learned from Plotinus and Henry More that sexual love would persist in the 'clarified body', ('Crossed fingers there in pleasure can/Exceed the nuptial bed of man'),[79] while Swedenborg taught him to believe literally that there will be no marrying or giving in marriage in the heavenly world, as he first explains in his unpublished novel *The Speckled Bird:*

> A happy community upon earth must be an image of the community of the angels, who as Swedenborg long ago pointed out know nothing of exclusive marriage.[80]

A literary source for his rejection of 'exclusive marriage' is of course Shelley's *Epipsychidion*, which taught him eloquently enough how the 'slaves' of 'modern morals'

> With one chained friend, perhaps a jealous foe
> The dreariest and the longest journey go.

There are also, of course, the noble defences of free love in Blake, whose early heroes cannot conceive that to 'turn my face to where my whole soul seeks' could be called a crime:

> For everything that lives is holy, life delights in life,
> Because the soul of sweet delight can never be defiled.[81]

Yeats understood that the exalted ideal behind these lines could never be realised in time, as Blake also came to do; 'you may do so in Spirit, but not in the body, as you pretend, until after the Last Judgment'.[82] Both poets, however, believed that a life of free and unforced giving would become possible beyond the grave, and the lines in Yeats's play have to be interpreted in such a spirit.

For all that is offered, Cuchulain cannot bring himself to 'alight at the comely trees and the lawn'—I am using the language of 'The Collar Bone Of A Hare'—or to look back from that Elysian landscape at the time-world that has been transcended. The moving lines with which the scene begins tell us that he will not be capable of it: Fand dances before him, but he sits crouched on the ground, in his grave-clothes, averting his eyes.

> Fand: Hold out your arms and hands again.
> You were not so dumbfounded when
> I was that bird of prey, and yet
> I am all woman now.
> Cuchulain: I am not
> The young and passionate man I was
> And though that brilliant light surpass
> All crescent forms, my memories
> Weigh down my hands, abash my eyes.

This statement is later repeated, as though Yeats were trying to bring home Cuchulain's weariness by a technique of reiteration:

> Fand: Because I long I am not complete.
> What pulled your hands about your feet
> Pulled down your head upon your knees
> And hid your face?
> Cuchulain: Old memories:
> A woman in her happy youth
> Before her man had broken troth,
> Dead men and women. Memories
> Have pulled my head upon my knees.

When he was young Cuchulain could have dared the attempt, but now he has not the heart for it. The argument here connects with the bitter 'Men Improve With The Years' and with the equally bitter 'A Song':

> O who could have foretold
> That the heart grows old?

With this we are told that Cuchulain is 'impure with memory', distracted by 'intricacies of blind remorse', and here other parallels suggest themselves. One thinks of the paradox 'repentance makes the heart impure' and of the counter-truth at the end of 'A Dialogue Of Self And Soul':

> When such as I cast out remorse
> So great a sweetness flows into the breast
> We must laugh and we must sing.
> We are blest by everything.
> Everything we look upon is blest.

Yeats knew from the disciplines of all world-religions that the perfection of one's own penitence, after which the sense of guilt can be discarded or cast out, is the indispensable preliminary to all mystical experience. Indian philosophy taught him that the mind of the religious must be a purified vacancy, and he learned also from St. John of the Cross that 'the mind must be empty of all sensible perception, resting on faith'.[83] But the ageing Cuchulain is distracted by a flood of memories he cannot stem, memories of the men he has slain and of the woman he has betrayed: he cannot make perfect his will.

Such, then, is the shaping logic behind Cuchulain's meeting with the Goddess, and his ultimate rejection of her love. Of course woman's beauty is a supernatural manifestation, the play tells us, and requires our love for its own sake; of course it is never in any ultimate sense pernicious; of course the idea of the merely dutiful wife is a 'deformed' thing by comparison; of course man is by nature a spiritual adventurer, and his tragedy is that when 'young and passionate' the absolute of woman's beauty is denied him and that, when in maturity it will give itself, he is no longer able to accept the gift. And yet, Yeats goes on to suggest, building upon this preliminary structure, where the pursuit of beauty is in itself so agonising, is there not some kindness in the denial; if it is in the nature of men to worship before Rodin's Eternal Idol, is there not something endlessly unrewarding in a loveliness which can only make demands on us, and has nothing, in the material sense, to give? This counter-suggestion is broached in the first lines of the play:

> White shell, white wing,
> I will not choose for my friend
> A frail unserviceable thing.

In this way Yeats turns the tables on his own idealism and sets off the resolute affirmation of his main argument with a sceptical worldliness; what Una Ellis-Fermor has called 'the tough matter-of-fact wisdom' of middle age.[84] But his play is not a negation; it is the maturest expression in our literature of the hard and demanding religion of Platonic love, not falsified (as Shelley's poetry sometimes is) by a young man's hope, but seen retrospectively and without any form of illusion after the undeviating allegiance of many years. And, as follows naturally from so mature an insight, it is a confession of human inadequacy; as we grow old, we know this painful discipline is not for us.

Yeats is the most humane of dramatists, and Emer herself is presented as an altogether sympathetic figure, though he stigmatises her as 'impure',[85] and though Bricriu, looking on life with the candid eyes of the spiritual world, pronounces her affection for Cuchulain to be quite worthless. She stands for natural and maternal affection, fidelity, all the virtues that can attach to the love of mere flesh and blood. For Emer of course is blind to the spiritual world, or antagonistic to what she can discern of it:

> We're but two women struggling with the sea.

Cuchulain's affection for her, and his remorse when he remembers the injuries he has done her, are deliberately pitched in a low style, but they are very real:

> O Emer, Emer, there we stand
> Side by side and hand in hand,
> Tread the threshold of the house
> As when our parents married us . . .

Emer's tragedy is that she loses Cuchulain's love, which he recovers from his trance to give to Eithne Inguba; once granted a vision of the perfect beauty man can never be content with merely natural affection but must search for the recollection of that beauty in whatever woman nearest approximates to it. Cuchulain's tragedy is that Eithne does not deserve and will not keep his love, for woman in the central incarnations is not a stable personality. But neither the man nor the woman is the central object of Yeats's compassion; beauty itself suffers the ultimate defeat, for it deserves of us a pure response which the tensions of time make it impossible for us to give. Fand is the dancer whom Yeats leaves to mourn among the waves; she is his tragic victim.

VI

The final chorus of Yeats's play follows immediately upon the *dénouement*, serves as a diminution of tension, and also underlines the arguments I have just been reconstructing by reviewing the whole of the action from the point of view of his tragedian, Fand. Yeats resorts for this purpose to a simple device of parallelism: he presents us with the sufferings of another woman who is Fand's similar, and in this way Fand's own predicament is obliquely brought home. His chorus completes the play in many ways besides, for example by fulfilling the pattern of colour-suggestion Yeats has been creating: we begin from the symbols of 'white bird' and 'white shell', combined with the more sombre imagery of sea and storm: the sea-imagery gradually darkens and grows more menacing till it is offset by the climax with its 'supernatural light'; now we are returned to the marble whiteness of Yeats's statue and to the calm classical archetypes—the myth of Pygmalion replacing that of Aphrodite—from which he began. To a certain extent, of course, a classical archetype has been kept before us throughout, by that reference to the *Iliad* by which Yeats associates Eithne and Helen, Fand and Aphrodite, and this aspect of the symbolism now also arrives at consummation. Helen is Yeats's consistent image for Maud Gonne, and he now makes it clear that his personal feeling for Maud Gonne has informed the whole play.

The mythological justification for this drama within a drama, where the chorus hold converse with a walking statue, lies in two very obvious connections: with the Pygmalion-Galatea myth, and perhaps secondarily with the story of Don Juan and the statue also (Yeats had used the image of 'Juan's sinewy thigh' a few years before).[86] It is as though Don Juan were being confronted with the Galatea-image, and by this network of suggestion Yeats gives his lyric archetypal depth. But, together with its archetypal suggestiveness, the song moves us by sheer urgency of personal feeling, and if we cast about for the source of the personal element, we are reminded of Maud

Gonne at once. Yeats thought always of her beauty as statuesque, 'Pallas Athene in that straight back and arrogant head';[87] a memory of her, as Vivienne Koch has shown, gave rise to his late poem 'The Statues'; and a passage from 'Autobiographies', written near the period of the dance-play, appropriates the statue-symbol to her beyond doubt. The passage may be a gloss on a sentence from Blake's *Laocoön*, where 'the Gods of Greece and Egypt' are presented as 'mathematical diagrams':[88]

> Her [Maud Gonne's] face, like the face of some Greek statue, showed little thought, as though a Scopas had measured and long calculated, consorted with Egyptian sages and mathematicians out of Babylon, that he might face even Artemisia's sepulchral image with a living norm.[89]

Here, as well as the statue-symbolism, we have the suggestion of those 'sepulchral' or as he says in 'A Bronze Head' 'supernatural' values which Yeats saw in Maud Gonne's beauty, together with an imagery of mensuration and computation that recur in 'The Statues';* and also (as if to point the relevance of the passage) in the present play. One remembers the first chorus of *Emer*, where the soul 'imagines' the body it will presently inhabit:

> In toils of measurement
> Beyond eagle or mole.

In the present context of his final chorus, it is Yeats's ultimate intention to expand his play's argument from the particular to the universal, and to show us that Cuchulain's rejection of Fand is every man's renunciation of the absolute; but his own personal knowledge and renunciation of the absolute, in the shape of Maud Gonne's perfect and inimical loveliness, is the individual experience which clearly directs the verse.

With this Yeats's notes give us another personal association for his statue-imagery, and one which reminds us how unlikely the sources of his poetry sometimes were: in this case, he is drawing upon the proceedings of the Society for Psychical Research. He had read, in a case history submitted by the distinguished scientist Sir William Crookes, of a 'phantom' which materialised in the seance-room, so tangible a presence that the researchers could feel its heart beating,

* For a fuller examination of the prose passage and Yeats's 'The Statues', see p. 290.

and Crookes's vivid description had filled him with horror.[90] This incident is used also in his later play *The Resurrection*, when the Greek meets with Christ risen from the tomb:

> There is nothing here but a phantom. . . . Look, I will touch it. It may be hard under my hand like a statue—I have heard of such things—or my hand may pass through it; but there is no flesh and blood. (*He goes slowly up to the figure and passes his hand over its side.*) The heart of a phantom is beating! . . . (*He screams. The figure of Christ crosses the stage and passes into the inner room.*)

The relevance of Crookes's narrative to the present chorus is obvious: 'Why does your heart beat thus', 'Its strange heart beating fast', 'O still that heart at last', are palpable reminiscences. The connection with psychical research is useful in another way as well, for it suggests that the 'walking statue' which materialises 'in a man's house' is a presence from the spirit-world. Yeats's attitude to his Galatea-figure is deliberately ambivalent: sometimes she seems to be a living woman, sometimes a ghost.

It ought now to be possible to take the full meaning of Yeats's chorus. It has been thought very obscure, but if we accept what the stage directions tells us, that all the words are chanted by the Musicians as if by a single voice (so that we cannot possibly read the song as a conversation between several personae), the symbolism will reveal itself easily enough:

> Why does your heart beat thus?
> Plain to be understood,
> I have met in a man's house
> A statue of solitude,
> Moving there and walking;
> Its strange heart beating fast
> For all our talking.
> O still that heart at last.

All these words have to be related to a single speaker, and it follows that all are 'about' the statue itself. By his statue Yeats symbolises perfect feminine beauty, beauty which manifests at his fifteenth, supernatural phase: the speaker is in a private house, where he meets either a perfectly beautiful woman or a phantom (both suggestions coexist, and Yeats is careful not to particularise); and he addresses her as 'a statue of solitude'. 'Why does your heart beat thus', he asks her, why do you choose to materialise in the living world, when the proper occupation of the ghost, as we have seen with Fand, is to attain to stillness, 'completeness', the condition of spirituality by which it may win freedom from the wheel of time? Or if you are a flesh and blood woman, how can such perfect spirituality of beauty be appropriate to the fallen world we live in? There follows a parenthesis of six lines in which, so as to be 'plainly understood' by the audience, he explains the circumstances of the encounter, and describes how the 'strange heart' of the mysterious visitant is beating; another circumstance which may point to her supernatural origin, since, 'for all our talking', the heart of a phantom has been known to beat. Then, as the verse ends, he again recommends her to turn from the kinetic excitement of the time-world to 'stillness'; whether she is in fact a living woman or no, it is unthinkable that her preoccupations should be those of a human being. Such is the substance of the first verse, its delicate suggestiveness balanced by Yeats's use of insolent colloquialisms: 'for all our talking', 'in a man's house'. This style of language, one should add, contrasts and blends very effectively with the dignified tenor of the main body of the narrative and first chorus.

Here, and at the end of each verse of his song, Yeats places a haunting and curiously Japanese-seeming refrain. The oblique phrasing and ambiguities are certainly part of his purpose, for such 'opaqueness' was a quality he much admired in the Noh plays.

> O bitter reward
> Of many a tragic tomb!
> And we though astonished are dumb
> Or give but a sigh and a word,
> A passing word.

The suggestion now is, I think, of a suicide's tomb; Shakespeare's Juliet and Marlowe's Hero and Leander were much in Yeats's mind at this period,[91] or perhaps he was thinking of some suicide in the Noh plays, where love often ends in such a way. A woman may die for love (and perhaps the woman-figure of the song is in fact a ghost who has done this); but the 'reward' of such an action is as bitter as the events that cause it. Beyond the grave the beautiful do not find peace, but merely new isolation, Fand's isolation, as indeed will also be their fate as subjectivity increases in their next incarnation. Thus they may leave the spirit-world, between rebirths, to manifest as lonely ghosts in search of companionship; rewarded for all their sufferings by having to take on the lineaments of 'a statue of solitude'. And we, the chorus—who may indeed now be witnesses at such a materialisation—have no consolation to offer, for indeed there is none; we can give no more than a mere gesture of compassion, 'a sigh or a word'. In an early poem, with Maud Gonne explicitly in mind, Yeats tells how the spectator even of Helen's and Paris's love will have had no comment to pass beyond 'a word and a jest'.[92]

The next verse of Yeats's song presents no real problems: it serves, in fact, to clarify what has gone before, for (if she is indeed a phantom) it gives his heroine the motive for her suicide:

> Although the door be shut
> And all seem well enough
> Although wide world hold not
> A man but will give you his love
> The moment he has looked at you,
> He that has loved the best
> May turn from a statue
> His too human breast.

These words are again addressed to Yeats's Galatea-figure, woman, statue or phantom as we may choose to think of her; and they summarise the tragedy of her situation, whether in life or in the ghost, should a man fall in love with her in either condition. Beginning in the urbane and insolently colloquial style of his first verse, Yeats describes the spirituality of beauty; once seen, there is no man in the world who will not offer it his adoration. But though we may adore perfect beauty, it is ultimately a quality alien and inimical to us; man 'human, all too human' in Nietzsche's sentence, in love with the 'imperfect' in the phrase of Balzac which the verse even more certainly remembers,* must ultimately finish by turning away from it. In these lines Yeats provides both a moving apology to Maud Gonne for his defection from her service, and an indication of the level at which we are to read his whole play.

The Musicians finish their song by restating the play's central theme in terms of Yeats's theory of reincarnation. By this means they pick

---

* 'I have lived from boyhood in the shadow, as it were, of that enumeration of famous women in *La Recherche de l'Absolu* ending with the sentence "Blessed are the imperfect for theirs is the kingdom of love". Dante might have made it or some great medieval monk' (*Essays* 1931-6). 'It is the imperfect that we love' stands as a kind of epigraph to *Emer* in one of Yeats's early drafts.

up the thread of the moon-symbolism so important to what has gone before:

> What makes your heart so beat?
> What man is at your side?
> When beauty is complete
> Your own thought will have died
> And danger not be diminished.
> Dimmed at three-quarter light,
> When moon's round is finished
> The stars are out of sight.

We are now shown Yeats's tragic victim with her lover, whose ghost, it may be, now materialises at her side, and the suggestion is that her heart beats as it does in mingled passion and fear that she will lose his love. All beautiful women have the most absolute need for man's companionship; it is their only escape from solitude. But beauty is no protection from loss; even in the fifteenth rebirth, when physical loveliness is 'complete' and all 'thought' dies in self-absorption, the 'danger' of dereliction and loneliness will remain; for man, loving the imperfect as he does, 'cannot bear very much reality', and will tend to turn away. All this Yeats now expresses by a symbolism of the moon rounding towards the full and blotting out the light of the stars. As woman's beauty increases from incarnation to incarnation, it will be increasingly difficult for man to entertain for her intellectual love, 'starlight', the emanation from the superior spheres; while at beauty's zenith it is unthinkable that true love should be experienced at all.

On this bitter note, for I think the colloquialisms mask a deep personal unhappiness, Yeats brings his dance-play to an end. It is indeed a play of many masks: a private sorrow is disguised in a universal statement, an elaborate metaphysical argument in a wild legend from Celtic folklore, a sombre poetry of renunciation in an elaborate aesthetic beauty of colour, spectacle and dance. The result is a work more intricate than any other of *Four Plays For Dancers*, its complexity narrowing to a single direct statement in the second verse of the last chorus; this blend of subtlety and directness seems to me extremely attractive and the play is perhaps the best of the series. Or we may say that *At The Hawk's Well* is the most concentrated and astringent, this the richest and most prodigal of concrete beauty: the choice between the two would be hard to make.

Fand, ideal beauty, is the victim of Yeats's play, and its logic connects closely with that of *Burnt Norton*:

> But the enchainment of past and future,
> Woven in the weakness of the changing body,
> Protects mankind from heaven and damnation
> Which flesh cannot endure.

Yet one ought not to think of Yeats's rejection of the Fand-archetype as permanent, or even that he permanently believed that any escape from the absolute was to be had. He soon reverts to his habitual idealism, telling us in the draft of *The King Of The Great Clock Tower* that 'love's image is a woman made of stone'; and we have seen that his late lyric 'The Statues' is founded on the same premise. There is further statue imagery in 'Among School Children'; there, we are shown a nun in adoration of a 'marble' or 'bronze' sculptural image; and the implication is that every lover must necessarily worship a heartless 'presence' of the same kind.

> O Presences
> That passion, piety or affection knows
> And that all heavenly glory symbolise—
> O self-born mockers of man's enterprise.

The image of the object of desire as something both 'heavenly' and mocking 'man's enterprise' was very deeply embedded in Yeats's mind, and I do not think he ever entirely transcended it.

CHAPTER FOUR

THE CAT AND THE MOON

I

YEATS WROTE *The Cat And The Moon* to exploit a vein of light comedy which runs through the Japanese Noh theatre. In that theatre, two separate dance-plays would be given in the course of a night's entertainment and the interval between them would be filled by means of a *kyogen*, or robust farce. *The Cat And The Moon* was designed to fulfil a similar function:

> I intended my play to be what the Japanese call a *kiogen*, and come as a relaxation of attention between let us say, 'The Hawk's Well' and 'The Dreaming of The Bones'.[1]

There were in fact two forms of *kyogen*, one in which the Noh plays themselves are burlesqued, and another in which the principal characters are the 'Daimyo' (feudal dignitary) and his comic servant. In the latter, the action is broad farce, and the Daimyo is normally shown at the mercy of his servant 'who hoodwinks him . . . but, in the end, the Daimyo usually triumphs and beats the delinquent severely'.[2] *The Cat And The Moon* is a play of the latter kind and, however much or little Yeats may have known of the *kyogen* themselves, it follows the Noh rules closely. At the simplest level, the amusement lies in the fact that the Blind Man is duped by his servitor the Lame Man, who takes advantage of his impediment to steal and skin his sheep. At the climax of the play, the Blind Man discovers the deception, beats the thief with his stick and makes an indignant exit. The low comedy of the play centres about this act.

The play, however, consists of much more than low comedy alone. Yeats makes it perfectly clear that all the action is highly symbolic: 'no audience could discover its dark mythical secrets'.[3] No *stage* audience, perhaps he meant, could do so; the play, written in 1917 for the drawing-room, was not given until 1925, when it was put on in the public theatre; and Yeats may have felt that the heterogeneous assembly a stage performance entailed would not be able to probe very deep. Or perhaps he wrote the words quoted in a moment of reaction against his symbolist intentions, one of those which I have discussed in my preface. For whatever reason, his notes play down the esoteric significance of his drama, though he does provide several clues which point towards it. In *Wheels And Butterflies*, Yeats goes so far as to point out that he has built upon the subjective tradition, but he interprets at what we shall find to be the simplest level:

> I found them (the blind man and lame man) in some medieval Irish sermon as a symbol of soul and body, and then that they had some like meaning in a Buddhist Sutra.[4]

In the first, Cuala, edition of his play, Yeats is more recondite:

> Minnaloushe and the Moon were ... an exposition of man's relation to what I have called the antithetical tincture, and when the Saint mounts upon the back of the Lame Beggar he personifies a certain great spiritual event which may take place when Primary Tincture, as I have called it, supersedes Antithetical.[5]

Primary Tincture, in Yeats's system, supersedes Antithetical at the moment in time at which a society or culture arrives at the highest point of achievement, so that the argument here suggests that the play is related to his theory of history. In *Autobiographies*, Yeats refers directly to it as illustrating his theory of history,[6] and there is therefore no doubt that it has this slant.

Yeats's symbols of Blind Man and Lame Man have in fact both a macrocosmic and a microcosmic application; they are related both to the life-cycle of an individual man and to the history of a civilisation at it approaches Unity of Being. The play consequently becomes one of the most concentrated pieces of symbolism in all Yeats's work, but it should not be forgotten that it is essentially, and centrally, a *kyogen*, a piece of light comedy. His imagery, Yeats says in his Cuala preface, may carry certain learned connotations, but he has tried to leave them as implicit as those underlying eastern arabesques:

> I have amused myself by imagining incidents and metaphors that are related to certain beliefs of mine as are the patterns upon a Persian carpet to some ancient faith or philosophy.[7]

This recalls the advice Yeats gave to his chorus on the production of another dance-play, *The King Of The Great Clock Tower*:

> Lose my words among patterns of sound as the name of God is lost in Arabian arabesques. They are a secret between the musicians, myself, yourselves. They are there in the book if the audience cares to look them up, but we will not thrust our meanings upon them.[8]

It is therefore quite clear that we have to take the story at two distinct levels: first as straightforward drama and only afterwards as philosophical statement. But it is equally clear that the concealed meaning, once found, will be considerable, and not (as a single glancing allusion has led some critics to suppose) in the direction of light satire on George Moore.[9]

In giving his play an ulterior meaning of whatever kind, and even in making it the stylish comedy that it is, Yeats went beyond his Japanese originals. The Noh *kyogen* are low farce merely, and there is nothing of tradition in them, nothing of symbolic significance or ancestral myth; they are improvisations, devised simply as a relaxation of tension, and the parts were not always written down. Yeats clearly did not imitate them as they were, but as they might have been: he realised potentialities the Japanese dramatists had not explored, but which he saw as latent in their form. Thus he says of his plot that he tried to write in the vein of 'Indian and Japanese legends', but he clearly does not mean by this the indifferent material from which the *kyogen* were put together: he means the beautiful folk-tales of Hinduism and Tantric Buddhism, as they are recorded, not in drama, but in the holy books of the East. The story of the priest and the *lingam* will serve as an example:

> A certain Hindu ascetic who lay down to rest beside the holy Ganges, placed his feet upon a Shiva-symbol [a *lingam*, combined phallus and vulva, symbolising, as in Yeats's own poem 'Solomon and The Witch', the union of God and His spouse]. A passing priest observed the man reposing there and asked him, 'How can you dare to profane this symbol of God by resting your feet upon it?' The ascetic replied, 'Good sir, I am sorry; but will you kindly take my feet and place them where there is no such sacred lingam?' The priest seized the ankles of the ascetic, but wherever he set them down a phallus sprang from the ground and they rested as before. 'Ah, I

see,' said the priest humbled, and he made obeisance to the reposing saint and went his way.[10]

With this story we may parallel the legends Yeats quotes in *A Vision* from *Memoirs Of A Japanese Priest*, or the story of the lama, the girl and the two donkeys, taken from Tantric Buddhism as I have shown elsewhere, round which he builds *The Herne's Egg*.[11] He had the most intimate knowledge of this folk convention which the Noh *kyogen* might have used but passed over, and knew it as a comedy both reverent and naïve, prolific with symbolic significance, a curious blend of the sacred and profane. Yeats himself accepted the whole of life and spoke of obscenity as 'the loam of Eden', and the very raciness of the Eastern legends will have attracted him to their use.

The actual myth on which *The Cat And The Moon* is based is a Celtic one, but it is a myth which Yeats thought curiously 'Asiatic' in quality. There was, he says, a 'tradition' in western Ireland that a blind beggar and a lame beggar once 'dreamed a well could cure them, and set out to find it, the lame man on the blind man's back'.[12] More details than this Yeats does not record, perhaps did not know, and the fact is probably fortunate: it left him free to embellish his plot as he chose, and to do so in such a way as to enforce symbolic meaning upon his text. Such local colour as he needed Yeats took from the holy well of the Burren near his home, where 'patterns' or pilgrimages had been made and votive offerings left, 'bits of cloth torn perhaps from a dress, hairpins, and little pious pictures'; Yeats describes this well and its worshippers, painting a picture half-satirical, half-affectionate, in the preface to his play.[13] The wellside of the Burren, for reasons I shall presently show, seemed to him to provide a suitably 'eastern' environment for his maimed beggars to inhabit, and he had thus ready to hand both the plot and landscape he required. What cost him more pains, as we must now turn aside to see, was to find a style appropriate to his subject.

II

Yeats himself, in his 1926 preface, pays homage to the writers from whom he learned his comic style, and he even 'places' his play by assigning it to a particular *genre* of the Irish drama. He relates it to the work of those writers who made up the 'peasant' school, as opposed to the 'realistic' school (a drama of 'provincial' bourgeois manners) which succeeded it in the Dublin theatre. If we are to come closer to the precise nature of what I shall call his play's 'humaneness', it will be necessary to investigate this rather difficult preface.

After explaining his sources in Celtic myth, Yeats's preface develops on lines I have discussed already, and explains that his play requires of us an 'Asiatic' emotion. He decided to publish, we are told, at a time when he was preoccupied with Eastern legend, playing with the idea of 'inventing for Cuchulain some youthful sojourn in the forest, and writing for him many love-poems like those Indian poets have put into the mouth of Krishna'; and these studies convinced him that his play had 'an odour, a breath' which was that of Indian folk-art.[14] 'Asiatic emotion', he goes on to say, had been a salient characteristic of a whole school of Irish drama, to which his own play stood in due relation: we are referred to 'the last act of Synge's *Well Of The Saints*, and your (Lady Gregory's) *Gaol Gate . . . The Grasshopper* by Mr. Padraic Colum and a play of Mr. Corkery's'.[15] In these lines Yeats confers on his play both an atmosphere and a pedigree, and it will be useful to investigate both the meaning of his sentences and the words in which this 'oriental' atmosphere is discerned.

When Yeats tells us that the Irish peasant 'lived in Asia till the Battle of the Boyne' he means that the two cultures are alike in their full 'subjectivity', and his argument can thus be related to his theory of psychological types. We need here to elaborate what my previous section may already have partly illustrated, the precise nature of the outlook Yeats associated with the Eastern mind. In the first place, he associated spirituality, but a spirituality quite divorced from asceticism; all peasant cultures seemed to him characterised by the nearness of *l'homme moyen sensuel* to the visionary state:

> They [the common people in such civilisations] have no asceticism, but they are more visionary than any ascetic, and their invisible life is but the life about them made more perfect and more lasting.[16]

Yeats also associated joy in the manifested world, profound wisdom in 'the science of beauty everywhere', and this is well shown from a celebrated passage in his later prose. He is comparing Irish and Indian attitudes to the life of contemplation, and contrasting the Russian mystic, who is taken as the type of the 'objective' saint:

> The Russian, like most European mystics, distrusts visions though he admits their reality, seems indifferent to nature, may perhaps dread it like St. Bernard who passed the Italian lakes with averted

eyes. The Indian, on the other hand, speaks continually of the beauty and terror of the great mountains, interrupts his prayer to listen to the song of birds, remembers with delight the nightingale that disturbed his meditations by alighting upon his head and singing there, recalls after many years the whiteness of a sheet, the softness of a pillow, the gold embroidery of a shoe.[17]

Yeats goes on to say that the primitive Irish mystics were of one kind with the Indian: that they 'made innumerable poems about bird and beast and spread the doctrine that Christ was the most beautiful of all men'.[18] And with this he associated also a certain radical belief in the equality of man and man, which was an article of religious, not at all of political faith. 'Kings, princes, courtesans, the beggar and the fool by the wayside', he says, are 'all equal' to the Indian saint, for 'everyone's road is different, everyone awaits his moment'.[19] By this Yeats implies, of course, a certain fixed tendency to see the holy behind the squalid, the divine image behind the beggar's rags.

We now have to relate Yeats's arguments to each of the Irish plays he mentions, since each will have contributed something to the atmosphere of his own play. We are referred, in the first place, to the last act* of *The Well Of The Saints*. The story of Synge's play is well known: the two old beggars sit at the side of the road, knowing too much, now, to wish to have their sight a second time restored; conscious of all the hostility of the visible world, the mortifications of desire, the squalid penury which normality would bring them, the misery of watching each other grow old. They are perfectly unregenerate as they sit there, and ready to quarrel at the least pretext; but from this nadir of squalor, a paean of what one can only call thanksgiving goes up. It is a small hymn in praise of the blessings which come with blindness:

Mary Doul: Well, we're a great pair, surely, and it's great times we'll have yet, maybe, and great talking before we die. . . . There's the sound of one of them twittering yellow birds do be coming up in the springtime from beyond the sea, and there'll be a fine warmth now in the sun, and a sweetness in the air, the way it'll be a grand thing to be sitting here quiet and easy, smelling the things growing up, and budding from the earth.

* The rest of this paragraph is concerned with Synge's last act only; I am not trying to say that his play as a whole communicates 'inner peace'.

> Martin Doul: I'm smelling the furze awhile back sprouting on the hill, and if you'd hold your tongue you'd hear the lambs of Grianan, though it's near drowned their crying is with the full river making noises in the glen.

This subjective self-sufficiency the saint does not comprehend, and when he tries to force healing upon them Martin knocks the stoup from his hand:

> What call has the like of you to be coming between innocent people that you're not understanding at all, and be making a great mess with the holy water you have, and the length of your prayers?

The saint is the type of what Yeats calls the 'European mystic', and their inner peace is an alien quality to him; but this peace, so beautifully communicated, blends perfectly with what one might call the Asiatic squalor of their circumstances; and this seems to me the central virtue of the play.

Lady Gregory's one true tragedy *Gaol Gate*[20] is less well known. An old Galway peasant woman comes with her neighbour to visit her son, who is in gaol because of activities subversive to the English administration. They are an illiterate couple, and their talk is of privation and the workhouse: Mary Cushin especially is a primitive creature, and her words merely echo her physical needs:

> Mary Cushin: It is very cold at the dawn. It is time for them open the door. I wish I had brought a potato or a bit of a cake or of bread.

The gaoler reads the letter that has brought them to the prison, which they cannot do themselves, and explains that its drift is not (as they suppose) to inform them of the young man's release, but to tell them that he has been hanged. He gives them the youth's few possessions, 'all he brought in with him, the flannels and the shirt and the shoes'. The two old women console each other, and with their sorrow, mixed as it is with pride in the young man's integrity, they recover something of the old heroic spirit of their race. At the end of the play, as in the neighbour's keen, this emotion overflows in the most passionate language:

> Gather up, Mary Cushin, the clothes for your child; they'll be wanted by this one and that one. The boys crossing the sea in the springtime will be craving a thread for a memory.

One word to the judge and Denis was free; they offered him all sorts of riches. They brought him drink to the gaol, and gold, to swear away the life of his neighbour.

Pat Ruane was no good friend to him at all, but a foolish, wild companion; it was Terry Fury knocked a gap in the wall and sent in the calves to our meadow.

Denis would not speak, he shut his mouth, he would never be an informer. It is no lie he would have said at all in giving witness against Terry Fury.

I will go through Gort and Kilbecanty and Drumdarode and Darode; I will call to the people and the singers at the fairs to make a great praise for Denis. . . .

Lady Gregory's is a woman's prose, and it is sometimes charged with emotion to an extent which I find unpalatable, but the intensity of passages such as this one can only admire. The play splendidly brings home the equality of man and man—a conviction Lady Gregory bases on purely spiritual values—as it may be discerned in the dignity and nobility of the Irish poor.

Yeats also mentions 'a play of Mr. Corkery's', and there are several plays which he may have had in mind. One is *King and Hermit* (1916)[21] which draws a close and, I think, an intended parallel between an Irish hermit and his gilly and an Indian holy man and his *chela*. There is something very Asiatic in Colman, the recluse, who has 'found peace and contemplation in the depths of the forest . . . with birds winging in it and sun-lit deer and golden fruit and running streams'. One remembers that Yeats planned to put love-poems into Cuchulain's mouth, and to set him to meditate in a similar forest. But I think that the play Yeats has in mind is more probably *The Yellow Bittern* (1917).[22] This tells of the sufferings and death of an old Irish beggar-poet, 'the likeness of the yellow bird, the same in habits and the same in colour; both of them would be out at night when other folk would be in their beds; and both of them were yellow'. The old man is portrayed with resolute unsentimentality: he is hideous and vicious and then we see him delirious, and he has nothing but his joy in life to recommend him. Even his masterpiece is an outrageous drinking-song where he compares himself to a bittern dead of the drought:

'Tis a fine song, surely—a dead bird, stretched on the flat of his back, and his feet sticking up to the sky.

The play consigns him to a sordid death, and he is 'a rascal and a stroller and a deceiver of women', cursed by the Catholic priest; but a pale, barefooted woman appears at his deathbed and is later identified with the Queen of Heaven. The moral is not enforced, but it can only be that self-sufficiency and joy in life are enough.

Padraic Colum, the last playwright listed by Yeats, is a less starkly uncompromising but a similarly orientated writer. Yeats refers us to what has proved to be an evanescent play, *Grasshopper*,* but the spirituality with which Colum invests his peasant characters is better shown from his lyrics, where it is very evident:

BRANDING A FOAL

Why do I look for fire to brand these foals?
What do I need, when all within is fire?
And, lo, she comes, carrying the lighted coals
And branding tool—she who is my desire.
What need have I for what is in her hands,
If I lay hold upon a hide, it brands,
And grass, and trees, and shadows, all are fire.

What Yeats calls the Asiatic element in Colum's art is, however, perhaps best illustrated from such a poem as 'The Honey Seller', in 'Reminiscences':

You went by, a man upstanding,
On your head a wide dish holding
Dark and golden lumps of honey;
You went slowly, like an old horse
That's not driven any longer
But that likes to take an amble . . .

Thus the old man moves across our vision like some figure in an Eastern bazaar; but no one ever bought his honey:

On you went, and in a sounding
Voice, just like the bell of evening
Told us of the dark and golden
Treasures dripping in your wide dish . . .

---

* It would be pointless to discuss *Grasshopper* here, since it was written after Yeats's play but before his preface and so cannot be an influence.

This poem shows particularly clearly the quality Yeats has in mind, an almost childishly simple blending of the dignified and the sordid into a whole moving, unEuropean, and strange.

Such are the influences on *The Cat And The Moon*, and it is important to note that it could not have been written without them. Yeats was not by nature a writer in this *genre*. He had, and demonstrates in *The Pot Of Broth*, a certain slender talent for low comedy, but when, in *The Unicorn From The Stars*, he tries to combine it with something more, a vein of rather excessive spirituality comes between him and success. There is something of the 'nineties aesthete in Martin, the central character of *The Unicorn From The Stars*, and this is a most inappropriate quality in an artisan hero:

> Martin: Does the body slip from you as it does from me? They have not shut your window into eternity?

Yeats had to learn, from the movement he speaks of, to dispense with this kind of writing, and to balance what spirituality remained with a compensatory earthiness. Synge no doubt taught him most, introducing him to a prose style which would carry the peasant idiom: he taught him also to be hard, even callous, in statement, and to blend the spiritual and the unregenerate in characterisation. And the other dramatists I have listed no doubt contributed their share: Corkery perhaps helped him towards starkness and forthrightness and Lady Gregory towards sincerity, while Colum may have assisted him to a style unforcedly simple, while at the same time curious and strange. Colum's very genuine naïveté, indeed, will have made him particularly attractive to Yeats, for they seem to me to have shared in a direct, basically religious vision denied to the other writers mentioned; I think it no coincidence that they wrote between them the two best modern Irish ballads in folk-idiom, 'Down By The Salley Gardens' and 'She Moved Through The Fair'.

The Cat And The Moon, then, is a derivative piece of writing and it is a slight and experimental play. But I will state here what I shall later try to prove, that it is nevertheless, a work of considerable stature. Yeats recognised the deficiencies as well as the merits of the writers from whom he profited, and it is interesting to observe how sedulously he avoids their faults. There is nothing in his play of what Henn calls the 'sadism' of Synge's drama, that harshness and violence of imagery which seem essential to his art; I think indeed that Yeats realised that this quality was not always a virtue, and it is instructive that his preface praises only the last, which is the gentlest, act of *The Well Of The Saints*. His own play is much more temperate, holding to a middle course in language with no very marked loss in peasant salt,★ and this seems to me indicative of his surer temperamental balance, as the affectionate generosity of his characterisation may be of greater maturity of mind. Humaneness and 'natural kindness' are after all the essential constituents of spiritual understanding, and they are not always the characteristics we associate with Synge's theatre.[23] And if Yeats's chronicle of blindness, for all its slightness, is a wiser play than his, it is more many-sided than any of the other works he names: there is a richer seam of poetry in it than anywhere in Corkery, more of a 'tough reasonableness' than is usual in Lady Gregory, while *Grasshopper* is the only play (as distinct from poem) by Colum which he could have cited, for Colum's other dramas are in an alien mode. If it is not the best, then, I think I can make out a case for *The Cat And The Moon* as the most spiritually adult production of the Irish 'peasant' movement; it is also perhaps one of the most *classical*, in the sense of the freest from defect.

III

If we now complete our study at the exoteric level by an examination of Yeats's text, it will be seen that his play is not satiric in any sense; I should call it a sympathetic portrait of the Irish folk-imagination. Yeats analyses that imagination from within: there is no scenery, and he presents most of the action through his characters' own eyes, so that we are forced to visualise the story as they themselves see it. His prose has toughness of fibre as well as an informing kindliness, and much amusement is derived from the distortions to which the folk imagination tends; but his intention is affirmative, and he stresses the essential dignity of all his characters, as also the unEuropean nature of the Irish peasant mind.

The 'Asiatic' qualities he discerned in his theme served Yeats to great advantage, for they entitled him to use to the full the resources of the Noh theatre: the more oriental and unfamiliar his technique, the more the analogy between Ireland and the cryptic East would be underlined. Thus the chorus-musicians are used to an extent unique in his drama, while every episode of the story is presented so as to provide

★ Yeats does not try for the richness and sonority of Synge's prose, though he captures something of its idiomatic flavour; his own style, when matter-of-fact, comes closer to Corkery's, while his lyrical effects are like those Colum sometimes brings off in verse.

a disturbing visual image. We begin with the weird ensemble of the two crippled, grotesquely masked beggars, which crosses the stage to muffled drum-taps; and Yeats opens further vistas of uncouthness before us by means of visual description:

> Lame Beggar: When you go out to pick up a chicken, or maybe a stray goose on the road, or a cabbage from a neighbour's garden, I have to go riding on your back; and if I want a goose, or a chicken, or a cabbage, I must have your two legs under me.

Then they come to the well, and we are asked to imagine the Saint (as surely nowhere else save in Eastern folk-lore) perched in the branches of an ash-tree; the saint heals Blind Beggar, who begins to beat the Lame Man, the beating taking the form of a dance 'accompanied by drum and flute'. Lame Beggar, however, refuses the proffered healing; he prefers sanctity, and another Eastern reminiscence has the saint climb on his back, after which they perform the pagan ceremony of blessing the road. His beatitude is complete when, still carrying his mount, he begins his dance:

> The lame beggar begins his dance, at first clumsily, moving about with his (i.e. Blind Man's) stick, then he throws away the stick and dances more and more quickly. Whenever he strikes the ground strongly with his lame foot, the cymbals clash.

In all this climactic scene, the part of the saint is spoken by the First Musician, as would be normal practice in the Noh: he speaks from the corner of the stage, and we have to imagine an invisible presence on Lame Man's back. This adds the last touch to Yeats's narrative, completing a whole which is by turns squalid and visionary, but which is always bizarre.

The sequence of events we are shown is apparently quite arbitrary and undirected, and we may at first 'place' the play in the region of simple farce, where it provides us with amusement of two distinct kinds. There is humour, as I have said, in the fantasy and naïveté of the Irish folk-imagination, where much of the incident has its merely hallucinatory existence: in the mentality which can site a saint in a tree, and which can describe the wellside of Yeats's preface in affirmative terms: 'the beads and the candles and the leaves torn out of prayer books and the hairpins and the buttons. It is a great sight, and a blessed sight'. Then also, there is entertainment to be derived from the unregenerate nature of the two pilgrims; one thinks of Lame Man, whose theft of the sheepskin is detected at the moment of his beatification, standing there, in Yeats's ingenious symbolism, a grotesque penitent: clothed in the wool of the lamb, the black sheepskin draping his guilty shoulders. Or one thinks of the Blind Man's unChristian sentiment at the moment when the saint touches his eyes:

> Lame Beggar: Am I not blessed, and it's a sin to speak against the blessed?
> Blind Beggar: Well, I'll speak against the blessed, and I'll tell you something more that I'll do. . . . I have been saying to myself, I shall know where to hit and how to hit and who to hit.

Here Yeats is tilting at Catholicism or the Irish peasants' response to Catholicism, but the irony is of the gentlest kind, and is in this respect a departure from his normal practice. *The Player Queen*, his other mature comedy, is in many ways a cruel, even an embittered play; and *The Herne's Egg* is as brutal as it is full of levity;[24] but here he is concerned with 'the book of the people', and this keeps his writing always humane.

Irony, in any case, is only one side of Yeats's theme: the other side is miracle. The saint, by whom Yeats's miracle is effected, is not (as in Synge) the type of the 'European mystic'; he is a subjective holy man whose spiritual home, one would say, is in Asia. Thus he is not preoccupied, as the Christian might be, with the enforcement of a moral code: he knows that 'everything that lives is holy', as is natural in one who has returned to a condition of undifferentiating innocence. This is made clear by what may at first seem a monstrous asseveration in Blind's Man's central speech, which we are explicitly told contains 'great wisdom':

> Now the Church says that it is a good thought, and a sweet thought, and a comfortable thought, that every man should have a saint to look after him, and I, being blind, give it out to all the world that the bigger the sinner the better pleased is the saint. I am sure and certain that Saint Colman would not have us two different from what we are.

And since the saint has this 'radical innocence', he can be presented much as the Irish folk-mind would envisage him, speaking in peasant dialect and adopting the most undignified postures, and his holiness will not seem to be in the least impaired. It is communicated in the reverence which the two beggars feel for him, the more valid for Yeats in being an instinctive emotion; and also by the gentle and fragile prose he is made to speak (a style Yeats had in common with Padraic Colum, who was gifted with a rather similar vision of sanctity and wrote poems on holy wells and St. Columbkille). For all this, Yeats's saint is not an abstract personification: he is carefully humanised, and we are reminded of his 'loneliness' and of the frailty to be associated with the solitary, attributes he shares with the later Ribh. Here is the dialogue as he mounts on Lame Beggar's back:

Saint: Bend down your back. . . . I'm up now.
Lame Beggar: I don't feel you at all.
Saint: I don't weigh more than a grasshopper.
Lame Beggar: You do not.

This is gently moving, and so is the simplicity of the play's conclusion:

Saint: Aren't you blessed?
Lame Beggar: Maybe so.
Saint: Aren't you a miracle?
Lame Beggar: I am, holy man.
Saint: Then dance, and that'll be a miracle.

The Lame Man dances, and his dance, the dance of recovered innocence, abstracts a dominant emotion from the play.

The spirituality of Yeats's play may be at its most unmixed when he is describing his saint, but there is nobility also in each of his two beggars. The Blind Man is a bully and a thief, he is physically repellent and morally has little to recommend him, but he is redeemed by a quality of intuitional wisdom, as we may see from his disquisition (already quoted) on the loneliness of the saint. We have always to remember that Yeats's saint is above all conventional distinctions of good and evil, sin and virtue; will prefer the natural and joyous to the unnaturally pious, and may even assent to that favourite maxim of Yeats's: 'Blessed are the imperfect, for theirs is the Kingdom of love.'[25] So at least the Blind Man characterises him, in a speech where there is perhaps some irony in the words 'holy company' and 'innocent'; they are applied, after all, to the worshippers who have strewed litter round the well:

Blind Beggar: What pleasure can he have in all that holy company kneeling at his well, on holidays and Sundays, and they maybe as innocent as himself?
Lame Beggar: That's a strange thing to say, and do you say it as I or another might say it, or as a blind man?
Blind Beggar: I say it as a blind man, I say it because since I went blind in the tenth year of my age, I have been hearing and remembering the knowledges of the world.

It is obvious that we are to attach weight to these words, and one remembers what a peasant told Yeats, as a young man gathering folk-lore, of the vatic powers of the blind. One remembers, too, his essay 'Why The Blind Man In Ancient Times Was Made A Poet',[26] where he stresses the connection between physical deprivation and spiritual wisdom, as also his confidence in 'the thinking of the body' and his conviction that philosophy should 'bulk animal below the waistline'.[27] The Blind Beggar's wisdom is partly of this order, though it is partly also a philosophy of bitterness and destitution, as we may see from his indecision whether or not to be restored. He knows that the gift of eyesight is hardly worth the having, and this article of his wisdom Yeats derives from Synge.

The Blind Man, however, is more than darkly gifted merely, and another aspect of his character emerges as he accepts his healing, and opens his eyes for the first time on the visible world. We know that he is quite unrepentant, and that he is about to use his restored eyesight to take revenge on the Lame Man, but the moment still has its spirituality, a power which derives from Yeats's very great awareness of what he calls in a lyric 'human dignity'. I have quoted some of the speech to illustrate Yeats's satire, but it will now be seen to be something very much more, though satire coexists with its opposite in the Blind Man's words:

Saint: In the name of the Father, the Son, and the Holy Spirit, I give this Blind Man sight and I make this Lame Man blessed.
Blind Beggar: I see it all now, the blue sky and the big ash tree and the well and the flat stone—all as I have heard the people say—and the things the praying people put on

> the stone, the beads and the candles and the leaves torn out of prayerbooks, and the hairpins and the buttons. It is a great sight and a blessed sight.

This is a mere vignette (and throughout the play Yeats is working, one might say, in miniature), but beneath all the levity he of course means precisely what he says: the wellside is indeed 'a great sight and a blessed sight' if we visualise it rightly, and our sense of this makes the speech telling on the stage. It takes its cathartic power from the quality of the writing: this is prose of the very simple and beautiful kind Yeats gives also to Teigue, the visionary fool of *The Hourglass*, in those descriptions of the heavenly world one does not forget:

> Everybody knows, everybody in the world knows, when it is spring with us, the trees are withering there, when it is summer with us, the snow is falling there, and have I myself not heard the lambs that are there all bleating on a cold November day—to be sure, does not everybody with an intellect know that?

And if Yeats thinks of Teigue as an undeveloped mystic, does not Blind Beggar in his turn see the world as Blake says humanity will do on the last day, 'when all shall be consumed and appear Infinite and Holy'? Behind the shabby and the workaday he perceives the eternal beauty, and this holiness coexists with and transcends the hairpins, buttons and the rest.

Less obviously moving, but equally effective in retrospect, is the scene in which Lame Man chooses to be blessed. Yeats's two beggars stand in relation much as do Fool and Blind Man in *On Baile's Strand*, the one slow, wise and full of a massive simplicity, the other 'flighty', cowardly and complex; but, as there, each has his respective spiritual talents, as indeed in Yeats's theology must always be the case:

> There cannot be, confusion of our sound forgot,
> A single soul that lacks a sweet crystalline cry.

In the scene in question, the low cunning with which Lame Man probes for the advantages to be gained from beatitude, and what I can only call the spiritual cupidity of his decision, are ironically painted in; but there is more than comedy in his 'flighty' conversation with the Saint:

> Lame Beggar: What would it be like to be blessed?
> Saint: You would be of the kin of the blessed saints and Martyrs.
> Lame Beggar: Is it true now that they have a book and that they write the names of the blessed in that book?
> Saint: Many a time have I seen that book, and your name would be in it.
> Lame Beggar: It would be a grand thing to have two legs under me, but I have it in my mind that it would be a grander thing to have my name in that book.
> Saint: It would be a grander thing.
> Lame Beggar: I will stay lame, Holy Man, and I will be blessed.

The simplicity of the last line here introduces the *motif* of Lame Beggar's humility, before the saint, and before the idea of his own beatitude, and this quality is made the dominant note of his character for the remainder of the play. It is, if one may call it so, a primitive and instinctual humility, but it is not the less moving for this. Thus, Yeats's hero, knowing his great demerits, can never be quite sure that he is really transfigured:

> Saint: Are you happy?
> Lame Beggar: I would be if I was right sure I was blessed.

I have already mentioned his simple acceptance of his condition at the conclusion of the play:

> Saint: Aren't you blessed?
> Lame Beggar: Maybe so.
> Saint: Aren't you a miracle?
> Lame Beggar: I am, holy man.

There is now that fragility in Lame Man's speeches, that delicacy of rhythm and cadence, which I have noticed as characteristic of the Saint's also; as there should be, since they are both proceeding to the same spiritual norm.

So much can be said of the affirmative element in Yeats's drama, and of the claims which can be made for it as a profound and even noble play. It shows us the essential dignity of the Irish peasant vision, a mentality pagan or subjective beneath the thinnest veneer of

Catholicism, and close to that pristine innocence which (as distinguished from mere goodness) seems to Yeats 'the occupation of the saint'. He is careful, of course, not to make too much of his two pilgrims, and the darker side of their personalities is unsentimentally etched in, but he wishes us to look through man's unregenerate nature to the purity which is at its root. His *kyogen* has thus a moral stature, a sense of the intrinsic worth of the individual, which makes it even at the exoteric level a considerable achievement; though this should not blind us to what have been called its faults. It is certainly very brief, and critics have thought it also much weakened by irrelevancies (as by the choruses, apparently with no relation to the main text, which describe Minnaloushe and the moon themselves); it has further been said that the basic situation is hackneyed, in that the comic beggar was even in 1917 a cliché of the Irish stage. Much of this, however, is seeming rather than real criticism, for *The Cat And The Moon* has a dimension of sheer depth which redeems it from any charge of mere triteness, and which no other work of the 'peasant' movement could reasonably be said to possess. It has, that is, a very definite and very beautiful ulterior meaning, to a study of which I shall now proceed.

IV

The esoteric meaning of Yeats's play is concerned with his theory of history, and this gives one salient reason why it could not be published before 1925. He could not bring it out with the rest of *Four Plays For Dancers*, for he had not then announced this side of his philosophy; as soon as he had finished *A Vision*, his dance-play appeared at once. I shall quote frequently from *A Vision* in the summary of Yeats's theory that follows, and in which I am less concerned to produce new facts than to arrange the known facts in a helpful order;* an order which will illuminate my text.

Yeats's philosophy of history is really an extension of his theory of reincarnation. He says in *A Vision* that an identical law may be observed in 'every completed movement of thought or life', from the vast cyclic round of history to the mechanics of 'a single judgement or act'.[28] For the process is in each case circular: in the sphere of physical action, from inertia to fulfilment, with a consequent return to inertia; and on the historical plane from primitivity to a peak of culture, after which there is a period of gradual relapse. Yeats learned his interpretation of

* This is not to say that I have nothing new to add. I intend this section as a supplement and corrective to the account given in *Yeats And Tradition*, which is rather scrappy.

history, in the first place, from theosophy, for the cyclic theory is axiomatic to Madame Blavatsky's thought:

> Ancient philosophy . . . divided the interminable periods of human existence on this planet into cycles, during each of which mankind gradually reached the culminating point of highest civilisation, and gradually relapsed into abject barbarism.[29]

Madame Blavatsky has here in mind Indian and Buddhist philosophy, and she might have added that the belief is characteristic of most of the religious systems of the world. Jungian psychology has demonstrated that there are powerful compulsions on mankind to envisage history in such a way, and that it is in the nature of the psyche to do so:[30] the theory originates from our tendency to reason by analogy, or as the mystic would say to perceive metaphysical truth in the harmonies of the visible world. The analogy drawn is precisely as in the theory of reincarnation: with the seasons, or with the cycle of day and night, or the phases of the moon; in the Mandukya-Upanishad, the comparison is with man's daily progress from sleep to full waking consciousness, and his relapse into the unconscious state.[31] Historians such as Vico tend similarly to proceed by analogy, as we shall see;[32] and that Yeats's historical theory had similar premises we know from his verse:

> The Primum Mobile that fashioned us
> Has made the very owls in circles move.[33]

It is thus hardly possible to dismiss Yeats's theory, with Toynbee's and Spengler's, as something merely topical in nineteen-twenties' thought. Much more than theirs, it is the expression of a central traditional teaching, persistent because it is based on the normal processes of the human mind.

Where Yeats's theory goes beyond Spengler's, as it goes also beyond the theory of 'identical recurrence' proposed by Nietzsche, is in combining the cyclic law and the law of the 'paired opposites'. This also was traditional, since it was traditional to believe that the opposites—Kant's antinomies—must be manifested in everything that partakes of generation; they can only be reconciled in God. Thus hot and cold, moist and dry, 'subjective' and 'objective', 'Chance' and 'Choice', are in the human sense irreducible dualities: male and female are opposites also, and their longing for union is a longing for a reconciliation which will come in the divine world. But if the opposites are to be manifested in everything human, they will be manifested in history as elsewhere; and, as Greek philosophy recognised, successive cycles will tend to display opposite characteristics. Thus Empedocles has a system of endlessly alternating cycles, characterised by 'love', and 'strife';[34] while Plato's system is of alternating cycles also, 'superior' and 'inferior', good and evil.[35] Yeats in turn recognises the need for such an arrangement, and discerns the opposites interacting to the beginnings of recorded history:

> There was everywhere a conflict between two principles or elemental forms of the mind, each 'dying the other's life, living the other's death'.[36]

He calls his two alternating cycles, in accordance with his theory of reincarnation, 'subjective' and 'objective', and imagines time as an endless conflict between his two opposite psychological principles, each winning dominance in turn. Thus in the subjective cycle from 2000 B.C. to the birth of Christ, the 'superior' subjective principle was in the ascendant, and the religion of the Self sprang up in Greece, India, pagan Ireland and throughout the world; in the inferior cycle then beginning Christianity supplanted its opposite, and would remain dominant until a reversal of the gyres. In conceiving of history as a process of this kind, Yeats had the sanction of Indian and Buddhist, even Jainist, tradition to reinforce the Greek: for there also there is an alternation between good and evil cycles, with epochs now 'bright' with religious affirmation, now 'dark' as the true religion falls into decay.[37]

As well as in relating history to the law of opposites, Yeats followed his perennial philosophy in adopting the theory of the Great Year, and in doing so he resolved an apparent anomaly in his thought. His 'subjective' and 'objective' cycles were each some 2000 years in duration, but the observable length of actual civilisations (the time between Homer and the Greek decadence or from the Norman conquest of Britain to 'this vile age') was characteristically not much more than half this period; and the discrepancy was not easy to explain. Yeats resolved it by applying the concept of the Platonic *Magnus Annus*, which is identical with the Great Year of Indian and Buddhist philosophy: a period many hundreds of thousands of solar years in length, which represents the time necessary for one complete evolution of the historical pattern in all its detail. This Platonic Year, an astrological computation, had four seasons like the secular (thus Aristotle says that Deucalion's flood came at a winter of the Great Year)[38] and all human time measurement followed its archetypal pattern. As Yeats himself says, it was inscrutable in itself, but its structure could be guessed at from that of its component parts:

> Whatever its length it divided, and so did every unit whose multiple it was, into waxing and waning, day and night, summer and winter.[39]

The one true historical measurement, then, was the *Magnus Annus*, and eras and civilisations are merely microcosmic entities obedient to its laws: we subdivide the Great Year and obtain historical cycles, further divide these cycles and obtain 'sub-cycles' or secular cultures, and can if we wish continue until we arrive at such 'units' as the calendar year, or month, or day. Yeats saw every cycle as containing within itself two 'sub-cycles' or major cultural periods,* each of which has its circular pattern and four seasons of maturation: its spring of heroic endeavour and midsummer zenith, followed by a period of autumnal intellectualism and a return to mid-winter decay. Or one could, if one chose, dissect them in more detail: thus he sometimes discerns in a culture twenty-eight 'lunar' phases, analogous to those of the reincarnating soul.

We have now to turn from Yeats's theory to his practice, for *The Cat And The Moon* presumes a very thorough knowledge of the actual workings of his system. It is necessary to demonstrate the process as he saw it from some one of his historical cycles, and I shall use for this purpose the present objective era, whose starting-point is the birth of Christ. Each of the two sub-cycles of this age begins from midwinter or the symbolic dark of the moon, and the seasons or lunar phases follow in regular succession until intellect begins to assert itself over spirit and emotion, and disintegration begins. Thus the sub-cycle from Christ's birth to A.D. 1050 begins with disorder (the gradual collapse of the classical empire); finds its heroic age in the great years of the primitive church, when ascetic and martyr perfected themselves as 'God's athletes'; reaches its zenith in the early Byzantine period and declines thence into the autumnal intellectualism of Byzantine theological dispute; and returns to winter as the feud of Church and State begins and the Christian solidarity, so painfully won, begins to fall apart Yeats elaborates his description of the era with great brilliance and ingenuity, but this is the essential framework on which he builds, both in *A Vision*[40] and in his play.

* He sometimes uses here his symbol of the double cone.

The Cat And The Moon is concerned with the historical period of summer or full moon, and I shall therefore concentrate here on Yeats's description of this period. He sees the manifestation of his climactic 'fifteenth phase' in the reign of Justinian, 'that great age of building in which one may conclude Byzantine art was perfected'. Culture had now arrived at the condition of Unity of Being, and the characteristics of the age are therefore precisely those which an individual would exhibit in an equivalent incarnation. Momentary contact with the mystical world would be the first of these, and Yeats consequently points out that the art of Byzantium was visionary:

> Byzantium . . . substituted for formal Roman magnificence, with its glorification of physical power, an architecture that suggests the sacred city of St. John.[41]

Yeats goes on to describe, in a famous passage, how the Byzantine craftsman felt 'the supernatural descending nearer to him than to Plotinus even'[42] and made it the subject of his art. With this, Yeats's theory of Unity of Being would incline us to look for a certain anonymity in Byzantine art, such a preoccupation with universals as he discerns in William Morris: the moon of the Self shines over Justinian's city, and we may expect of its craftsmen that transcendence of all merely personal values which accompanies spiritual fulfilment. Yeats makes it clear that this was indeed a characteristic of the period:

> The painter and the mosaic worker, the worker in gold and silver, the illuminator of sacred books, were almost impersonal, almost perhaps without the sense of individual design, absorbed in their subject-matter and in the vision of a whole people.[43]

'The work of many', as Yeats puts it, 'had become the work of one', so that 'building, picture, pattern, metalwork of rail and lamp seemed but a single image'.[44] The lower Self, that is to say, was attained with consummate ease, and we should therefore predict also a perseverance beyond such fragmentated vision of the divine beauty, and a discovery of the full discipline of escape. Yeats completes his description by establishing that this was so, and that sanctity was the preoccupation of both of emperor and common people.[45]

Beyond this spirituality lay the gradual decline of four hundred years, and at the end of the sub-cycle we meet with a strange anomaly. The year A.D. 1050 falls within the twenty-eighth phase of Yeats's minor era, and falls therefore at the dark of the moon; but it is also the fifteenth or central phase of the Christian dispensation considered as a whole. Two contrary impulses thus manifest at this time, and Yeats has a fascinating paragraph on their interaction. The age, from the full moon of its major era, has a considerable spiritual potentiality, but this spirituality is distorted by the malevolent influence of its dark moon until it becomes merely grotesque:

> All creation has ceased, and man has come to terms with the supernatural . . . saint or angel does not seem very different from themselves, a man thinks his guardian angel jealous of his mistress . . . three Roman courtesans who have one after another got their favourite lovers made Pope have . . . confessed their sins, with full belief in the supernatural efficacy of the act, to hands that have played with their own bodies. In monastery and in hermit cells men freed from the intellect seek their God upon all fours like beasts or children.[46]

There is also that curious sense of stagnation which we associate with the fifteenth phase of Yeats's cycle of reincarnation: with Fand, for example:

> All that is necessary to salvation is known, but there is apathy everywhere. Everywhere man awaits death.[47]

Yeats's arguments here are highly relevant to *The Cat And The Moon*, though they are so largely in a negative sense. We have to remember that the fifteenth phase of the greater era is not a period of spiritual achievement, but an apathetic, 'inferior' age.

The second sub-cycle of Yeats's era points towards disintegration; and it leads man steadily away from God. It has, however, a phasal development, as before, and rises to a peak in the early Renaissance before its final decline. The 'heroic spring' of this period is the age of the Crusades, which finds its intellectual counterpart in Dante's Florence, and the zenith is achieved a little after A.D. 1450. Then the 'strangeness' sensed by the artist everywhere as the full moon of the Self comes round lends his work an 'emotion of mystery' that is new in painting; the art of the period, however, is secular rather than religious, for vision is beginning to deteriorate as the cycle moves towards its end. The lower Self, however, is found with the same ease as before:

Botticelli, Crevelli, Mantegna, Da Vinci, who fall within the period, make Massaccio and his school seem heavy and common by something we may call intellectual beauty or compare perhaps to that kind of beauty Castiglione called 'the spoil or monument of the victory of the soul'. Intellect and emotion . . . are for the moment one.[48]

The discovery of the Self was made at all levels of the community, as it had been in the Byzantium of the preceding age:

> Men attained to personality in great numbers, Unity of Being, and became [Yeats uses Dante's phrase] 'like a perfectly proportioned human body', and as many men so fashioned held places of power, the nations had it too, prince and ploughman sharing that thought and feeling. What afterwards showed for rifts and cracks were there already, but imperious impulse held all together. Then the scattering came, the seeding of the poppy, bursting of the seedpod, and for a time personality seemed all the stronger for it.[49]

Thus Shakespeare and Rembrandt, though they stand on the verge of the abyss, preserve something of the memory of the integrated Self. But the wheel could not be halted, and after them came the autumnal intellectualism of the eighteenth century, and then the gathering darkness of our own age. Yeats's system takes the modern period as the beginning of the final winter, though there are phases still to run before the degeneration is complete.

Yeats expounds his theory in all detail in his Irish *kyogen*, and I am now in a position to demonstrate this from the play itself. It is concerned with the progress of a culture from primitivity to Unity of Being, and there is at least some suggestion of the downward course it will subsequently take. Yeats had no particular cycle in mind when he wrote his play, and we can relate it to the Renaissance· or the Byzantine culture at will; we can even, if we choose, interpret in terms of the previous, 'subjective' era, when Unity of Being was achieved in the age of Pheidias and Scopas. The time-interval between any two of these manifestations (since the intervening millennium is merely a period of 'apathy'), is a little over a thousand years; and this fact is alluded to in the text; we have also to know that the first centuries of a cycle are a period of heroic and some extent disorientated struggle, and that Unity of Being is followed immediately by 'the seeding of the poppy', when the communal solidarity begins to weaken and finally to decay. The 'image' of Yeats's play is thus as complex as his terms of reference are vast, but we may now proceed with some confidence to dissect it.

V

The esoteric meaning of Yeats's play turns on his symbols of the well, the two beggars, blindness and lameness, and some of these symbols have already been discussed. If I am right in presuming that Yeats's symbology is for the most part fixed and constant, then the well must represent Unity of Being here as in *At The Hawk's Well*; while the beggar I have shown to be the traditional Noh symbol for humanity generally. It carries this meaning, of course, in almost all the branches of Yeats's perennial philosophy; in Platonism, it is the symbol for man's soul, dressed in 'the rags of mortality'; and one might instance also the great Gaelic tradition of the spiritual beggar, 'full of hope and love', walking the roads of the world.[50] Yeats's two beggars thus represent two complementary divisions of humanity, which he characterises as being in its nature either 'blind' or 'lame', and we must now consider what is implied by this dichotomy.

Yeats's most extended commentary on the traditional symbolism of the eyes may be found in his notes on Blake's *Tiriel*. In that highly relevant poem Tiriel is blind, and he walks on a stick supported by his daughter Hela. Yeats explains that the eyes in symbolism are the place of mystical 'marriage', perfect eyesight symbolising visionary potentiality, because in them the union of 'Subject and Object', of 'thought and nature, spirit and matter' first takes place.[51] Behind this statement lies no doubt the convention inherited by Greece from ancient Egypt, and passed down to the medieval occultists, by which the left eye represents love and the right wisdom; perfect vision, love and wisdom acting in absolute concord, makes possible direct apprehension of the mystical world.[52] This beautiful symbolism connects with the universal tradition—drawn on in *Calvary*—of the single eye of deity; the eye of Horus, or of Odin, or of the Morrigu in Yeats's own *The Death Of Cuchulain*: divinity, as Yeats himself explains, perceives by the great eye of intuitive wisdom,[53] but humanity has to rely upon the purification of its natural faculties. Blindness thus represents man's deficiency in visionary intelligence, and in that love for all created things which proceeds from the Self. As Yeats wrote of the loveless despot who is Blake's Tiriel, it symbolises a separation from all spiritual values, and the consequent 'deprivation'.[54]

THE CAT AND THE MOON

In Yeats's dance-play, one beggar can walk but not see, while the other has the use of his eyes but is a cripple. The meaning of this latter symbol, which would be perfectly apparent to any student of the tradition, can be demonstrated most clearly from elemental symbolism. As Yeats understood the connotations,[55] earth—the element which concerns us here—was the symbol for instinctive perception and water for 'emotion and passion'; the region of air represented the intellect and fire the condition of perfect spirituality. Lame Beggar, we may use these correspondences to confirm, represents that division of humanity which has vision, intellectual and spiritual perceptivity, but which is crippled in the lower, earthier faculties, deficient in the rich wisdom of instinctive life. This is Yeats's symbol for the intellectual, gifted with all the acumen of superior understanding, but cut off from the wisdom of the people. Blind Beggar, who can walk but has lost his sight, is the symbol of the proletariat: he has his instinct to support him, but knows nothing of the life of the mind. The two divisions of humanity are shown as natural enemies, but have been brought together by the sense of their respective limitations; society cannot progress unless they act as friends.

We are now in a position to take the full meaning of the play, in which Yeats develops his initial symbolism with astonishing ingenuity. The esoteric significance of what we are to see is made clear in the first few lines:

Blind Beggar: One thousand and six, one thousand and seven, one thousand and nine. Look well now, for we should be in sight of the holy well of St. Colman. The beggar at the cross-roads said it was one thousand paces from where he stood and a few paces over.

Here the crossroads, associating as it does with the concept of the *Conjunctio oppositorum*, serves Yeats in precisely the sense of his holy well as a symbol for Unity of Being; and the central meaning is that the pilgrimage of history between any two such 'points of highest civilisation', between Byzantium and Botticelli's Florence, lasts a little over a thousand years. Each pace Blind Beggar takes represents a year's progress towards the millennium, and he has already taken over a thousand; by this means Yeats indicates that he is beginning his play *in medias res*. We are not to be told much of the early history of a culture, its emergence from winter and its aboriginal strivings; the action begins when aristocracy and plebs have almost completed their long journey, and with the zenith already near.

Yeats foreshortens his action, of course, to avoid complexity, and he uses his first few speeches to define the identity of his characters beyond all doubt. I have shown how Blind Man, 'hearing and remembering the knowledges of the world', is presented as the type of peasant wisdom, and Lame Man, who is at once the passenger and the guide in Yeats's ensemble, is obviously the type of the aristocrat. He has humility only before God, none before his companion, and he has shown his powers of leadership in the journey to the well:

> Lame Beggar: I have brought you the right way, but you are a lazy man, Blind Man, and you make very short strides.

For the masses are slow to progress and they have to be guided from above, though they are willing, in the early stages of social development, to accept the aristocracy that will direct them, and the Blind Man knows it is not in his interests to use the 'stick' of inherent power which is always at his side. Yeats carefully divides his sympathies between 'prince and ploughman': he certainly feels no disdain for his proletariat, whose 'own goods' are so often stolen from them because they 'are blind'; and the Lame Man, despite his airs of superiority, is characterised both as a parasite and a 'rogue'. He has, however, his own characteristic virtue of 'flighty talk', an expression Yeats uses nowhere else save of Septimus, the artist-hero of *The Player Queen*:[56] the intellectual has the soaring imagination which enables him not only to lead the way to the well, but to understand, as the Blind Man cannot, the real purpose of the journey. The artists and savants of the Middle Ages, poets, schoolmen, and the architects of the great cathedrals, were never in any doubt that the goal of human existence is sanctity. Yeats's Lame Man expresses their convictions in the low style typical of the play, but the symbolic meaning is there beneath the surface:

> Lame Beggar: And maybe we'll see the blessed saint this day . . . and maybe that will be a grander thing than having my two legs, though legs are a grand thing.
> Blind Beggar: You're getting flighty again, Lame Man; what could be better for you than to have your two legs?

Soaring imagination and primitive intuition, then, have combined in uneasy partnership to arrive at their symbolic well, though the journey has been marked by many quarrels. In the grotesquerie of their wanderings Yeats images the 'heroic spring' of a race, which is a period of purposive but disorientated struggle.

Lame Man, though always 'flighty', does not fully understand the purpose of the journey until they are near the well, for man recognises his destiny only as Unity of Being approaches. A little after his mentor, Blind Beggar, similarly awakens to a new understanding of life, though it is one of a very different kind. He is no longer content to be a mere subordinate:

> Blind Beggar: If we were whole men and went our different ways, there'd be as much again between us.

This symbolism connects with a prose passage already given, where Yeats explains that the 'rifts and cracks' in a society begin to manifest at its climactic period. At this time the masses shake off their trance-like peasant stupor and, acquiring a new intellectualism, make the irrevocable decision that they will rule themselves. Thus the gift that the well brings the Blind Man is that of his lost sight; he uses it first, as in his beautiful speech on opening his eyes, for purely visionary perception, and 'prince and ploughman' are for the moment one; but his sense of accumulated injury, and the natural brutality of his nature, soon distract him from contemplation. He notices his lost sheepskin, recognises in its theft clear evidence of the parasitic nature of his companion, raises his 'stick' against Lame Man for the first time, and goes out. The recovery of the sheepskin, at this level, no doubt symbolises a reversal of roles: the masses discover the idea that they and not their masters are in fact God's chosen people, though Yeats communicates his dislike of such Rousseauesque idealism by making the sheepskin black. The first stirrings of the 'enlightenment', however, persuade the people of their 'radical innocence', and precipitate the final breach between rich and poor.

The Lame Man, as against this, uses the moment of unity to better purpose, and the Saint descends and gives him his blessing. By this means Yeats symbolises the condition of the intellectual aristocracy of a community as its moon nears the full, and shows us (to revert to his prose) 'the supernatural descending nearer' to man's mind 'than to Plotinus even'. The choice before the artist at this time is between integration into the community and momentary sanctity, and his decision is conditioned by his essential spirituality: Lame Man turns from his companion to take the Saint on his back, and the artist and the mystic are for the moment one. And as the fusion takes place, his deformity is for a moment by miracle removed, and he dances what we must take as the dance of his beatitude. With the splendid subtlety of this detail Yeats makes the chief point of his play: this is Unity of Being, and Lame Beggar has become a living illustration of Dante's symbol for such a moment, 'a perfectly proportioned human body'.

What seems at the exoteric level low comedy becomes noble and moving as Yeats's meaning unfolds, and this is especially true of the ending of his play. As the moment of his transfiguration approaches, Lame Man is told to perform the ceremony of 'blessing the road':

> Saint: What do you want words for? Bow to what is before you, bow to what is behind you, bow to what is to the left of you, bow to what is to the right of you. [*Lame Beggar begins to bow.*]

At the moment of Unity of Being, the total meaning of history becomes clear, and man learns to accept all the bitterness of the struggle, the hard centuries ahead as much as those behind, for the sake of the divine purpose momentarily discerned beneath the pattern. And so the Lame Man dances in praise of the whole process of human history, and his ecstasy is converted into philosophical statement by the words of the closing song.

The Cat And The Moon thus ends on a note of absolute rejoicing, but Yeats was not altogether satisfied with his conclusion. He planned at one time to extend the scope of his symbolism:

> (The play) is probably unfinished, and must remain unfinished until it has been performed and I know how the Lame Man is to move. Is he to remain . . . upon one knee, or crouching till he can pick up, as I have no doubt he does, the Blind Man's stick? Or is he but to walk stiffly, or limp as if a leg were paralysed?[57]

I take these lines to refer to incident to take place after the Saint has climbed down from Lame Man's back, and to symbolise the disunity in man's mind as Unity of Being recedes from him. Lame Man, as he rises from his knee, is either to revert to his earlier state of deformity, or more probably to be shown usurping the power which Blind Man has formerly possessed: the élite will rule, in the centuries of man's decline, by legal enforcement, and will compel in the masses an obedience they are no longer willing to give. Here Blind Man's staff has precisely the significance of Tiriel's rod: it is the symbol for unimaginative oppression. As Blake did, Yeats no doubt had in mind the century preceding the French Revolution, and he had also before him the continuing pattern of the whole nineteenth century, and even the 'terrible drill' of the Fascists at Fiume. The world around him made very clear the meaning of modern tyranny, which was the expression of a society irrevocably at war.

VI

Yeats's historical symbolism surely transfigures what had seemed a mere light comedy, and his play would emerge as a major production even if there were no meaning beyond. There is, however, still another facet of his intention, a third thread in the fabric, and this will most readily appear from a consideration of the Musicians' song. Yeats's lyric is nothing if not philosophical—I will beg the question here by calling it a Vicoesque performance—and it extends even more the dimensions of his play.

There is no reference to Vico in the notes in the Cuala edition, where Yeats first explains his symbol of the cat fascinated by the moon: Minnaloushe, he says, symbolises 'the natural man' and the moon may be taken as 'the opposite he seeks perpetually' or may be given 'any meaning' he has conferred upon it elsewhere. Vico's philosophy, however, is certainly implied by the long commentary in *Wheels And Butterflies*, where there are unacknowledged quotations on every page; and the shortest of notes on his theory will show why he seemed so relevant.* Vico attracted Yeats, centrally, because he was something more than a mere historian; he concerned himself centrally with the pattern to be discerned in history, but he also applied his cyclic theory on two supplementary planes. His Catholicism held him back from any theory of reincarnation, but he believed that the different psychological types predominated in fixed order, springing up in large numbers as history had need of them: the hero, the many-sided savant, the intellectual and the psychopath seemed to him the cyclic series,[58] and this is of course the order in Yeats's system of the personality also. Vico perceived an analogous pattern in the cycle of experience from birth to death:

---

* Vico is 'relevant' to the play; he is not an actual source. Yeats discovered Vico between writing his text and publishing it in *Wheels And Butterflies* and the allusions to Vico are there because Vico seemed to bear him out in all his (independently evolved) arguments.

The mind, rising from sensation successively to the imaginative and the rational, . . . is bound in conformity with its eternal nature to retraverse its course.[59]

Yeats saw in all this, of course, the rediscovery of a very ancient law, and he points out in *Wheels And Butterflies* that his own lunar symbolism has a parallel significance. All the cycles are one; the successive rebirths of the soul, as also the phasal development of man's mind, each following the pattern which can be discerned in history:

I . . . saw in the changes of the moon all the cycles: the soul realising its separate being in the full moon, then, as the moon seems to approach the sun and dwindle away, all but realising its absorption in God . . . the mind of a man, separating itself from the common matrix, [passing] through childish imagination, through struggle— Vico's heroic age—to roundness, completeness, and then externalising, intellectualising, systematising, until at last it lies dead, a spider smothered in its own web.[60]

We have not understood Yeats's mind if we take this passage as idle speculation, where it has so transparent a relation to the imagery of his own lyric. He is using Vico's logic to illustrate the premise round which he has written: all the cycles are susceptible of an identical symbolism, so that all will at once be implied by the moon-symbolism of his play.

If we may here glance back from Yeats's lyric to his general plot, we shall see that even his narrative is susceptible of extended interpretation, and can in fact be taken on each of Vico's three symbolic planes. The historical argument is of course central, and several passages of dialogue have no meaning apart from it, but the imagery carries subsidiary connotations also, as it is normal for the productions of the symbolist to do. Yeats uses his notes to attach to his two beggars the significance of soul and body, and it is easy to read their pilgrimage as an account of the circumstances of man's life; soul and body keep their precarious balance until the years of full maturity, while afterwards the body rebels and the soul has to impose its will. There is also the cycle of reincarnation, which Yeats implies in the note I have last given. At this level, the Well becomes the symbol of the perfected Self, to which the soul attains with its fifteenth rebirth; it is then separated from the body, since this is a supernatural incarnation; and in the subsequent objective rebirths has to stave off its own degeneration, 'intellectualising' and 'externalising' until it is 'absorbed' in the idea of a Christian Saviour-God. Such then, is the wealth of meaning that can be read into Yeats's *kyogen*; and it follows that the lyric which holds all together will have something of the function of the 'control' in a scientific experiment: it will set out a typical pattern, from which the characteristics of all three cycles can be read. If we now return to the song of Minnaloushe, we shall find it to be a generalisation of precisely this kind: Yeats gives it a significance at once cosmic and particular, all-embracing and vague.

Yeats took his Minnaloushe from real life, and the preface to *Per Amica Silentia Lunae* shows him captivated by the animal's graceful movements; but his poem derives its central symbolic correspondence from ceremonial magic, where the cat and the moon are traditional antagonists. In magic, as Yeats knew from Agrippa, the cat's eyes symbolise the fact that it is a lunar beast, for they 'become greater or less according to the changes of the moon';[61] a superstition on which the last verse of his own song depends. But if Yeats's two *personae* are as he says 'kindred', they are also in a sense opposites, and this is brought home by the lines with which he begins:

> The cat went here and there
> And the moon spun round like a top,
> And the nearest kin of the moon,
> The creeping cat, looked up.
> Black Minnaloushe stared at the moon,
> For, wander and wail as he would,
> The pure cold light in the sky
> Troubled his animal blood.

Several details here serve to point the contrast: the black and white colour symbolism and the adjectival stresses which balance 'animal blood' and 'pure cold light'; there is also an implicit elemental symbolism of earth and sky. The central meaning of course is that man is in love with his opposite; he may 'wander' from the path that will lead to their reconciliation, or 'wail' like black Minnaloushe in his rebellion against the compulsive attraction he feels, but he cannot ultimately escape from its influence. The symbolism is significant at all levels of Yeats's narrative: the individual man is compelled to a course of life that will unite him with his 'antiself' and so complete his personality; the 'black' soul has to seek its antithesis in the fulfilment it can only find at the fifteenth phase; and primitive society to develop towards that sophistication which is its opposite and goal. For as Blake paraphrases the tradition 'without contraries is no progression'; humanity is drawn to the saint's well by its sense of its own lack.

The first verse of Yeats's song is used to motivate the action which is to follow, and the second is spoken as his beggars approach the well. The climactic excitement of the moment is conveyed by means of rhythm:

> Minnaloushe runs in the grass
> Lifting her delicate feet.
> Do you dance, Minnaloushe, do you dance?
> When two close kindred meet
> What better than call a dance?
> Maybe the moon will learn,
> Tired of that courtly fashion,
> A new dance turn.

Our initial response here may be to the mimetic gaiety of the verse more than anything else (and Yeats had reasons I shall explain for stressing the concrete beauty of his image), but there is also a strong undercurrent of metaphysical suggestion. Minnaloushe 'runs in the grass' as he seems to be about to 'meet' his opposite, and we are clearly to think of man's ecstasy as the moment of Unity of Being approaches. If man can use that moment to best advantage, perhaps the wheel of becoming may be diverted from its course and escape from all the cycles be won: the moon may tire of its symbolic progress through the sky, and the opposites be reconciled in the ecstatic cosmic dance. Thus the individual may escape by perfect union with the Self, and the reincarnating soul by achieving 'completeness' in the central phases, while at the climactic moment of a culture the communal sanctity must make it seem that a whole civilisation is in process of being saved. All this, however, is presented as no more than pathetic fallacy, for the round of history can never really be halted nor merely 'natural' man escape the toils of reincarnation, however near liberation may seem when the moon of the Self is in the sky.

The last lines of the lyric follow immediately upon Lame Man's dance. They centre upon the imagery Yeats inherits from ceremonial magic:

> Minnaloushe creeps through the grass
> From moonlit place to place.

> The sacred moon overhead
> Has taken a new phase.
> Does Minnaloushe know that his pupils
> Will pass from change to change
> And that from round to crescent
> From crescent to round they range?
> Minnaloushe creeps through the grass
> Alone, important and wise,
> And lifts to the changing moon
> His changing eyes.

These lines have the responsibility of conveying all that Yeats hoped to bring within the action proper by lengthening his play: they are the only indication his published text provides that Lame Man's ecstasy is to be shortlived. For Unity of Being is lost as soon as won, and the 'sacred moon' of generation soon hurries us on beyond the moment of fulfilment: man, Minnaloushe, has to continue his journey through the early objective, though still 'moonlit' phases of Yeats's system. And this is the inflexible law of all the cycles, as Yeats indicates under his symbolism of the cat's widening and narrowing eyes: individual man is driven on from the 'round' of achieved personality to the 'crescent' of old age, the soul from the fifteenth phase to the winter of extreme objectivity, society from a Byzantium or an Italian Renaissance to the moment of disintegration. When the cycles are complete, or so the symbolism suggests, the whole process of development from 'crescent' to 'round' will in each case begin again.

So much may be said of the content of Yeats's lyric, and I will conclude by demonstrating what has often been denied, that it is aesthetically in harmony with the body of his narrative. Yeats's normal method is to integrate his choruses through their symbolism; they may be tangential to the main text in point of subject, but they usually persevere in the imagery round which the drama proper has devolved. Thus the lyrics which end *At The Hawk's Well* explore images we have met with in the narrative, the dry well of disillusion and the green tree of religious affirmation; the idol-symbolism in *Emer* is elaborated in the statue-imagery with which it ends; while the bird-symbolism of *Calvary* is developed from an otherwise dissociated main text. And thus in *The Cat And The Moon* also: the image of 'black' Minnaloushe reiterates the theme of man's unregenerate nature, symbolised in the narrative by the black sheepskin; Yeats's insistence on the earthbound nature of his creeping cat connects with the elemental symbolism on which the whole play is founded; while the last lines of the song, in telling us that Minnaloushe's eyes change with the moon, are a reversion to his symbolism of blindness also. At one level these imply what the whole body of the play has been written to tell us, that man has eyesight, spiritual vision, only at the symbolic zenith or full moon, and that his understanding diminishes as that zenith recedes. Yeats's method in all this is one he had learned from the Noh, where the device of 'playing upon a single metaphor' serves to impart unity to a play.[62] His own practice, moreover, is functional in every respect, for his songs entrench him in symbols which may be imperfectly established in the main text.

If the symbolism of Yeats's lyric is corroborative, his main intention is none the less to point a contrast. The angle of vision is changed, and all that we have seen as squalor is converted into beauty. I do not think that the beggar-imagery of Yeats's main text was forced upon him by the laws of his form, for he had perfect freedom whether or no to imitate the grotesquerie of the Noh *kyogen*: one feels rather that he envisaged history precisely as his play presents it, as a sorry procession of human deformity in all its shapes. Any medieval satirist would have recognised the picture he paints: we may compare the caricature-humanity of Bosch's 'Millennium' and 'The Haywain', or the simpler and perhaps even harsher allegory of 'The Ship Of Fools'. But if man's lower nature made him the 'ape' of Shakespeare's paradox,* his 'glassy essence' was unimpaired by this: he was Minnaloushe, the creature of mystery, as much as the maimed beggar. He might carry his rags through eternity, or he might move through all the cycles in perfect inner harmony, aloof, knowledgeable and content. Another poet might have chosen between these two polar images, but Yeats knew too much of philosophy to do so: he merely presents us with history in each of its eternal aspects, which are the aspects of dry well and green tree.

* I am thinking of the medieval cartoon 'Aristotle And Phyllis'.

CHAPTER FIVE

CALVARY

I

Calvary has never been the most popular of *Four Plays For Dancers*, though there is fine poetry in the lyrics with which it begins and ends. For the rest, it is perhaps more thoroughly philosophical than any other of the series, and narrative, chorus and dance are harnessed in the service of an idea. Yeats thought that his coldly intellectual play might succeed as ritual, hoping especially to obtain dramatic forcefulness through his masks: both Lazarus and Judas are characterised with this in mind, and Yeats presents them as 'images' on which the sculptor's dispassionate art might build. He hoped for great things from a collaboration:

> Perhaps in the end one should write plays for certain masks. If some great sculptor should create for my 'Calvary', for instance, the masks of Judas, of Lazarus and of Christ, would not this suggest other plays now, or many generations from now, and possess one cannot tell what philosophical virility?[1]

The 'stony face' of Judas particularly excited Yeats's imagination, and he played with the idea of writing another drama in which his ghost might appear. The slums of Dublin seemed a suitable setting, and the people could mistake Judas for 'the ghost of an old rag-picker':

> A Sinn Feiner will have a conversation with Judas in the streets of Dublin. Judas is looking for somebody to whom he may betray Christ in order that Christ may proclaim himself King of the Jews. The Sinn Feiner has just been persuading a young sculptor to leave his studio and shoulder a rifle.[2]

This macabre idea was never utilised, but it does indicate a characteristic dramatic preoccupation Yeats inherited from the Noh theatre: his play would have been a study in what is there called 'the aesthetics of ugliness'.[3] *Calvary* has a similar orientation, though the effect is less than complete in that no great sculptor has yet been attracted to the text; if we had the masks and music the plot requires, Yeats's cold style and low imagery might seem virtues.

Yeats knew that the intellectualism of *Calvary* might make it difficult to follow, and the notes he wrote on the meaning are the fullest we have for any play. They are, as we might expect, both sophisticated and evasive. Yeats was determined to suggest, rather than to betray, his intentions, and his commentary consists largely of anecdotes with no apparent relation to the text: there are stories from the folk-lore of his imaginary Arab tribe of Judwalis, interspersed with a few sentences on his symbolism and a number of difficult passages on the limitations of the Christian faith. The anecdotes, however, are as important to the dance-play as the rest of Yeats's argument. In one of them he tells of the Arab theory of the daemon, and in another sets out the Judwali philosophy of Chance and Choice. All this is in fact intended to help in the interpretation of *Calvary*, which turns upon precisely these themes.

Yeats's theory of chance may be left until later, but it will I think help to discuss his philosophy of the daemon here. The substance of his anecdote is very simple: it is merely that the guardian angel may materialise in animal shape. Judwali folk-lore is quoted to show that any 'hyena' met with in the desert, any great bird that crosses the traveller's path, may be a supernatural visitant; and Yeats goes on to say that these apparitions are of two kinds:

> (if one) is interested in things, in places, likes to be with many people, his Daemon has the form of a beast, but your (Robartes') Daemon will have a bird's shape because you are a solitary man.[4]

Yeats's symbolism here seems to me forceful rather than learned, and I do not suppose that he is building upon any very profound knowledge of primitive Arabic religion. The source which commends itself to me is Doughty's *Arabia Deserta*, which Yeats loved, and whose influence may be traced on his own desert poetry, as on the bird imagery in 'The Second Coming' and similar passages in the present play:

> Call on your father now before your bones
> Have been picked bare by the great desert birds . . .

> Make way for Lazarus, that must go search
> In the bare desert places where there is nothing
> But howling wind and solitary birds . . .

Doughty has long passages on the *djinn*, which is the Arab equivalent of the daemon; he tells how the 'jan' are of two kinds, half of them 'malicious spirits' and the others benevolent; and he explains that they take the form of animals at will, so that 'many a house-cat and many a street-dog . . . are jan'.[5] One of the most charming stories in his book tells of a man who has to deliver a letter to his angel, which materialises in the shape of a ghetto dog.[6] Doughty does not speak of the jan manifesting as birds, but Yeats will have known from the *Arabian Nights* that they did so; in the story of Princess Budur, for example, Maymunah's characteristic disguise is as a hawk. We have 'The Gift Of Harun Al-Rashid' to show the relevance of such stories, and since Yeats's dramatic method was to build round the symbolism of folk-lore, we can hardly object if desert folk-lore is used for his one near-Eastern play.

The Arabic symbolism used in *Calvary* is peculiar to that play alone, but the theory which underlies it is important to all Yeats's work. While Christianity may support him in his belief in the guardian angel, his angels are not those of the orthodox West, for Greek, Indian and Swedenborgian philosophy combined to enforce a different complexion upon his thought. According to Yeats's subjective tradition, 'there are no angels by original nature', but 'only those beings which have once been men'; the soul after death undergoes an elaborate process of purification, after which it may choose to return to the time-world as 'the schoolmaster of the living'.[7] Thus in 'Vacillation', for example, the purified spirit is shown descending to perform a service for mankind: Yeats meditates upon the body of St. Teresa, 'undecayed' in the tomb, and suggests that the ghosts of ancient Egyptian embalmers may have been sent in the astral body to preserve it:

> Those self-same hands perchance
> Eternalised the body of a modern saint that once
> Had scooped out Pharaoh's mummy.

In 'A Nativity', where he describes the second coming of Christ, he imagines that the purified spirits of actors and artists, Talma, Irving, Landor, Delacroix, may be sent back into the world to decorate the manger in which Christ will be reborn.

What made the drapery glisten so?
Not a man but Delacroix.

In *Calvary*, as I shall later show, the daemon of Judas descends to perform a similar service on his behalf, but I will content myself here with what is relevant to the prose commentary. When Yeats there distinguishes two kinds of daemon, he does so because of his two psychological types. Subjective man, after being finally purified, may return to the world in the shape of a bird, and there are also the daemons of objective or orthodox Christian nature, whom he will represent by animal symbolism.

Since Yeats's angels are no more than the perfection of his two psychological types, a natural extension of his symbolism will make it cover those types generally, and the notes make it clear that this is the case in his play. Beast-symbolism, he says, is used for objective humanity as well as for the spirits which preside over it, while the 'lonely' subjective temperament is always symbolised as a bird, simply because it lives primarily in the zone of pure intellect, or 'air':*

> Certain birds, especially as I see things such lonely birds as the heron, hawk, eagle and swan, are the natural symbols of subjective life . . . while the beasts that run upon the ground, especially those which run in packs, are the natural symbols of objective man.[8]

Yeats speaks in *A Vision* of having made 'too little' of the objective phases in his system, and this, one feels no doubt, is one of those places where a natural antipathy makes itself felt. There is almost certainly an allusion to the Kabbala, and to the famous passage on which Yeats draws also for the bird-tree symbolism of 'Byzantium' and 'At Algeciras'. I give the translation he himself quotes in *Ideas of Good And Evil*:

> In the branches of the Tree the birds lodge and build their nests; that is, the souls and angels have their place; and beneath it those animals which have power seek the shade; [that is, impure souls and fallen angels promote the ends of evil]; for in it [the shade of the tree] every beast of the forest doth walk.[9]

---

* I hope it will not be thought irregular in me to insist on elemental symbolism as I do throughout this chapter: Ellman first showed that reliance on the elemental correspondences was second nature to Yeats. As I shall show, the correspondences are particularly relevant when Yeats is using bird-symbolism.

Yeats did not believe in absolute evil, and the souls and angels which stalk through the 'forest' of generation will have seemed to him imperfect rather than vicious; but he obviously intends a slur on the objective temperament, and this is conveyed even in the phrasing of his *Calvary* note. His own beast-symbolism implies primitivity and ugliness, together with abstraction and a blind herd-instinct, as we may confirm from the later verse. There the Sphinx, the type of arid intellectualism, serves as one symbol for objectivity,[10] while 'What Magic Drum' adds to the beast image the connotation of undifferentiated instinctive striving; in 'The Statues', Yeats represents objectivity by the primitive image of Grimalkin, the witch's cat. This glance at the alchemical tradition of the familiar is doubly interesting, since it reminds us that East and West join in belief in the animal daemon, a fact which no doubt confirmed Yeats in using Arabic folk-lore as he does.

When *Calvary* represents angels as manifesting in animal shape, the imagery is thus as traditional, and dramatically as defensible, as the alchemical symbolism by which Goethe has Mephistopheles materialise as a poodle; and the comparison may help us to establish right perspectives for Yeats's play. *Calvary* is less centrally concerned with animal symbolism, or with theories of Chance and Choice, than with comparative religion, and Yeats uses it to express the mingled respect and disaffection he felt for the Christian faith. In one sense he was its bitter opponent; I have shown that he placed objective religion at the dark of his symbolic moon, and the distaste he felt for orthodoxy is at the root of his play's argument. But he knew, at the same time, that another personality might find the Christian mediation necessary, and I have shown him acknowledging that final escape could be achieved by its aid. *Calvary* is in part his respectful recognition of this fact, but it is also an attempt to adjudicate between the two disciplines. Yeats's ultimate intention is to present a very careful statement of his theory of the human psyche, and to prove what he is so often content merely to state: that Christianity is polar to his own subjective synthesis, and that it is inferior in kind.

In making the prior assumption that he had two polar disciplines between which to adjudicate, Yeats was parting company with most of the authorities on whom my previous essays have been building, and it is interesting to see how far his disagreement went. Jungian psychology presupposes, and Blake would have agreed with its findings, that the religion of the Self is the one true faith, and that orthodox modern Christianity is an attenuated and corrupt statement of its teachings.[11] Yeats whether rightly or wrongly did not share this view: he held that there were two paths to the spiritual world, and that the Christian way and the subjective constituted the ultimate expression of the Platonic theory of opposites, being two contrary disciplines each of unquestionable validity. When Yeats took up this position, which he did in early life, he had scant support within his tradition; instead, we find him building on the findings of modern philosophy, on Nietzsche especially and, beyond Nietzsche, Schopenhauer. *Calvary* is thus interesting as being the one play in Yeats's sequence to be based upon modern, as opposed to traditional logic, and will enable us to estimate Yeats's stature as a post-Nietzschean philosopher. I will say here without reserve that I consider Yeats a much safer and saner theorist of religion than Nietzsche, and leave the pages which follow to bear me out.

If *Calvary* goes beyond Nietzsche, it is largely in that it is an expression of Yeats's resolute polytheism, as when the Roman Soldiers invoke the classical pantheon while they mock Christ on the cross. Yeats's polytheism is not what it may appear, a contradiction of his theory of the Self, but a substantiation of it; and it will be useful to explain here how this can be so. The Universal Self, with which the individual Purusha is to be identified, was not for Yeats an indivisible entity; it had its *essences*, or transcendent characteristics, and also its *energies*, or immanent powers, by which it manifested itself in 'everything that lives'. Yeats fluctuated between describing the Self as unity and as multiplicity (this fluctuation is reflected in *Calvary* itself), but in so far as he thought of it as multiple, it gave rise to his theory of a pantheon of divine powers. He followed the traditions of Platonism, Kabbalism and the religions of the East in representing the transcendental Self as a *deus absconditus*, while its energies, divine wisdom, justice, beauty and the other Platonic Ideas, he symbolised by his 'visible' gods. These energies, present in every human soul as in the spiritual world, are invoked in his final tableau, and Yeats contrasts his theology and the Christian concept of a single supreme deity, accessible and indivisible as He is conceived to be.

If only because *Calvary* is concerned with the Self as multiplicity, it is obviously a more complex philosophical statement than *At The Hawk's Well*; and it is also a much more radical one. *At The Hawk's Well* begins in *medias res* with the Christian position already repudiated; now we have to go back in time to see in detail why Yeats rejected it, and precisely how he evolved the contrary discipline that takes its place. It is easiest to look first at the very early alchemical stories, since these provide us with the germinal statement of his religious tenets, and his theory of opposite disciplines is mooted in them. Not only must we turn from these stories to modern philosophy, but we must bear in mind in doing so all Yeats's salient beliefs; especially his theory of reincarnation, where man's 'phase' determines his choice between Christianity and the religion of the Self. The result will be an essay which may appear complex, but will in fact be simpler and more direct than any other in this series. *Calvary*, though a highly intellectualised statement, is not a particularly oblique one.

II

Yeats took the materials for his dance-play from two main sources. The plot itself derives from a story by Oscar Wilde, but much of the symbolism is elaborated from his own early stories, 'Rosa Alchemica' and 'The Tables Of The Law'. Since *Calvary* embodies a restatement of metaphysical theories first broached in these stories, they were naturally much in Yeats's mind as he wrote; the resemblances extend to small points of local colour, and even to turns of idiom and phrase.

Yeats's early work is much confused by refinements in his theory of polytheism, and the stories in question can only be approached when these have been explained. I have said something of the underlying philosophy, which led him to think of the divine emanations, beauty, wisdom, justice, as visible gods; but the position is complicated by the nomenclature he uses, derived as it is from the Order of the Golden Dawn. The initiates thought of the Gods in terms of the great archetypal images of antiquity, Aphrodite (if one chose the classical pantheon) serving as the type of divine beauty, Athene of wisdom, Apollo of harmony and sanity; thus Yeats speaks of the visible Gods as the idealisations of human emotion—which is of course what archetypal images are—and refers to them often as 'the Moods'.[12] They would be approached by means of contemplation, though in reverie and even in dreams their images might materialise in the human mind; in such heightened states of being, the visionary would penetrate to Anima Mundi, and the great archetypal symbols would emerge in his consciousness, and seem indeed, Yeats thought, to live with a life independent of his own. All this, with the exception of the last detail mentioned, is of course in accordance with modern Jungian psychology, which teaches that the archetypal world is approached in such a way, and that the disciplines I have explained underlie all true religion. The Order went beyond Jung in that they believed literally in the theory of emanations: they did not worship the idealisations of human emotion for human emotion's sake, but as functions of deity discoverable in and through the soul; living, mobile powers.

Yeats felt, as his Order generally did not, that the Christian God and the subjective Gods were distinct though it might be complementary entities;[13] and having to choose, and despite the fact that he might be pinning his faith in false Gods, he gave himself up to the idea of a divine pantheon. He wrote several stories to proclaim this, and to express a quite personal theory for which he later found philosophical sanction, that in an objective cycle of civilisation men would see God as One, or as Christians see Him, and in a subjective cycle as Many. One of these stories is 'Rosa Alchemica', where we are introduced to an imaginary alchemical order under the patronage of Michael Robartes, a man lacking in all the orthodox Christian virtues, 'something between the debauchee, the saint, and the peasant'. The worshippers make contact with the visionary world through contemplation; Yeats symbolises the ecstasy which is the goal and end of subjective contemplation by a dance; and in the course of that dance, the 'immortals' descend to their votaries, 'beautiful Grecian faces and august Egyptian faces'. We are told that the initiates of the Order, as the members of the Golden Dawn indeed believed themselves to be, are the precursors of a new religion; the old order of things is about to perish, and the world 'to plunge into a night as obscure as that which followed the downfall of the classical world'. In the new cycle which will eventuate, humanity will return to the worship of a pantheon of Gods, and the transition will be especially easy in Ireland, where the people have never been fully Christianised:

> They will sacrifice a mullet to Artemis, or some other fish to some other divinity, unless indeed their own divinities, the Dagda with his overflowing cauldron, Lug with his spear dipped in poppy-juice, lest it rush forth hot for battle, Aengus with the three birds on his shoulder, Bodb and his red swineherd, and all the heroic children of Dana, set up once more their temples of grey stone.

Yeats had of course ample support, even at this stage in his reading, for his belief that history was nearing the end of a cycle: he found similar beliefs in Swedenborg and in Indian and Buddhist religion, and in the slender Platonism he had acquired from Madame Blavatsky. 'Rosa Alchemica' is really a propagandist piece of writing, and its function is to express Yeats's acceptance of these traditionalist theories.

Another such story, also relevant to *Calvary*, is 'The Tables Of The

Law'. Yeats's hero Owen Aherne is a lapsed Catholic, a man of great learning and piety, but whose faith in orthodox dogma has been vitiated by his reading of Joachim de Flora's *Liber Inducens In Evangelium Aeternum*, and who is now in despair. The book is not a figment of Yeats's imagination, though it is now lost, having been burned by the public hangman in the early middle ages: it set out Joachim's cyclic theory of history, in which the present cycle is one of legal enforcement and oppression, while in the coming era God will be manifested in many forms and there will be absolute freedom, pure spirituality and joy. Joachim's theory gave rise to the heretical sect of the Adamites, to which the great painter Hieronymus Bosch is said to have belonged:[14] the Adamites, trying to live in the spirit of Joachim's teachings, practised free love, believing that the act would be purified through *acclivitas*, the contemplation of the divine Self at the moment of sexual union; and Yeats seems to have been aware of this essentially noble doctrine. His own story rehearses long paragraphs of Joachim's hypothetical book, explaining the spirituality which may attach to free love and to anarchic freedom of action in all its forms, and we are asked to believe that Aherne has been converted from orthodoxy by this very Blakean philosophy. When the change is complete, he is visited by the 'immortals', and recognises in those 'mild eyes' and august lineaments the Gods of the coming age.

Yeats draws heavily upon both these stories in *Calvary*, and upon 'Rosa Alchemica', if we may take this first, in all the dance-plays with which this study is concerned, I have shown in my previous essays how Cuchulain is horrified by Fand's 'unfaltering, unmoistened eyes' and is later given by her the 'Kiss of Death'; these are concepts which can be traced back to the early story. During Yeats's alchemical dance, his narrator gives himself to an 'immortal woman':

> Suddenly I remembered that her eyelids had never quivered, and that her lilies had not dropped a black petal, or shaken from their places, and understood with a great horror that I danced with one who was more or less than human, and who was drinking up my soul as an ox drinks up a wayside pool; and I fell, and darkness passed over me.

Calvary draws as heavily upon 'Rosa Alchemica' as the rest of 'Four Plays For Dancers', and the resemblance is particularly marked in two places. His dance is of course the centrepiece of Yeats's story and, like the Roman Soldiers in his later play, the subjective worshippers dance round the effigy of 'a pale Christ on a pale cross'. We are told, and I shall show later the significance of the statement, that they dance 'to trouble His unity with the multiplicity of their feet'. With this, the story provides us with the genesis of Yeats's theory of the daemon, in the lines in which Robartes speaks of the inadequacy of the Christian angelology; he says that the Christian angels have renounced the divine Self, and that they therefore wear robes of a uniform 'greyness':

> They had renounced their divinity and turned from the unfolding of their own separate hearts out of love for a God of humility and sorrow.

There is respect in this passage, of course, but there is also disaffection, as it is natural there should be in a writer of Yeats's subjective temperament. This disaffection deepened in later life and, in the stronger language of his dance-play, the angel who serves such a God materialises as a 'beast'.

Beyond these particular instances, 'Rosa Alchemica' is of considerable overall interest to the student of Yeats's philosophy, since it presents us with his theory of subjectivity and objectivity in what I shall call its intermediate form. Yeats had clearly already decided that there were two polar forms of worship, and he says himself that his story exists to balance the discipline of 'Eleusis' against that of 'Calvary', but we must understand that, at this stage in his development, his arguments tended to be vitiated by an unhealthy romanticism. The daring of the subjective religion, and especially the magical rites by which his order reinforced the process of *contemplatio*, obviously aroused in him mixed emotions; and he began by wondering whether the whole alchemical synthesis might not be fascinatingly evil. Thus 'Rosa Alchemica' concludes with a piece of rather disingenuous writing, heavily 'decadent' in flavour, in which Yeats renounces all his half-glimpsed visions:

> There are moments even now when I seem to hear those voices of exultation and lament [that is, the 'immortals', lamenting that men have turned aside from their worship], and when the indefinite world, which has but half lost its mastery over my heart and my intellect, seems about to claim a perfect mastery, but I carry the rosary around my neck, and when I hear, or seem to hear them, I press it to my heart and say that he whose name is legion is at our doors deceiving our intellects with subtlety and flattery and our

hearts with serenity, and then the war which rages within me at other times is still and I am at peace.

Yeats indulged himself in this kind of writing without believing what he asserted, as we may confirm from the early poetry, where the 'immortals' are celebrated without the sense of guilt; but he certainly found it histrionically convenient to conclude his prose stories with recantations. Here, for comparison, is a passage from 'The Adoration Of The Magi', a story to which I have not so far referred:

They may, for all I and any man can say, have been immortals, immortal demons. . . . Whether they were or no, I have turned into a pathway which will lead me from them and from the Order of the Alchemical Rose. I no longer live an elaborate and haughty life, but seek to lose myself among the prayers and sorrows of the multitude. I pray best in poor chapels, where the freze coats brush past me as I kneel [ETC.].

Melodramatic as this is, and certain as it is that Yeats never did retreat from his alchemical Order, what is real in such passages is the sense of conflict. There was clearly a choice before the man's soul, between the way of 'exultation' and the way of humility and compassion; knowing himself to be of 'mixed' temperament, Yeats was not absolutely convinced which road was his.

If we now conclude this survey with an examination of 'The Tables Of The Law', this story also will be seen to be immediately relevant to Yeats's dance-play. There is only one exact textual parallel, when Yeats speaks of Joachim and his followers, as they explore the kingdom of heaven, as soaring to 'the blue deep of the air'; a vivid phrase which occurs nowhere else in his work save in the closing song of *Calvary*. But in general argument there are close correspondences: the two works cohere in seeing 'solitude' and 'freedom' as the essential constituents of subjective spirituality; while the closing phrases of Yeats's story are also taken up in his play. Inevitably, Aherne recants, but the words in which he does so are much less histrionic than before. We may imagine that they fairly reflect the conflict in Yeats's mind:

At first I was full of happiness, for I felt a divine ecstasy, an immortal fire, in every hope, in every desire, in every dream. . . . Then all changed and I was full of misery. . . . In my misery all was revealed to me: that man can only come to that Heart through the sense of separation from it which we call sin, and I understood that I could not sin, because I had discovered the law of my being [i.e. the Self] and could only express or fail to express my being. . . .

I am not among those for whom Christ died, and that is why I must be hidden. I have a leprosy that even eternity cannot cure. I have lost my soul because I have looked out of the eyes of the angels.

In these words, if we can purge them of their odour of the confessional, we have the gist of all Yeats's later religious theories, and also the preliminary statement of some of the key-phrases in his later plays: 'God has not died for the white heron'; 'God has not appeared to the birds'. Yeats's development between 'The Tables Of The Law' and *Calvary* was largely in the direction of philosophical stability: the prurient ecstasy that underlies Aherne's words had to be sloughed off.

Yeats came on the theme of his dance-play when he was writing his alchemical stories. He found it in a 'fairy tale' by Oscar Wilde, 'The Doer Of Good'. Yeats greatly admired Wilde's prose-poem, and told Dorothy Wellesley, shortly before his death, that it was 'the most beautiful fairy-story in the world'; he also refers to it in *Autobiographies*, but there he makes it clear that the story lost in being written down. He first heard it over the dinner table:

Wilde published that story a little later, but spoiled it with the verbal decoration of his epoch, and I have to repeat it to myself as I first heard it before I can see its terrible beauty.[15]

This passage does more than introduce us to the source of Yeats's plot; it also gives us the key to his deliberately austere treatment. He tells us that Wilde did not alter the content of his story, and we may conclude that his germinal anecdote presented the narrative we now have in a more direct and 'terrible' way; Yeats would have sacrificed any quality to *terribilità*, and he probably decided on the bare style of his dance-play as a device by which this original starkness might be retrieved.

'The Doer Of Good',[16] like *Calvary*, is an episodic piece of writing, though it is very succinct. Christ comes to a (nameless) 'city', and the sound of music takes him into a house:

He saw lying on a couch of sea-purple one whose hair was crowned with red roses and whose lips were red with wine. And he went behind him and touched him on the shoulder and said to him:

'Why do you live like this?'

And the young man turned round and received him and made answer and said: 'But I was a leper once and you healed me. How else should I live?'

Powerless before such a question, Christ goes back into the street, where a man and girl approach him. But the woman has 'the fair face of an idol' and the young man's eyes are 'bright with lust':

'Why do you look at this woman and in this wise?'

'Lord, I was blind once and you gave me sight. At what else should I look?'

The woman for her part explains that he once forgave her her sins 'and this way is a pleasant way'. And so Christ leaves the city in despair, only to come on a young man weeping outside the gate. He asks him the reason for his grief:

I was dead once and you raised me from the dead. What else should I do but weep?

Recognising in these words the ultimate explanation of all he has seen, Christ goes sadly away.

The most obvious resemblance between Yeats's dance-play and Wilde's story is one of underlying sentiment. Wilde's theme is that Christ is powerless against psychological suffering, that life itself is not worth living, and that man is driven to vice by his consciousness of his despair. Very similar arguments are put forward in the notes to *Calvary*:

Christ . . . only pitied those whose suffering is rooted in death, in poverty, or in sickness, or in sin, or in some shape of the common lot, and he came especially to the poor who are most subject to exterior vicissitude. I have therefore represented in Lazarus and Judas types of that intellectual despair that lay beyond his sympathy.[17]

Yeats goes beyond Wilde here only in writing 'beyond his sympathy' where Wilde would have said 'beyond his reach'—justifying the extension by a glance at the Anglican service of the Mass[18]—and by relating the whole argument to his theory of reincarnation, as his note next proceeds to do. Where Wilde saw no solution to the problem of 'intellectual despair', and no God to whom the sufferer could turn,

Yeats—by the time he wrote Calvary—saw a very obvious remedy: subjective suffering could only be staunched by a subjective God, and the problem before its victim was to discover the 'religion of the Self', with which, by virtue of his 'phase', he would be in affinity. The strength of Wilde's story, as Yeats saw it, was that it served forcibly to bring home this point; Wilde himself might not have seen the logical culmination of his argument, but it was nevertheless implicit in his narrative.

Yeats had to make slight adjustments in plot to adapt Wilde's story to his own purposes, and he had aesthetic as well as dramatic reasons for reshaping it as he did. I imagine that his sense of theatre made him take Lazarus and Judas, characters from whom his imagination could catch fire, as his types of intellectual suffering, and that a similar preoccupation with stage effect made him place his action at the stations of the cross. Aesthetic considerations, on the other hand, will have made him wish to purge Wilde's narrative of its heavily 'period' atmosphere, and to rid it of an unhealthy preoccupation with vice. Yeats does this by making his subjective *personae* the representatives of a pure, unmixed despair, while his only characters to take refuge in vice are the three Roman Soldiers, whom he uses to represent a form of objectivity beyond even Christ's help. The Roman Soldiers stand at the extreme dark of his symbolic moon, a little before his last, subhuman incarnation, and are too fallen even to be conscious of their need for grace. Apart from these changes, Yeats follows Wilde closely; in building upon the story of a man raised from the dead; in presenting his theme in the form of three anecdotes and in adopting the same episodic manner; in everything by which Wilde communicates his 'message'. Stripped of its gilded aestheticism the story seemed to Yeats a terrible exposition of the inadequacy of the Christian doctrine; he had too much experience of life to dismiss it as mere dilettantism.

Calvary thus becomes one of the several plays Yeats wrote which lean heavily upon Wilde's talent: one might parallel *A Full Moon In March*, which takes much from Wilde's *Salomé*, while the prose style of *The Resurrection* seems to me to owe something to such plays as *La Sainte Courtisane*, although I can do no more than glance at this fact here.[19] Apart from the debt to his art, there is even a sense in which Wilde's own personality may be remembered in the play. The Lazarus of *Calvary* is a heroic and designedly dehumanised figure, but Yeats may nevertheless have based himself upon particular observation. He was one of the few friends who stood by Wilde during his trial, and he records how Wilde's disdainful 'fantasy' then took a 'tragic turn';

how he 'tried to sleep away as much of life as possible', then wasted 'the rest of the day at the Café Royal'.[20] Yeats took Wilde as the type of subjective solitude, 'the enemy of the crowds in the street'; he was 'one of the men who belong by nature to the nights near the full moon', and it seemed an irony of history that this doomed minority should still be born into an age hardening into complete objectivity. Yeats's Lazarus, like Wilde, is a subjective born 'out of phase' into an objective age, and we can only speculate whether a current of personal sympathy for Wilde or for his similars in the 'tragic generation' may have informed the hollow image of 'Lazarus who cannot find a tomb'. It would be characteristic of Yeats's method if it were so.

III

At the time Yeats first read Wilde's story, he will have attached to it the kind of romantic significance I have demonstrated from 'The Tables Of The Law', but before he wrote *Calvary* he had systematised his theory of personality. His main authority was Nietzsche, whom he read in the years following 1903. When Yeats says that Nietzsche's thought 'flows in the same bed as Blake's, but still more violently',[21] he may seem to misrepresent, and the critics have speculated widely on the nature of his indebtedness to Nietzsche's work; it has been variously suggested that Nietzsche's theory of history, or of the mask, or of the superman, lay at the root of this enthusiasm. Yeats of course can hardly have learned from Nietzsche's doctrine of eternal recurrence, for he knew already the much more coherent and consistent theory of Indian philosophy; he may have learned something concerning the mask; but *The Unicorn From The Stars*, where the hero is made to turn from a life of anarchic action to one of mystical contemplation, seems to me a clear sign of his rejection of the superman theory, and was probably written in his reaction from it. Yeats did not go to Nietzsche for his political philosophy, but for his knowledge of the human psyche, though even here we shall find him preserving his essential independence and interpreting Nietzsche's sometimes rather febrile speculations through his own more stable logic. Nietzsche's theory as his works present it is vitiated by prejudice, but Yeats refashioned it out of his own eminently fair mind.

Yeats's favourite reading in Nietzsche was the early work *The Birth Of Tragedy*, which he refers to obliquely in several letters written in 1903.[22] The book owes a good deal to Schopenhauer, and it is Nietzsche's first and fullest statement of the theory of the personality which lasted him all his life. Nietzsche saw two contrary tendencies in the psyche, and he speaks of them as the 'Apollonian' and 'Dionysiac' characteristics; all thought and all art is the manifestation of one or other of these tendencies, though in the greatest music and literature the two may be combined. By the Apollonian state Nietzsche meant that tendency in man's mind to see the material world as good and life in the world as joy. Homer, 'the aged dreamer sunk in himself', 'the type of the naïve artist', is cited as the perfect illustration of a response to experience of this kind. By the Dionysiac instinct Nietzsche implies that contrary and as it seemed to him more philosophical tendency to see life as terrible, and he points out that this response also was common in Greek civilisation. He quotes the myth later used by Sophocles in *Oedipus At Colonus:*

> The old story runs that King Midas hunted long in the forest after the wise Silenus, the companion of Dionysus. . . . When at last he fell into his hands, the King asks, what is the best and most desirable of things for man? [The God replies]: 'The best thing of all is for thee quite unattainable: not to be born, not to be, to be nothing, But the second best thing is for thee—soon to die.'[23]

We may turn aside here to notice how deeply Yeats remembered his Nietzsche: how close to this the phrasing of his own translation of Sophocles' chorus comes. There are other, parallel reminiscences, as when Nietzsche attacks Plato and Socrates as having lost completely the power of instinctive response of whatever kind, and ironically speaks of them as typifying 'the abstractly perfect man, good, wise, just, a dialectician—in a word, the scarecrow'. These words I am sure lie at the root of the famous stanza in 'Among School Children', and I think they are also responsible for the reserve with which Yeats approached Plato in later life. He admired the Platonic philosophy but found it sterile, deficient in natural joy: 'to die into the truth is still to die'.

Nietzsche is at pains to do justice to both his warring instincts, though it is clear that the influence of Schopenhauer inclines him to a radical pessimism. The Apollonian response, he says, is the natural result of reverie, a state in which primitive man projected the Self into an elaborate fantasy world. This dream-world manifested as a higher reality, the perfection and goal of consciousness; Lucretius is quoted to show the nature of the Apollonic condition, and how the archetypes, 'the glorious divine figures', thus first appeared to 'the souls of men'. And indeed this kind of meditation has always been common and is so today; in it 'We take delight in the immediate perception of form; all forms speak to us; there is nothing indifferent, nothing superfluous'; and we are conscious of 'freedom from the wilder emotions' and of 'philosophical calmness'. Nietzsche makes it clear that the contemplative condition is not to be despised:

> Indeed the man of philosophical turn has a foreboding that underneath this reality in which we live and have our being another and altogether different reality lies concealed, and that therefore it [consciousness] is also an appearance. Schopenhauer actually designates the gift of occasionally regarding men and things as mere phantoms and dream pictures as the criterion of philosophical ability.[24]

In any case, Nietzsche thought that the ecstasy induced by this fantasy-world underlay and gave logical coherence to the Homeric joy in life:

> So vehemently does the will, at the Apollonian stage of existence, long for this existence, so completely does the Apollonian man feel himself at one with it, that the very lamentation [caused by our separation from the condition in ordinary waking consciousness] becomes its song of praise. . . . In the midst of a world of sorrows the individual sits quietly supported by and trusting in his *principium individuationis* [Self].[25]

Nietzsche sees Apollo, the God of harmony and symbol, as the 'glorious divine image' of the individual Self, and he says that the Greeks worshipped him as the spiritual exemplar of their own 'inner joy in contemplation'. But, he says, modern philosophy has to turn back from reverie to the 'only partially intelligible physical world', and the disinterested enquirer will agree that the Apollonian state is essentially a condition of 'Maya', illusion.

At this point we may leave Nietzsche's text and consider what Yeats will have made of the arguments I have so far reconstructed. Yeats knew much more of Indian philosophy than either Nietzsche or Schopenhauer (from whom Nietzsche derives his reference to Maya), and he will certainly not have supposed that they have its sanction for dismissing the Apollonian state as illusory; for a thinker in harmony with the Upanishads, as for a Platonist, the physical world will be seen as Maya, and the contemplative world, evoked through the Self, as the one trustworthy reality. But for all Nietzsche's sudden and illogical transitions, Yeats will have learned much from his thought; he will have found in it what he had previously found only in his own esoteric reading, authority to think of the Self as a demonstrable psychological reality. Nietzsche makes it clear that *contemplatio* is a historical spiritual discipline, and that it has informed most of the religions of the world; he at least suggests, and does so in passages of great beauty, that it may bring man in contact with 'higher truth', and he also explains its importance in the sphere of aesthetic creation. Homer is used to illustrate the way in which the subjective artist will visualise the world, and this I am sure is of particular importance to Yeats's thought; immediately after reading Nietzsche, he began systematically to allude to Homer in his own poetry, and he makes it clear that Homer is his own ultimate model as an artist:

> Homer is my example and his unchristened heart.[26]

But, centrally, the importance of these passages is that they helped Yeats to translate his own theory of the Self into what (despite the unsatisfying nature of Haussmann's translation) is essentially an atmosphere of sober and disinterested philosophical speculation. Nietzsche taught Yeats to think calmly and to have confidence in his thought and his subjective synthesis; his suspicions that the religion of the Self might be 'evil' could be finally laid at rest.

If the Apollonian condition, for Nietzsche, means the apotheosis of the Self, the Dionysiac state is made possible by its destruction. It is 'the conquest of the subjective, the redemption from the ego and the cessation of every individual desire' and it takes the form of a return to primal unconsciousness. One type of man, Nietzsche says, will always need some more powerful and kinetic joy than he will find in the symbolic and harmonious Apollonian landscape, and he will tend to find this by merging his identity in all that is not the Self, by which he will achieve oneness with the external world and a sense of primeval awe. For there are Gods of the 'not-self', just as there are Gods within it:

> Add to awe the blissful ecstasy which rises in the innermost depths of man, aye of nature, at the collapse of the *principium individuationis*, and we shall gain an insight into the being of the Dionysian, which is brought within closest ken perhaps by the analogy of drunkenness.

It is either by the influence of the narcotic draught or by the powerful approach of [desire] ... that these Dionysian emotions awake, in the augmentation of which the subjective vanishes to complete self-forgetfulness.[27]

Nietzsche obviously prefers this form of escape from the 'world of appearances' to the Apollonian, and he is at pains to point out that its dark rituals have been practised from the beginning of history:

In the German middle ages, singing and dancing crowds, ever increasing in number, were borne from place to place under this same Dionysian power. In these St. John's and St. Vitus's dances we again perceive the Bacchic choruses of the Greeks, with their previous history in Asia Minor, as far back as Babylon and the orgiastic Sacaea.[28]

Such primitive rituals, he says, are not 'folk-diseases', but signs of 'glowing health'; they and their more modern counterparts are honest attempts to gain strength and unity by assimilation into the non-ego and by the destruction of the inhibitive 'I'. Nietzsche's theory is primarily aesthetic, and he now turns to the study of literature and music: the development of his argument is to assert that, in the greatest art, 'the two worlds of dreamland and drunkenness are one'. Attic tragedy he says combines a dark Dionysiac wisdom of choric song with an archetypal, Apollonian fantasy-plot and a 'subjective' harmony of general structure; while Wagner, in whom the Dionysiac talent is so prominent, might be about to achieve a similar fusion in his own sphere.

We now have to consider what Yeats will have made of this side of Nietzsche's theory, and we must first realise that he will have seen both the escapes proposed as acceptable religious disciplines. The Apollonian path, which he accepted for himself, was a way upwards through consciousness and beyond the ends of consciousness, to a state where the mind received impressions from Anima Mundi and was united by the virtue of 'present immortality' with all created things. In this way it learned the 'science of beauty everywhere', or the immanence of God in every object of the material world. And the alternative was a discipline of self-abnegation which would end in contact with Anima Mundi also, and in another, more strenuous form of mystical experience through 'awe'; beyond awe, there would be participation in the 'non-ego', which seemed to Yeats, who understood that all spiritual truths must be paradoxical, no more than another expression of the divine. With this Yeats will have seen the essential vulgarity of Nietzsche's synthesis, which illustrates the Dionysiac discipline by all its most orgiastic manifestations, and specifically excludes the Christian religion from consideration. Nietzsche's argument is corrupted by a prejudice against Christianity, which he saw as a degenerate and unmanly cult. Yeats was too widely read in the early Christian writers[29] to consent to this, and he will clearly have wished to relate the orthodox faith to Nietzsche's general scheme; at the same time he will have been chary of the more barbaric of his authority's examples, though his natural generosity will have made him accept that there may have been some virtue in all. Yeats went to Nietzsche, then, with elaborate reservations, but I think it clear that he accepted his central thesis: there were these two polar states, positive and negative, at war through history but reconciled in God.

We are fortunate in having some of Yeats's private notes on Nietzsche,[30] which show how he arrived at his own very much extended synthesis. Having to find Christianity some place within the general system, Yeats substituted it for Dionysus worship at his negative or 'objective' pole: it taught as much of any of Nietzsche's preferred faiths the extinction of the individual will and personality, culminating in the absorption of the 'I' in Godhead in its extroverted aspect, while in purity as in universality it was clearly the most significant faith of its kind. Remembering that Socrates also thought of the One or Good as something external to man, Yeats finds objective tendencies in his philosophy also. He notes as objective characteristics 'denial of Self' and belief in a single, indivisible God, symbolises the negative pole as 'night', and repudiates Nietzsche's suggestion that Christianity and Platonic thought are of no value:

> Why does Nietzsche think that the night has no stars, nothing but owls and bats and the insane moon? [31]

In later life Yeats wrote *The Resurrection* out of his confident belief that Dionysus worship, in its pure form as a mystery religion, was a more primitive faith of the same order as Christianity, and this of course is a natural development of the arguments I have set out above. As for the subjective synthesis, Yeats's annotations do no more than cite Homer as its poet, and to list as characteristic virtues belief in 'many Gods', affirmation of the 'Self' and of 'life': attributes which enable us to associate Indian, Shintoist and pagan Irish religion with the Homeric Greek. All this is expressed in the notes Yeats wrote on Nietzsche, in the following form:

> Night: Socrates, Christ—one god—denial of Self—the soul turned outwards towards [the external aspect of] spirit, seeking knowledge.
> Day: Homer—many gods—affirmation of Self—life.[32]

We have in these words a complete system of world-religions, in which any creed can be found a place.

I have hardly the space to say more here of the relation between Yeats's and Nietzsche's thought, but it will be useful to conclude this survey with a general comparison. Nietzsche rationalised Yeats's opinions and converted what had been loose emotion into intellectual substance: he gave him the core of his theories both of human personality and of religion, for *The Birth of Tragedy* is concerned with man's mind at least as much as God. He gave him even the terms 'subjective' and 'objective' for the divisions of the human psyche, and (since Dionysus-worship is an Asian and Homeric religion an Aryan emanation) the substance for the Yeatsian belief that subjective and objective religion originated respectively in the *west* and *east*.* Both *Calvary* and *The Resurrection*, works concerned with God and the psyche, are owed to Nietzsche's influence, while we may trace a considerable debt in Yeats's later experiments with the Dionysus myth, *The King Of The Great Clock Tower* and *A Full Moon In March*. At the same time we must remember how thoroughly Yeats transformed his authority. Nietzsche, it seems to me, was a man of violent and thus unphilosophical temperament; Yeats was far more tolerant and, on metaphysical questions, far better informed. In the field of subjective religious experience, Nietzsche had of course everything to learn from him, and in the negative or objective field, though both men had to build upon merely theoretical understanding, Nietzsche deliberately alienates the whole body of Christian mysticism, which Yeats retrieves. The result, if I am not mistaken, is that Yeats converted a minor and erratic theory into one of first importance,[33] and conferred on Nietzsche's arguments a distinction they do not in themselves perhaps deserve.

Having perfected his theory Yeats naturally turned to the traditional

---

* Yeats's position here is confused (or may seem confusing) in that he thought of Indian civilisation as Western, 'Aryan'. See my section on 'The Statues', below.

philosophy for precedent (he would not willingly have broken with its teachings); and the cycles of rebirth in the Upanishads, with their detail of the moon's 'brightening' and 'darkening' fortnights, persuaded him that corroboration was to be found. The cycle of the 'brightening fortnight' Yeats equated with Nietzsche's subjective temperament, so that it follows that the soul has fourteen 'Apollonian' lives; while the inferior, 'darkening' cycle was one of self-abnegation, and these would be the Dionysiac rebirths. Beyond the Upanishads, Yeats found precedent in the psychological theories of Heraclitus and Philolaus, both of whom had divided humanity into two opposite spiritual types: they had named these the 'lunar' and 'solar' personalities, and there were the strongest reasons for identifying the lunar and Apollonian temperaments, and for seeing in the 'solar' personality a soul dominated by an (external) God.[34] Yeats had thus both Indian and Greek authority for taking Nietzsche's as the traditional theory, or at least as a theory which the traditionalist might reasonably believe.

When Yeats had aligned himself to the traditional doctrine of reincarnation, he still had a further problem of integration: he had to establish a connection with his cyclic theory of history also. Nietzsche had presented his two principles as alternating through recorded history, citing Babylon and the German Middle Ages as objective periods and heroic Greece as a subjective culture, and it was necessary to find proper sanction for such beliefs. Plato's system of 'superior' and 'inferior' cycles provided a convenient means by which this could be done: in an inferior (objective) cycle the Dionysiac temperament would predominate, and in a superior the Apollonian. A further passage in Plato, with the commentaries in Burnet's *Early Greek Philosophy*, seemed to Yeats to authorise even his polytheism. In a celebrated text in his *Sophist*, Plato gives Empedocles and Heraclitus as his sources in affirming that 'in one cycle of civilisation' God will be seen as unity and 'in the next' as 'Many';[35] a statement which Yeats takes to mean that the Apollonian will worship the archetypal, 'visible' Gods, and the Dionysiac the concept of the Victim-Saviour. Here is his own commentary on the passage:

> I think that two conceptions, that of reality [sc. 'Godhead'] as a congeries of beings, that of reality as a single being, alternate in our emotion and in history and must always remain something that human reason, because subject always to one or the other, cannot reconcile. . . . I think that there are historical cycles when one or the

other predominates, and that a cycle approaches when all shall be as particular and concrete as human intensity allows.[36]

And Yeats goes on to present himself as the Virgil of that approaching cycle, its vatic singer, conditioned by its proximity to envisage divinity always as multiplicity:

> Again and again I have tried to sing that approach, 'The Hosting Of The Sidhe', 'O sweet everlasting voices', and those lines about 'The lonely majestical multitude', and have almost understood my intention. Again and again with remorse, a sense of defeat, I have failed when I would write of [a single] God, written coldly and conventionally.[37]

In this way Yeats found authority for an early and quite personal theory, with which I have shown him occupied in the alchemical tales.

By the time that Yeats wrote *Calvary*, he had already made all the connections I have been indicating, and his theory of the psyche was consequently complete. He had arrived, that is, at a fixed and considered attitude towards Christianity and those opposite faiths he set against it, and I will end this section with a brief *résumé* of what this attitude implies. For Christianity, it implies a very definite disaffection: the religion was only possible in an inferior cycle, and for inferior personalities born into that cycle, such souls as were progressing through the objective or 'darkening' phases. These souls will be characterised by a certain primitivity, for they are either in their very early incarnations (before they have acquired any tincture of subjectivity) or in procress of disintegration and so of return to that primitivity from which they began. In the central incarnations, as against these, and even in the sophisticated phases of any civilisation, the Christian discipline becomes unthinkable; as Yeats himself writes, it is satisfying only to the crude and untutored spirit:

> Does not every civilisation, as it approaches or recedes from its full moon, seem as it were to shiver into the premonition of some perfection born out of itself? . . . Does not every new civilisation, on the other hand, imagine that it comes from dependence upon dark and unknown powers, that it can but open its eyes with difficulty after some long night's sleep, or winter's hibernation? [38]

Christianity, then, was for Yeats in the truest sense one of the dark religions, demanding a primitive response of surrender to the 'non ego' or in his own words to 'the black night of oblivion'. Against the rigour of this discipline one could set the subjective synthesis, tranquil, sophisticated, achieved.

IV

The tranquillity and sophistication of subjective worship are qualities well illustrated from *Calvary*, for Yeats discusses these virtues in his opening and closing songs. He begins with an image infinitely remote from Jesus himself; a white heron brooding over a shallow stream. This heron serves as the type of subjective humanity, and the harsher Christian discipline is contrasted in the middle section of the play.

Yeats introduces his heron in accordance with his promise to build on bird-symbolism, and it represents subjective man in his character as a *contemplative*. In this sense it has a long pedigree in his earlier verse and prose. Yeats first broaches his visual image in a story in *The Secret Rose*, where he describes one of several herons 'standing with lifted leg in the shallow water . . . with bent head and motionless feathers as though it had slept from the beginning of the world'.[39] These birds are the pagan men of learning in the court of King Laoghaire, who have been bewitched into heron-shape by St. Patrick. Gaucheness and a certain pontifical dignity are the values Yeats at this stage saw in his symbol, and they are also the dominant values as he uses it in his poem 'The Three Beggars'. He is describing, not without *Selbstironie*, the tragicomic aloofness which distinguishes him and his 'companions of the Cheshire Cheese' from the gregarious masses; and his heron has now become a crane:

> 'Maybe I shall be lucky yet,
> Now they are silent', said the crane,
> 'Though to my feathers in the wet
> I've stood as I were made of stone
> And seen the rubbish run about,
> It's certain there are trout somewhere
> And maybe I shall take a trout
> If but I do not seem to care.'

Calvary uses the heron much as here as an image of lonely introspection, and its appearance presages, as always in Yeats's verse, a clash of personalities: the image is later set off against that of Christ's disciples just as the pagan wise men are contrasted with St. Patrick, and as the crane is with the objective crowd. But there is a clear shift in the emotion with which Yeats charges his symbol, and in this it looks forward to the God-imagery of *The Herne's Egg*. Where the earlier crane-image (as also the related image of the *fisherman*) denotes no more than an arrogant intellectualism, we are now in the region of visionary discovery and ultimate truth. This change perhaps reflects the development of Yeats's own spiritual personality: what had begun as a painful and unrewarding discipline may now have arrived at fulfilment. At any rate, the meaning in *Calvary* is richer than ever before, while the coarseness and bitterness which characterise 'The Three Beggars' have vanished from the verse.

Beauty and even elegance are the values *Calvary* attaches to the heron-symbol, though gaucheness may also be implied by way of *Selbstironie*. The heron is shown fishing in the waters of *Sangsara* or physical life, and perhaps the traditional Indian term is here to be preferred; *Sangsara* carries with it the thought that the phenomenal world is illusory, and Yeats's play goes on to assert that nothing exists save in the mind of God. To these unreal waters, then, the opening of the play consigns us, and its first words connect with a prose passage I have given; where Yeats speaks of the subjective soul 'shivering with the premonition of some perfection to be bred out of itself':

> First Musician: Motionless under the moon-beam,
> Up to his feathers in the stream,
> Although fish leap, the white heron
> Shivers in a dumbfounded dream.
> Second Musician: God has not died for the white heron.

These lines present us with a symbol for man rapt in contemplation, engrossed in the reverie which Nietzsche confirmed Yeats in believing was the road to the visionary world. The heron is made 'white' to confirm the essential purity of the discipline; the moon represents both the full moon in March at which Christ died and rose from the dead, and the central symbol of Yeats's own system of reincarnation. It is only by supernatural sanction, by virtue of his phase among the phases near the full moon, that man is able to discover the Self through contemplation. But if he can do so, Christ has not died for him: he is spiritually immune from all externalities, even from the sacrifice of an external Saviour-God.

The second verse of the song now becomes relatively simple. We are given a beautiful image for man in meditation, discovering his *Purusha* or Higher Self, that spiritual personality which the subjective mystic tries to resuscitate. The Higher Self, for Yeats, is of course identical with God, and later in the play he will divide his God-image into its constituent energies: but now he is content to image it as an *alter ego* merely, a pure reflection floating on the tide of *Maya*, illusion.

> First Musician: Although half-famished, he'll not dare
> Dip, or do anything but stare
> Upon the glittering image of a heron
> That now is lost and now is there.
> Second Musician: God has not died for the white heron.

It is worth noticing how much these lines are concerned with the *difficulty* of the subjective discipline: that elongated image in the water, which is the only 'reality' that the white heron can worship, flickers and is gone, or is glimpsed only momentarily. Yeats shows us also the price the discipline demands: solitude, terror—the heron is 'dumbfounded' by his dream—and that famine which we may take to symbolise the subjective's endlessly frustrated desire for the companionship of his fellow-men. 'For triumph would but mar his solitude': the laws of his nature inhibit him from social success. The last verse develops this side of the argument, suggesting that if the moon did not change, if objective incarnations did not follow the subjective, humanity could not survive the discipline the Self demands:

> First Musician: But that the full is shortly gone
> And after that is crescent moon,
> It's certain that the moon-crazed heron
> Would be but fishes' diet soon.
> Second Musician: God has not died for the white heron.

Yeats's *Selbstironie* here breaks surface in a crackle of sharp colloquialisms, 'moon-crazed', 'fishes' diet', which temper what might otherwise have seemed the romanticism of his visual image; and the lyric is surely as beautiful as it is meaningful. It is exciting at whatever level one takes it, atmospheric, haunting and strange; every detail is appropriate both literally and on the plane of ulterior meaning, which is of course the mark of the great symbolist.

Yeats keeps the imagery of his first chorus active in our minds by returning to it at crucial moments of the drama. When Christ appears, carrying his cross, the mockers in the crowd shout insults at him, and the effect is described in a passage of lyrical commentary:

> Chorus: O but the mockers' cry
> Makes my heart afraid,
> As though a flute of bone
> Taken from a heron's thigh,
> A heron crazed by the moon,
> Were cleverly, softly played.

Yeats's imagery here is peculiarly subtle, and carries several distinct connotations. The first implication is that the cries of the crowd are subjective, bird-like; the high voices are like music played on a heron-flute; these are the cries of men born near enough to the full moon for the spectacle before them to have no meaning. The imagery carries also powerful overtones of death—the mockers are, if anything, the *dead* herons—so that it is even possible to relate them to the nineteenth or twentieth phases of Yeats's system, when the Self, though still a memory, has begun to die. And beyond this there is the suggestion that supernatural forces are responsible for this terrible music, playing upon the merely passive instrument of the crowd; a suggestion we may parallel from *The Herne's Egg*. In that play, we have an identical heron flute, and the imputation is that Attracta's angel, if not indeed the God she loves, plays upon it to summon her to her mystic marriage. The image in *Calvary* has to be interpreted in a similar spirit, and I take it that Yeats's supernatural instrumentalists are the daemons of the crowd.

Later in the play, we have another, simpler, allusion. Christ stops for a moment during his long climb up the hill, and his lamenting disciples gather round him:

> Chorus: Take but His love away,
> Their love becomes a feather
> Or eagle, swan or gull,
> Or a drowned heron's feather,
> Tossed hither and thither
> Upon the bitter spray
> And the moon at the full.

Whether Yeats owes this passage to personal observation or to the famous image of the 'swan's down-feather' in *Antony And Cleopatra*,[40] it is clearly the antithesis of what has gone before. His white heron maintains and even worships its separate identity; but in Christ's adherents the Self has died, has been submerged in the ocean of unconsciousness, and nothing but a single feather remains. Here one remembers Nietzsche's analysis of objective religion, and how the worshipper seeks mystical union through self-oblivion. The disciples have made this sacrifice: they are the *drowned* herons; and what is personal in them has lost its original virtue, or recovers it only by contact with the external, guiding love of Christ himself. As they walk, the light of Yeats's full moon in March is shed on them, and the force of this detail is now as the symbol of God's death and resurrection, and so of cyclical change.

In this way Yeats tries to suggest the 'fabulous, formless darkness' of the coming objective cycle and the effect is much heightened by naturalistic scene-painting. Here is his description of the scenes which follow Christ's meeting with Lazarus:

> The crowd shrinks backward from the face that seems
> Death-stricken and death-hungry still; and now
> Martha, and those three Marys, and the rest
> That live but in His love are gathered round Him.
> He holds His right arm out, and on His arm
> Their lips are pressed and their tears fall; and now
> They cast them on the ground before His dirty
> Blood-dabbled feet and clean them with their hair.

These lines seem to me particularly Nietzschean in temper; such accented words as 'dirty' and 'blood-dabbled' convey an atmosphere of ugliness; there may be something orgiastic in the scene as Yeats sees it and there is certainly an element of primitivity. One feels that he was conditioned to regard the whole terrible ritual, infinitely more spiritual though it may have seemed to him, in terms of primitive Dionysus worship or the German folk-diseases of the Middle Ages. He certainly stresses the gregarious nature of the worshippers and their emotionalism; we are intended to contrast these qualities with the pure self-sufficiency of his subjective white heron. And of course Christ and his adherents are as 'death-hungry' as Lazarus, or as any face they meet: Christ is their leader on the road to self-annihilation.

Against this background of contrary religious tensions Yeats projects his narrative, in which the two opposite temperaments are to be shown in open conflict. We begin with a long passage of *récitatif*, where Yeats underlines both the dignity of his Christ and the hysteria by which he is surrounded. The chorus then describe the meeting with Lazarus, using words which will serve to illustrate how necessary masks are to the play:

> Who is this from whom the crowd has shrunk
> As though he had some look that terrified?
> He has a deathly face, and yet he moves
> Like a young foal who sees the hunt go by
> And races in the field.

It is worth turning aside at this point to confirm how consistently Yeats uses low imagery, here and throughout the anecdotal part of his drama:

> Lazarus: 'Come out', you called;
> You dragged me to the light as boys drag out
> A rabbit when they have dug its hole away.

Thus also we are told colloquially that Christ 'had but to whistle' to enforce obedience; the Roman Soldiers are presented in the most unglamorous terms as 'three old gamblers who have asked for nothing'; and Yeats characterises his Judas in words which enforce the later comparison to 'an old rag-picker':

> ... I'd go with my old coat upon me
> To the High Priest, and chuckle to myself
> As people chuckle when alone, and do it
> For thirty pieces and no more, no less.

I find Yeats's grotesque masks and deliberately unpoetic imagery functional beyond any effect of forcefulness or *terribilità* he may have hoped to achieve by them: the ugliness is that of an 'inferior cycle', intensified now at the moment of cyclical change. Yeats saw Christ's rule for all its spirituality, as something essentially sordid; a manifestation, like Dionysus-worship, to 'the dregs of the population'; to penury and deformity in all its shapes. And the Christian discipline itself seemed to him as deformed as its adherents, since it could not but reflect the 'inferiority' of its age: a cancelled note stigmatises it as unhealthy, preoccupied with scourge and birch and its other implements of pain; in short as a perversion of spiritual and natural joy.[41]

Or we may parallel those speeches in Yeats's later *The Resurrection*, where the Greek upbraids the Hebrew:

> [Christianity] makes me shudder! The utmost possible suffering as an object of worship! You are morbid because your nation has no statues.

In *Calvary*, even the miraculous is infected with this taint of squalor, lest there should be some aspect of Christ's regimen where *morbidezza* might not seem to reach. We hear of Him raising a Lazarus 'bound up in cloths' like a mummy, swathed in gravecloths from head to foot.

The virtue of Yeats's narrative consists largely in its atmosphere: the argument itself could perhaps have been done better. Yeats had meditated Wilde's story for years before the Noh form enabled him to use it, and I think he stood closer to his theme, when he wrote, than makes for successful dramatic treatment. We are certainly presented with an argument both involved and obscure, and which seems as it unfolds to be less 'terrible' than eccentric:

> Judas: If a man betrays a God
>   He is the stronger of the two.
> Christ: But if
>   'Twere the commandment of the God himself,
>   That God were still the stronger.

Yeats's involvement in problems of this kind is hardly to the advantage of his dance-play, but the dialogue develops only to become more prolix:

> Christ: But my betrayal was decreed that hour
>   When the foundations of the world were laid.
> Judas: It was decreed that somebody betray you—
>   I'd thought of that—but not that I should do it
>   I the man Judas, born on such a day
>   In such a village, such and such his parents.

The conversation with Lazarus is better, but it does not altogether avoid a merely intellectual complexity of the same kind:

> Lazarus: You travel towards a death I am denied
>   And that is why I have hurried to this road

And claimed your death.
Christ: But I have conquered death.

The argument here, that Lazarus is frustrated in the only ambition left him, to die and find peace in the grave, is perfectly defensible; but Yeats seems to be lost in the intricacies of his own argument. So abstract and elliptic a style can only end in confusion, and I cannot imagine why the lines were allowed to stand.

Yeats's argument is more successful when it is informed by a current of emotion. His main thesis I have explained from the notes: his characters are types of an intellectual despair which Christ cannot help or even understand. Thus Lazarus has always found life insupportable, as must be the fate of the subjective 'born out of phase' into an alien world; Christ has raised him from death and from the 'comfortable mountain cavern' where he has found the solitude he longed for, and returned him to a suffering it is beyond His power to annul. This suffering is intensified in that Lazarus has no longer any possibility of solitude; he asks only to be alone, and now Christ's protective care, which is in fact no protection but merely stifles his individuality, is everywhere in the world. He cannot even escape into death, for Christ's unwanted solicitude will extend beyond the grave:

> ... now you will blind with light the solitude
> That death has made; you will disturb that corner
> Where I had thought I might lie safe for ever.

This sense of the intrusive nature of objective religion is perhaps better expressed in The Resurrection, where Yeats stigmatises all such faiths as alien to the Western temperament. He traces them back to a common origin in Asia Minor:

> The Greek: I cannot think all that self-surrender and self-abasement
> is Greek ... when the Goddess came to Achilles in the
> battle she did not interfere with his soul, she took him
> by his yellow hair.

And in that context Yeats does what he does not attempt in *Calvary*: he sets up against the Christian concept of Deity his own subjective Gods, the eternal archetypal figures of divine Wisdom, Justice, Beauty. The words in which he does so clearly derive from *The Birth Of*

Tragedy; and (as Nietzsche does before him) Yeats quotes Lucretius to define the nature of the visible Gods:

> The Greek: Lucretius thinks that the Gods appear in the visions of the day and are indifferent to human fate; that, however, is but the exaggeration of a Roman rhetorician. They can be discovered by contemplation, in their faces a high keen joy like the cry of a bat, and the man who lives heroically [sc: 'in conformity with the divine energies within him'] gives them the only earthly body that they covet. He, as it were, copies their gestures and their acts. What seems their indifference is but their eternal possession of themselves. Man too remains separate. He does not surrender his soul. He keeps his privacy.

In *Calvary*, while this contrast is not brought out, it is implicit in Yeats's argument, and we must understand that Lazarus is by nature in harmony with these same subjective ideals. Born out of phase as he is, however, he is forced into the service of a quite opposite God, and is denied for ever the loneliness he needs to achieve the Higher Self.

One result of Yeats's reorientation of Wilde's original story, and of his reaction against the 'decadence' it contains, is a certain sameness in the pattern of his narrative. Where Wilde varies his characters by making them escape into the different cardinal vices, Yeats insists on their absolute purity of intention, with the result that his personae are identical psychological types. Judas is born out of phase as much as Lazarus, and the suggestion is that he could never have found life worth living; association with Christ has merely increased his misery, for the 'all-powerful' personality of the God has sapped his intellectual freedom. We are asked to believe that he has betrayed Christ to regain his independence, and to prove to himself that he has perfect liberty of choice:

> I could not bear to think you had but to whistle
> And I to do: but after that I thought,
> 'Whatever man betrays him will be free'
> And life grew bearable again.

Here again the argument is better done in *The Resurrection*, where Yeats has a terrible speech on the nature of Christian obedience. We

CALVARY

are told that what Christ requires is a complete evacuation of the personality, after which a form of supernatural possession will take place:

> The Hebrew: One had to sacrifice everything that the divine suffering might, as it were, descend into one's mind and soul and make them pure. One had to give up all worldly knowledge, all ambition, do nothing of one's own will. Only the divine could have any reality. God had to take complete possession. It must be a terrible thing when one is old, and the tomb round the corner, to think of all the ambitions one has put aside; to think perhaps a great deal about women. I want to marry and have children.

Instead of humanising his hero as these lines do, Yeats diverts *Calvary* from its course to discuss predestination; he does this in the abstract and rather naïve speeches I have quoted, and concludes by allowing Judas his free will. God cannot have prejudged any soul sent into the world, and so Christ's betrayer is not bound by necessity of any kind:

> I did it!
> I, Judas, and no other man, and now
> You cannot even save me.

Thus Judas sacrifices his soul to preserve his individuality, and to defend himself from 'possession' by an external power.

Solitude and freedom are the qualities Yeats presents as essential to the subjective nature, and these qualities are re-examined in the final chorus of his play.* He uses the symbols of eagle, gull and swan, all of which have already been introduced into the main text, and the notes tell us that such birds are as much the symbols of subjectivity as the heron, 'especially when floating upon the wind alone or alighting upon some pool or river'.[42] If we apply Yeats's elemental symbolism, which operates together with his bird-imagery whenever it is employed and where the region of air denotes intellect and water emotion, the

---

* The rest of this chapter is concerned to make out the *most* that Yeats's final chorus, and his daemon-symbolism, and his dance, can be construed to mean. They can be construed to mean less without injury to the dramatic experience, but I am concerned with maxima. So also with my readings that follow of 'The Second Coming' and 'The Wild Swans At Coole'; we do not have to take these poems at this level, but we can if we like; and Yeats no doubt wanted to make readings at my level a possibility, while not a necessity.

meaning of his note becomes clear. Birds seem to him the images of subjectivity particularly when, like the subjective soul, they soar into the zone of intellect and the free spirit, or, in equal solitude, rest proudly and peacefully upon the waters of mundane emotional life. It is in this sense that the first verse of Yeats's song makes use of water symbolism:

> First Musician: Lonely the sea-bird lies at her rest,
> Blown like a dawn-blenched parcel of spray
> Upon the wind, or follows her prey
> Under a great wave's hollowing crest.
> Second Musician: God has not appeared to the birds.

There are at least two earlier poems where Yeats uses the gull as symbol,[43] and in each of those it serves as an image for 'lonely wildness', so that we may safely give it this connotation here also. The subjective soul cherishes its loneliness and freedom above all things, especially when it is at peace, content to drift passively on the foam of the sea of life,[44] asking no more than Unity of Being and allowing the wind of destiny to blow it in whatever direction it will. Even when some momentary impulse draws it down into the tumult of mere everyday living, 'under a great wave's hollowing crest', it remains essentially separate from the world it enters. We may confirm this precise reading from 'Upon A Political Prisoner', where the 'sea-borne bird' which is the symbol of Yeats's heroine is shown rejecting what Yeats speaks of elsewhere as 'common life': staring 'upon the cloudy canopy', and conscious of that symbolic sky alone,

> While under its storm-beaten breast
> Cried out the hollows of the sea.

Here once again is the sea of common living, or Sangsaric 'emotion and passion', though the bird in this case turns from it (directing its gaze instead upon the 'air' of intellectual beauty) in aristocratic disdain.

The second verse of Yeats's chorus shifts from water to air symbolism, and the eagle, which Yeats understood as traditionally the emblem of 'genius',[45] replaces the gull as the image for the soul itself. We are shown it soaring to the 'blue deep' of the 'upper air'; the phrase Yeats had used previously for the mystical *Erhebung* of Joachim de Flora:

CALVARY

> Third Musician: The ger-eagle has chosen his part
> In blue deep of the upper air
> Where one-eyed day can meet his stare.
> He is content with his savage heart.
> Second Musician: God has not appeared to the birds.

The subjective genius, these lines imply, chooses to leave mundane emotion behind him and to live always in the rarefied atmosphere of the noetic intellect. In that climate of spirituality, he boldly challenges the 'sun', or makes the nature and attributes of God his proper study. I have shown elsewhere that the single eye of intuition is a traditional emblem of deity.[46] If Yeats's image of a hero confronted with a one-eyed antagonist suggests anything beyond this, it is (just conceivably) the legend of Odysseus challenging Polyphemus, and this may be a less arbitrary association than it at first appears. I am convinced that Yeats has Homer in mind as the type of subjective genius, which would make this a last reminiscence of Nietzsche within his play.* We may compare his fourth line with one from 'Vacillation':

> He is content with his savage heart . . .
> Homer is my example and his unchristened heart . . .

In any case, Yeats's central argument is that the subjective soul preserves its individuality and freedom even when it comes closest to God.

The song concludes with the image of the swan, which has a particular significance in at least two cultures. In Celtic myth the swans of Aengus symbolise the souls of lovers, and in Indian traditional symbolism this association persists: it is prominent in several Sanscrit plays which Yeats had read.[47] It is also prominent in Indian visual art, and Yeats himself speaks of 'the bride and bridegroom in Rajput painting, sleeping upon a housetop, or wakening when out of the still water the swans fly upwards at the dawn'.[48] In such paintings, the swans image the lovers' souls, leaving the waters of emotion and passion for the air of spiritual contemplation, where their love will be transmuted to the plane of intellectual beauty. I think this symbolism impressed Yeats deeply, for his own usage is very similar:

---

* Does not Yeats commonly combine allusions to Homer with his bird-symbolism? In 'Upon A Political Prisoner', he stresses that the gull is 'rock-bred', and since he apostrophises Homer elsewhere as 'that rock-born, rock-wandering foot', this may indicate that the heroine of the poem is of Homer's subjective tribe. A more definite juxtaposition occurs in the famous last verse of 'Coole Park And Ballylee, 1931'.

> First Musician: But where have last year's cygnets gone?
> The lake is empty: why do they fling
> White wing out beside white wing?
> What can a swan need but a swan?
> Second Musician: God has not appeared to the birds.

Yeats's image here associates with that of 'The Wild Swans At Coole', where we are explicitly told that the swans symbolise lovers, though in that poem I think he is primarily concerned with reincarnation. We are shown his emblematic swans drifting together over the still waters of life, 'lover by lover'—a phrase Yeats had used previously to describe an audience of Platonic lovers, sitting together at a play;[49] then these swans rise and leave the waters for ever behind them, journeying through the pure air of spirituality to some other lake or subsequent incarnation. It was of course Yeats's belief that lovers are united in each of their lives on earth, and the poem's last verse, in which the swans take wing together to the 'pool' of their next rebirth, is used to convey this idea:

> ... now they drift on the still water,
> Mysterious, beautiful;
> Among what rushes will they build,
> By what lake's edge or pool
> Delight men's eyes when I awake some day
> To find they have flown away?

The meaning in *Calvary* is much less complex than in Yeats's lyric, though the swan-symbol carries the same overtones of 'passion and conquest' and a mysterious inwardness. The play gives us an image for early manhood, and shows the subjective soul rising to the sphere of intellectual beauty in the process of choosing a lover. The argument is that the subjective, even in first youth, has no need of externalities; the most he can require of the world is a lover as subjective as himself.

'God has not appeared to the birds.' Yeats's last line leaves the suggestion, which the notes reinforce, of a crucifixion taking place under the indifferent eyes of all the birds in the world. It is important to realise that these are both natural and supernatural watchers. I have left until now the relation of *Calvary* to Yeats's theory of the daemon, but he has referred to that theory consistently throughout the play, as can most easily be demonstrated from a speech given to Judas. Judas describes how he made up his mind to betray Christ, and felt a sense of perfect freedom as he did so:

> ... When I planned it
> There was no live thing near me but a heron
> So full of itself that it seemed terrified.

This is clearly a supernatural bird, and we must take the meaning to be that Judas, arriving at the moment of decision, passes from the power of an external God into the power of his subjective angel: the angel, as it is its function to do, directs him as to the course of action by which he can best make his separate soul. I detect here a slight shift in the emotional values with which Yeats charges his symbol: we are now perhaps to think rather of the gaucheness of the heron than of its solitary beauty; and it is appropriate that so ragged a figure as his Judas should have this bird for daemon. The angel given to the emaciated Lazarus is more terrible:

> Make way for Lazarus that must go search
> Among the desert places where there is nothing
> But howling wind and solitary birds.

If we care to read symbolism into this passage (we need not unless we wish) it is clearly about man's quest for a transcendental god: the desolation of the apparently naturalistic imagery mimes the desolation of this enterprise. On one level, Lazarus goes in search of the *deus absconditus*, the non-entity beyond human comprehension from whom the divine energies emanate; Yeats called an early story on the theme of the *deus absconditus* 'Where There Is Nothing' and these lines very possibly refer us back to it.[50] His solitary angels encourage Lazarus in his search, taking the form of kites and vultures as they do so. The lines thus become the clearest application in Yeats's poetry of the belief he derived from Doughty, that the great desert scavengers might be supernatural.

Yeats's closing refrain must be read with these passages in mind, and the full meaning he attached to it may be confirmed from his prose commentaries. Here is the gloss he published on the line 'God has not appeared to the birds':

I have surrounded Him with the images of those He cannot save ...

with the birds, who have served neither God nor Caesar, and who wait for none or a different saviour.[51]

In the original manuscript, however, Yeats wrote 'daemons' where we now have 'images', and after emending this phrase made several casts of the sentence in an attempt to insert 'daemon' elsewhere into the text.[52] There is therefore a possible connection between his play and 'The Second Coming', where daemonic birds flock round the new Messiah, born as he is from the Sphinx's loins or from the abstraction of a degenerating era. At that subjective rebirth, the bird-daemons are precipitated into action, but Christ's crucifixion moves neither them nor their human charges (the symbolism operates on both planes); subjectivity 'waits for a different Saviour'. And so in *Calvary*, Christ makes what for half humanity is a meaningless sacrifice; watched by the subjectives of the world and their daemons, He dies a death whose significance they cannot comprehend.

V

I have left until now the dance of the Roman Soldiers, which has the most elaborate symbolic significance. Its function is that of all the dances in Yeats's drama; to isolate, and to present in a concentrated form, the central emotion of the play.

One aspect of the dance has already been indicated: it connects with that other dance in *Rosa Alchemica* where the worshippers of Yeats's alchemical order encircle Christ and 'trouble His unity with the multiplicity of our feet'. Yeats's Roman Soldiers are in a late objective incarnation, which makes them so fallen as to be impervious to Christ's sufferings; but they preserve at least the outward forms of classical religion, and it is indicated in the text that they are polytheists. They cast lots for Christ's garments, dancing round the Cross as they do so:

Second Roman Soldier: Come now, let us dance
    The dance of the dice-throwers, for it may be
    He may not live much longer and has not seen
        it.
Third Roman Soldier: If he were but the God of Dice he'd know it,
    But he is not that God.

These lines make it clear that what is to follow will be no common ritual: the play is to culminate in what the Noh theatre calls a God-dance (a dance in honour of some deity and in mimesis of his characteristic actions), the God in this case being the Soldiers' patron, Mercury. By this means Yeats's tableau opposes the two contending forces of his drama: monotheistic Christianity and the pluralism which he saw as the true subjective faith. At one level of the symbolism we are to see Christ's death as the last triumph of the classical Gods, of a culture founded not on abnegation, sin and pain but on the external archetypes. With His resurrection the position will be reversed: 'unity' will triumph over 'multiplicity', and the objective cycle begin.

The scope of Yeats's tableau, however, extends to 'minute particulars', and if the mere fact of the dance itself serves to juxtapose two cultures, the figure the dancers trace will have its own, ulterior significance. Yeats tries to suggest his intentions through the last of his notes to the play, an anecdote to explain his philosophy of 'Chance and Choice'. An old Bedouin meets with every kind of misfortune; his wife and children are murdered by robbers, his house and lands are sequestered, and he himself is brought to his deathbed, but he dies singing a hymn in praise of God. The people ask him how he can do so, and the old man explains that the glory of God has been manifested in everything that had befallen him, for God's Chance, if we can understand it, is as holy as His Choice. He uses the analogy of the dice-box.

> If I should throw the dice-box there would be but six possible sides on each of the dice, but when God throws He uses dice that have all numbers and all sides.[53]

For we worship God, he goes on to say, when we recognise that He is infinite, and one way in which we may do this is by recognising infinite, God-given variety in the events of our lives:

> Some worship His Choice; that is easy; to know that He has willed for some unknown purpose all that happens is pleasant; but I have spent my life in worshipping His Chance, and that moment when I understand the immensity of His Chance is the moment when I am nearest to Him.[54]

We are told that the old man has recognised the greatness of God in the infinite unlikelihood of the events which have combined against him, and on this very Jungian note[55] the anecdote ends.

When the soldiers throw before Christ, there is imagery to relate tableau and prose commentary, and obviously the Bedouin anecdote is there to show the symbolic significance which their dicing is meant to carry. The dice, at the symbolic level, are symbols of 'God's Chance'; and in the draft version of the play are said to have supernatural virtue, which connects them the more closely with those of the anecdote 'that have all numbers and all sides'. We must understand that ivory is traditionally a magical material:

> Third Roman Soldier: Some play with wooden dice and some with stone.
> But ours are ivory; the merchants bring it
> In boats along the Nile, and after that
> On camels through the desert.
> Second Roman Soldier: I knew a man
> That dealt in ivory, and he slept sound
> Because he had seen the marvels of the world.[56]

In the version he finally published, the need for concision and Yeats's determination to use low imagery made him alter this passage as follows:

> Second Roman Soldier: Our dice were carved
> Out of an old sheep's thigh at Ephesus.

This very amusing imagery carries a significance similar to that which it supersedes, and it is worth turning aside to explain how this is so. Yeats uses Ephesus simply because of its traditional associations with gaming,* but the image of the 'sheep's thigh' is used to associate with the 'heron's thigh' that has gone before. That symbol had daemonic associations, so that the present image ought to be interpreted at the same level, and, since the soldiers are objectives and will have animal daemons, the malicious suggestion probably is that their daemon would have the shape of an old sheep. One could parallel a similarly ironic passage in *A Vision* where Yeats speculates whether the ghost of a certain 'abject religious' might not manifest with a sheep's head,[57] but it is hardly necessary: we have only to know his mind to recognise the joke as characteristic. The dice, at all events, retain their daemonic connections, and the suggestion is much as before.

* Also with subjectivity; see my note on the Seven Sleepers of Ephesus below (p. 269). Imagery of 'sound sleep' is there also in the draft version, carrying with it a suggestion of subjective self-sufficiency.

Beyond the malice of Yeats's symbol lies his usual human generosity; we are to understand that his soldiers' apparent brutality is merely the result of their obtuseness. None of his characters is ever finally condemned, even if he can only excuse them by giving them defective guardian angels; thus the soldiers are observed with an amused tolerance, and a similar spirit of tolerance informs the climax of his play. Yeats could have concluded by worshipping God's choice, man's knowledge that He has willed Christ's death for reasons of His own; the idea of the divine inscrutability is indeed implicit in his argument, just as it is conceded in his old Bedouin's private philosophy. Yet a convenient conclusion of this kind would not have justified all Yeats's characters, Lazarus, Judas and the rest, and it would also have been out of keeping with the main theme, which is the relation of personality to religion. The one suitably dignified alternative was to celebrate God's chance, and this is what Yeats does in his final tableau: the ritual in honour of the 'God of Dice' begins, the participants throwing as they dance, and we are to see in this a mime of the divine bestowal of variety upon the world. I think Yeats may have in mind the special field of the human psyche, and that the traditional Indian symbol of the dice of personality[58] may conceivably be remembered in his verse. Thus the dance represents a 'quarrel', a single naturalistic detail if we like, yet one which may also typify in miniature the quarrel between subjectivity and objectivity, the soldiers representing, at this level, the divergent psychological types. But the symbol of human disunity is replaced, as the dance continues, by that of the Great Wheel of Becoming:

> In the dance
> We quarrel for a while, but settle it
> By throwing dice and, after that, being friends,
> Join hand to hand and wheel about the cross.

I think that Yeats's choice of the unusual verb 'wheel' is enough to suggest that my interpretation is correct, and that we must see an ingenious representation of the Buddhist Great Wheel in the pattern of his dance. At one level the psychological types are enemies, but all twenty-eight rebirths are reconciled in the symbol of God's chance, and in another, deeper sense they 'join hand to hand' in the cycle of human existence, each of them an integer in the many-spoked wheel of reincarnation. And (at this deep level) they are friends, for we are all God's dice, the symbols of his infinite multiplicity, and the contradictions of human psychology are reconciled in Him.

CHAPTER SIX

THE DREAMING OF THE BONES

I

YEATS MADE SEVERAL draft versions of *The Dreaming Of The Bones*, and he seems to have found it hard to decide on a location for the play. He first planned to site it in the Wicklow mountains, but later preferred the battlefield of Corcomroe, in that part of the ancient kingdom of Thomond where Clare borders on Galway. The change gave him a setting in the desolate hills of the Burren, where the terraced limestone 'stretches for miles in grey nakedness'[1] and is almost destitute of vegetation save for a few scattered hazels and thorns, and this landscape gives the play its characteristic atmosphere:

> Sometimes among great rocks on the scarce grass
> Birds cry, they cry their loneliness.
> Even the sunlight can be lonely here,
> Even hot noon is lonely.

This is clearly an apt environment for a ghost-play, and the sombre setting blends excellently with the laborious style Yeats chooses, and with the heavy pedantry of his several references to the occultists: to Agrippa and Henry More:

> Have not old writers said
> That dizzy dreams can spring
> From the dry bones of the dead?

And if there is something very un-Japanese in Yeats's indecisiveness as to setting in what we shall see is the most Japanese of all his plays—the Noh legends are always traditionally associated with some particular *genius loci*, and cannot conceivably be transplanted at a dramatist's whim—his plot left him no alternative; the ghosts of Dermot and Dervorgilla have no traditional habitat, but are thought of as 'wandering' from place to place. It is logical that they might come to Corcomroe and to the tomb of Donough O'Brien, who shares with them the stigma of having called in a foreign army against the Irish people; and the location was also useful to Yeats in relating his play to contemporary politics and working in allusions to the Easter rising. Heavy fighting took place in this part of the west during the 1916 rebellion[2] and the play contains a bitter commentary on the vandalism of the English troops.

If Yeats took some freedom with the geography of his play, his notes claim rather sententiously that he has allowed himself none with its history; every allusion he tells us, he has carefully checked. I will quote Lady Gregory's synopsis of the shaping story:

> Dervorgilla, daughter of the King of Meath, wife of O'Rourke, King of Breffny, was taken away, willingly or unwillingly, by Diarmuid MacMurrough, King of Leinster, in the year 1152. O'Rourke and his friends invaded Leinster in revenge and, in the wars that followed, Diarmuid, driven from Ireland, appealed for help to Henry II of England, and was given an army under Strongbow, to whom Diarmuid promised Leinster as reward. It is so the English were first brought into Ireland. Dervorgilla, having outlived O'Rourke and Diarmuid and Henry and Strongbow, is said to have died at the abbey of Mellifont, near Drogheda, in the year 1193, aged 85.[3]

There is no proof whether Dervorgilla eloped with Diarmuid of her own free will, but Lady Gregory clinches the matter from folk-lore by giving a Kiltartan peasant version of the story:

> As for Dervorgilla, she was not brought away by force, she went to MacMurrough herself. For there are men in the world that have a coaxing way, and sometimes women are weak.[4]

Yeats sees the abduction similarly; indeed as an Irish parallel to the rape of Helen:

> The man she chose, the man she was chosen by,
> Cared little and cares little from whose house
> They fled towards dawn amid the flights of arrows...
> And how, if that were all, could she lack friends
> On crowded roads or on the unpeopled hill?
> Helen herself had opened wide the door
> Where night by night she dreams herself awake
> And gathers to her breast a dreaming man.

He follows what literary convention has made the canonical, if hardly the proven, form of the legend here, and allows himself some further tinge of romanticism in making Dervorgilla a 'young girl' at the time of her rape, whereas she was as we have seen a mature woman of over forty; but there is not much in his play to offend the historian. In the one passage where serious research might really have been called for, the lines on Donough O'Brien, he is I believe perfectly accurate. In the Abbey churchyard where Yeats's ghosts bring his hero:

> Close to the altar,
> Broken by wind and frost and worn by time,
> Donough O'Brien has a tomb, a name in Latin.
> He wore fine clothes and knew the secrets of women
> But he rebelled against the King of Thomond
> And died in his youth.
>   —And why should he rebel?
> The King of Thomond was his rightful master.
> It was men like Donough that made Ireland weak.

This prince was a discontented Irish noble of the early fourteenth century, one of a group of such nobles who invited the Scots, after Bannockburn, to invade Thomond and take it from the King. After the defeat and withdrawal of the Scots, Donough and his followers had to shift for themselves and the prince escaped from the field of Athenry only to fall, fighting bravely, in 1317 near the abbey of Corcomroe.[5] Yeats imagines that the ghosts of his soldiers relive this battle after death or, as the impetus to hatred dies, join hands with their former enemies in the air above the churchyard:

> They and their enemies of Thomond's party
> Mix in a brief dream-battle above their bones
> Or make one drove, or drift in amity.

They are afforded this relatively mild purgatory, we are told, because they are not to blame for their master's crime in calling in 'the alien from oversea'.* He suffers a severer penance; his grave, indeed, may have attracted Dermot and Dervorgilla, his fellow-traitors, to Corcomroe.

---

* Alternatively, Yeats's rather cryptic verse here may mean that O'Brien himself suffers a milder penance than Dermot and Dervorgilla, because his treachery at least did not extend to inviting 'the alien' to Ireland—the Scots and the Irish being thought of as kindred. Yeats's whole drift is ambiguous, and he may even be following some authority who disputes whether Donough sponsored the Scottish invasion at all.

In the hills of the Burren, we are told, Dermot and Dervorgilla continue to expiate a crime against patriotism now seven hundred years old, and which can only be absolved if some living man of their own people can bring himself to forgive them. Their sufferings made a familiar theme for Yeats, who had described them years before in a story in his *Red Hanrahan*.[6] Hanrahan, his peasant hero, goes into a valley, where, 'the gateway to eternity' opening for him for 'one beat of the heart', he has a momentary vision in which the valley fills with ghosts of dead lovers. First he is shown the blessed condition of those who have loved the divine goodness and beauty in one another; and then he sees pass in a blast of wind the penitential throng of those whose love has been selfish or carnal. Presently this procession too disperses and he supposes the vision to be at an end:

> He stood up trembling and was going to turn away from the valley when he saw two dark and half-hidden forms standing as if in the air just beyond the rock, and one of them that had the mournful eyes of a beggar said to him in a woman's voice, 'Speak to me . . . I am Dervadilla, and this is Dermot, and it was our sin brought the Norman into Ireland, and the curses of all the generations are upon us. It was but the blossom of the man and the woman we loved in one another, the dying blossom of the dust and not the everlasting beauty. When we died there was no lasting unbreakable quiet about us, and the bitterness of the battles we brought into Ireland turned to our own punishment. We go wandering together for ever, but Dermot who was my lover sees me always as a body that has been a long time in the ground, and I know that is the way he sees me. Ask me more, ask me more, for all the years have left their wisdom in my heart, and no one has listened to me for five hundred years. [This story has to be thought of as taking place in the eighteenth century.]

Most of this detail recurs in Yeats's dance play, but what is perhaps more obvious here than there is the eclecticism of his writing; as Hone first pointed out,[7] he is clearly and consciously engaged on creating a Celtic parallel to the legend of Paolo and Francesca. He needed no great Dante scholarship to conceive this ambition in the 'nineties, when its peculiar fusion of the sensual and the spiritual made the episode standard reading; and the Dantesque influence, transmitted through his own story, persists in *The Dreaming Of The Bones*. Thus in Dante, the loneliness of the damned lovers is a prominent *motif*: the poet calls them to speak with him, and they thank him in well-known lines:

> Se fosse amico il Re dell' universo
> Noi pregheremmo lui per la tua pace
> Poi che hai pietà del nostro mal perverso.[8]

If the King of the Universe were our friend, we would pray him to grant you peace, since you have so much compassion on our perversity as to speak with us.

Yeats takes up this *motif* both in his prose tale and his play: though in his version, the past treason of the lovers adds trenchancy to their present solitude:

> Until this hour no ghost or living man
> Has spoken, though seven centuries have run
> Since they, weary of life and of men's eyes
> Flung down their bones in some deserted place,
> Being accursed.

In Dante, the lovers still have desire—'ancor non m'abandonna'— though it is now a torment to them, and in Yeats also inhibited desire is Dermot and Dervorgilla's special punishment:

> These have no thought but love, nor any pang
> That is so bitter as that double glance,
> Being accursed.

There are other traces of Dante in the story which disappear in the dance-play: in the prose and in Dante alike, the procession of guilty lovers is whirled along on a black wind, 'la bufera infernal, che mai non resta'; in both, again, two penitents of a vast concourse remain behind to explain their state. And, as happens with Hanrahan, Dante's vision ends when he faints with pity and horror, after which the lovers melt disconsolately away:

> Mentre che l'uno spirto questo disse
> L'altro piangeva sì, che di pietade
> Io venni men così com'io morisse,
> E caddi come corpo morto cade.[9]

All the time that the one spirit spoke, the other wept, until out of pity I swooned away like a stricken man, and fell as a dead body falls.

The one salient detail in the play that is absent from Yeats's earlier story is that of Dermot and Dervorgilla asking, and being refused, absolution from the young revolutionary on the run who is his hero. In 'Red Hanrahan's Vision', the faint that recalls Hanrahan to the waking world merely prevents him from speaking with the lovers and ending their ostracism; Yeats's concern is simply with their loneliness and not with any possibility of forgiveness. He may have added his new matter, if indeed it is necessary to find a source beyond his own invention, from Lady Gregory's play *Dervorgilla* (1911), which he will naturally have pondered deeply; Lady Gregory and he were not only collaborators in several stage productions, but she had helped him to formulate his own philosophy of the ghost. Her one act play tells of Dervorgilla in old age living at the abbey of Mellifont, and much of the action is quite off our subject, but it is centrally concerned with that problem of the lovers' eventual absolution with which Yeats had not concerned himself previously but which was later to interest him so much:

> Dervorgilla: Suppose there was some person who had done a great wrong, had brought, maybe, a bad neighbour into his house, or a hard stranger in among kindred; it might be a race, an army, into a country. Could that person ever gain forgiveness, praying and sorrowing?

As in *The Dreaming Of The Bones*, Dervorgilla conceals her identity to ask this question, and the whole point of the play is that while the leniency of the old (which is a form of weakness) may persuade them to agree that 'there is an excuse for everyone', the fiercer mettle of youth can never be brought to forgive her, and she reads her eternal damnation, from generation to generation, in 'the swift, unflinching, terrible judgment of the young'. In Yeats's play, though we ourselves as spectators are meant to be swayed by pity, the young man knows immediately and instinctively that there is no possible forgiveness for the damned lovers, and the 'swift, unflinching, terrible judgment of the young' is made the theme.

In 1917, with this climax to build towards, Yeats returned to a situation which must have seemed ideal subject-matter for a Noh play, and his immediate impulse to do so was clearly the unsuccessful

Easter Rebellion, which made his theme only too topical. With a young man escaped from the Dublin Post Office as hero, he wondered in fact whether his play might not be too incendiary for the Irish stage.*
We ought not to forget, at the same time, the subsidiary factors in his new enthusiasm, and one of these was clearly his resurgence of interest in Dante and in the Paolo and Francesca myth. That he was rereading Dante at this time, and imitating him as he read, is obvious, and follows from such poems as 'Broken Dreams', which not only alludes to the 'mysterious, always brimming lake'—'che si deriva perchè vi s'immegli' —of the *Paradiso*,[10] but seems to me peculiarly Dantesque in the quality of its emotion; from the more fiercely urgent, but equally Dantesque, prologue to *Responsibilities*, written in a variant form of *terza rima*;[11] and from 'Ego Dominus Tuus', where Dante serves as exemplar of the deprived and even vicious artist composing from his mask or anti-self:

> Being mocked by Guido for his lecherous life,
> Derided and deriding, driven out
> To climb that stair and eat that bitter bread,
> He found the unpersuadable justice, he found
> The most exalted lady loved by a man.

It has not yet been noted that this attitude of Yeats to Dante probably derives from his readings in Landor (another stylistic model of the period) and in particular from Landor's commentary on the Paolo and Francesca myth:

> The features of Ugolino [are] reflected full in Dante. The two characters are similar in themselves; hard, cruel, inflexible, malignant, but, whenever moved, moved powerfully. In Francesca, with the faculty of divine spirits, he leaves his own nature (not indeed the exact representative of theirs) and converts all his strength into tenderness. The great poet, like the original man of the Platonists, is born double, possessing the further advantages of being able to drop one half at his option and to resume it. Some of the tenderest on paper have no sympathies beyond; and some of the austerest in their intercourse with their fellow creatures have deluged the world with tears. It is not from the rose that the bee gathers her honey, but often from the most acrid and the most bitter leaves and petals.[12]

---

* For this reason, as the draft shows, he at one stage thought of backdating the action to the eighteenth-century risings.

With this essay of Landor's in mind, we may reasonably suppose that Yeats returned to the Paolo and Francesca legend, and that a recrudescence of the old ambition to emulate it followed; or if this seems too hypothetical, at least the story will have taken on a new importance in his thought.

For proof of the general direction in which Yeats's mind was turning there are certainly allusions to Dante's Italy within the play; the Italianate strain is as strong as in *Emer*. It breaks surface when Yeats's young revolutionary looks down on the Galway landscape, devastated by the fighting during the 1916 rebellion, when Athenry was at one time in the hands of a 'republican army'.[13] The British troops sent in have 'toppled roof and gable' and 'torn the panelling from ancient rooms':

> What generations of old men have known
> Like their own hand and children wondered at,
> Has boiled a trooper's porridge.

To set off this bitter perspective the young man calls up a mental image of what the landscape might have been if Dermot and Dervorgilla had never betrayed their country; and the picture that forms is of a city in the mould of Dante's Florence or of Peter Bembo's Urbino:

> That town had lain
> But for the pair that you would have me pardon,
> Among its gables and its battlements
> Like any old admired Italian town
> For though we have neither coal nor iron ore
> To make us wealthy and corrupt the air,
> Our country, if that crime were uncommitted,
> Had been most beautiful.

These lines of course illustrate Yeats's political as well as his literary ideals at the period, and it is interesting to see this early pointer to what has been called the 'fascism' of his mature verse. Yeats's aristocratic bias took direction at this time, when he reacted away from his disillusion with Irish popular politics to their antithesis in the courtesy and order of the medieval or early renaissance city-state (he idealised Coole Park as an Irish Urbino);[14] it is, I think, pure of any infection of 'power politics' and originates, more than from any other single source, perhaps from his admiration of the social structure mirrored in Castiglione's *The Courtier*.[15] And so here, his appeal is to the social norms of the 'great house' and the autocratic Italian renaissance community, and he opposes them to the 'formlessness' of modern democracy. It is because the English have destroyed the aristocratic feature of the Galway landscape that his young revolutionary is so bitter here: they are shown as bringing hierarchic Ireland down to their own vulgar, egalitarian level.

The Dreaming Of The Bones, then, brings together several strands in Yeats's thought: his passionate nationalism and I think his advocacy of small self-contained communities on the renaissance model; of the hierarchy of 'workman, noble and saint', where the 'Aran fisher' in his 'coracle' and the great prince who 'wore fine clothes and knew the secrets of women' might each have his individual dignity. There are also his ambition to emulate Dante, his partisan's interest in aboriginal Irish history and the fascination he experienced for supernatural phenomena and the metaphysics of the ghost. Of these the notes make it perfectly clear that we must think of his play centrally as an exercise in metaphysics, and that its theology is something in which the poet literally believed:

> The conception of the play is derived from the world-wide belief that the dead dream back, for a certain time, through the labyrinth of conscience.

We have thus Yeats's own sanction for reading his play as a ghost play, and only secondarily as a political document; as literature it is certainly at its best on the former level, for it contains no political *poetry* so moving as, say, 'Easter, 1916' or 'The Rose Tree', though it does contain a *situation* of great inflammatory potential. The political verse is used to build up this gesture rather than for any more genuinely aesthetic end, and, if it is fiercely sincere, it is also orotund:

> Police
> Are out upon the roads. In the late Rising
> I think there was no man of us but hated
> To fire at soldiers who but did their duty
> And were not of our race, but when a man
> Is born in Ireland, and of Irish stock,
> When he takes part against us . . .

> I have no dread (of the dead)
> They cannot put me into gaol or shoot me,
> And seeing that their blood has returned to fields
> That have grown red with drinking blood like mine,
> They would not, if they could, betray . . .

I therefore propose to approach the play as Yeats wishes, as an attempt to write in the *genre* of the Noh of ghosts, which need not be to lose sight of the political thread. The play's ingenuity lies in the skill with which the two aspects of the theme are integrated, eventually, I will anticipate myself to say, being united in a single symbol.

II

As a ghost play, *The Dreaming Of The Bones* may owe something to Dante, but it is eclectic in another way as well: it reflects Yeats's admiration of the Noh play *Nishikigi*. His plot may be Irish, and he may have hibernated over it for years, but the form in which he cast it as a dance-play is no doubt owed to this work, which provided him with an exact model in his parent theatre. The resultant parallelism is very close, running deeper than any other in *Four Plays For Dancers*; indeed, there is a very real sense in which *The Dreaming Of The Bones* is not an original play at all, but the recreation of a Japanese original.

Nishikigi, though very successful, would not seem to a Japanese critic one of the greatest pieces in the Noh; but it is easy to find reasons for Yeats's enthusiasm. He read it in the singularly beautiful translation of Fenollosa and Ezra Pound,[16] may even—it seems to me from the idiom of the opening speeches—have had a hand in what is by far the most successful of Pound's Japanese translations; he saw in it a philosophy of the ghost which would bear out his own; and he will also have found much solace in its philosophy of sexual antagonism and reconciliation. *Nishikigi* is a study in unrequited love; it is a play both courtly and learned, in its *awaré* (gentle spirituality) often reminiscent of Dante or Guido Cavalcanti; and Yeats, coming to the text in his Italian period and at the moment of his break with Maud Gonne, will hardly have read it without emotion. It turns on a question central to his own life: whether sexual loss is final and irrevocable, or whether the lover may hope to find the peace that has been denied him, either beyond the grave or in a subsequent incarnation. We can hardly be surprised that Yeats should have been uniquely attracted to his play, since it explores this theme with a tenderness and sympathy perhaps unique in dramatic literature; and it is equally predictable that he should have wished to write in the same mode, for which he must bitterly have allowed himself a special *métier* and talent. One imagines that this was the first stage in the genesis of his dance-play, which took shape as suitable subjects occurred to him: first, he says, a story from the Aran Isles of two ghosts who were married by a priest,[17] and when he had decided against that his favourite legend of Dermot and Dervorgilla, carrying with it the literary and political attachments we have seen.

Nishikigi, as is normal in the Noh ghost-plays, consists of two scenes bridged by a passage of choric recitative, and we now ought to examine its story in some detail. Here is Yeats's own synopsis of the opening speeches, as he retails them (rehearsing the theme, ostensibly, for the philosophy of the ghost it embodies) in an essay in *Visions And Beliefs*:[18]

> In a play still more rich in lyric beauty [than *Motomezuka*, the play which became a source for 'Byzantium', which Yeats has previously been paraphrasing], a priest is wandering in a certain ancient village. He describes the journey and the scene, and from time to time the chorus sitting at the side of the stage sings its commentary. He meets with two ghosts, the one holding a red stick, the other a piece of coarse cloth, and both dressed in the fashion of a past age, but as he is a stranger he supposes them villagers wearing the native fashion.

The ghost-lovers, separated in purgatory as in life, next explain their predicament to the audience, and they do so in a beautiful but embittered speech which will have meant much to Yeats. The young man tells how he loved the girl with a 'visionary' passion to which she never for a moment responded, and, he says, this is normal enough in love; there is always a lover, who gives everything that he has, and a beloved, who gives absolutely nothing in return. After death, however, this young girl has to expiate her cruelty by experiencing unrequited love for him exactly proportionate to his own; now they are both 'entangled' in the 'consequence' of his emotion, and both suffer equally from the denial of any consummation:

> Tangled, we are entangled. Whose fault was it, dear? We neither wake nor sleep, and, passing the nights in a sorrow which is in the end a vision, what are these scenes of spring to us? This thinking in sleep of someone who has no thought of you, is it more than a dream? And yet surely it is the natural way of love.

Yeats's essay singles out for quotation these lines—I think he had a hand in their translation—after which he continues with his paraphrase:

> To the priest they seem two married people, but he cannot understand why they carry the red stick and the coarse cloth. They ask him to listen to a story. Two young people had lived in that village long ago, and night after night for three years the young man had offered a charmed red stick, the token of love, at the young girl's window, but she pretended not to see and went on sewing. So the young man died and was buried in a cave with his charmed red sticks, and presently the girl died too, and now because they were never married in life they are unmarried in death.

The priest, who does not yet understand that it is their own story, asks to be shown the cave, and this brings to an end the first scene of the play.

There follows a bridge passage to represent a day-long journey, for it is many miles from the village to the love-cave. There is no action, but during the recitative the players perform the Noh ceremony of 'making a journey', which I shall later explain:

> The chorus describe the journey to the cave. The lovers go in front, the priest follows. They are all day pushing through long grasses that hide the narrow paths. They ask the way of a farmer who is mowing. Then night falls and it is cold and frosty. It is stormy and the leaves are falling and their feet sink into muddy places made by the autumn showers; there is a long shadow on the slope of the mountain and an owl in the ivy of the pine tree. They have found the cave and it is dyed with the red sticks of love to the colour of 'the orchids and chrysanthemums which hide the mouth of a fox's hole', and now the two lovers have slipped into the shadow of the cave.

The ritual journey is now complete and, though the stage is exactly as before, the audience have been imaginatively prepared for the climax of the play.

The second scene, as always in the Noh ghost-plays, takes place on the supernatural plane. The priest says a prayer which serves to liberate the two lovers, and is shown, first a masque of their past sufferings, and then one of their heavenly marriage:

Left alone and too cold to sleep, the priest decides to spend the night in prayer. He prays that the lovers may at last be one. Presently it seems to his wonder that the cave is lighted up. . . . The ghosts creep out and thank him for his prayer and say that through his pity 'the love promises of long past incarnations' find fulfilment in a dream. Then he sees their love-story unfolded in a vision. . . . A little later he is shown the bridal room and the lovers drinking from the bridal cup. The dawn is coming. It is reflected in the bridal cup and now singers, cloth and stick, break and dissolve in a dream, and there is nothing but 'a deserted grave on a hill, where morning winds are blowing through the pine'.

This is the end of the Noh play, the priest having dispelled by his prayer the evil *karma* caused by the girl's cruelty, and enabled the lovers to escape from purgatory and be reconciled in heaven. Their beatitude is not of course final, for eventually they will suffer rebirth into the world, where they will meet and love, perhaps prosperously now, once again.

The resemblances between this play and *The Dreaming Of The Bones* are very obvious. Yeats replaces the wandering priest who is the *Waki* (interlocutor) of *Nishikigi* by his young revolutionary, but his *Shite* and *Tsure* (hero and heroine) are ghost-lovers as in his original. The young man at first mistakes this couple, 'dressed in the fashion of a past age', for country folk of the district, and, as in the Japanese, they tell him their whole story under the pretence that it is merely a legend of the neighbourhood, and without his guessing their identity. Yeats also follows *Nishikigi* in having them lead him to the 'haunted stones' where they have made their home, though in his play it is the need for shelter from police and English troopers, and not mere curiosity, that makes him go with them to the Abbey. The ritual of their journey is imitated in all detail from the Noh play; Yeats substitutes the eerie landscape of the Galway hills for the romantic nightpiece of his original, but in point of technique follows *Nishikigi* closely. The young man asks Dermot to show him his path:

> *They go round the stage once. The first musician speaks.*
> And now they have climbed through the long grassy field
> And passed the ragged thorn-trees and the gap
> In the ancient hedge; and the tomb-nested owl
> At the foot's level beats with a vague wing. . . .

> *They go round the stage once,*
> They are among the thorns above the ash,
> Above the briar and thorn and the scarce grass.
> Hidden amid the shadow far below them
> The cat-headed bird is crying out
>
> *They go round the stage. Diarmuid speaks.*
> We're almost at the summit and can rest.
> The road is a faint shadow there; and there
> The Abbey lies amid its broken tombs. . . .

Here (for contrast as well as comparison) is the same scene in *Nishikigi*, in the pauses of which the chorus also symbolically circle the stage. This is the Noh ritual of making a journey.

> Waki: I will go to that love-cave.
>   It will be a tale to take back to my village:
>   Will you show me the way there?
> Shite: So be it, I will tell you the path.
> Tsure: Tell him to come over this way
> Both (performing a mime): Here are the pair of them
>   Going before the traveller.
> Chorus: We have spent the whole day until dark
>   Pushing aside the grass
>   From the overgrown way at Kefu,
>   And we are not yet come to the cave.
>   O you there, cutting grass on the hill,
>   Please set your mind on this matter. . . .
>   Very well, then, don't tell us,
>   But be sure we will come to the cave.
> Shite: There's a cold feel in the autumn.
>   Night comes. . . .
> Chorus: And storms; trees giving up their leaf,
>   Spotted with sudden showers.
>   Autumn! Our feet are clogged
>   In the dew-drenched, entangled leaves.
>   The perpetual shadow is lonely,
>   The mountain-shadow lying alone.
>   The owl cries out from the ivies
>   That drag their weight on the pine.
>   Among the orchids and chrysanthemum flowers,

> The hiding fox is now lord of that love-cave,
> Nishidzuka,
> That is dyed like the maple's leaf.
> They have left us this thing for a saying.
> The pair have gone into the cave.[19]

Yeats's own ritual-journey is much simpler and less impressionistic than this, as it had to be where the audience would not be familiar with the technique he was using. But though his verse may seem laboured and even pedestrian beside the freshness and natural cadences of his original, the ceremony as he presents it remains dramatic and exciting, and is indeed one of the successes of the play.

When the young man has reached the ridge above the Abbey where he is to hide, the ghosts who are his guides give up the attempt at subterfuge and explain that, as in *Nishikigi*, they need the prayers of a living man:

> If someone of their race forgave at last
> Lip would be pressed on lip.

Here we have to use *Nishikigi* to come at the metaphysical implication beneath the verse, which must be—since Yeats tells us that everything in his play has philosophical validity—that the prayers of one of their race are needed to dispel the evil *karma* that Dermot and Dervorgilla have stored up for themselves. Yeats of course believed in the law of *karma*, by which the good or evil actions in which it participates during life condition the soul's destiny between incarnations and in its next rebirth, and applies it in *A Vision*. As once again in *Nishikigi*, however, the young man does not properly understand the identity of the supplicants until it is revealed to him by their dance:

> Why do you dance?
> Why do you gaze, and with so passionate eyes,
> One on the other; and then turn away,
> Covering your eyes, and weave it in a dance?
> Who are you? What are you? You are not natural.

The dance in the Noh play is of consummated love, and here of love's frustration, the distinction reflecting the one radical difference in orientation; and, after the young man has refused Dermot and Dervorgilla his forgiveness, the play ends with first light and the crowing of the cock. This is a last point of comparison with *Nishikigi*, which finishes similarly:

> Shite (*crowing like a cock*):
>> Ari-aki.
>> The dawn.
>> Come, we are out of place;
>> Let us go ere the light comes.
>> We ask you, do not awake,
>> We all will wither away,
>> The wands and this cloth of a dream.
>> Now you will come out of sleep,
>> You tread the border and nothing
>> Awaits you; no, all this will wither away.
>> There is nothing here but this cave in the field's midst.
>> Today's wind moves in the pines.
>> A wild place, unlit and unfilled.

Thus the priest wakes from his vision to the 'nothingness' of the empty cave, symbolic of the worthlessness (maya) of all life in the material world.

One might here usefully develop the comparison of the two plays into a study of their relative merit, since we now have a yardstick by which to measure Yeats's achievement. His own play is full of atmosphere, and effective on the stage, but in comparison with *Nishikigi* it does I think reveal itself as an inferior imitation. *Nishikigi* is a very much more natural and spontaneous work, as airy as Yeats's play is earthy, and it combines, as in the scene where the priest prays for the dead lovers, a profundity of philosophical content with a delicacy and lightness of touch quite beyond Yeats's reach. The Tsure appears and explains that all our acts have spiritual consequence; one cannot even dip a hand in a river without setting a sequence of *karma* in motion:*

> Waki: It seems that I cannot sleep
>> For the length of a pricket's horn
>> Under October wind, under pines, under night.
>> I will do service to Butsu.
>> (*He prays for the dead lovers.*)

---

* So Yeats will have understood the meaning, but Pound's lines in fact contain a mistranslation.

> Tsure: Aie, honoured priest.
> > You do not dip twice in a river
> > Beneath the same tree's shadow
> > Without bonds in some other life.
> > Hear soothsay.
> > Now is there meeting between us,
> > Between us who were until now
> > In life and in after-life kept apart.
> > A dream-bridge over wild grass.

Yeats's explanation of the metaphysics of his own dance-play seems laboured beside this, largely because he could not, as the Noh dramatist could, build on a religious tradition that would be immediately and unquestioningly accepted by his audience; he had no opportunity to be urbane:

> Their manner of life were blessed could their lips
> A moment meet; but when he has bent his head
> Close to her head, or hand would slip in hand,
> The memory of their crime flows up between
> And drives them apart.

His symbolism of 'March cock', 'airy music' and dry bones seems, I think, equally laboured (and in the latter instance, perhaps excessively macabre also) beside that of the Noh play: the wild grass, in which the lovers are entangled like small birds, the phallic love wands and the woven cloth:

> As the cloth Hosunono is narrow of weft,
> More narrow than the breast,
> We call by this name any woman
> Whose breasts are hard to come near to.
> It is a name in books of love.

Nor has Yeats anything so visually effective as the love-cave miraculously illuminated as a symbol of the spiritual world; an effect he later incorporated into his own symbol of the miraculously lighted house:*

---

* In *Purgatory*, 'Crazy Jane On God' and 'The Curse of Cromwell'. Did the wand-cloth symbolism of *Nishikigi* influence the sword-cloth symbolism of 'A Dialogue of Self and Soul'?

> Waki: Strange, what seemed so very old a cave
> Is all glittering bright within
> With the flicker of fire.
> They are setting up a loom
> And heaping up charm-sticks. No,
> The hangings are out of old time.
> Is it illusion, illusion?

With this, of course, the love-poetry in Yeats's play is markedly inferior to that of his model. He has nothing to match the first speech of the Japanese lovers, at once so visionary and so bitter:

> This thinking in sleep of someone who has no thought of you, is it more than a dream? And yet surely it is the natural way of love.

Nor has he anything of the urgency of the passionate chorus following, where the Chorus sum up the situation:

> Chorus: Narrow is the cloth of Kefu, but wide is that river, that torrent of the hills, between the beloved and his bride,
> The cloth she had woven is faded, the thousand one hundred nights were love-trysts watched out in vain.

Beside this pure poetry and the sheer felicity of the love-masques which come later, Yeats's descriptions and dance of frustrated love can only be called mechanical; lifeless set-pieces.

The Dreaming Of The Bones, then, has nothing of the lyricism of its Japanese counterpart, but it may not be altogether fair to Yeats's play to condemn it on these grounds. The sombre and portentous Galway landscape which is felt behind the verse demanded perhaps a certain heaviness of statement; and the strength of Yeats's play is that it has this weighty quality, a quality of grave metaphysical deliberation. The best poetry of the play arises out of this metaphysical element; a poetry at once ponderous and bizarre, the theories behind the verse being painstakingly, even sententiously explained; a poetry which I shall compare to the finest passages in Blake's *Tiriel*:

> Young Man: My Grandam
> Would have it they [the penitential shades] did penance everywhere;
> Some lived through their old lives again.

> Stranger: In a dream.
> And some for an old scruple must hang spitted
> Upon the swaying tops of lofty trees;
> Some are consumed in fire; some withered up
> By hail and sleet out of the wintry north
> And some but live through their old lives again.

And the solemnity of this verse is counterpointed in the more pictorial writing; in the description of the 'ridge' below which:

> the cocks
> Of Aughanish or Bailevelehan
> Or grey Aughtmana shake their wings and cry

and in those other passages where Yeats makes use of the poetry of place-names as never before or after; when, for example, he describes an 'Aran coracle' putting in

> At Muckanish or at the rocky shore
> Under Finvara.

Or we may gauge the timbre of his play from the ritual journey to the mountain-side, where his death-motif and his feeling for place join hands:

> They have passed the shallow well and the flat stone
> Fouled by the drinking cattle, the narrow lane
> Where mourners for five centuries have carried
> Noble or peasant to his burial

We may say, then, that the poetry of the play stems from Yeats's keen sentiment for 'cold Clare rock and Galway rock and thorn'; and from his doing full justice in it, as perhaps only here in his poetry, to that feeling for bizarre and exotic religious speculation which is another side of his talent.

One might comment at this point also on the language of the play, on that strange blending of archaisms and slang phrases by which Yeats achieves the bizarre effect which is his aim: 'drove' (as a noun), 'amity', 'moidered', 'coracle' mingling with such colloquialisms as 'dizzy dreams', 'my rascal heart', 'I'd let the whole world go' and Irish provincialisms such as 'the flannel bawneen and the cowhide shoe'.

His style is similarly mixed; there are reminiscences of Macbeth—
'Who are you? What are you? You are not natural'[20]—and even of
Milton:

> their two hearts are wrung
> Nearest to breaking, if hearts of shadows break.[21]

There are medievalisms, 'they fled towards dawn amid the flights of
arrows', and there are also deliberate orientalisms, such as the metaphor
of the valley, overflowing with the dreams of the dead, like a 'grey-
green cup' of agate or of jade; together with a number of speeches of a
matter-of-fact bluntness:

> I was in the Post Office and, if taken,
> I shall be put against a wall and shot.

By such odd fusions Yeats triumphantly conveys the fantastic atmosphere of the purgatorial landscape; we are lost in a world of shifting
stylistic and linguistic values, where the obsolete and the colloquial
word meet and many manners merge into one. Time present and time
past do indeed blend in this haunted valley, and, consciously or unconsciously, the language Yeats uses underlines this uneasy conjunction.

III

One certain way to a misreading of *The Dreaming Of The Bones* is
to take Yeats's metaphysical poetry for something it is not, and to
think of it as the product of his personal imagination. If we read, for
example, his descriptions of the 'shape-changer' (the spirit, in the post-
mortem condition, changing into 'what shape it will'), and think of
them as verse in the same *genre* as, say, Shakespeare's 'Full fathom five',
we shall regret Yeats's incapacity for airy fantasy, for free play of subconscious association, and we shall be regretting the absence of virtues
he had no intention to inculcate. Yeats's descriptions of the Dreaming
Back are not, like Shakespeare's astonishing lyric on a dead man's
metamorphosis, intended as graceful entertainment; we ought if anything to read them as the productions of a conscious antiquarian, much
as we read some of the prose of Sir Thomas Browne. They are largely
the almost literal versification of some of the finest writing of Cornelius
Agrippa, whose morbid and obsessive prose inspired Blake as well as
Yeats. The two poets, however, did not go to Agrippa out of mere
connoisseurship in antiquarian learning, or because the sinister beauty

of his imagery was eminently conversible into verse; they went to him because they thought he was in the right and that his philosophy of the ghost was literally true. In *The Dreaming Of The Bones* as elsewhere, Yeats is always the didactic poet; and we ought at this point to be aware of the philosophy he is urging, especially when it is important in *Emer* and the rest of *Four Plays For Dancers* as well as in the present play.

My previous book contains a detailed study of Yeats's philosophy of the ghost,[22] and I need only recapitulate here. He had clearly entrenched himself in his theory by the time he wrote his two essays in *Visions And Beliefs*, which give a complete list of his sources and a coherent account of his beliefs (quoting, indeed, the chapter in Agrippa to which *The Dreaming Of The Bones* stands in relation), as well as providing the summary of *Nishikigi* quoted and containing a number of references to Dante which confirm his influence on the play. Yeats explains that his primary source was Neoplatonism and the Cambridge Platonists Cudworth and Henry More; and that he found confirmation of his theories in orthodox Christianity, Zen Buddhism (the philosophy of many Noh plays), Paracelsus, Agrippa and most of the primitive religious traditions of the world.* Since, like Paracelsus, he was not too proud to 'learn a philosophy from midwife and hangman', he had investigated the superstitions of the Irish peasantry and found much there to bear him out in his theory, and he had also found corroborative evidence in the manifestations at those séances he did not discredit. Finally, he had happened to reread Swedenborg, a visionary independent of the traditions he had been using, and had found there a theory astonishingly similar to his own.

Yeats's philosophy of the ghost may strike the modern reader as the most dubious of his tenets, but this I feel is because of the current tendency to discredit all theories of the life after death of whatever kind: once accept the initial postulates of a purgatory and a condition of beatitude, and Yeats's conception of their nature loses much of its strangeness. His theory is syncretic, and may for this reason seem both difficult and arbitrary, but it is an honest attempt to reconcile the traditions of Christianity with the beliefs of Neoplatonism and the oriental faiths. From Christianity, Yeats took the concepts of purgatory and heaven, though he could not accept the orthodox belief in eternal damnation: hell was for him a condition of eternal fixation in the purgatorial state, which is precisely the situation of his Dermot and Dervorgilla. From Neoplatonism he took the doctrine that the business

* Later, when he knew them better, the *Upanishads* gave him much support.

of the shade is the conquest of emotion; for the unsentimental Platonic philosophy, thinking as it does of all human affections as impure, teaches that they continue to 'obstruct the soul' after death. In Yeats's Dreaming Back, his equivalent for the purgatorial state, the shade consequently relives all the actions and emotions of its past existence, until it is able to purge itself equally of joy and pain, 'pleasure and remorse', the will to good and the will to evil; then it returns to its pre-natal condition of 'pure intelligence', which equips it to enter heaven. Purgatory thus becomes what is essentially a condition of *illusion*—here there is an influence from Zen Buddhism, for example from the Noh play *Motomezuka*—the soul lives among phantasmagoria and confused images from its past life, though it can banish these images at once by an act of pure intelligence; it has only to overcome the emotions, whether of guilt or joy, which cause them to materialise. While the phantasmagoria last, on the other hand, it may be drawn down to those places on earth it associates with them, and then it will manifest, clothed in what Platonism calls the 'body of air', in the form of the ghost. When all emotion is at an end, the body of air will be exchanged for the 'celestial' or 'etherial' body and, after a temporary sojourn in heaven, the soul will be reincarnated into the world. Souls of extreme purity can earn permanent liberation from the wheel of rebirth, and remain in Yeats's condition of the *Marriage*—beatitude— for ever.

Some of the most obviously didactic passages in *Four Plays For Dancers* will resolve directly from this basic summary. The whole plot of *Emer*, for example, is based on what Yeats saw as the soul's condition during the first few days of the Dreaming Back, when—as he learned from Swedenborg, though he could have found similar beliefs in Tantric Buddhism and Tibetan theology—it is not yet 'accustomed' to its 'freedom' and is irresistibly drawn down, clothed in the 'body of air', to the side of its relatives and those it loves:

> All that are taken from our sight, they say,
> Loiter amid the scenery of their lives
> For certain hours or days.

Thus in Yeats's extraordinarily effective dramatic representation, the ghost of Cuchulain, dressed in 'graveclothes', 'crouches' at the bed's foot so as to be near his wife Emer and mistress Eithne Inguba, while his corpse lies on the pillows. The shaping premise of *The Dreaming Of The Bones* is a later phase in this same condition of the Dreaming Back, and we are now able to give names to the authorities the poet hints at:

> Have not old writers said
> That dizzy dreams can spring
> From the dry bones of the dead?

It is in this same process of 'unloosing the knot' of memory, that the dead:

> ... fill waste mountains with the invisible tumult
> Of the fantastic conscience.

And just as Yeats's symbol for purgatory is *dreaming*, so his symbol for beatitude, where the soul escapes from its individual memory into the unselfconscious condition of union with God, is *dreamless sleep*. Thus we are told in *Emer*:

> The dead move ever towards a dreamless youth*
> And when they dream no more return no more.

Thus also Dermot and Dervorgilla long for:

> the sleep
> That lingers always in the abyss of the sky,
> Though they can never reach it.

A similar longing for forgetfulness comes to the ghosts of the soldiers buried in the Abbey churchyard, as their mild purgatorial penance draws to an end:

> They and their enemies of Thomond's party
> Mix in a brief dream-battle above their bones
> Or make one drove, or drift in amity,
> Or, in the hurry of the heavenly round,
> Forget their names.

The movement here is from the Dreaming Back, where the soldiers live among memories of their past battles, to 'amity' as these frenetic dreams die; and finally to a condition of complete unselfconsciousness and oblivion.

So far there could be no reason to confront Yeats's theories with

---

* 'Youth' because the soul resumes in heaven the appearance of its early manhood: the symbol of its spiritual, as once of its physical, perfection.

particular sources, and I cannot see that it was markedly eccentric in him to envisage purgatory and heaven as he did. There is, however, a darker and more macabre element in *The Dreaming Of The Bones* which cannot be normalised so easily. The ghost, we are told, both here and (in more detail) in *A Vision*,[23] not only has a real existence, but is able to transform its plastic and malleable 'body of air' into various shapes, inanimate as well as animate, manifesting as readily as an animal or a plant, a tree or even a stone. Thus the unclean spirit tends to assume 'a monstrous image', while in Yeats's Cuchulain plays, the spirit who is Fand 'dreams herself' first into a hawk and then into the semblance of a beautiful woman so as to thwart his hero. Judas, in the unwritten play Yeats envisaged, was to materialise as 'an old ragpicker', and in *Calvary* ghosts and angels appear in the form of herons, kites and vultures, even as 'an old sheep'. And not only is the ghost subject to these metamorphoses, one often succeeding another at the speed of thought, but it can manufacture an entire hallucinatory world around it in which to suffer punishment; so that, though in fact it may be in some familiar place on earth, 'hovering between a thorn-tree and a stone', it may seem to itself to be enduring death by freezing, burning or immolation, or to be in even more macabre ways 'harried and consumed'. These horrific details, whose intermittent emergence in *The Dreaming Of The Bones* give it so much of its characteristic atmosphere, clearly stand in need of precise exegesis.

We ought to be perfectly clear, first, that Yeats did not concoct his beliefs out of any credulous interest in the sensational; he did so out of an unsqueamish and, I think, profound understanding of the psychology of hallucination. The sufferings and metamorphoses of his ghosts have no *objective* reality; they are, to use Blake's words, 'States that are not but, ah! seem to be'; and they are hallucinations so deeply entertained that they may momentarily impose themselves on the witness as well as on the sufferer. Once we accept the proposition that the post-mortem life is one of dreams, it follows in all logic that the dreamer will build these fantasy-worlds around himself; and Yeats studied this logic in a 'learned school': namely, in the works of Cornelius Agrippa. The precise passage in the *De Occulta Philosophia* on which he founded himself is indicated in *Visions And Beliefs*:

> Agrippa's *De Occulta Philosophia* was once so famous that it found its way into the hands of Irish farmers and wandering Irish tinkers, and it may be that Agrippa influenced the common thought when he wrote that the evil dead see represented 'in the fantastic reason'

those shapes of life that are 'the more turbulent and furious . . . (dreaming) sometimes of the heavens falling upon their heads, sometimes of their being consumed with the violence of flames, sometimes of being drowned in a gulf, sometimes of being swallowed up in the earth, sometimes of being changed into divers forms of beasts'.[24] [Agrippa in fact goes on to list numerous examples of transformation, to tiger, swine, bear, dragon, lioness, fire and running water. Orpheus, he says, has called them the people of dreams, saying, 'The gates of Pluto cannot be unlocked; within is a people of dreams.']

Yeats not only adapts to his play the striking expression here attributed to Orpheus (but by other writers to Pythagoras), saying that Dermot and Dervorgilla are 'now but of the people of dreams', but founds on this text in Agrippa his own description of spirit hallucination:

> Some for an old scruple must hang spitted
> Upon the swaying tops of lofty trees.
> Some are consumed by fire, some withered up
> By hail and sleet out of the wintry north,
> And some but live through their old lives again

And we have only to turn up Agrippa to find other relevant material also:

> the soul being left to the power of a furious phantasy . . . may seem to itself sometimes almost to obtain its delights but to be driven from them . . . into bitter torments, as in the poets, Tantalus from a banquet, Sardanapalus from embraces, Midas from gold, Sisyphus from power.[25]

Thus the whole conception of Dermot and Dervorgilla's penance, so forcibly (and, also, didactically) described in Yeats's dance-scene:

> . . . Why do you dance,
> Why do you gaze, and with such passionate eyes,
> One on the other; and then turn away,
> Covering your eyes?

It is, as I have said, the *karma* or evil consequence of their crime that flows up between them and keeps them separate, and here there are echoes of *Nishikigi*, but the idea of their seeming 'sometimes almost to obtain their delights but to be driven from them' is clearly a detail culled (for its dramatic potential, as previously Yeats had built *Emer* out of a thought in Swedenborg) from the *De Occulta Philosophia*.

It may now be more obvious why I say that the proper comparison for *The Dreaming Of The Bones* is Blake's *Tiriel*, and particularly that seventh section where Tiriel comes 'at eventide' to the 'caves of Zazel'. This means that the death-wish comes over him and beckons him towards the grave; for Blake is building on Agrippa, in whom Zazel is the ruler of the purgatorial condition.

> The flesh being forsaken, and the body being defunct of life . . . is left to the care of the Demon Zazel . . . the dust of the earth is his bread.[26]

Thus 'old Zazel' and his sons 'run from their caves' as Blake's blind old man, led by his daughter, passes, clanking their chains, mocking him and throwing 'dirt and stones' over him, inciting him to join the people of dreams:

Where are you going? Come and eat some roots and drink some water.
Thy crown is bald; the sun will dry thy brains away
And thou wilt be as foolish as thy foolish brother Zazel.

And Tiriel passes on into a wood of 'wild beasts'—ghosts who have taken the shapes of tigers and other 'monstrous images'—his daughter driving them away with her lamentations. Earlier in the poem there is another description of the ghost as shape-changer, and of a living man's struggle against its insinuations, where Blake has Agrippa and the Proteus myth in mind. Proteus, as Yeats says in *Visions And Beliefs*, is in fact the archetype of the ghost, and in Blake's verses a protean apparition 'approaches a living man through his dream-hallucinations':*

. . . sometimes (he) roars a dreadful lion,
Then I have rent his limbs and left him rotting in the forest
For birds to eat; but I have departed from the place
But like a tiger he would come; and so I rent him too.
Then like a river he would seek to drown me in his waves
But soon I buffeted the torrent: anon alike to a cloud
Fraught with the swords of lightning; but I braved the vengeance too.
Then he would creep like a bright serpent, till around my neck

---

* Kathleen Raine, 'Some Sources of Tiriel', Huntingdon Library Quarterly XXI, 1, p. 34; and for my whole paragraph, pp. 25-34. Yeats suspected all that Miss Raine's essay has proved.

While I was sleeping, he would twine: I squeez'd his poisonous soul.
Then like a toad, or like a newt, would whisper in my ears;
Or like a rock stood in my way, or like a pois'nous shrub.

Like much of *The Dreaming Of The Bones*, this is really didactic poetry meant to show the spiritual condition of the evil dead, and if Blake's verses quoted, however incoherent, remain the more imaginative recreation of their common source, Yeats's play is at least fitfully illuminated by flashes of the same intensity. Perhaps he had *Tiriel*, as well as the *De Occulta Philosophia*, in his mind's eye as he wrote.

One respect in which his play is, I think, suggestive beyond *Tiriel* is in Yeats's blending of peasant folk-lore with his medieval occultism; a process which goes on even where he seems most obviously to have a single source.* This does I feel strengthen and deepen his atmosphere, giving his play roots in 'the wisdom of the people', and clearing him from any charge of archaising pedantry. He has several patent allusions to west of Ireland superstition: to the belief that ghosts are only visible to those 'born at midnight'; to the tradition that a cock born in March has particular strength to ward off the powers of darkness; and, centrally, in his sinister recurrent image of the 'cat-headed bird', which is worth a little elaboration. The image connects with the 'man-headed birds' of *The Shadowy Waters* and with many such apparitions in Celtic folk-lore and heroic myth; with the 'catheads' and 'dogheads' with whom Finn did battle; also perhaps with the man-headed bird, the Eanchinn-duine, in the eighteenth-century peasant story which Yeats himself anthologised. This bird was an oracle and demi-god, lived in a cave in the mountains, and very possibly suggested to Yeats his own later bird-god, the Great Herne:

> If there is any possibility of relieving you, that bird can do it, for there is not a bird in the western world so celebrated as that bird, because it knows all things that are past, all things that are present and exist, and all things that shall hereafter exist.[27]

The function of Yeats's own image is of course purely atmospheric, to point the atmosphere of dark expectancy against which his action is played out:

> Why does my heart beat so?
> Did not a shadow pass?

* Against what is said of the psychology of hallucination in the *De Occulta Philosophia*, for instance, we might set the argument in McAnally's *Irish Wonders*.

If we want to rationalise his symbol, however (and we should remember here his belief that Agrippa's theories influenced the course of Irish peasant supernaturalism), we ought probably to see the cat-headed bird as one of Yeats's shape-changers: as a dreaming ghost whose plastic body has momentarily taken on this shape. There are several weird hybrids of this sort among the apparitions described in *A Vision*, and the 'man-headed birds' of *The Shadowy Waters* are certainly the spectres of the dead.*

A more complex blending of occultism and folk-lore takes place in the beautiful song which ends the play, and which tells of the music of purgatory:

> At the grey round of the hill
> Music of a lost kingdom
> Runs, runs, and is suddenly still.

Here Yeats is very obviously thinking of Irish fairy music, whose power to traduce the living man 'moidered in its snare, is one of the commonest of west of Ireland superstitions, and on which he had collected much data for *Visions And Beliefs*. Fairy music is not mentioned anywhere in the song, but we can recognise its cadences, 'soft and low and plaintive' as Lady Wilde describes them,[28] in Yeats's rhythms; and if his spirit harpists seem to be influenced by ancient Irish folk-music also,† we ought to remember that the Irish think even of their traditional airs as supernatural:

The Irish airs, so plaintive, mournful and tear-compelling, are but the remembered echoes of that spirit music which had power to draw souls away to the fairy mansions.[29]

Fairy music is also irresistibly suggested in Yeats's final stanza, despite its faintly biblical undertones:

---

* We ought also to remember Swedenborg, whom Yeats was reading with such assiduity at this time, and whose descriptions of the 'mental state of the damned' are full of such 'terrible birds of night'. He tells for example how the dead create worlds of illusion around them: 'The deserts where they live are merely heaps of stone or barren gravel with bogs full of croaking frogs, *while birds of ill omen fly screeching over their miserable hovels.*' Swedenborg, who understood the psychology of hallucination as thoroughly as Yeats, explains these birds as the 'representative images of their fantasies'.—*The True Christian Religion*, Pars. 45, 661. We know from both Indian and ancient Egyptian art that most primitive peoples believed that gods or ghosts, when they materialised, did so as strange hybrids of the type Yeats represents.

† We may associate here that music for strings played by 'mad fingers' in 'To A Friend Whose Work Has Come To Nothing'.

> Those crazy fingers play
> A wandering airy music.
> Our luck is withered away
> And wheat in the wheat-ear withered.
> And the wind blows it away.

He had learned from Robert Kirk's *The Secret Commonwealth* that fairy merrymaking is the index to a plentiful harvest in their world, and equally to famine in ours: 'when we have plenty, they have scarcity in their homes; and on the contrary'.[30] Thus to the vague suggestion of ill-luck which fairy music always carries could be added the particular prognostication of starvation and dearth.

There is, nevertheless in Yeats's closing song a special gravity, an obsessive weight of melancholy, which no commentary that dismisses it as a fanciful evocation of fairyland can properly explain. There are the biblical cadences which I have mentioned, reminiscent possibly of *Ecclesiastes*, and beyond this the general atmosphere of disconsolate morbidity, as also Yeats's own statement that the instrumentalists are the 'dry bones of the dead':

> What finger first began
> Music of a lost kingdom?
> They dream that laughed in the sun.
> Dry bones that dream are bitter.
> They dream and darken our sun.

If we want to understand how the song acquired its character, what moved Yeats to finish his play with it and to pitch it in the key he did, we shall have to look beyond his sources in folk-lore to his secondary source in Platonic philosophy, which we shall find in Henry More. The Cambridge Platonists were an important influence on Yeats's theory of the ghost, and he was at this time particularly occupied with More in that he found in him much material on the 'body of air'. The dead, More tells us, change their shape at will:

> It being so easy for them to transform their vehicle into what shape they please, and to imitate the figures as dexterously as some men will the voices of brute beasts, whom we may hear sing like a Cuckow, crow like a Cock, bellow like a Cow and Calf . . . and indeed imitate the cry of almost any Bird or Beast whatsoever. And as easie a matter is it for these lower Genii to resemble the shapes of all these Creatures.[31]

Yeats therefore cites More to support Agrippa in those sections of *Visions And Beliefs* which tell how the ghost adapts its shape to its fluctuating dreams; and continues directly to explain that not all the dreams, even of the impure dead, are tormented and evil:

> But there are good dreams among those doing penance, though we cannot properly name that a dream which is but analogical of the deep unattainable virtues and has, therefore, stability and a common measure. Henry More stays himself in the midst of the dry, learned and abstract writing of *The Immortality of the Soul* to praise 'their comely carriage ... their graceful dancing, their melodious singing and playing with an accent so sweet and soft as if we should imagine air itself to compose and send forth musical sounds without the help of any terrestrial instrument' and imagines them, in the thin upper air where the earth can but seem 'a fleecy and milky light' as the moon to us, and he cries out that they 'sing and play and dance together, reaping the lawful pleasures of the very animal life, in a far higher degree than we are capable of in this world, for everything here does, as it were, taste of the cask and has some measure of foulness in it'.[32]

The beginning of this extract does not do justice to More's picturesque and masculine style, from which Yeats's imagination clearly caught fire as much as from the darker vision of Agrippa, but it does show how strongly he was drawn to the charming and moving digression he mentions. More does indeed speak of that mood which comes to the penitential shade 'when the fancy consorts with that first exemplar of Beauty, Intellectual Love and Virtue, and the body is wholly obedient to the imagination of the mind, and will in every Punctilio yield to the impresses of that inward pattern'; and tells how, so moved, 'they cannot but enravish one another's Souls, when they are mutual Spectators of the perfect pulchritude of one another's persons'.[33] Their bodies, we must understand, have changed now to the semblance of that perfect beauty they are meditating. Captivated thus, they make music of their delight and longing, not with instruments, for 'the tenderer Ear cannot but feel the rude thumpings of the wood and gratings of the rosin, the hoarseness, or some harshness or untunableness or other, in the best consorts of Musical Instruments and Voices';[34] but as if from the air itself. This amusing and truly imaginative passage, written with much emotion by a philosopher who himself loved music and thought it the highest function of intellectual beauty, gave Yeats the metaphysical explanation he sought for his Celtic folk-superstition.

What the peasant called 'fairy music', then, could be rationalised—at least to the poetic imagination—as the music of purgatory, born out of a spiritual longing in the shade for the peace that was withheld from it. Perhaps Yeats's own song remembers More's 'music of the lower and more deeply lapsed Daemons', which More says is more gloomy and disconsolate than that described above;[35] there is certainly a note of *morbidezza* in it, and it conveys with almost frightening success the aimlessness and mental vacuousness of the instrumentalists. Its function in the play is both to contrast and combine with the main action; to image the more negative and passive aspect of the purgatorial condition, which has been understressed in the need to enlarge on the violent torment of Dermot and Dervorgilla (though it has been suggested in the first chorus, where the valley 'overflows' with a strange, nameless emotion); and also to show the nearness of the ghost to the heavenly condition of 'dreamless sleep', as we have previously been shown its agonising separation from that condition. And indeed I think it is beautifully integrated into the text; it completes it by sounding a note for which we have long been listening:

> Even the sunlight can be lonely here,
> Even hot noon is lonely.

For this loneliness Yeats has now provided the perfect symbol.

IV

The ghosts of Dermot and Dervorgilla, their memories fixated on the moment of their betrayal of Ireland, need the good karma that will follow upon the intercession of the living if they are to progress through the Dreaming Back. They materialise before a young rebel, on his way to a hiding-place in the Aran islands, and he answers for all the youth of Ireland in turning away from them. The logic of all this should by now be perfectly clear, but what is needed, to make the play an artistic unity, is a clinching symbol: a device which will weld together aesthetically, and not by arbitrary and melodramatic association, Yeats's two themes of politics and ghosts. This device is provided, if we care to read the play at any deep level, in the image of the 'red March cock'.

We are not *forced* to read any such significance into Yeats's central recurrent symbol, whose immediate, and I do not dispute central, function, is to establish a simple day-night antithesis. Everyone has enough folk-lore in their veins to know the cock as an emblem of consciousness and sanity, at whose awakening all the apparitions of the night must disperse; it is used so in *Hamlet*, and of course (like the owl, which stands at the other pole of Yeats's antithesis) it is there in *Nishikigi*:

> Ari-aki
> The dawn.
> Come, we are out of place.
> Let us go ere the light comes.

Yeats's own bird is more explicitly a *March* cock, and this is in deference to a west of Ireland belief that a 'cock of the springtime' (perhaps because of its gospel associations) is a more powerful defence against the supernatural than any other. Yeats has a passage that is relevant in *Visions And Beliefs*:

> There was a man walking one night and he felt a woman come and walk behind him, and she all in white. And the two of them walked on till sunrise, and then a cock crowed, and the man said, 'There's a cock crowing.' And she said, 'That's only a weak cock of the summer.' And soon after another cock crowed, and he asked did she hear it and she said, 'That's but a poor cock of the harvest.' And the third time a cock crowed and when the man asked her she said, 'That's a cock of March. And you're as wise as the man that doesn't tell Friday's dream on Saturday.'[36]

For Friday's dreams, in west of Ireland superstition, are peculiarly sacrosanct: the ghost is commending the man on his diplomatic reserve, and on the tact with which he has suggested that she might disappear. She saw no reason to do so for a summer or an autumn cock, but the behest of a March bird has to be obeyed.

If we take the symbolism beyond this, it will probably not be on first watching the play; but Yeats wanted an audience to meditate his choruses after leaving the theatre, and we may do so if we wish. One possible extension of meaning—and it is the virtue of symbolist poetry that multiple associations do simultaneously arise from it in this way— is suggested by the traditional symbolism of 'Byzantium'. There I have shown in my previous book that the cock serves as a reincarnation emblem: the cock of Hades, of Hermes Psychopompus, had this significance in Greek and Roman religion, as Yeats knew from Eugenie

Strong; and he also remembered it as a rebirth symbol from his own Order of the Golden Dawn.[37] In his poem the soul, imaged as a golden bird, reaches beatitude or the apex of the tree of life, and there by the symbol of cockcrow announces its desire to be reborn into the time-world (or, the poem goes on, if it is 'embittered' against the 'moon' of generation, 'scorns' the time-world altogether):

> Miracle, bird or golden handiwork,
> More miracle than bird or handiwork,
> Planted on the star-lit golden bough
> Can like the cocks of Hades crow
> Or, by the moon embittered, scorn aloud
> In glory of changeless metal
> Common bird or petal
> And all complexities of mire or blood.

There is also the poem 'A Last Confession', where Yeats says, if we will give his verse symbolic dimension, that when lovers are united in heaven no thought of reincarnation can come between them. No cock dare crow to remind them of this eventual separation:

> There's not a bird of day that dare
> Extinguish that delight.[38]

With these usages in mind, we may concede a possible (though by no means definite) undertone of the same kind in Yeats's play; and that his invocations of cockcrow may embody a pious prayer for Dermot and Dervorgilla's eventual escape from the Dreaming Back and rebirth into time. The audience, after all, is expected to feel compassion for their sufferings, and the play would not realise its full potential if this pity-motif were not allowed to work itself out.

The third connotation of Yeats's image is less hypothetical and I think follows inevitably, for the reader versed in the traditional symbolism, from the guiding adjective in his phrase *red* March cock. Why should this colour adjective be used, if not to stress that the bird is the red symbolic bird of Mars, regent of war and in Yeats's system (as we know from the poem 'Conjunctions') of the first bloody phases of a new historical cycle?* We know from many poems and plays[39] that Yeats expected the 'cycle of freedom' to begin with world-wide

---

* 'Red' can also mean 'lusty', which gives the adjective a meaning at the exoteric level, but in itself hardly justifies Yeats's choice of it.

wars—involving among other things the liberation of Ireland—at a full moon in March, the month of Mars; nor will it have escaped his notice that the Easter Rising of 1916 came almost exactly at this time, a fact which would make it ominously portentous of the new order. We also know that the cock is his frequent symbol for the herald of a new era, as for example in his poem 'Solomon And The Witch', written at the same period as *The Dreaming Of The Bones*:

> He that crowed out eternity
> Thought to have crowed it in again.

He had used the symbol in the same way, years before, in 'The Adoration Of The Magi', where an old woman prophesies the coming of the new historical cycle; first a cock crows through her mouth, and then she is possessed by the God:

> I am Hermes the Shepherd of the Dead, and you have heard my sign that has been my sign from the old days.

Yeats had learned that the cock was the emblem of cyclic change from Hermes Trismegistus, where the symbol is traced back to ancient Egyptian religion, while G. R. S. Mead had taught him to think of the cock of the gospels (which crows as the Christian historical era is about to begin), in a similar light;* and he had later parodied the Christian aspect of the image in his farce *The Player Queen*. There, at the moment of cyclical change, an old man rolls in the straw and brays like an ass;[40] a comic substitute for the cock of tradition:

> Old Man: When I bray I like a donkey, the crown changes (viz. a new cycle eventuates). . . . It is the donkey that carried Christ into Jerusalem, and that is why he is so proud.

With all these instances before us, I think a similar reading in the present context inevitable.

Yeats's cock is for me on one plane the symbol of heroic martial endeavour and of that universal anarchy that he thought would usher in the collapse of the present 'objective' age; which the Dublin rebellion seemed to him at this time to presage. Any reading which ignores this connotation seems to me to fall down, and this simply because it must

---

* The Mead passage is prominently quoted in *A Vision*.

reject certain passages as meaningless. The first relevant chorus admittedly is not complex in this way: it takes up a phrase from the play's opening (itself a reminiscence of the final chorus of *Emer*), and is an invocation of dawn, sanity, the safe material world:

> Why should the heart take fright?
> What sets it beating so?
> The bitter sweetness of the night
> Has made it but a lonely thing.
> Red bird of March, begin to crow!
> Up with the neck and clap the wing,
> Red cock, and crow.

The chorus following, however, can hardly be taken at this level: it is no longer an expression of fear, but of joy:

> My head is in a cloud.
> I'd let the whole world go.
> My rascal heart is proud
> Remembering and remembering.
> Red bird of March, begin to crow!
> Up with the neck and clap the wing,
> Red cock, and crow.

I see no possible reading here save in the context of the Easter Rising, the reference, perhaps, being deliberately veiled in Yeats's anxiety not to make his play too inflammatory for the stage; there is certainly no allusion to ghosts, daybreak or returning normality. We must surely interpret: 'I exult in the thought of the Rising [which the Young Man has been discussing on the previous page]; nothing else in the world seems to matter. My heart is full of pride at the memory of the courage that was shown during those few days, and I pray that the new era, when Ireland will regain her liberty, will soon begin.' This theme is presently reintroduced with the fourth line of the following stanza:

> The dreaming bones cry out
> Because the night winds blow
> And heaven's a cloudy blot.
> Calamity can have its fling.
> Red bird of March, begin to crow!
> Up with the neck and clap the wing,
> Red cock, and crow.

Here the two aspects of Yeats's theme are conjoined, and the cock is *both* the herald of daybreak and of the historical reversal approaching. We have three lines to establish the former connotation, but the fourth must mean that the 'calamity' of the unsuccessful Easter rebellion is only a phase and that the final victory is certain. And even the three lines apparently off the subject carry a secondary inflection (though I would not myself stress this): together with the literal meaning, one might think of the bones of the Irish heroic dead 'crying out' with anguish at the failure of the rising, when the 'night winds' of calamity 'blot out' the 'heaven' of their ambition for a free Ireland. All the symbols used recur in this precise political sense in Yeats's later poem 'The Black Tower';[41] and he has even prepared for this reading by explaining, a few lines earlier in his play, that the fields of Clare-Galway are red with the blood of the heroic dead:

> I have no dread (of the dead)
> They cannot put me into gaol or shoot me
> And seeing that their blood has returned to fields
> That have grown red with drinking blood like mine
> They would not, if they could, betray.

When, in the final chorus, Yeats goes on to say confidently that

> Now the night *is* gone.
> I have heard from far below
> The strong March birds a-crow

I take him on one plane to be fortifying himself in his earlier political prophecy, a belief which is strengthened by the bold heroic cadences of the musical score.

That Yeats wished us to see layer below layer of meaning in his symbolism there can be no doubt; unpopular as his technique may be at the present time, he tells us again and again that this was his method of communication. His cock emblem thus becomes, in a sense, a creaking piece of mechanism; it makes a laborious finale to a laborious play. The action, indeed, might be said to creak in other respects as well: there are Dermot and Dervorgilla themselves, who remain always stage ghosts, never winning our total and unforced acceptance like the lovers in *Nishikigi*; and there is Yeats's climax—'Never, never, Shall Diarmuid and Dervorgilla be forgiven'—which offends an audience's aesthetic susceptibilities as it does, I think, because it is so stridently theatrical. If tempers had not been inflamed at the time he wrote, perhaps Yeats might have seen that his lovers ought for aesthetic reasons to have been absolved,* or at least to have been denied their peace in some less militant formula: purgatory, after all, is realler than local patriotism. There is also Yeats's recurrent bone-imagery, which I have not studied in detail, largely because it is not one of the successes of the play. He concentrates here rather unimaginatively on the obvious macabre values of the symbol, which becomes one of his great emblems only much later with the poem 'Three Things', where a 'wave-whitened' bone, cast up by the Sea of Eternity, sings its paean to love and pleasure.

All this does not really amount to a condemnation of Yeats's dance-play, for I am pointing out no more than the defects of its qualities. The cock-symbol, for instance, seems laborious only because it is a fully realised traditional image, and would not seem so to a reader at home in that symbology: the cycles of day, rebirth and history are of course complementary, and (as in his song of Minnaloushe) Yeats has done nothing more devious than explore each aspect of his image fully. His other apparent failures similarly mask hidden strengths: if Dermot and Dervorgilla move stiffly, the shades which move behind them remain frighteningly real; while as for his political rhetoric, it is partly the spontaneous overflow of his intense feeling for place, in which the true patriotism of the play resides. Perhaps this is not enough to save the play on the stage, where I think it a successful melodrama in proportion to its artistic failure. As a dramatic poem, however, the descriptive and metaphysical verse redresses the balance, and (for me at least) it gains in stature each time that it is read.

* We have, after all, his own splendid epigram in *Ideas Of Good And Evil*: that art ought not to be the 'accusation', but the 'forgiveness of sins'. 'Accusation', Yeats thought, made for rhetoric, since writing thus orientated would hardly rise from the deepest human emotions. But of course, in the months after the Easter Rising, it is not strange that he should have departed from his own axiom, and I would not want it thought that I undervalue the bitterness and suffering an Irishman must have experienced at this time.

APPENDIX TO PART TWO

THE BRIDEGROOM (*1923*)

THERE ARE FOUR drafts[1] of the nameless unfinished dance-play to which I have given this title. Yeats began it in verse but continued in prose and the final form might well have been a simple, naïve prose like that of *Fighting The Waves*. The play has five scenes and in this respect is unlike any Noh play; its loose, episodic construction is something like that of the *The Herne's Egg*. None of the characters has been given a name.

After the rough draft of a chorus, where Yeats planned to work in allusions to the Irish myth of Cloona of the Wave, the action begins with an old fisherman sitting down to rest after mending his net. A young girl runs down the hill to ask whether he has a letter for her from her lover. The old man has a letter, but conceals it so as to keep her in talk; he is attracted to her and persuades her to sit down on his net—a piece of patent sexual symbolism. He asks her story. She says that she is an orphan who lives in an old abandoned tower on the hill, and that she would marry her lover if his mother would allow it, but the mother hates her. The old man says that the mother is probably jealous of her beauty and youth; and he tells her how bitterly he regrets the loss of his own youth, and the transience of those love-affairs he once thought would be eternal. The young girl falls asleep while he talks, and the old man amuses himself by imagining how it will be when her lover comes to visit her at the tower; the tower is clearly symbolic, resembling on one plane the tower in which Hero waited for Leander; on another plane we are reminded of Dante's winding stair where only 'goodness' can bring man to the summit of the stairway, of Axel's Castle and even perhaps of the alchemical tower of Olympus;* while there is also an imagery of turning which may associate the penetration of the stairway with the sexual act. While the old man talks the girl cries out in her sleep; she is dreaming of a lover who is a prince and comes with a retinue of horsemen. Her real lover

* The girl's chamber is at the summit of the stairway, like the elixir in the Rosicrucian myth.

is a young fisherman, and the old man thinks that her dream is wish-fulfilment and that she would really like a richer husband. She wakes; he gives her the letter and she leaves him. The scene closes with the old man predicting a great storm.

The rather scrappy second scene shows the girl's lover quarrelling with his mother, who is a bitter old woman and is said to play the hawk to the young girl's dove. He plans to row over to the tower, which is at a river-mouth, and his mother prays that he may be drowned in that night's storm if he does so.

The third scene shows the young man knocking at the tower door. The girl, half-awake, speaks through the door and (still engrossed in her dream) says that he cannot be her lover, for her lover is with her already: his horsemen are bedded in the ante-rooms and their horses, shod in gold and silver, are in the stables. The young man puts the natural interpretation on all this and goes off in a rage. Then the old fisherman comes with a lantern bringing bad news for him: his boat has been washed away in the storm. Grasping what has happened he is afraid the young man may attempt suicide and goes with the girl to look for him.

Scene Four takes place at the river-mouth where, after some rather unsqueamish comedy as the old fisherman discusses where a corpse might most likely be washed up, he finally sees the young man being carried downstream by the waves. He has thrown himself into the river and they hear his dying prayer, invoking blessing on the girl and on the other man to whom she has given herself; a prayer that they may be happy together always. He dies with a broken phrase about the lark, a reminiscence of one of their partings in the tower. The girl takes up the phrase, saying that it is no lark but the nightingale, that the whole night is theirs and it will be eternal, and throws herself into the river and dies trying to reach him. The *Romeo And Juliet* reminiscence recurs in Yeats's poem 'Parting'; and the relevance of the myth of Cloona now also becomes clear, since Cloona also drowned for love. One should add that this is the dance scene of the play: there would have been no river, no death struggles or impossible stage effects, but simply a lantern and a darkened stage and two masked dancers playing out a dance of suicide by drowning. This daring and brilliantly dramatic device will not seem strange to anyone versed in the Noh, and it would have made this perhaps the most exciting dance scene in all Yeats's plays.

The old fisherman buries the lovers under two crossed sticks (the symbol, together with its religious connotations, of sexual passion) and the last scene shows him pointing out the grave to the young man's mother. As he does so, the ghost of the young girl materialises, dressed in graveclothes: she has come to forgive the mother, saying that beyond the grave she and her lover are reunited: he is with her, her prince is with her, with all his carriages and horsemen. The mother ignores this strange last phase, announcing angrily that the girl has returned from the dead to triumph over her; and the draft finishes with the old woman's bitter speech of self-justification. Yeats was not generally given to the 'accusation of sins' and, here as in *Deirdre*, he gives his villain the last word.

I have not quoted Yeats's text because Mrs. Yeats does not wish it, and I want to stress that, while the prose version especially is distinguished by what the Japanese call *awaré* (gentle sympathy), what we have is in every sense an unfinished, inadequate play, undeserving of publication as an independent work. The *meaning*, however, is of very considerable interest and indicates the answer to what Virginia Moore thinks a central problem in Yeats's art: 'What did love, Agape (as opposed to Eros), mean to him, love in the high caritative, charismatic sense?'[2] The play is clearly about the doctrine of the image, used in the Noh play *Awoi No Uze*.[3] This piece of mystical doctrine will be familiar from Shelley's *Prometheus Unbound*, while a modern play that turns on it is Eliot's *The Cocktail Party*. The very ancient tradition is that every human being has an image or *ka*; a purer self which does not participate in the tumult of mere everyday living but stands always a little outside it; the personality is united with the *ka* after death. Yeats's argument is that every lover is really in love with this higher self as he discerns it in the beloved; in waking life we cannot come very close to the higher self, but in dreams we can; thus the young girl dreams of her prince (Yeats's symbol for the higher self) and it is this higher self, her true bridegroom, whom she loves beyond the grave. But in using the symbol of the prince Yeats makes his argument more complicated: the prince is traditionally the symbol of Christ in his character as Rex Mundi and the horsemen, in Christian iconography (as in Yeats's *The Unicorn From The Stars*), will be Christ's attendant angels. Thus Yeats is boldly saying that the higher self in every man is identical with Christ; it is the Christ in man that a woman discerns and gives her love to; and this tremendous statement is meant in a quite literal sense. Yeats had read, in the Syriac Christian *Hymn of Bardesan*,[4] that the higher self may be identified with Christ, and this is true, he says, even of a goat-girl and a young fisherman, even of adolescent passion and what the world calls illicit love.

The symbolism of bride and bridegroom is on one plane, and that a very relevant one, specifically Christian, and I think I detect an influence from the *Songs* of St. John of the Cross, where the symbols of tower, nightingale and divine horsemen also occur.[5] The knocking at the door and the lantern are also symbols with a Christian aura. Finally, the play probably owes something to Flaubert's *La Spirale* (cited in *A Vision*),[6] where a young man unluckily in love has dreams of a princess, and his love for the princess prospers despite his failure in real life. Yeats, I think, took this story as an unconsciously projected narrative of the higher self, and not as a case-history of Freudian wish-fulfilment.

PART THREE

POEMS

'Some little song about a rose . . . those hard symbolic bones under the skin.'—*A Vision*.

CHAPTER SEVEN

TWELVE RELATED POEMS

THIS SECTION OF the book is bound to contain some reiterative matter, for some (not all) of the poems in question have been glossed in the previous essays; but I want now to look at each in a new context, the context of Yeats's developing thought as opposed to that of his plays. The first four poems chosen connect with *At The Hawk's Well*, and enable me to subject the image-cluster used for the play to a more thorough scrutiny than I have so far had space for; also to go into detail on the origins and genesis of Yeats's tree-symbolism. 'The Collar-Bone Of A Hare', 'At Algeciras', 'Mohini Chatterjee' and 'The Statues' all in different ways connect with *Emer*. 'The Wheel', 'The Hour Before Dawn' and 'Demon And Beast' are poems about objectivity and thus associate with *Calvary*. Finally 'Solomon And The Witch' bears out my interpretation of the cock-symbol in *The Dreaming Of The Bones*, which I take to be the least thoroughly substantiated of my conclusions so far. In a sense the essay as a whole is 'about' Yeats's tree-symbolism and thus is meant both as a supplement and a corrective to Kermode's valuable study.

THE TWO TREES
MONGAN THINKS OF HIS PAST GREATNESS
TOWARDS BREAK OF DAY
MEDITATIONS IN TIME OF CIVIL WAR I

I am glad to begin this chapter with two of Yeats's very early poems, if only because the beautiful poetry of his early period has sometimes been undervalued in the past. The poems I have chosen both connect with *At The Hawk's Well*, which is why I am treating them; and beyond this they are I feel representative of Yeats's method in his early verse. They may not be among the *best* work of this period— 'Aedh Wishes For The Cloths Of Heaven' is perhaps Yeats's most consummate early lyric and 'The Man Who Dreamed of Faeryland' (especially in the revised version) his most sustained achievement, while, for sheer delight in the narrative aspect of myth, one might single out 'Under The Moon'—but they are I would say characteristic undertakings and show particularly well the kind of poetry he was trying to write. The sophistication of Yeats's early poetry, what makes his sensuous and highly-coloured lyrics at least potentially adult where so many similar productions of the period fail to affect us today, is a direct consequence of his knowledge of myth; he writes with full reliance on his esoteric archetypes, and out of an extensive study of comparative symbolism, so that even his early poetry has an intellectual substructure as well as a surface richness. The lyrics under consideration illustrate this fact, while they also represent his first strivings towards that tree-symbolism so important to his mature art, and which reappears in such poems as 'Solomon And The Witch', 'Among School Children', 'Byzantium', 'At Algeciras' and 'Vacillation'. What I write here will presently be seen to be commentary on these works as well, and it is for this reason that I go into so much detail.

The two trees in the poem of that name present no problems of identification, for they are very obviously the scriptural Tree of Life and Tree of Knowledge, the first of which gave our 'original parents' the token of beatitude while the second brought about their fall. Kermode suggests that Yeats's first verse has a part-source in Blake,[1] and quotes one of the songs from 'Poetical Sketches', where the Tree of Life symbolises the 'creative imagination', joy and 'divine energy'. Here is the beginning of the poem:

> Love and harmony combine
> And around our souls entwine
> Whilst thy branches mix with mine
> And our roots together join.
>
> Joys upon our branches sit
> Chirping loud and singing sweet;
> Like gentle streams beneath our feet
> Innocence and virtue meet.

And Blake goes on to describe how, when lovers are thus united to become an image of the Tree of Life, 'golden fruit' are borne and 'love himself' has his nest among the 'lovely leaves'; details which are certainly remembered in Yeats's own text. In the same way Yeats's second verse will owe something to Blake's elaborate descriptions of the Tree of Knowledge or of Mystery, which is his symbol for the fallen world and fallen morality, all that 'barrenly discursive and prudential knowledge' that the 'brigand apple' brought into the world.

> Urizen fix'd in envy sat brooding & covered with snow
> His book of iron on his knees ... till underneath his heel a deadly root
> Struck through the rock, the root of Mystery accursed shooting up
> Branches into the heaven of Los.[2]

Blake situates his Tree of Mystery in a landscape much like that with which Yeats's poem ends, making it branch over the 'dismal abyss' among snows and 'gloomy rocks'; and any man, we may infer from his poem 'A Poison Tree', can convert himself into its image, as readily as into that of the Tree of Life.

For all this it would not be responsible scholarship to suggest that Yeats took over his tree directly from Blake, for this was quite simply not his method. Blake confirmed him in believing that the traditional symbolism could be used in modern poetry, and indeed showed him how to use it, but Yeats borrowed no image from his poetry simply because it was there; he worked backwards from Blake to Blake's sources in myth and wrote in conformity with what he believed to be the shaping religious conventions of the world. In this case he made an elaborate excursion into comparative symbolism, which convinced him that the tree was an archetype in all the world's religious symbologies; and for this reason he adopted it, incorporating in the process many details which Blake does not use and indeed may not have known. He began from a passage in Rhys's *Celtic Heathendom* important also to *At The Hawk's Well*, and where the well and hazel of Connla are connected with the Norse Yggdrasil as symbols of the ubiquitous Tree of Life; Rhys also calls into question the oak and spring of Dodona, and associates the spring with the *soma* or waters of regeneration in Indian myth.[3] Yeats presently read the long description of Dodona in Ennemoser's *History of Magic*,[4] which is the source of his famous allusion in *The Cutting Of An Agate*. From these works he went on to d'Alviella, a scholar in symbolism famous in the 'nineties, and found in his *The Migration of Symbols* an elaborate and extremely accurate account of tree-symbolism throughout the world. The scriptural tree of beatitude is associated with the tree of the Buddha—a correspondence several times celebrated in Yeats's mature verse—as symbols of 'eternal life, productive power, perfect happiness, supreme knowledge'; the Vedic heaven-tree is compared with that guarded by the dragon of the Hesperides, and this gave Yeats the raw materials for his lyric 'Aedh Pleads With The Elemental Powers' while the tree of knowledge is connected with the cross on which Christ died, a commonplace of theosophy on which he several times draws.* There are especially important references to the 'bird', emblem of resurrection or reincarnation, which is sometimes shown 'perched in the tree's fork', and to tree-symbolism in Justinian's Byzantium, where the esoteric significance is said to have been imparted by architects from the east.[5]

The tree, then, was in every sense an archetypal symbol, and Yeats's central source of all those known to him was beyond doubt the Jewish Kabbala, which he imagined (probably wrongly) had also influenced Blake. In his translation of *Kabbala Unveiled*, Mathers explains that the typical Kabbalistic representation of the Tree of Life is as an *apple tree*,† which grows from the earth to the apex of heaven and bears the sun and moon for fruit; its image grows within the soul of every man and connects him with God. In the branches of the tree, birds perch, or the 'souls' of the dead and 'angels' have their place, and beneath it the 'beasts' or fallen angels lurk in the shade.[6] There are many seeming reminiscences of this tree in Yeats's early verse, as when he speaks of 'The silver apples of the moon/The golden apples of the sun'; the Kabbalistic image gives his comparisons of Maud Gonne's hair to 'apple-blossom' their mystical connotation; and a song in *The King's Threshold* establishes his indebtedness beyond doubt. It is interesting to see how Yeats incorporates the 'well' symbolism of Irish myth, as also the 'root' symbolism connected with Yggdrasil, into this description of 'the four rivers of paradise'.

> The four rivers that run there
> Through well-mown level ground
> Have come out of a blessed well
> That is all bound and wound
> By the great roots of an apple
> And all the fowl of the air
> Have gathered in the wide branches
> And keep singing there.

---

* Much that Yeats read was naturally confirmed for him in conversations with his associates in the occult, but I am concerned here only with what he learned from those books he himself mentioned as important to his early thought.

† This passage was clearly of crucial importance in Yeats's iconography, as can be gathered from the several occasions on which I have already had to gloss it.

This, according to the fable of the play, is part of a song by Seanchan:

> It's out of a poem I made long ago
> About the Garden in the East of the World
> And how spirits in the images of birds
> Crowed in the branches of old Adam's crab-tree.

An equally obvious later allusion comes in 'Vacillation':

> From man's blood-sodden heart are sprung
> Those branches of the night and day
> Where the gaudy moon is hung.

My last book has explained the obliquer reference in 'Byzantium'[7] and there is another in the last verse of 'Among School Children', where a memory of *Wilhelm Meister*—'boughs, leaves, buds, blossoms and fruit . . . are they not all one and there by means of each other?' —is probably appropriated into Yeats's image for *unitum mundum*, the essential identity of all life.[8]

The first verse of 'The Two Trees' is a clear gloss of the Kabbalistic image, as we can see from Yeats's insistence that the tree grows 'within' the human heart and the suggestion that the sun and moon are its fruit. He is describing the religious discipline of 'joy', of subjective thought where the 'intellect' does not operate alone but is co-ordinated with the other faculties into 'imagination'; the process by which God may be discerned as present within the human personality. In the same way the Kabbala intends symbolism of the 'Way' leading from the human heart through the 'Sephiroth' (or archetypal ideas), to union with the divine.* By subjective contemplation, Yeats says, we can discover the radical law of the universe, that all manifested and all interior life, the stars, the sea, music, spiritual peace, are united in one chain of affirmation; affirmation of a God who is intrinsically present within the Self:

> Beloved, gaze in thine own heart,
> The holy tree is growing there;
> From joy the holy branches start
> And all the trembling flowers they bear.

---

* For a discussion of this 'Way', see part one of my *Calvary* essay. A diagram of the 'Sephirotic tree' is given in Mathers; and, though a Jewish Kabbalist might find the definition of the Sephiroth as 'Ideas', rather loose, we have to remember that Yeats derived his early knowledge of the Kabbala entirely from Mathers, from whom my phrase is taken.

> The changing colours of its fruit
> Have dowered the stars with merry light
> The surety of its hidden root
> Has planted quiet in the night.
> The shaking of its leafy head
> Has given the waves their melody
> And made my lips and music wed
> Murmuring a wizard song for thee.*

The Celtic tincture of the last lines here serves to remind us that Yeats's symbol is, on one level, the hazel of Connla, and his imagery becomes even more syncretic in the continuation, where he takes up with some of the detail of Blake's song already rehearsed:

> There, through bewildered branches, go
> Winged loves borne on in gentle strife
> Tossing and tossing to and fro
> The flaming circle of our life.
> While looking on their shaken hair
> And dreaming how they dance and dart
> Thine eyes grow full of tender care;
> Beloved, gaze in thine own heart.

These 'winged loves' are of course the 'divine ideas', materialising, by a process explained in my *Calvary* essay,[9] in concrete form and tracing the pattern of the 'eternal dance'; they are the 'immortal Grecian faces and august Egyptian faces' of the early alchemical stories; the pantheon of the Gods or the emanations of the Sephiroth. The end of 'joy' is to perceive them and they are shown tossing from bough to bough, like some hoop, the 'circle'—'flaming' with spirituality—of the lovers' united lives. On one plane this is a reference to the magic protective circles of Druidism, for the Immortals will work to keep their votaries from harm; but Yeats also glosses the fact (which he had already learned from Madame Blavatsky) that man's life is a microcosm of the cycle of history; and there is even allusion to the circle as an emblem of eternity, and of the immortality of the soul.

The second verse presents us with another tree, which we shall be right to equate with Blake's Tree of Mystery; but Yeats's precise justification for his new symbol is probably an esoteric detail of Kabbalistic tradition. The Sephirotic tree, as Ellmann has noted,

* I quote the versions of these early poems that Yeats published in the 'nineties: later he revised them stylistically. Here, 'wizard' has for me a Celtic tincture in that it suggests a bardic incantation.

presents two faces to the world, 'one benign, the reverse side malign ... on one side are the Sephiroth, and on the other the dread Qlippoth'.[10] The Qlippoth are evil spirits antithetical to Yeats's 'Immortals'; or we may say that they represent the divine ideas in their dark or malevolent aspect, for the Kabbalists were well aware of what Jung calls 'the bipolarity of all archetypes'; that they may manifest for good or ill. Yeats represents the Qlippoth naïvely as 'demons', and shows them holding up a magic looking-glass of the kind familiar from many fairy stories—there is one such in his unpublished novel *The Speckled Bird*[11]—where the Tree of Life presents a distorted and misshapen reflection. This new image is the external temporal world as the untutored senses may perceive it; a desolate landscape in which the sense of unity and divine purpose has been lost. Yeats follows Platonism (as for example the myth of Dionysus)[12] in insisting that this fallen world is nevertheless a distorted mirror-image of the real; the Kabbalists also represent the 'world of evil' as an inverted image of the good;[13] and his symbol for the 'objective' universe is thus perfectly traditional:

> Gaze no more in the bitter glass
> The demons, with their subtle guile,
> Lift up before us when they pass,
> Or only gaze a little while;
> For there a fatal image grows
> With broken boughs and blackened leaves
> And roots half-hidden under snows
> Driven by a storm that ever grieves.
> For all things turn to barrenness
> In the dim glass the demons hold,
> The glass of outer weariness
> Made when God slept in times of old.

Having by this rather Blakean detail established himself in his new symbolism, Yeats completes his poem with imagery suggestive of the Yggdrasil of Norse myth, where like Cuchulain in his dance-play Odin comes in search of wisdom and purchases it at the cost of an eye. Yggdrasil is perhaps the nearest approximation in myth to the 'evil aspect' of the tree-archetype, and the choice is therefore appropriate:

> There, through the broken branches, go
> The ravens of unresting thought;
> Peering and flying to and fro
> To see men's souls bartered and bought.

> When they are heard upon the wind
> And when they shake their wings, alas!
> Thy tender eyes grow all unkind;
> Gaze no more in the bitter glass.

In this way, with a reference to Odin's ravens and a reminiscence (which he later deleted) of *The Countess Cathleen*,[14] Yeats brings his delicately emotional and at the same time elaborately learned little poem to an end.

'The Two Trees' is an engaging enough piece of immature verse, and it is interesting to the student of Yeats's mind as the first statement we have of his theory of subjectivity and objectivity, even though he had not yet read Nietzsche and could not have attached to his theory these names. It also points forward to the whole range of his later tree symbolism, which implies always a simplified form of the antithesis postulated here. Whenever life is presented as joyous activity, as in 'Among School Children' or the second part of 'Vacillation', Yeats is likely to bring forward his symbol of the green tree in full leaf. Whenever bitterness and a sense of failure are to be stressed the dry tree is chosen, as in *Purgatory* or even the simplest of his beggar poems, 'The Lamentation Of The Old Pensioner', for instance:

> Although I shelter from the rain
> Under a broken tree . . .

The 'blasted oak' under which Crazy Jane stands is a variant on the dry tree image, and so is the symbol in 'A Meditation In Time Of War':

> For one throb of the artery
> While on that old grey stone I sat
> Under the old wind-broken tree
> I knew that one is animate,
> Mankind inanimate fantasy.

For almost the whole day the absolute is unattainable and Yeats therefore presents his image in its negative aspect, but there is 'a moment in each day that Satan cannot find' and for this moment we may, if we wish, imagine the tree growing green.

If we now want to come closer to *At The Hawk's Well* and see Yeats in act of identifying his Kabbalistic tree and Connla's hazel, and connecting both with a philosophy of the Self and of 'present immortality' similar to that of his dance-play, we could do worse than look at 'Mongan Thinks Of His Past Greatness'. This is usually taken as a poem 'about' metempsychosis, and an analogy has been drawn with the slightly earlier 'Fergus And The Druid', some lines from which are worth quoting here:

> I see my life go drifting like a river
> From change to change; I have been many things,
> A green drop in the surge, a gleam of light
> Upon a sword, a fir-tree on a hill,
> An old slave grinding at a heavy quern,
> A king sitting upon a chair of gold.

I doubt whether Yeats ever took metempsychosis* very seriously, and 'Fergus And The Druid' is hardly evidence to the contrary; he uses the theory there because it is ornamental and 'mystical' (in time, of course, the poet who begins by playing at mysticism is likely to become a visionary in earnest, for he is demonstrating a natural propensity); and the imagery is of course not symbolic in any sense. 'Mongan Thinks Of His Past Greatness' evidences a change to a more familiar manner:

> I have drunk ale from the Country of the Young
> And weep because I know all things now:
> I have been a hazel-tree, and they hung
> The pilot star and the crooked plough
> Among my leaves in times out of mind.
> I became a rush that horses tread;
> I became a man, a hater of the wind,
> Knowing one, of all things, alone, that his head
> May not lie on the breast nor his lips on the hair
> Of the woman that he loves, until he dies;
> Although the rushes and the fowl of the air
> Cry of his love with their pitiful cries.

Unsatisfactory though this poem may be, and imminently as the seeming naïveties of the first seven lines may court disaster, Yeats's 'hazel-tree', 'pilot star', 'plough' and 'rush that horses tread' are all

---

* As opposed to reincarnation. I am using metempsychosis to mean the migration of spirit between inanimate, animal and human forms.

full symbols simply and directly presented, and this technique of spare and total symbolism clearly looks forward to the mature verse. If the symbols fail to communicate, this is because of over-subtlety and a habit of cryptic utterance, vices which account for most of Yeats's failures at the time of 'The Wind Among The Reeds'.

The full title of Yeats's lyric, by which 'Mongan thinks of his past greatness *when a part of the constellations of heaven*', is a clear pointer to the *Mabinogion*, for Taliesin begins his account of his own past lives by saying that his 'original country' was '*the region of the summer stars*'.[15] And if Taliesin's transformations are not much like those of Yeats's wizard-king, at least there is a technical resemblance, for in each case the drama consists of the alternations of majesty and indignity. A few lines from the Welsh poem will show what Yeats will have learned from it:

> I was with my Lord in the highest sphere
> On the fall of Lucifer into the depth of hell.
> I have borne a banner before Alexander . . .
> I have been on the White Hill in the court of Cynvelyn
> For a day and a year in stocks and fetters.[16]

A pagan Irish poem in some ways similar to Taliesin's song, which Yeats knew well, and from which I feel sure that some of the imagery in 'Fergus And The Druid', at least, derives, is 'The Song Of Amergin'. Here are some of Amergin's transformations; though I should say here that the poem is only seemingly about metempsychosis:

> I am the wind which blows over the sea;
> I am the wave of the ocean;
> I am the murmur of the billows;
> I am the ox of the seven combats;
> I am the vulture upon the rock;
> I am a tear of the sun;
> I am the fairest of plants;
> I am a lake in the plain.

> *

> I am a word of science;
> I am the spearpoint that gives birth;
> I am the god who creates in the head of man the fire of thought.[17]

The use of the present tense here is a key to the meaning; Amergin is all these things *at the same time*, which means that we are not concerned with reincarnation but with participation. Yeats knew as a very young man, and from the great Celtic scholar de Jubainville,[18] that the Druidic 'science' had much in common with the religion of the Self; the adept learned to identify himself, by the *participation mystique*, with 'every thing that lives'; and Amergin, as much as any Taoist, is celebrating the 'oneness of nature' and his own achievement of 'present immortality', by which he becomes equal with 'god'. The fact that there is this coherence between Druidic 'science' and Schopenhauer's 'science of beauty everywhere' (or of the unity of all manifested being) will clearly have counted for much in Yeats's early thought, and he will have been predisposed to accept the religion of the Self in that it had special associations for his own race.*

I am sure that 'Mongan Thinks Of His Past Greatness' derives from the two songs of Taliesin and Amergin, and Yeats keeps a foot in each of their respective worlds, for his poem is about *both* the rebirth of the soul and the *participation mystique*. King Mongan drinks the magical ale of fairyland, which Rhys had taught Yeats to connect with the Indian *soma* of regeneration and wisdom, and remembers how, in some past life or perhaps in the prenatal state before his incarnations began, he participated in the whole of the Tree of Life, or had the religious sense of oneness with everything that lives. Yeats goes beyond 'The Two Trees' in openly adopting the symbol of Connla's hazel, and in that his hazel bears sun, moon and stars for fruit we may detect a Kabbalistic influence; though in giving it also the attributes of Pole Star and Great Bear, I imagine he is glancing at the Kalevala, which he was reading at this time. In the Kalevala, the enchanter Wainamoinen 'sings aloft', by magical conjuration, a 'wondrous fir-tree' equivalent to the Tree of Life; after which he stations the moon and stars among its boughs:

> . . . sings the moon to shine forever
> in the fir-tree's emerald branches,
> In its top he sings the great bear.[19]

North star and great bear are occult symbols for the 'way of the saint', or the desire for escape from the time-world into the mystic marriage,

---

* Some modern scholars (for example Joseph Campbell; *The Hero With A Thousand Faces*) see Taliesin's song also as 'about' the religion of the Self; but of this we cannot be certain.

and the 'way of the natural man', or his acceptance of the necessity of reincarnation,* and their juxtaposition on the tree symbolises Mongan's sense that these contrary tendencies are 'reconciled among the stars'. Later, Mongan loses his spiritual eminence and becomes a 'rush', which may variously be read as one of a series of metempsychoses, or as an image for the loss of the 'higher Self' or even for the fall of man; but we ought not to think of his separation from the mind of God as absolute, since the humility in the image suggests openness to the divine influence.† The real separation comes about when Mongan becomes 'a man, a hater of the wind', or is driven into rebellion against the divine purpose; after which Yeats can conclude with a statement of his own personal sufferings that grows the more poignant if read in the light of Mohini Chatterjee's celebrated axiom,‡ which clearly could not help him here. The real interest of the poem, for all this, is in that it anticipates by eighteen years the philosophy and symbolism of *At The Hawk's Well*, which ought thus to be thought of as a miracle of patience as well as of acquired technique.

During those eighteen years Yeats wrote several minor works associated with the grail legend, and in them his scheme of symbolic reference broadened. *The Withering Of The Boughs* is a lyric that associates with *Red Hanrahan*, located as it is on Slieve Echtge where Hanrahan failed in his grail adventure; and the title-image presents us with the negative aspect of Yeats's tree-symbol, brought into proximity now with the symbol of the grail-cauldron.[20] Much later, in 'Towards Break Of Day', we find him developing the alchemical symbol of *aqua vitae* also to be used in his play. This poem tells of identical dreams that came to his wife and himself; bitter dreams reminding them of the inadequacy of sexual possession, when the higher Self that each loved in the other could never be possessed:

> Nothing that we love overmuch
> Is ponderable to our touch

Thus his wife dreamed of the 'marvellous stag of Arthur' evading her from 'mountain steep to steep'; and this image (which Yeats took

---

* For the Pole Star as a symbol for the object of mystical vision, see 'A Dialogue Of Self And Soul'; the Plough symbolises the 'crooked way', *hodos chameliontis*, the 'path of the serpent'. Ellmann is not altogether wrong when he sees here a symbolism of 'guidance' and 'conflict'.

† There may be a reminiscence of the 'clod of clay' 'trodden by the cattle's feet' which speaks for noetic intelligence in Blake's 'The Clod And The Pebble'.

‡ That (in the fullness of a man's incarnations) all his sexual ambitions would be realised. See p. 288 below.

always as a full symbol where it occurred in Arthurian myth)[21] clearly represents the elusive spiritual beauty which a woman may discern in a man. Yeats's own dream is of a waterfall on Ben Bulben, but its symbolic significance is as an image of the *fons vitae*, the water of life. Thus his dream indicates that the elixir or *summum bonum* of woman's spirituality is equally outside the scope of sexual possession.

> I would have touched it like a child
> But knew my finger could but have touched
> Cold stone and water . . .

The *fons vitae* and the grail are now identified (this is my justification for having interpreted *At The Hawk's Well* from alchemy) and a tactile image like that on which the play turns has been projected in verse.

After *At The Hawk's Well* Yeats does not use fountain-symbolism very often, but I ought at least to gloss the most interesting of his usages, which occurs in part one of 'Meditations In Time Of Civil War'. In this sequence, which contains some of his most starkly austere lyric writing (and is thus very much in the spirit of his play), he is concerned with his cyclic theory of history; and the 'tough reasonableness' of his traditional argument is communicated through the austerity of the verse. The first poem, 'Ancestral Houses', is 'about' Unity of Being and that 'violence' and 'bitterness' which is the expense of greatness; which has always disqualified the great aristocrats of history from the pursuit of the Self. The quintessence of life, Yeats says, might be expected to yield itself to the rich; they have the means to cultivate the 'lower Self' as it should be cultivated: in leisure and freedom:

> Surely among a rich man's flowering lawns,
> Amid the rustle of his planted hills,
> Life overflows without ambitious pains
> And rains down life until the basin spills,
> And mounts more dizzy high the more it rains
> As though to choose whatever shape it wills
> And never stoop to a mechanical
> Or servile shape, at others' beck and call.

Here, clearly, we have a very beautiful and individual representation of the *fons vitae*, and later in the poem Yeats entrenches himself in his image. There is no Unity of Being in the degraded modern world, we are told, and perhaps after all it never has been feasible, since even the men who planted these hills were too violent and bitter to 'seize the moment'; yet life would not be worth living if men did not think of Unity of Being as a possibility. The fountain symbol now reappears, significantly linked with Homer as the type of subjective contemplation:

> Yet Homer had not sung
> Had he not found it certain beyond dreams
> That out of life's own self-delight had sprung
> The abounding glittering jet;

But, Yeats continues, at all events the modern aristocracy do not possess their souls, and the fitting emblem for their way of life is less the fountain than the shell; not the conch of Aphrodite, but a shell that is empty: sterile, spiritually dead. The modern great house is lovely, for it is the monument of a moment when spiritual beauty was at least desired, when true civilisation was tossed up out of the dark womb of history; but it has become a mere façade:

> now it seems
> As if some marvellous empty sea-shell flung
> Out of the obscure dark of the rich streams,
> And not a fountain, were the symbol which
> Shadows the inherited glory of the rich.

In this astonishing passage, the dominant symbols of *At The Hawk's Well* and *Emer* are juxtaposed, the addition of one word serving to invest the meaning of the latter, though its rationale is not changed. There could be no clearer evidence of their interrelation, or of the function each fulfils in Yeats's art.[22]

THE COLLAR-BONE OF A HARE

I have said that this poem connects with *Emer* in being about Yeats's doctrine of free love in heaven, and in the sturdy opposition it offers to the idea of exclusive marriage. One does not need to reiterate all Yeats's sources in Plotinus, Swedenborg, Henry More and Shelley, and I will content myself with one further quotation from Blake which connects with the argument of *The Bridegroom* as well as with the present lyric, elucidating as it does the special compassion Yeats feels for the young goat-girl of his play. She of course images the 'radical innocence' of all sexual passion, and free love brings her to the mystical union. Thus similarly in Blake Oothoon says that marriage is unnecessary to her when she reflects the divine image of her lover, and Blake ends with a great image for the incorruptibility of human affection, since (to revert to Yeats's own phrase) 'virginity renews itself like the moon'.

> How can I be defiled when I reflect thy image pure?
> Sweetest the fruit that the worm feeds on, and the soul preyed on by woe,
> The new-wash'd lamb ting'd with the village smoke, & the bright swan
> By the red earth of our immortal river. I bathe my wings
> And I am white and pure to hover round Theotormon's breast.[23]

In this essay I shall take for granted the theorists of free love who inform Yeats's verse, and try for a line-by-line interpretation of his meaning.

Yeats has this in common with Baudelaire, that each had a particular aptitude for *la poésie des départs*; they consent in a special nostalgia for the sea-voyage from earth to heaven.* I will not catalogue here all Yeats's adventures in the field, but the present lyric is a worthy forerunner to 'News For The Delphic Oracle', which I take to be his most consummate representation of the voyage. In both poems, most of his symbolism is Platonic; the soul crosses the *sea* of Anima Mundi in a *boat* symbolic of its 'aerial body', and arrives eventually at an *island paradise* which connects both with the Celtic Islands of the Dead and the Greek Isles of the Blessed. And where Baudelaire is an ironic and disillusioned cartographer, and we are never sure that his paradise will not turn out to be some *Eldorado banal de tous les vieux garçons*. Yeats's naïver vision of beatitude has a purity probably unrivalled in modern literature; he does not, like so many visionaries, inflict on his heaven a crabbed morality born of the Tree of Good and Evil, and which reflects his own prejudices and grievances, but enforces in every line the undeniable truth that the essence of heaven is perfect freedom. 'For there the king *is* but as the beggar', he tells us in 'Running To Paradise'; and the words are meant both to deflate the claims of a merely political idealism (for nowhere else save in paradise is such liberty feasible), and also to introduce us to a heaven which can

---

* I should like to think of this paragraph being read against Eliot's *Selected Essays*, 'Baudelaire', pp. 428-9, which suggested to me the comparison I am pursuing.

truly be what heaven must be, at once an image of 'the unpersuadable justice' and 'the land of heart's desire'.

At the centre of Yeats's lyric, together with 'images of heaven', lies the symbol from which it takes its name, and the idea that the pierced bone of a hare may have magical virtue is an Irish superstition retailed in *The Celtic Twilight*:[24]

> A peasant found the shin-bone of a hare lying in the grass. He took it up; there was a hole in it; he looked through the hole and saw the [fairy] gold heaped up under the ground.

In the poem, however, the image is of looking through the hole, drilled by a 'gimlet', in a hare's collar-bone rather than a shin-bone, and there is a clear visual resemblance to a detail in the slightly earlier lyric 'The Dawn'. There, Yeats is concerned with the brooch of Emain Macha, who is 'a kind of Celtic Atalanta', and whose breastpin and brooch are the arms of the city of Armagh:

> I would be ignorant as the dawn
> Which has looked down
> On that old queen measuring a town
> With the pin of a brooch.

Yeats's image here is chosen for the sheer arrogance of the gesture that is described, and the critics have put down his later usage to a similar preoccupation with the aristocrat as *poseur*, but a very slight act of the imagination should convince us that it is functional beyond this. What begins with 'The Dawn' as merely decorative imagery is converted, with 'The Collar-Bone of A Hare', into an equivalent for Yeats's own dominant symbol of 'the needle's eye':

> God's pity on the rich!
> Had we been through as many doors, and seen
> The dishes standing on the polished wood
> In the wax candle-light, we'd be as hard,
> And there's the needle's eye at the end of all.

This is *The Countess Cathleen*, and the biblical symbolism broached here is common usage in the mature poetry; we learn that 'all the stream that's roaring by' came through the eye of a needle, and that men's guardian angels 'thread the needles' eyes', or have free passage between the spiritual and material worlds.[25] In the present poem, the hole drilled through an object of magical virtue has an equivalent connotation, and to look through it is to pass through the strait gate dividing timelessness and time.

Before one can perform the insolent gesture of scanning the time-world through such lorgnettes, the sea-voyage to perfection has to be undertaken, and the first lines of the poem, in which this journey is accomplished, are very heavily symbolic indeed:

> Would I could cast a sail on the water
> Where many a king has gone
> And many a king's daughter.

The king and princess imagery here connects with *The Bridegroom*, and stands also in a definite relation to Yeats's early poem 'The Happy Townland'. In this charming fantasy, Yeats's generous and uninhibited vision makes him choose Cockayne as a symbol for beatitude, and the atmosphere of his landscape over-flowing 'with red beer and brown beer' is thus rather like that Mahler achieves with his 'A Child's Dream Of Heaven', but there is also much traditional symbolism of a highly syncretic order. Valhalla is obviously intended in the second verse, when the blessed 'unhook their heavy swords' for the recreation of 'intellectual war'; the Kabbalistic Tree of Life is suggested when Yeats speaks of the 'golden and silver boughs' of paradise; while the first verse ends with what is essentially the Rosicrucian symbolism of the Queen and the princess. The Rosicrucians imaged the soul after death, when it arrived at its full dignity and stature, as either a prince or a princess, or even as a king or a queen where it achieved total union with God in either his masculine or feminine aspect;[26] and that is why Yeats uses the image he does for souls swept up into 'the eternal dance':

> Queens, their eyes blue like the ice,
> Are dancing in a crowd.

In 'The Collar-Bone of A Hare' similarly, the purified souls which cross the sea of Anima Mundi are imaged as kings and princesses, and their voyage leads to the Isles of the Blessed and to a dance already in progress. Yeats, 'weary of time', wishes that he himself could 'cast a sail' as they do:

> And alight at the comely trees and the lawn
> The playing upon pipes and the dancing,
> And learn that the best thing is
> To change my loves while dancing
> And pay but a kiss for a kiss.

The adjective 'comely' here suggests a source for the whole passage in those pages of *The Immortality Of The Soul* concerning the music of the spirit world where Henry More speaks of 'the comely carriage (of the blessed) . . . their melodious singing and playing with an accent so sweet as if we should imagine air itself to compose lessons and send forth musical sounds';[27] we have to remember that More goes on to speculate that 'the amorous propensity' will be 'recreated' in heaven.[28] In the lyric, it is more precisely the formal landscape of beatitude that is 'comely', but this takes us no further from More than to Yeats's commentary on him in *Visions And Beliefs*, where he points out that More, Swedenborg and Blake consent in thinking of heaven as a place of formal terraces and lawns where 'the good are amid smooth grass and garden walks and the clear sunlight of Claude Lorraine'.[29] Perhaps the image in his poem is in fact composite, for the passage in *Visions And Beliefs* develops into a discussion of Blake's woodcuts to Thornton's *Virgil* and of several other visionary artists as well:

> Always in his [Blake's] boys and girls walking or dancing on smooth grass and in golden light, as in pastoral scenes cut upon wood or copper by his disciples Palmer and Calvert, one notices the peaceful Swedenborgian heaven.[30]

Whether or not they derive from More, the assertion in Yeats's last lines that the blessed 'change' their 'loves' in the course of the eternal dance is a clear statement of his belief that love in heaven will be free. The *idea* of 'bride' and 'bridegroom' 'exchanging partners' while dancing Yeats tells us was suggested to him by 'a Gaelic play'; but the *symbolic meaning* of the act as he presents it makes the lyric a palpable gloss on Swedenborg, or on what Yeats understood by the Swedenborgian doctrine that there will be 'no marriage or giving in marriage' beyond the grave.

One does not have to fight hard for the idea that Yeats's world-weariness grew out of some quarrel with Maud Gonne, and this conjecture is reinforced by the now perfectly accessible second verse. Having earned his freedom in heaven, Yeats imagines himself looking back through his magical quizzing-glass on the institutions of the time world, which are now seen as ridiculous and trivial but which had seemed so important to him in the past:

> I would find by the edge of that water
> The collar-bone of a hare
> Worn thin by the lapping of water
> And pierce it through with a gimlet, and stare
> At the old bitter world where they marry in churches
> And laugh over the untroubled water
> At all who marry in churches
> Through the white thin bone of a hare.

Here we see the poet shaping his magical bone into a similitude of the 'needle's eye', and passing in imagination through that gateway of heaven so as to gain a new and ironic insight into the time world. From the liberty of those formal gardens where the 'untroubled waters' of Anima Mundi lap, the bondage of contractual church marriage seems both absurd and 'bitter', as the fruit of the Tree of Good and Evil would naturally do; and all this externality of discipline reveals itself as superfluous. There is a slight edge of hyperbole in Yeats's contrast which reminds us that his lyric is less than philosophical in that it is the expression of a passing mood, but the subtle monotony of the phrasing reassures us that it is, nevertheless, concerned with the real nature of heaven as Yeats envisaged it: the repetitions go, very successfully, to create an atmosphere of reverie and thus of quasi-visionary sensibility and insight much as they do in the earlier 'Aedh Wishes For The Cloths Of Heaven'. And the formal structure of the second verse is exquisite; Yeats establishes himself in his central bone-image, turns from it, then returns to it so as to point the fact that it *is* a full symbol, and so as to end his crystalline and unassuming little poem on a last delicacy of rhythm.

THE WHEEL
THE HOUR BEFORE DAWN
DEMON AND BEAST

A Vision, Yeats felt, did scant justice to the 'objective' temperament simply because he himself was repelled by it; and certainly the failure of *Calvary* can be partly blamed on his lack of sympathy for the type. For all this, there are a number of early poems which are concerned with objective religion; with the desire for 'annihilation of the personality' and for union with the not-self. These poems exist because Yeats was slow in arriving at self-realisation; he may have been early aware of the bipolarity of religious experience, but he did not make any final choice between his two opposite disciplines until relatively late in life.

'The Wheel', the first text I shall take to illustrate these arguments, is a deceptively direct little poem, the versification of an idea that had occupied Yeats in the 'nineties. Its interest is largely in what it shows of his method and his theories, as in the fact that it brings home the cyclic structure of man's life. It might be the application of a symbolism familiar in Neoplatonism, where the time-world is thought of as the circumference of a circle whose centre is God:

> Through winter-time we call on spring
> And through the spring on summer call
> And when abounding hedges ring
> Declare that winter's best of all.
> And after that there's nothing good
> Because the springtime has not come.
> Nor know that what disturbs our blood
> Is but its longing for the tomb,

But where the Platonic circle of existence revolves about the positive concept of God, Yeats's here centres in the negation of the tomb: the poem is about the death wish, the desire of the perceiving ego for its own extinction; and as such its objectivity is evident.[31]

It may seem hard to believe that so simple a poem could have an esoteric root, but Saul has pointed out that it resembles a thought in 'The Tables Of The Law',[32] and one which Yeats there had 'attributed' to Leonardo da Vinci. A passage in Leonardo's *Notebooks*, not previously noticed by the critics, does indeed provide us with Yeats's source, and it is interesting to read this passage against the commentary on it given in Neumann's *The Origins And History Of Consciousness*, which is an important text in Jungian psychology. It is rather saddening to reflect that no Yeats critic before Saul can ever have read this informative work on myth, which quotes da Vinci in the following translation:

Now you see that the hope and desire of returning to the first chaos is like the moth to the light, and that the man who with constant longing awaits with joy each new springtime, each new summer, each new month and each new year—dreaming that the things he longs for are ever too late in coming—does not perceive that he is longing for his own destruction. For this desire is the very quintessence, the spirit of the elements, which finding itself imprisoned within the soul is ever longing to return from the human body to its giver. And you must know that this same longing is that quintessence, inseparable from nature, and that man is the image of the world.[33]

Neumann points out that this 'tendency to self-destruction', regarded by da Vinci as the quintessential longing of the entire universe, is a very primitive religious predisposition (Yeats of course thought of objectivity as a primitive and of subjectivity as a sophisticated discipline); and he compares the similar primitivity of emotion which pervades D. H. Lawrence's 'The Ship Of Death':

> Drift on, drift on, my soul, towards the most pure
> Most dark oblivion
> And at the penultimate porches, the dark-red mantle
> Of the body's memories slips and man is absorbed
> Into the shell-like, womb-like, convoluted shadows.

Yeats himself, of course, in maturity opposed all this striving towards the not-self, 'pure oblivion and utter peace', with a belief in self-development and crystallisation: he was more interested in the living reality than the death-wish; and his own *poésie des départs* is less concerned with absorption into 'convoluted shadows' than with the waking landscape of heaven, 'the comely trees and the lawn'. But there were moments of reaction, and in one of these[34] his paraphrase of da Vinci still seemed to him an accurate statement of his own religious position.

Da Vinci is also a source for the much more considerable lyric 'The Hour Before Dawn', where a beggar enters a cave and breaks upon a figure like one of the Seven Sleepers of tradition, of whom Yeats knew from works as far apart as *The Well At The World's End*[35] and the Koran. We are told that Yeats's sleeper at first wanted only a winter's oblivion, but that this oblivion was so sweet that he later decided to 'sleep all time away'; for life is simply not worth living. Thus he explains himself to the beggar:

> You cry aloud, O would 'twere spring
> Or that the wind would shift a point
> And do not know that you would bring
> If time were suppler in the joint
> Neither the spring nor the south wind
> But the hour when you shall pass away
> And leave no smoking wick behind.
> For all life longs for the last day
> And there's no man but cocks his ear
> To know when Michael's trumpet cries
> That flesh and bone may disappear
> And souls as if they were but sighs

This, with the exception of the last line given, seems to me great poetry: a perfect example of the spare and arrogant austerity of Yeats's middle period, when his octosyllabics at least had come into their own and needed only a certain augmentation of verbal colour (together with a certain diminution of preciosity) to be able to support such poems as 'Wisdom' and the lyrics from *The Resurrection*. But we ought to remember that it is great *objective* poetry, and that the poet's religious intuition had clearly not matured to the same extent as his technique.

Perhaps we may see some signs of a reaction in Yeats's symbol of the *intruder*, to whom the whole scene in the cavern is obnoxious and who MacNeice[36] takes to represent the poet's own desire to stand aloof from the morality he is delineating; and in the sordid detail Yeats brings to his description of the sleeper himself, which underlines the essentially unwholesome nature of the objective discipline. In his later 'On A Picture Of A Black Centaur', of course, Yeats uses the image of the Seven Sleepers again, and I ought at least to gloss this poem because of the shift in symbolic values it reflects. The relevant passage begins with a reference to the exploitation of Egyptian tombs, an operation in which (as 'The Gyres' also bears witness) Yeats showed a great deal of interest. Mummy wheat was discovered in the course of the diggings, and we are asked to think of it being collected and baked into bread:

> I . . . gathered old mummy wheat
> In the mad abstract dark and ground it grain by grain
> And after baked it slowly in an oven; but now
> I bring full-flavoured wine out of a barrel found
> Where seven Ephesian topers slept and never knew
> When Alexander's empire passed, they slept so sound

The first three lines of this complex piece of symbolism refer to Yeats's accumulation of his system, in which process he 'ground' and 'baked' the 'old mummy wheat' of his traditional doctrine; and the rest is concerned to tell of the ease and spontaneity of the poetry subsequently generated out of that system, and out of that 'wine' which is Blake's familiar symbol for emotion as bread is for the intellect. This freedom and 'aimless joy' of creation,[37] and this total disinterest in the world external to the self, are clearly the manifestations of subjectivity, and the image of the Sleepers thus has now a *subjective* significance, a meaning diametrically opposite to that it previously carried in Yeats's verse. It changes as it does, I think, because of the suggestions of exhilaration and excess it can be made to convey, for excess and inebriation are associated with the religion of the Self as early as the wine-symbolism of 'The Blessed' and 'The Secret Rose'.

In the middle period, however, Yeats had not yet fastened upon his theory of self-delight, and this is well shown by his poem 'Demon And Beast'. The point of this difficult lyric is that all spiritual exaltation bred out of the self is illusory, and that the only reliable discipline is the mortification of the Christian saint. This obstinate conviction, so difficult for Yeats to shake off, is a legacy of Victorian asceticism, and if we want a representative objective poet of the period we could do worse than look to Tennyson, whose 'St. Simeon Stylites' illustrates well enough the kind of ethos from which Yeats had to fight free. Tennyson's saint, unfashionable as the thought may be, seems to me to provide a true index to the poet's own religious intuition, and his starting-point is from a perception that human personality is quite worthless and that he himself is 'the basest of mankind':

> From scalp to sole one slough and crust of sin,
> Unfit for earth, unfit for heaven, scarce meet
> For troops of devils, mad with blasphemy.

For three years he has lived on a mountain-side, his 'right leg chained into the crag'; and 'for many weeks' he has 'haled the buckets from the well' by a rope twisted about his loins; finally he has decided upon 'pillar punishment', and the curious dignity Tennyson imparts to what might have seemed a regimen of simple insanity derives its strength from the fact that it is in harmony with the spirit of the age:

> Then, that I might be more alone with Thee,
> Three years I lived upon a pillar, high

> Six cubits, and three years on one of twelve,
> And twice three years I crouched on one that rose
> Twenty by measure; last of all I grew
> Twice ten long weary weary years to this
> That numbers forty cubits from the soil.

Noble as Tennyson's poem is, and moving as we may find such kindred manifestations as the immolation of Tolstoy's last period or the more secular philosophy of Dostoievsky, it is one of Yeats's central achievements as a religious thinker that he found a way back to normality and stability. For though there is nothing abnormal in the desire of, say, Indian ascetics to master the rebellious body so as to enjoy uninterrupted communion with the Self, there is in much Christian asceticism a tendency to attack the total human personality through the body: to regard the living organism as intrinsically and wholly evil, and reducing it as far as possible to a nonentity, to await an infusion of grace from without. This sterile discipline Yeats eventually rejected, but 'Demon And Beast' shows how difficult it was for him to do so.

The source of 'Demon And Beast' is also Yeats's principal source for his knowledge of early Christian monasticism, and it is the *Lausiac History* of Palladius, a work which inspired Cavafy also to a famous poem.* This contemporary study of the fellowship of St. Antony is one of the most frightening accounts of austerity ever written, and Yeats frequently refers to it, with a grim relish of its nobility, in his mature prose. The penances are almost beyond belief, as for example is that of Macarius of Alexandria, whose sin was to have killed a mosquito that had settled on his foot:

> He condemned himself to sit naked for six months in the marsh of Scete, which is in the great desert. The mosquitoes there are like wasps and even pierce the hide of wild boars. . . . He returned unrecognisable but for his voice.[38]

Thus Ammonius 'when desires arose in him . . . heating an iron in the fire would apply it to his body till he became a mass of ulcers';[39] and Stephen is shown 'working with his hands and weaving palm-leaves and talking to us while the rest of his body was undergoing an operation' for cancer.[40] The object of all this mortification is explained in the central anecdote of the book, when Diocles the philosopher addresses the monks of Antinoe.

---

* 'The Tomb of Ignatios', in *The Poems of C. P. Cavafy*, London, 1952, p. 87.

He told us this . . . 'Intelligence which is separated from the thought of God becomes either a demon or a brute beast'. But since we were anxious to know his manner of speaking he explained thus: 'intelligence separated from the thought of God inevitably falls into concupiscence or anger.' And he said concupiscence was beast-like and anger demoniacal. But when I objected 'How can human intelligence continually be with God?', this same man said, 'Whenever the soul is engaged on a thought or action which is pious and godly, then it is with God.'[41]

All the austerities of the desert are a penance to fortify the soul; a regimen not in the least sterile or objective as Diocles outlines it, but easily *becoming* so for the unwary practitioner. Yeats came to feel, and remarks in his later *A Vision*, that such objectivity was commonly the rule among the desert fathers.

The *Lausiac History* clearly took a strong hold on Yeats's imagination, for there are several reminiscences of this passage in his mature writings. The beginning of the present poem very obviously derives from it:

> For certain moments at the least
> That crafty demon and that loud beast
> That plague me day and night
> Ran out of my sight
> Though I had long perned in the gyre
> Between my hatred and desire
> I saw my freedom won
> And all laugh in the sun.

Another allusion, whose relevance within the general structure of the poem can hardly be ascertained unless we know the source, comes with the magnificent tribute at the end:

> O what a sweetness strayed
> Through barren Thebaid
> Or by the Mareotic sea
> When that exultant Anthony
> And twice a thousand more
> Starved upon the shore
> And withered to a bag of bones.
> What had the Caesars but their thrones?

There are other references in the prose: those I have noted in 'A Vision', and another in the 1930 diary; while Yeats's late lyric 'The Spur' has at least a tangential relevance to the *Lausiac History*, telling as it does how the poet has become a prey to concupiscence and hatred with old age:

> You think it horrible that lust and rage
> Should dance attendance on my old age.
> They were not such a plague when I was young.
> What else have I to spur me into song?

What else is there indeed, save only the idea of God, if one accepts the doctrine of the desert fathers? Eliot is another poet preoccupied with 'the saint in the desert', 'the loud lament of the disconsolate chimera', and he has called this poem 'unpleasant',[42] but it is interesting to note that it is sanctioned by the precepts of the fellowship of St. Anthony, the 'athletes of Christ'.[43]

'Demon And Beast' begins with the stanza which I have given, and which tells how Yeats felt a momentary 'freedom', generated, it seemed, from within and thus from the Self, from the warring antinomies of 'hatred and desire'. The second verse is perfectly simple and hardly very interesting save to students of the Irish heritage of portrait-paintings: it does not rise above the discursive level and shows Yeats, in his newly-earned freedom, moving among the portraits in the Dublin Municipal Gallery; observing the Ormondes, Strafford and the picture of Luke Wadding, the description of whose 'glittering eyes in a death's head' is subtly functional, characterising as it does the company in the Thebaid as well as the sitter. Everything that Yeats looked upon was blessed.

> Now that the loud beast ran
> There was no portrait in the Gallery
> But beckoned to sweet company.

The third verse, whatever we may think of that preceding, is charming and inventive; less than symbolic in scope, but carrying symbolic potentiality for those who are minded to look for it:

> But soon a tear-drop started up
> For aimless joy had made me stop
> Beside the little lake
> To watch a white gull take

> A bit of bread thrown up in the air;
> Now gyring down and perning there
> He splashed where an absurd
> Portly green-pated bird
> Shook off the water from his back;
> Being no more demoniac
> A stupid happy creature
> Could rouse my whole nature.

In this vignette we may see, if we like, an emblematic representation of the poet earning his victory over demon and beast, whose symbols are the white bird and the green. The daemon flies down from the 'air' of intellect, mollified by the 'bit of bread' which symbolises Yeats's momentary propitiation of the antinomies, whilst the comatose 'beast' is engaged on rising above its element, shaking off the water of generation from its back. That this symbolism is intended, or half intended, follows from Yeats's reiteration of his 'gyre' imagery, which leads us back to the first verse.[44]

The last part of the poem is concerned with the moment of reaction, when Yeats's fleeting sense of stasis deserts him. At this period he had convinced himself that subjective man had no 'right mastery of natural things', no hope of winning absolute spiritual freedom, and so he concludes bitterly that there can have been nothing of spiritual significance in his experience, which he prefers to attribute to the poverty of an old man's emotions:

> mere growing old, that brings
> Chilled blood, this sweetness brought.

And yet, he movingly continues, he has

> no dearer thought
> Than that I may find out a way
> To make it linger half a day.

Then, with a sudden blaze of passion, the poem completes itself in a reminiscence of some who could make spiritual 'sweetness' linger; by cultivation of the objective austerities, and of that regimen of ferocity which (we are told in the later *A Vision*) is the counterpart of 'hatred of the Self':

> O what a sweetness strayed
> Through barren Thebaid
> Or by the Mareotic sea
> When that exultant Anthony
> And twice a thousand more
> Starved upon the shore
> And withered to a bag of bones.
> What had the Caesars but their thrones?

The last line here bears some relation to a paragraph in *Per Amica*, where Yeats says that the objective saint every day 'renounces' a temptation like Christ's in the wilderness, when he is offered in exchange for his austerity 'the kingdoms of the world'.[45] This thought also recurs in 'The Saint And The Hunchback', where Yeats couples an imagery of flagellation borne in on him by such works as the *Lausiac History* with an interest in classical history stimulated by Plutarch's *Lives*:

> The Saint: I lay about me with the taws
> That night and morning I may thrash
> Greek Alexander from my flesh
> Augustus Caesar, and after these
> That great rogue Alcibiades.

'What had the Caesars but their thrones?': no monk in the desert would barter his spirituality for so barren a gift as the world.

'Demon And Beast', after an unsteady beginning, develops into one of the most poignant of Yeats's minor poems, but we ought nevertheless to be thankful that he eventually replaced the image of St. Anthony with that of the subjective hermit Ribh, who knows that love, and not self-immolation, is the light of the world:

> by that light
> I turn the pages of my holy book.

Boehme, I think, above all mystical writers convinced Yeats of the adequacy of subjective religious experience, and it is worth giving a final paragraph to explain how he did so. Boehme's theory of 'centres' teaches that 'manifested life expands like a tree, or a cloud of smoke, from a little grain or seed'; and that there is a kernel, or central knot of pure being, to every object in the natural world, where. if we can perceive it, 'the Deity stands as it were hid, yet forming, imaging or imprinting himself powerfully on all things':

> The Eternal Centre and the Birth of Life are everywhere. If you make a small circle (as small as a little grain or kernel of seed) there is the whole birth of the Eternal Nature.[46]

This is the source of Blake's own theory of centres, which, he teaches as Boehme does, the regenerate man who has attained to the Self will be able to perceive; we should remember that the Self in turn is a centre within the psyche, 'less than an atom, greater than immensity'. Blake sees the centre everywhere:

> The vegetative universe opens like a flower from the Earth's Center
> In which is Eternity . . . within that Center Eternity expands
> Its ever-during doors that Og and Anak fiercely guard . . .[47]
>
>> There is a Moment in each Day that Satan cannot find
>> Nor can his Watch Fiends find it; but the Industrious find
>> That Moment, and it multiply, and when it once is found
>> It renovates every Moment of the Day if rightly placed.[48]

This 'centre' or 'moment' is of course Eliot's 'still point of the turning world'; and it is also the timeless moment of Yeats's *At The Hawk's Well* and his 'needle's eye' which is the gate leading from earth to heaven. When Yeats had Boehme's philosophy to reinforce Blake's vision, he began to have confidence in the religion of the Self, and he clearly assimilated it in the period between *The Unicorn From The Stars* (where the hero is modelled on Boehme himself) and the final draft of *The Player Queen*, which is full of allusions to Boehme's writings. It had certainly become a part of his own thought by the time he wrote 'Stream And Sun At Glendalough', where he does not doubt that the subjective can achieve present immortality. Yeats shows himself doing precisely this and living, for a moment, like one of the regenerate: and he has no longer any doubt of the metaphysical validity of the experience.

> What motion of the sun or stream
> Or eyelid shot the gleam
> That pierced my body through?
> What made me live like those that seem
> Self-born, born anew?

I think I see glancing reference to Boehme in this stanza, for his 'waking trance' was precipitated by a chance reflection of sunlight on a pewter vessel, just as Yeats suggests his own vision may have been by a reflection of sunlight on water; and 'Stream And Sun At Glendalough' is a fitting tribute to Boehme's influence.[49]

SOLOMON AND THE WITCH

The cock symbolism in 'Solomon And The Witch' connects it with *The Dreaming Of The Bones*, and there is a further link with *Calvary* in this third poem of a sequence, for while Yeats's first Sheba poem, 'On Women', had been 'about' passion and his second, 'Solomon To Sheba', about love, he is now occupied with nothing so much as his theory of Chance and Choice. His poem is also remarkable as an example of Yeats's syncretism, Hermetic, Kabbalistic and Indian symbols coexisting in the text, even though his intentions may be less than serious. A comparison here might be with Donne, who sometimes manipulates his scholastic learning with a kindred lightheartedness; and the analogy is probably an apt one, for I agree with Henn[50] in tracing an influence from Donne on Yeats's text.

Yeats's diaries contain references to Solomon and Sheba as early as 1909, and he uses them then as the types of 'perfect love'. This was of course their conventional significance in the 'nineties, when the legend and the Song of Solomon were rehearsed as assiduously as the myth of Paolo and Francesca; probably the best work produced on the subject was Arthur Symons's play 'The Lover Of The Queen Of Sheba', and this seems to me to have exerted a very definite influence on Yeats's thought.* So much has been made of Symons's importance within the symbolist tradition that it is strange that so many of Yeats's debts to him have been missed: his translation of Verlaine's 'Colloque Sentimental' may have suggested Yeats's early lyric 'Ephemera'; his version of Catullus' 'Attis' connects with both 'Vacillation' and *A Full Moon In March*; while his 'Dance Of The Daughters Of Herodias' may perhaps bear more directly on several of the mature lyrics than the critics have yet allowed. Where all this is so, we ought not to be surprised that his verse play should remain deeply embedded in Yeats's memory, as I believe to have been the case.

Symons presents his Sheba, as is conventional, as a young girl precociously learned in the occult sciences, who gives herself to

* A copy of the magazine in which this one act play first appeared is still in Yeats's library.

Solomon because he is wiser than she. She loves 'not him, but wisdom', and her fulfilment is to become the receptacle of his knowledge:

> Sheba: I have unburdened all my soul
>   And he has filled my soul with his.

Symons's further characterisation of his heroine may remind us of the precocious young bride who, in Yeats's 'The Gift Of Harun Al-Rashid', gives herself and her metaphysical ambition to **Kusta Ben Luka**:

> Sheba: O king, I have given up my youth
>   To wisdom; I have sought to find
>   The secret influences that bind
>   Star unto star, the grain of truth
>   Shredded in sand beneath the wind. . . .
>   And talked with those Arabians
>   Whose memory is more than man's
>   And read with them the books that teach
>   The lore of the Egyptians.

Like Kusta Ben Luka's bride, or like Yeats's own Sheba, Symons's heroine tries to divert her husband from passion into the sphere of metaphysical disquisition, but he tells her that 'wisdom' is 'weariness' to him and that the end of knowledge is to discover that love is worth more than all the wisdom in the world. Here again we have a parallel in Yeats's own verse:

> Sang Solomon to Sheba,
> And kissed her Arab eyes,
> 'There's not a man or woman
> Born under the skies
> Dare match in learning with us two,
> And all day long we have found
> There's not a thing but love can make
> The world a narrow pound.'*

But it is with the culmination of Symons's play that we begin to see how thorough an influence it was on 'Solomon And The Witch', and the parallelism is so close that I will quote the relevant lines at length:

* 'Solomon To Sheba.'

> Solomon: When thou art I, and I am thou
> Time is no more; the heavy world,
> As we among the lilies, we
> Under the vine and almond tree,
> Wake to that slumber, might be hurled
> Into the void eternity
> And we not know. Beloved, come
> Into the garden dim with spice,
> Let us forget that we are wise,
> For wisdom, though it be the sum
> Of all save love, is love's disguise.
> Let us forget all else that is
> Save this, that joy is ours to know
> A moment, ere he turn and go,
> And that that moment, love, is this.

Yeats substitutes the 'sacred grove' for this garden 'dim with spice', but his own poem, like Symons's, is about timelessness, and about the timeless moment as it presents itself to lovers, and I think there can be no doubt that it has a main source in this speech.

Symons may not be the only influence on Yeats's Sheba poems, for the years just before Yeats's marriage found him reading Flaubert's 'Temptation Of St. Anthony', which, though 'objective', he calls a 'sacred book'. On one plane he will have read the novel against the *Lausiac History* (which is one of Flaubert's sources) and for the sake of the ascetic self-maceration so strongly featured in the book.

> Anthony: Like Eusebius I have carried thirty-eight pounds of bronze upon my loins; like Macarius, I have exposed my body to insects; like Paconius, I have passed fifty-three nights without closing my eyes (etc.).[51]

But one of Anthony's temptations is by the Queen of Sheba, and Yeats will have been fascinated by Flaubert's Sheba with her 'great dark eyes deeper than the mystic caverns' and her 'body cold as the skin of a serpent'; with her robe ornamented with the twelve signs of the zodiac and her two immense blonde pearl ear-rings; her nails pointed like needles and her 'mouth opening in breathing as if her corset inconvenienced her'; her green parasol with its ivory handle, her silver bells that tinkle as she walks, and her train carried by 'twelve woolly niggerboys' assisted by an ape.[52] We have to remember that Yeats's own Sheba, learned as she is, contrives to be also an erotic, a 'perverse creature of chance', and that her beauty arouses a gamut of protective emotions:

> . . . tenderness and care,
> Pity, an aching head,
> Gnashing of teeth, despair.

At the same time, of course, Flaubert's Sheba is a 'sorcerer' whose familiar is a man-headed bird, and even her beauty has a mystical or quasi-mystical tinge. She is 'not a woman', she tells Anthony, she is 'a world'; and her 'cloak has only to fall in order that thou mayest discover a succession of mysteries'.[53]

'Solomon And The Witch' begins with an anecdote which has clearly an autobiographical cast. Sheba cries out in her sleep, much as we know Yeats's own wife to have done, frequently, in the early days of their marriage:

> And thus declared that Arab lady
> 'Last night, where under the wild moon
> On grassy mattress I had laid me,
> Within my arms great Solomon,
> I suddenly cried out in a strange tongue
> Not his, not mine.'

Solomon interprets the incident, clearly light-heartedly, as an instance of daemonic possession: either a cockerel has crowed through Sheba's lips or (perhaps we ought rather to understand) a spirit has spoken through her mouth to tell of a symbolic cockcrow in heaven. The passage that tells how the King, knowing as he traditionally does the language of all the animals, applies himself to the translation of this 'strange tongue' in which his wife has spoken, makes it very clear that the whole poem is less than seriously intended:

> Who understood
> Whatever has been said, sighed, sung,
> Howled, miau'd, barked, brayed, belled, yelled, cried, crowed,
> Thereon replied: 'A cockerel
> Crew from a blossoming apple bough
> Three hundred years before the Fall
> And never crew again till now,

> And would not now but that he thought
> Chance being at one with Choice at last
> All that the brigand apple brought
> And this foul world were dead at last.
> He that crowed out eternity
> Thought to have crowed it in again.'

In these lines we can recognise the Hermetic cockerel which is the harbinger of all the cycles, 'planted' as in 'Byzantium', and as d'Alviella and his own Order of the Golden Dawn had taught Yeats was traditional, in the boughs of the Tree of Life, for which Yeats uses the orthodox Kabbalistic symbol of the 'apple-tree'. The usage is a very obvious *jeu d'esprit*, and we may compare the farcical comedy of the cycle's end in *The Player Queen*,[54] or even Yeats's first metaphysical amusement with the cock-image, in *The Countess Cathleen*:

> Sign with this quill,
> It was a feather growing on the cock
> That crowed when Peter dared deny his master
> And all who use it have great honour in hell.

This is a comic detail in an entirely serious episode, and 'Solomon And The Witch' has a similar orientation, and is in fact a charming fantasy on a doctrine of the timeless moment in which Yeats at least half-believed.

This doctrine is that man and woman, at the climax of 'perfect love', become 'images' of the original world parents, the divine father and the celestial matrix. The belief that divinity contains both male and female elements, and that the first creation took place by an act analogous to human sexual union, is of course to be found in Boehme as it is also a convention in both Kabbalistic and Indian theology; and Yeats wrote 'Ribh Denounces Patrick' on this subject, which he later expounded in prose:

> In the Tantric philosophy, a man and a woman, when in sexual union, transfigure each other's images into the masculine and feminine character of God . . . the man seeks the divine Self as present in the wife, the wife the divine Self as present in the man.[55]

Yeats speculates whether there may not have been some parallel to this 'meditation' in medieval Europe, in 'the poets of *amor courtois*' 'in Parzifal and in Chrétien de Troyes';[56] and he may also have seen an allusion in Symons's learned verse-play, where the lovers are said to typify 'love' and 'wisdom' and thus serve excellently as images for the primary creative ideas. When they 'wake to that slumber' which is sexual fulfilment, Symons tells us that 'time is no more', and Yeats seizes upon this detail, greatly expanding its significance, for his own lyric. If Solomon and Sheba can perfect themselves as they make love, and become unflawed images of the divine parents, the sexual act may assume the properties of a ritual invocation* and the time-world (as every lover would wish) may come to an end.

This is why the cockerel that 'crowed out eternity' has prophesied through Sheba's lips. Solomon and Sheba have so nearly transfigured themselves into the divine images that it seemed to him for a moment as though all time might cease. Yeats makes this point in a blaze of magnificent poetry, and it is instructive to notice how easily, at this period, what begins as a fantastic disquisition appropriate to his 'learned lovers' can overspill into great art. The poetry is spare, concise and has tremendous impact:

> He that crowed out eternity
> Thought to have crowed it in again.
> For though love has a spider's eye
> To find out some appropriate pain—
> Aye, though all passion's in the glance—
> For every nerve, and tests a lover
> With cruelties of Choice and Chance;
> And when at last that murder's over
> Maybe the bride-bed brings despair,
> For each an imagined image brings
> And finds a real image there;
> Yet the world ends when these two things,
> Though several, are a single light,
> When oil and wick are burned in one.
> Therefore a blessed moon last night
> Gave Sheba to her Solomon.

These lines begin with the allusion Henn has noticed to Donne's 'Twick'nham Garden'—'that spider love that transubstantiates all/And can convert manna to gall'†—and they continue with a very bitter

---

* It is because of this detail that I say Yeats 'half-believed' in the theory of his poem. Of course he wholly believed in all the doctrine I have reconstructed up to this point.

† One might also compare Yeats's 'three hundred years before the fall' with Marvell's 'Love you ten years before the flood'.

allusion to the sufferings Yeats himself had experienced at the hands of Maud Gonne. How literally Yeats believed that the preliminaries of courtship were ritual murder, where the man dies a symbolic death from 'beauty's cruelty', may be seen from my essay on his later *A Full Moon In March*. Man suffers to this extent because of the opposition between chance and 'choice', which in the sphere of sexual selection manifests largely in the difference between the 'imagined' (or chosen) and the 'real' (or fated) image which the beloved presents. What is at stake may be ascertained from a beautiful passage in the early prose, whose profundity has already been remarked by Cyril Connolly:

> It seems to me that true love is a discipline and needs so much wisdom that the love of Solomon and Sheba might have lasted for all the silence of the scriptures. Each divines the secret self of the other and refusing to believe in the mere daily self creates a mirror where the lover or the beloved sees an image to copy in daily life; for love also creates the mask.[57]

When the 'imagined image' has been fused with the 'real', or the lover has been able to divest himself altogether of the 'daily self' and realise the mask, the 'despair' of the bride-bed may be overcome and the union of lovers become a 'perfect light'. Solomon and Sheba, Yeats imagines in his poem, have fulfilled this discipline and converted their love into that divine symbol whose religious counterpart is the *lingam*; 'where the world ends'.

Or at least they have almost done this, but perhaps their love still contains some residual element of dross, for the material universe stubbornly refuses to disappear as it ought.

> 'Yet the world stays'
>   'If that be so
> Your cockerel found us in the wrong
> Although he thought it worth a crow.
> Maybe an image is too strong
> Or maybe is not strong enough.'

These lines contain a direct allusion to the virtue attributed to the 'image' in ceremonial magic, but what makes them so charming is the perfect blend they achieve of metaphysical learning and urbanity. 'Although he thought it worth a crow': all Yeats's easy familiarity with the metaphysical world is summed up in this bland insolence.

By such devices as this Yeats completes the circular structure of his poem, and is able to end on that note of light levity with which he began. This he does with the subtle romanticism of Sheba's last speech, where there is that sense of 'identity' between speaker and landscape that we ought to expect where the Self has been achieved. (The *idea* of an ending of this kind Yeats clearly took from Symons.)

> 'The night has fallen; not a sound
> In the forbidden sacred grove
> Unless a petal hit the ground,
> Nor any human sight within it
> But the crushed grass where we have lain;
> And the moon is wilder every minute
> O! Solomon! Let us try again.'

With these exquisitely coquettish words Sheba leads her lover back into the moonlight for another act of sexual invocation, and the image of the 'forbidden' sacred grove is a last pointer to the religious meaning of the whole. Profane lovers ought not to enter this temple garden, but the regenerate may even make love there: the *lingam* is worshipped within its precincts.

One ought not to leave Yeats's lyric without a note on the general principle it illustrates, which is that his system is by no means injurious to his poetry. Whenever Yeats's metaphysics are properly irrigated by emotion, they are very readily convertible into art, 'the rock and loam of his Eden', and it is not at all necessary for the dry bones of his logic to be concealed from view beneath the verse, as we may see from this poem, where they are perfectly apparent. 'Solomon And The Witch' is a small but consummate poem and an almost total success, and it improves in proportion as the systematic meaning is understood.

AT ALGECIRAS
MOHINI CHATTERJEE

'At Algeciras' has already been discussed in the context of the bird symbolism of *Emer*, and I am going to study it here in relation to the tree symbolism of such poems as 'Solomon And The Witch', a process by which further dimensions of meaning should unfold. This lyric and 'Mohini Chatterjee' were originally planned as two sections of the one poem, and though Yeats eventually separated them, it is clear that they are to be associated as two statements of his theory of reincarnation. One reason for his having disjoined them will have been his fear lest the symbolic significance of 'At Algeciras' might fail to communicate (as indeed has hitherto been the case) and I am juxtaposing them here in the belief that it can be fully made out.

'Solomon And The Witch' had brought Yeats's tree symbolism to a certain pitch of sophistication: the apple-tree and the bird-herald of reincarnation, or of the renewal of all the cycles, are presented without a hint of their traditional genealogy, though here as elsewhere, 'he who runs may read'. Yeats wrote so obliquely because of his firm faith in the collective unconscious, which he thought would interpret any archetype for the reader who cared to meditate it, and because the Kabbalistic tree of gold and silver, where the birds perch and the sun and moon hang as fruit, seemed to him a peculiarly accessible archetype in that it had its counterpart in almost every religion and race. In Irish myth, for example, a tree of gold and silver, to which he will have attached the traditional significance, grows in the courtyard of Manannan;[58] and a similar tree, its symbolic function no doubt thoroughly understood, was built from gold and silver in the courtyard of the Caliph of Baghdad.[59] Yeats wrote 'Sailing To Byzantium', he says, when he 'read somewhere' that the Byzantine Emperor had a similar tree; an allusion which has suggested to some critics Hans Andersen's fairy tales,[60] but which the present writer is disposed to take more seriously. When Yeats read in Gibbon's *Decline And Fall Of The Roman Empire* of the project set in hand by the Emperor in emulation of the Caliph's magnificence, 'a golden tree, with leaves and petals, which sheltered a multitude of birds, warbling their artificial notes',[61] he will clearly have welcomed such a perfect delineation of his archetype, especially since d'Alviella had assured him that the Byzantines appreciated its esoteric significance: and he will have been drawn to the idea of using the image for a poem. Gibbon thus becomes a main source for 'Sailing To Byzantium', which in turn gave the radical idea from which 'At Algeciras' took fire.

Byzantium, of course, is a symbol in the central current of 'nineties thought; a typical recreation of that polyglot city is Rider Haggard's *The Wanderer's Necklace* (one of the novels which Madame Blavatsky recommended to her initiates); and Yeats imports the 'holy city' into his verse, giving it a precisely similarly orientation, as early as his 'The Old Age Of Queen Maeve'. It is not to my purpose to discuss the later development of Yeats's symbol, which becomes of course a very highly complex usage in the great period; but the accolade of responsibility for 'Sailing To Byzantium' goes nevertheless to Gibbon, who gave Yeats the image to which his whole poem is keyed. The entire last verse depends from his prose passage given, and I will quote it all because all is relevant to 'At Algeciras'.

> Consume my heart away; sick with desire
> And fastened to a dying animal
> It knows not what it is; and gather me
> Into the artifice of eternity.
>
> Once out of nature I shall never take
> My bodily form from any natural thing,
> But such a form as Grecian goldsmiths make
> Of hammered gold and gold enamelling
> To keep a drowsy Emperor awake;
> Or set upon a golden bough to sing
> To lords and ladies of Byzantium
> Of what is past, or passing, or to come.

Byzantium is of course in this poem the city of *regeneration*, and the bird which sings on a golden bough in that city is primarily a symbol for the enduring work of art, forged in the 'refining fire' of the spirit for the delectation of those who have attained to a regenerate way of life: the 'lords and ladies' of the city. But the tree that was manufactured in Byzantium was meant as the paradigm and complement of the tree that grows in heaven, and this fact is surely glossed in Yeats's poem: the soul's image, the work of art, sings *here* and for the regenerate precisely as the soul itself, when it is freed from the 'dying animal' of the body, will sing in Eden to delight the 'lords and ladies' of heaven and their emperor: that is to say, purified human souls and their King who is God.[62] Similarly, Yeats symbolises man's pilgrimage to regeneration as a *sea-voyage*; and this voyage is the earthly paradigm and complement of that on which the soul must once more embark after death, to heaven, the Isles of the Blessed. This system of analogies and *doubles entendres* brings home the fact that the state of regeneration *is* the temporal counterpart of the heavenly condition; and sets up an interior logic of extraordinary subtlety and resilience.

'At Algeciras' takes up what I would call the unstressed aspect of this symbolism, by which I mean the soul's post-mortem flight from earth to the Kabbalistic tree where 'the angels have their place'; though Yeats enforces the fact that beatitude is followed by rebirth into the body and that the escape is merely a phase. He begins at the moment when the spirit leaves the physical vehicle:

> The heron-billed pale cattle-birds
> That feed on some foul parasite
> Of the Moroccan flocks and herds
> Cross the narrow Straits to light
> In the rich midnight of the garden trees
> Till the dawn break upon those mingled seas.

Of course this is on one plane an evening landscape, the subdued colouring serving Yeats to establish a dominant mood; and of course it is also a piece of diagrammatic symbolism, and if we like, a commentary on the 'Byzantium' poems. I have already interpreted most of the traditional symbolism, by which the white bird of the soul crosses the straits of Anima Mundi on its journey to heaven, where it arrives at midnight. Midnight is Yeats's symbol for the hour of death, in 'Byzantium', where souls enter the purgatorial flames at this moment, and in several other poems also:

> At stroke of midnight God shall win . . .[63]

> At stroke of midnight soul cannot endure
> A bodily or mental furniture.[64]

We can now see more clearly that the 'garden' is Eden and that the 'trees' image the Tree of Life which grows there, in whose branches the soul finds what solace is allowed it between death and birth. It cannot stay there for ever; dawn, the moment of cock-crow and so of reincarnation, summons it back, and it recrosses those straits where the tides of life and death merge, to be 'tethered' once more to its 'dying animal' as it is reborn into the body and into the world.

Such is the symbolism Yeats saw in his straits of Gibraltar, and the second and third verses of his poem are equally dense with significance, proceeding by means of the related images of the *shells* and the *child*. There are several allusions to this symbolic conjunction in Yeats's prose, and the chief will be found in his commentary on a poem by Tagore, whose *Gitanjali* Yeats was glad to introduce because he admired the traditional Indian symbolism. Tagore's poem describes 'children playing', 'on the sea-shore of endless worlds', 'with empty shells' 'weaving their boats with withered leaves' and 'smilingly floating them on the vast deep'.⁶⁵ Yeats understands the shells to be images of 'divine truth', which is their function in Kabbalistic as well as Indian symbolism, and the children who have their 'great meeting place' on the verge of Anima Mundi he takes to represent the saints:⁶⁶ they come there in their recovered innocence to investigate the 'divine ideas' and to embark their toy boats on voyages over the collective unconscious, 'the mind of God', because their way of life is to explore 'strange seas of thought, alone'. I quote Wordsworth's lines on Newton designedly, for Yeats includes reference to Newton in 'At Algeciras', and the metaphor he refers to has marked affinities with Tagore's poem:

> I do not know how I may appear to the world, but to myself I seem to have been only like a boy playing on the seashore and diverting myself now and then by finding a smoother pebble or a prettier shell than the ordinary, whilst the great ocean of truth lay all undiscovered before me. (Newton: *Notebooks*.)[67]

This passage in fact serves as a key to several of the images in Yeats's text, though sanctity, rather than simple naïveté, is the implication behind his own symbol of the child. For this he had precedent in Greek as well as Indian religion, for Dionysus, imaged as the *puer aeternus*, represents the human soul returned to its pristine innocence beyond the grave.[68]

Either we allow the second verse of 'At Algeciras' symbolic inflection or the poem appears as a series of rambling *non sequiturs*; but the symbolism is of a peculiar cast. Yeats first presents a perfectly naturalistic memory of his own boyhood, and the last lines of the poem then force us to see it in a symbolic context also; as an action that will have to be repeated on the far side of death:

>   Often at evening when a boy
>   Would I carry to a friend—
>   Hoping more substantial joy
>   Did an older mind commend—
>   Not such as are in Newton's metaphor
>   But actual shells of Rosses' level shore.
>
>   Greater glory in the sun,
>   An evening chill upon the air,
>   Bid imagination run
>   Much on the Great Questioner:
>   What he can question, what if questioned I
>   Can with a fitting confidence reply.

The shells of verse two may be 'actual' and concrete, but Yeats finishes with a glance at their ideal counterparts, for at the moment of death he will once more become a boy carrying trophies to an 'older friend' in hope of commendation: in the 'radical innocence' of the spiritual world he will have to show the Great Questioner what he has made of the divine ideas (his symbolic shells) as they have manifested in his consciousness during life.* If he can justify his use of them with 'fitting confidence', he may be admitted to that 'substantial joy' whose symbol in recovered Eden is the Tree of Life.

The sequence of Yeats's poem is that the flight of birds suggests to him the ideas of paradise and reincarnation, and he then speculates gravely on his chances of temporary beatitude beyond the grave. The chain of logic is less than complete in that the concept of reincarnation is broached only to be abruptly dropped, and 'Mohini Chatterjee' was no doubt devised to complete it by showing precisely why man's sojourn in paradise has to be temporary and why reincarnation is for the good of the soul. The latter poem begins with a formula that Yeats had been taught by 'the Brahmin' of its title, who was a dignitary of the theosophical society, and whose teachings he had already versified in the bad early poem 'Kanva on Himself'.[69] The formula consisted of the novice's repeating to himself a credo of his own rebirth: 'I have lived many times; I have been a slave and a prince. Many a beloved has sat upon my knees and I have sat upon the knees of many a beloved. Everything that has been shall be again.' This credo Yeats now rehearses, though my own feeling is that he is concerned with the melodrama rather than the poetry of reincarnation, and that the first verse of 'Mohini Chatterjee' is not in itself great art:

> I asked if I should pray
> But the Brahmin said
> 'Pray for nothing, say
> Every night instead
> "I have been a king,
> I have been a slave
> Nor is there anything,
> Fool, rascal, knave,
> That I have not seen;
> And yet upon my breast
> A myriad heads have lain."'

* One might compare the New Testament parable of the servants rendering account for their talents.

The connection with 'At Algeciras' lies in Yeats having tacitly posed there the question: ought one to pray for clemency to the Great Questioner? His answer is in the spirit of 'A Dialogue Of Self And Soul', that one ought rather to ward off the fear of death by taking delight in the prospect of return to the world: 'I am content to live it all again.'[70]

The separation of the two poems injures, in leaving incomplete, 'At Algeciras', but it benefits 'Mohini Chatterjee' in making it a unified statement on the theme of unrequited love. 'I asked if I should pray' is, of course, Yeats's agonised (and deeply moving) reaction to the thought that he might lose Maud Gonne for ever, and the Brahmin sets his 'turbulent days' 'at rest' with the assurance that the beloved never can be lost, since the wheel of time brings all things round again. Yeats now adds to this doctrine a thought of his own, and a thought that generates all the magnificent poetry of his second verse: that the whole process of reincarnation was devised in God's care for unlucky lovers, and so that their wasted lives may be retrieved. The symbolism he uses is traditional: both Plotinus and the Geeta had taught him that the symbol for life in the fallen world is *warfare*,[71] and in 'Byzantium' he uses *drunken soldiers* and *prostitutes* as emblems for the two sexes ensnared by the tensions of time; in 'What Was Lost' he echoes the Geeta more directly in saying that life is endless conflict, a 'battle fought over again'. Love also is conventionally imaged as warfare—I will give only such casual examples, well enough known to Yeats, as Donne's 'Kill me as woman, let me die/As a mere man' and Marlowe's 'In such wars women use but half their strength'—and Yeats of course responded to this symbolism of the antithetical opposition of the sexes. Primarily, however, the 'battleground' of the poem is the classical symbol for reincarnation, and all humanity are the 'old campaigners', as appears well enough from the words on the page:

> I add in commentary
> 'Old lovers yet may have
> All that time denied—
> Grave is heaped on grave
> That they be satisfied—
> Over the blackened earth
> The old troops parade,
> Birth is heaped on birth
> That such cannonade

> May thunder time away,
> Birth-hour and death-hour meet,
> Or, as great sages say,
> Men dance on deathless feet.'

Here we are faced with an idea in which Yeats did not really believe in the image of 'birth-hour' and 'death-hour' meeting—the concept of the soul, at the moment of leaving the body, entering directly upon its next incarnation—but it justifies itself poetically as a simile for the gradual acceleration in the process of living which will take place as the absolute makes haste to 'thunder time away'. This will happen, we may infer, when all the world's lovers are united and such a salvo of rebirths and of requited passion rises to heaven as to break down the divisions between the worlds, a tremendous statement appropriate to what is perhaps the most affirmative of all Yeats's poems. The affirmation of life is so strong that, in the end, Yeats transfers to the material world (as a paradigm of the spiritual) the image of the 'eternal dance'.

THE STATUES

'The Statues' is a poem which one reads by the light of Vivienne Koch, whose reconstruction of the sources is perhaps her best piece of Yeats scholarship.[72] It is not for all this a final or even in the last resort an adequate analysis: it falls down in the third verse, where Miss Koch is simply not a good enough art-historian to follow the ramifications of Yeats's logic. My other objection to her work is that she over-rates her text aesthetically, a contention I would justify from the arguments of my *Emer* essay. I have spoken of the structure of the poem, how it begins from stasis and from the 'cold, hard' image of the Greek statues themselves, and proceeds by way of an extensive peregrination until the clinching image of Cuchulain presents itself and it can end in declamation. For my part the peregrination is too involved to make for perfection of form (it is possible to put too much material into a poem, and this is Yeats's error here); and the final peroration itself cannot be passed by without comment, for the apologist has to dispose of a criticism which has been voiced: that there is something immoral and 'sadistic' in the piled-up adjectives of Yeats's invective:

> We Irish, born into that ancient sect,
> But thrown upon this filthy modern tide
> And by its formless spawning fury wrecked . . .

Whatever one's attitude to this stanza, some rather careless technique in the second verse makes 'The Statues' an imperfect poem; but it remains, by sheer size, one of the most monumental of *Last Poems* and indeed of all Yeats's achievements.

It may be as well to begin from the imputation of 'inhumanity' (the word is Mr. D. S. Savage's)[73] and I will say frankly that I began, like him, by being antagonised by what seems to be the intransigence and race-prejudice of the last period. The position Yeats had taken in his early verse and prose had been that spirit (*atma*), undifferentiated and incorruptible, is a constituent of 'every thing that lives'; that all human life is dignified and 'holy' and that art ought consequently to be 'forgiveness' and never 'accusation'; and how much his position changed can be seen by juxtaposing the early 'Paudeen' and the late 'A Bronze Head':

> There cannot be, confusion of our sound forgot,
> A single soul that lacks a sweet crystalline cry . . .
>
> Or else I thought her supernatural,
> As though some sterner eye looked through her eye
> On this foul world in its decline and fall,
> On gangling stocks grown great, great stocks run dry
> Ancestral pearls all pitched into a sty,
> Heroic reverie mocked by fool and knave,
> And wondered what was left for massacre to save.

Terrible as that sibilant last alexandrine may be, the transcendentalism of 'A Bronze Head' justifies the invective, as we shall see if we penetrate into the myth of the poem. It is in fact a last application of that theory of daemonic possession I have discussed in relation to *At The Hawk's Well*: Maud Gonne is possessed by an angel, which descants through her lips and with the terrible unsentimentality of heaven, on the degradation of spirit in the modern world. For spirit in the material world necessarily passes through what Blake calls 'states', as in the present century it seemed to Yeats to be passing through the state of extreme objectivity; and these states, when they are abject or degraded, one must concede to be a proper subject for invective. The 'modern tide', in 'The Statues' also, is judged transcendentally and therefore purely, and if it should be maintained that Yeats overlooks the essential sanctity of all spirit in his universal condemnation of humanity sunk in its present state, we have to allow that, from the point of view of the subjective tradition, he would have been much more seriously at fault (and would have courted sentimentality) if he had neglected to condemn the 'state' for the sake of the individual. The issue is complicated by the terminology Yeats uses, as when he contrasts subjective or 'Aryan' culture (by 'Aryan' Yeats means 'Indo-European', the Hindu as well as the Graeco-Roman civilisation) with the inferior and objective non-Aryan or as he confusingly terms it 'Asiatic', ethos; terms which may seem to imply ugly racial theories. And indeed I cannot dispute a fascist influence on his *nomenclature*;[74] but his *meaning*, which is entirely pure, is simply that the major subjective religions have owed their inception to the Indo-European race, while his 'Asiatics'—the peoples of Asia Minor and the steppe and desert country beyond—have normally thought of God objectively, and have not been able to rise above the 'many', 'the multiplicity of the generative universe', to a sense of the 'One' or of the archetypal world.* Now in the twentieth century and as the world cycle nears its end, Yeats tells us, the 'objective' or Asiatic impulse has won dominance over men's minds everywhere in the world; and the ultimate intention of his poem is to combat this inadequate intuition and to set up against objective 'multiplicity' a great image of 'the One'; which seems to me an entirely justifiable undertaking.

Before we can approach Yeats's text, a further digression is needed into his theory of sculpture, on which all eventually depends. The sculpture, like the poetry, which attracted Yeats most was that which seemed to have been created from the integrated Self. 'The end of art', for him as for Patmore, 'is peace', and he loved best those artists who had experience of that 'peace which the world cannot give', or at least of that preliminary condition which he called Unity of Being and which resembles the alchemical discipline of *perfectio* in demanding the fusion of energy and spirituality, and the realisation and unification of all the four faculties, emotion and intellect, spirit and sense. *Perfectio* was the preliminary to *contemplatio*, Unity of Being to visionary attainment, and the subjective artist who had earned this inner harmony would produce works characterised by spiritual fulfilment and affirmation, by the 'stillness' that proceeds from an insight into the visionary world and the 'anonymity' which comes from the sense of oneness with all created life. These qualities Yeats early found in archaic Greek sculpture, as he tells us (in prose characteristically free from any false 'soulfulness') in his descriptions of those 'statues of Mausolus and Artemisia in the British Museum', 'private half-animal

* This makes Islam objective. But I have no space to dissect Yeats's sweeping generalisation.

half-divine figures' 'images of an unpremeditated joyous energy that neither I nor any man racked by doubt and enquiry can achieve'; and he 'wanted to create once more an art where the artists' handiwork would hide as under those half-anonymous chisels'.[75] 'The Statues' represents the imaginative fulfilment of this ambition, for it presupposes that Irish sculptors of the coming era will probe the collective unconscious and resurrect the archetypal images of 'stillness' from its depths.

In sculpture, as in poetry, Yeats felt that there was a subjective tradition, and to this now unfashionable 'sect' he argues that the Irish sculptors of the next generation are the natural heirs. The earliest ascertainable traces of his sculptural tradition Yeats found in ancient Egypt, and in work which seemed to him indicative both of spiritual self-realisation in the artist, and of an elaborate metaphysical discipline imposed on him from without:

> In Egypt that same age that saw the village headman carved [objectively] in wood, for burial in some tomb, with so complete a naturalism saw, set up in public places, statues full of an august formality, which implies traditional measurements, a philosophic defence.[76]

'Formality', or stylisation, seemed to Yeats the hallmark of his sculptural tradition, while the image of ideal human beauty that (by visionary insight) it achieved seemed to him its greatest glory; and from Egypt he saw penetrating into classical Europe a pure idea of physical pulchritude which combined 'immobility, dignity and power'; an archetypal 'face' that 'seems all the nobler for lacking curiosity, alert attention, all that we sum up under the famous word of the realists, "vitality" ', but which seemed instead to approximate to that pure 'being' which is possessed only by 'the mystic' and 'the dead'.[77] This sculptural archetype (in Yeats's lovely phrase 'like some phoenix at the end of its thousand wise years, awaiting in condescension the burning nest'),[78] he saw as imported by Ionian artists, who had contact with Egypt, into the Greek world. Thus it pervaded archaic Greek art; was combined by Pheidias and Scopas with their Doric technical accomplishment, for 'in Pheidias and Scopas Ionic and Doric unite . . . and all is transformed by the full moon (of their subcycle) . . . and all abounds and flows';[79] and is once more separated from Doric influence in Kallimachos, in whose 'stylistic management' of the 'falling folds of drapery' and 'lost masterpieces' 'known to us by a description of Pausanias' 'pure Ionic revives'; 'for Kallimachos was an archaistic workman and those who set him to work revived an older form'.[80] After this Yeats believed the Egyptian archetype to have been carried by Alexander's armies into India, where the authorities of his day thought, rightly or wrongly, that Greek influence could be detected on the Buddhas of Gandhara; and he supposed that in this way the 'traditional measurements' were imposed on the conventional image of the Buddha throughout the East.* They were by now well established in both branches of the Aryan consciousness and as such Yeats believed them to have remained accessible, through the collective unconscious, to later artists of East and West.

Yeats's sculptural tradition has not been taken seriously, but at least as far as Kallimachos he had authority for all his statements in the art-historian, Furtwängler, on whose work, and especially on his *Masterpieces of Greek Sculpture* he largely drew. Furtwängler supposed that a convention of stylisation originated in Egypt; was carried by Ionian traders to the Greek world; was handed down with the Ionian influence in archaic Greek art; and was fused with a Doric incisiveness and purposiveness in the works of Pheidias and especially of Scopas.[81] In Kallimachos, Furtwängler says, Ionic was clearly dominant, as we may judge from 'Pausanias' descriptions' of his 'tightly archaic manner combined with great elegance and a free treatment of the draperies', and especially from 'the most valuable objects kept in the Erechtheon, . . . the golden lamp of Kallimachos surmounted by the palm-tree of brass'.[82] The lamp according to tradition 'passed through the roof', while the palm symbolised 'the east vanquished by the Greek militia';[83] and how thoroughly Yeats remembered this and the preceding matter may be seen from his poem 'Lapis Lazuli', where much of the detail is pure Furtwängler:

> No handiwork of Callimachus
> Who handled marble as if it were bronze,
> Made draperies that seemed to rise
> When sea-wind swept the corner, stands;
> His long lamp chimney shaped like the stem
> Of a slender palm, stood but for a day . . .

And in the previous lines Yeats describes the coming, on 'camel-back'

---

* Coomaraswamy would not accept this, and I believe that modern scholarship would assert that the two branches of the Indo-European race discovered the traditional measurements in mutual independence. But the 'myth' of Yeats's poem largely depends on the theory of direct cultural influence and it has therefore to be borne in mind.

TWELVE RELATED POEMS

or on 'ship-board', of the Aryan tribes to Europe, and tells how they evolved a sculptural tradition, a 'wisdom', that—as he reiterates in 'The Statues'—now has gone 'to rack'.

Whatever the intellectual basis of Yeats's theory of Greek sculpture, we ought not to overlook the personal element in his assertion that the subjective artists penetrated to the Idea of beauty itself. There is always in the background that strange passage that compares Maud Gonne, through whom Yeats himself penetrated to the Idea of beauty, to a sculptural figure; and more especially to those statues of Mausolus and Artemisia which I have mentioned 'standing in the middle of the crowd's applause or sitting above it measuring out unpersuadable justice':[84]

> Her face, like the face of some Greek statue, showed little thought, as though a Scopas had measured and long calculated, consorted with Egyptian sages and mathematicians out of Babylon, that he might face even Artemisia's sepulchral image with a living norm. But in that ancient civilisation abstract [*sc.* 'objective'] thought scarce existed, while she rose but partially and for a moment out of raging abstraction.[85]

This passage ends with a variant image for Yeats's 'filthy modern tide', and another occurs (together perhaps with a further reminiscence of Maud Gonne's beauty) in a passage from *On The Boiler* whose immediate relevance to 'The Statues' was first pointed out by MacNeice. Yeats's intention is now to show how the European sculptural tradition was born and why it is necessary that artists should return to it, and he suggests that the Pythagorean theory of number (which Pythagoras, he believed, derived from Egyptian metaphysics and Egypt in turn derived from Babylon) gave the calculation and mensuration of the Doric studios its philosophical justification:

> There are moments when I am certain that art must once again accept those Greek proportions which carry into plastic art the Pythagorean numbers, those faces which are divine because all there is empty and measured. Europe was not born when Greek galleys defeated the Persian hordes at Salamis, but when the Doric studios sent out those broad backed marble statues against the multiform, vague, expressive Asiatic sea, they gave to the sexual instinct its goal, its fixed type.[86]

The Aryan sculptors were the real conquerors of objective Asia simply because they opposed to Asiatic formlessness that beauty whose origin is in the divine world, and which the subjective is able to discern by means of contemplation. It should by now be clear that the symbolism of 'The Statues' is precisely that of *Emer*; the 'marbles' and 'bronzes' of the poem symbolise that perfect and demanding loveliness which Yeats's Platonism made him worship,* and which it was the business of the subjective sculptural tradition to delineate.

Yeats's poem, like the last passage given, presumes that the Pythagorean theory of qualitative number gave the Greek sculptors a mathematical basis on which to work. In this sense Pythagoras is the 'onlie true begetter' of the statue so dramatically set before us in the first few lines:

> Pythagoras planned it. Why did the people stare?
> His numbers, though they moved or seemed to move
> In marble or in bronze, lacked character.

Classical statuary is philosophy in action, but though the metaphysics of harmony and right proportion have enabled the artists to penetrate to the ideal beauty, to that Galatea-image which is the likeness of the divine Aphrodite herself, they do this at the apparent expense of 'character'. 'Character' was of course a term charged in Yeats's vocabulary with a certain contempt, one of those 'famous words of the realists' we have seen him attacking; it seemed to him a function of 'becoming' as opposed to 'pure being'; an expression of the isolated individuality of the ego as against that passionate 'anonymity' that goes with the discovered Self. In his poem, he says that the common people may require such vulgar individuality, but that adolescence, with its intuitive insight into the ideal world, will understand that 'character' is irrelevant to passion; for love can infuse an ideal personality into the object of desire:

> But boys and girls, pale from the imagined love
> Of solitary beds, knew what they were,
> That passion could bring character enough,
> And pressed at midnight in some public place
> Live lips upon a plummet-measured face.

Here Vivienne Koch is right to see reminiscence of Blake, and of some lines in *Visions Of The Daughters Of Albion* which tell us that 'desire' once it is divorced from living flesh and blood and becomes desire for an image, is a form of 'religion'. Yeats, of course, is concerned with the

* Equally (of course) they symbolise ideal masculinity.

visionary propensity of adolescence at its highest and noblest reach, while Blake's business is merely with the impure 'image' generated by simple lust, so that there is matter for contrast as well as for comparison in the relevant passage:

> The moment of desire! The moment of desire! The virgin
> That pines for man shall awaken her womb to enormous joys
> In the secret shadows of her chamber: the youth shut up from
> The lustful joy shall forget to generate and create an amorous image
> In the shadows of his curtains and in the folds of his silent pillow.
> Are not these the places of religion, the rewards of continence
> The self-enjoyings of self-denial?[87]

Yeats's adolescents are less fallen than these; 'imagined love' has led them beyond the sexual into the archetypal world and they are therefore able to understand the true religious significance of Pythagoras' statues; and they go out 'at midnight to some public place' to pay homage to that beauty whose spiritual depth has required such niceties of scientific measurement. We may compare that profound insight into adolescence communicated in *On The Boiler*, where Yeats says that a young man choosing a lover seeks always some image 'opposite' to his own vitality: he needs to 'take his own death into his arms' and beget upon pure being 'a stronger life'.[88]

This verse seems to me great poetry and the second is of almost the same stature, but I find in the development of Yeats's poem a certain coarseness of rhythmical texture. This was an inevitable expense, for 'The Statues' stands at the end of a long sequence of poems in *ottava rima* and its variants, and Yeats's self-delight in his form had diminished by a process of habituation; after the unselfconscious artistry of 'A Prayer For My Daughter' and the deeper resonances of 'The Tower' and 'Sailing To Byzantium' the keen edge of the verse becomes blunted, and some of the rhythms of 'Parnell's Funeral' for example ('An age is the reversal of an age . . .') are merely mechanical. In his last period, his Steinach operation could give him new energy, but it could not bring back his first refinement of ear: the *ottava rima* is now characterised by rhythmical crudities, of which the worst is perhaps in 'The Municipal Gallery Revisited':

> . . . all that we said or sang
> Must come from contact with the soil, *from that*
> *Contact everything Antaeus-like grew strong* . . .

Yeats's most consummate rhythms, in *Last Poems*, come when he is working in the smaller, more ephemeral, forms, and the *ottava rima* of 'The Statues' can be as grating as elsewhere:

> No, greater than Pythagoras, for the men
> *That with a mallet or a chisel modelled these*
> *Calculations that look but casual flesh*, put down
> All Asiatic vague immensities . . .

The *logic* of this verse is perfectly simple, and corresponds exactly with what is said in *On The Boiler*: Pheidias and Scopas, or whatever Greek sculptors made the marbles and bronzes of the poem, are in retrospect 'greater' than Pythagoras, and more deserving of the credit which the first verse gives to him. They are creators where he was a mere theoretician, and they excavated from the collective unconscious, in its purest and most developed form, that archetype of ideal beauty which has been the fixed type of European sexual-religious contemplation ever since. They, consequently, and not 'the banks of oars' that fought at Salamis, set a limit on Asiatic formlessness by realising that hard definite image of which the oriental imagination was incapable. After them, subjective man could 'put off' the 'foam' of the 'many-headed' objective tide ('many-headed' is Aeschylus's term for the sea and is thus appropriate, but it also stigmatises Yeats's Asiatics as the worshippers of multiplicity):

> Europe put off that foam when Pheidias
> Gave women dreams and dreams their looking-glass.

Woman had not been able to evolve, out of the shifting, indefinite, 'multiform' sea of the Asiatic consciousness, an 'image' towards which to adapt herself, but after Pheidias she could. His masculine archetype could give her 'dreams' and provide those dreams of the ideal manhood with their concrete 'objective correlative'; while his feminine archetype, the lines may also imply, would provide her with the idea of a new and perfect femininity, towards which (by a conscious process of endeavour and between incarnations by the process explained in my *Emer* essay) she could evolve. In this way Greek art bridged the gap between the ideal and the real and canalised desire into desire for the heavenly beauty.

One reason for the rhythmic constriction of Yeats's second verse is that he quite simply had too much to say in it, and this is transparently the case in his continuation. We have been shown the process by which the European consciousness broke free from Asiatic domination, and now Yeats proposes to show us how his 'resolute European image' eventually conquered the East. This involves him at once in a vast historical panorama, which he presents as follows:

> One image crossed the many-headed, sat
> Under the tropic shade, grew round and slow,
> No Hamlet thin from eating flies, a fat
> Dreamer of the middle ages. Empty eyeballs knew
> That knowledge increases unreality, that
> Mirror on mirror mirrored is all the show.
> When gong and conch declare the hour to bless
> Grimalkin crawls to Buddha's emptiness.

Vivienne Koch's analysis of this verse becomes a shambles because she does not understand (though Yeats explains it in a letter to Edith Shackleton Heald)[89] that these lines describe the importation of Greek statuary into India by Alexander's armies and the influence that (it was believed) such statuary had exerted on 'the figure of the great seated Buddha'. Yeats describes how this variant form of Pheidias' archetype became the central image of Eastern religion, and explains how the Buddha was envisaged sitting under his bo-tree like some contemplative Hamlet; not, he says, like the lean and hungry 'intellectualised' Hamlets of modern stage convention, but like Hamlet as Shakespeare saw him, 'fat and scant of breath', 'a dreamer of the Middle Ages'. And together with the Indian image went spiritual values much like those which Pythagorean religion had independently evolved: the Buddha did not stand for the merely rational intellectualism and 'unreality' of 'abstract' modern thought, but for the spiritual condition of the religious, whose mind is made a 'purified vacancy' by the discovery of the Self: he stood for *contemplatio* and *perfectio* and for that state of 'pure being' where the external world ceases to exist. In this sense, Yeats concludes, the Buddha is still worshipped, even though modern India may be in process of abandoning its traditions and falling victim, like all the world, to objectivity (so that the modern worshipper may be materialist, ego-centred, misshapen like the witch's cat). If we are connoisseurs in Eastern art we shall connect with his last line those illustrations where the material world is symbolised by dragonish monsters and misshapen beasts, who prostrate themselves before an empty space symbolic of the Buddha's holiness, itself too sacred for pictorial delineation.* In such a way the 'multiform' objective consciousness of degenerate modern India abases itself before the image imported by Alexander 'where all is divine because all is empty and measured'.

In case this reading is thought conjectural, I had better confirm it by cross-references to Yeats's prose, and to do this is to establish a connection between 'The Statues' and *At The Hawk's Well*. Morris is a dominant influence on Yeats's play, as a writer who had achieved the Self and whose 'heroes and heroines' are 'always in the likeness of Artemisia and her man';[90] and a memory of Morris informs the present stanza. Here, from *Autobiographies*, is the description of his portrait painted by Watts, and it is clear that the detail of the prose constituted an image-cluster of great importance to Yeats himself:

> Its grave wide-open eyes, like the eyes of some dreaming beast, remind me of the open eyes of Titian's Ariosto, while the broad vigorous body suggests a mind that has no need of the intellect to remain sane, though it give itself to every fantasy: the dream r of the Middle Ages. It is the 'fool of faery, wide and wild as a hill', the resolute European image that yet half remembers Buddha's motionless meditation, and has no trait in common with the wavering lean image of hungry speculation, that cannot but because of certain famous Hamlets of our stage fill the mind's eye.[91]

Here Yeats establishes a connection between what he clearly saw as several variant forms of the one archetype (or 'resolute European image'): Titian's Ariosto, Shakespeare's Hamlet, and Watts's 'William Morris'; and calls into question also the symbols of the Buddha, the medieval court-fool, and the Irish Amadán or fool of faery, who is said to sit 'wild and wide as a hill' cupping in his hands his magical vessel or emblematic grail. All these, it is probable that Yeats supposed, are at one level conscious or unconscious reminiscences of the sculptural archetype delineated by Pheidias, and all would no doubt have found a way into Yeats's poem had there been room for them: Hamlet and the fool of the Middle Ages in fact do so, and are contrasted with the objective Hamlet of the modern theatre, abstracted, unheroic and 'thin from eating flies', an antipathy Yeats elaborates elsewhere.[92] In this rather confusing way the antithesis between subjective *contemplatio*

---

* Yeats's own misshapen beast, his Grimalkin, ought not to be connected with Minnaloushe, so much as with the 'objective' Sphinx that contends with the Buddha in 'The Double Vision Of Michael Robartes'; *v.* infra.

and objective intellectualism is introduced, and it is reinforced by the contrast between the Buddha's 'empty eyeballs' (Yeats speaks in *A Vision* of the eyes of Greek statues 'staring at nothing')[93] and what he calls elsewhere the 'photographic' vision of objective man, who is preoccupied with that wilderness of reflecting mirrors which is the physical world. This image of reflecting mirrors is also one developed in Yeats's prose, and especially in the preface to 'Fighting The Waves', where it is used to typify the objective mentality of Stendhal and the nineteenth century.[94] Finally, the image of Grimalkin is one coined in an essay of this period on 'Parnell', where Yeats contrasts the Goddess Astraea as the symbol of pure subjectivity and the coming cycle, and her antithesis in 'the brindled cat'.[95] The witch's cat of the poem connects with this passage as the symbol of absolute objectivity, the 'dark of the moon', and it humbles itself before Gautama as primitive and inept intuition must before what is tranquil and achieved.

On The Boiler contains a strong attack on modern egalitarian India, and this bears me out in enforcing on the final couplet above the interpretation I have done: 'the modern Indian worshipper, who has been caught up in the materialist "tide" and has become almost wholly objective, so that his true gods are the witch's cat and the dragon-monster of Eastern art, even today at the hour of prayer is ironically compelled to pay homage to subjective religion'. The contrast of Yeats's two religious types and the contemporaneity of his allusion thus pave the way for his last stanza, where the decadent modern world becomes the theme:

> When Pearse summoned Cuchulain to his side
> What stalked through the Post Office? What intellect,
> What calculation, number, measurement, replied?
> We Irish, born into that ancient sect
> But thrown upon this filthy modern tide
> And by its formless spawning fury wrecked,
> Climb to our proper dark, that we may trace
> The lineaments of a plummet-measured face.

Here Yeats's immense peregrination rights itself, as if by miracle, on the image of Cuchulain, and on the episode of the Easter Rebellion that so often inspired him to great art. We are shown Pearse, during that last stand, invoking the ancient hero of his race—Yeats tells us elsewhere that Pearse 'had a cult of Cuchulain',[96] which explains why he should have done so—and asked whether the image that materialised to his imagination will not have had the lineaments of some Greek statue, its every feature precisely calculated and numbered according to the Pythagorean laws. Yeats then takes this particular heroic defeat as an index to the state of the world and tells us that the many-headed sea of Asia has now everywhere reasserted itself against the European consciousness. The Irish, he says, are the rightful heirs of the 'ancient sect' of subjectivity—the word 'sect' here may suggest to us the Pythagorean community at Crotona—and, while the words may mean no more than that the Celtic peoples have kept alive their original traditions, we may if we like read them as a reference to the origin in Egypt of the Milesian race who were the first colonists of his country.[97] For this reason the heredity of the Irish especially equips them to resuscitate the laws of intellectual beauty; they preserve an unconscious knowledge of the great Indo-European archetype; and they will climb proudly to their proper eminence in that 'darkness' from which the new cycle must emanate, until the time comes for them to emulate Pheidias and bestow the laws they guard upon a new world.

'The Statues', as Vivienne Koch has said,[98] is in the last resort an *oracular* poem: out of the sheer drama of his beginning, and by means of an 'almost primitive' 'machinery of questions' 'in the style of the ancient oracles in the Greek anthology', Yeats manufactures a prophecy of the nearness of the moment of cyclical change, when humanity will revert to the religion of Platonic beauty and ideal love. As such, the poem both completes and compensates for the underlying logic of *Emer*, which is perhaps that aspect of Yeats's metaphysics most central to the present book. *Emer*, one has always to remember, is in many ways a negative statement, for though it is Yeats's fullest investigation of the philosophy of physical beauty, it concludes by saying that the demands of the ideal world are such that we cannot measure up to them, and that the end of the discipline of love is the abandonment of the quest.

> He that has loved the best
> May turn from a statue
> His too human breast.

'A Prayer For My Daughter' takes this argument a stage further in that it is a deliberate rejection of the archetype of ideal beauty; Yeats prays specifically that his daughter may *not* be given 'beauty to make a stranger's eye distraught', lest she lose 'natural kindness' and 'heart-revealing intimacy' and 'never find a friend': and he asks for her instead Unity of Being and the discovery of the Self, which can convert her into a living image of the Tree of Life:

> May she become a flourishing hidden tree . . .

In *The Bridegroom*, finally, whose metaphysic of love is for me Yeats's profoundest statement on the subject, he says that the physical personality is irrelevant to the act of loving; that the secret Self of the man will divine the secret Self of the woman; and that love is the act of adoration of that aspect of the human personality where the beloved is identical with Christ.

Beyond this sequence of poems lies Yeats's disaffection for Maud Gonne: for there is of course no reason, save that the poet himself in private life had found it necessary to do so, why he should have divorced the adoration of ideal beauty from the love of the Self. Yeats's attempt to reintegrate beauty and the Self begins, as I have already suggested, with 'Among School Children'; continues during many of the last poems and completes itself with 'The Statues', which ought I think to be read against *The Bridegroom*, and perhaps 'Solomon And The Witch' also, for the understanding of his philosophy of intersexual love in its totality. 'The Statues' is thus at the deepest level a poem of inner reconciliation, and suggests that Yeats's personal suffering may eventually have resolved in peace.

APPENDIX TO PART THREE

Notes to *W. B. Yeats and Tradition*

LARGELY IN RESPONSE to particular criticisms by Helen Gardner, a few corrections have already been made in the American edition of my book. What follow are additional corrections and acknowledgments, and the page-references are to the Gollancz edition.

Of my essays on the last plays, that on *The Herne's Egg* now satisfies me least. The play owes more to Ferguson's *Congal* than I once thought (there is room for a scholarly comparison of the two): the detail, for example, that I saw Yeats as taking over from *Julius Caesar* (p. 101) more probably derives from Shakespearean reminiscence within Ferguson's epic. My criticism of Swedenborg on p. 108 is unfair to him, since he uses the term *self* in a sense quite different from Yeats (to mean the ego), but my general argument is not affected by this: Yeats certainly saw Swedenborg as an objective and the propagator of an objective philosophy, as may be seen from *Visions And Beliefs* (II). I should also bring out the point that *The Herne's Egg* is a play of a radically different kind from, say, *A Full Moon in March*: it is in a sense an immediate response to new study, while the iconography of the earlier play had been in Yeats's mind for years. Though he knew his Indian bird-symbolism from Madame Blavatsky, there is no doubt that his studies in the *Upanishads*, undertaken concurrently with the play, triggered off *The Herne's Egg*; whereas Julian and the other sources of *A Full Moon In March* had been for some time part of his experience when he wrote; the *Mabinogion*[1] from as long previously as 1898. Yeats's works generally do tend to fall into these two categories, what I will call the 'immediate' and the 'considered', and I suggest it will one day be critically necessary to contrast the kinds. I do not say that the 'considered' works need be better, but they do tend to be more densely and variously symbolic.

My study of 'The Black Tower' is insufficient in that it does not include proper reference to Arthurian myth. The return of Arthur, heralded or preceded by the winding of a horn, is one of the traditional emblems of the millennium, and I am grateful to Mr. W. J. Keith for suggesting that Yeats may allude to it. I should also mention Virginia

Moore's suggestion (in *The Unicorn*) that Yeats may have had Kabbalistic symbolism in mind. Her interpretation of the poem is more complex than mine and, while I doubt whether the Kabbala is absolutely *essential* to the text, I would not dispute that Yeats may have been thinking of it. This is one of the many places where Virginia Moore interprets from a level nearer than mine to theosophic ritual (i.e. the ritual of Yeats's Orders); and by this means she frequently confirms and amplifies my own readings, which rely often on more 'literary' sources.[2]

I hope presently to publish an essay comparing 'Sailing To Byzantium' and 'Byzantium' and (since neither is centrally relevant to this present study) perhaps I need not anticipate it here. But I will say that, precisely because the world of regeneration is a microcosm of the heavenly world, I think it perfectly possible to take both poems as 'about' regeneration. In 'Byzantium' we have a perfect symbol for the regenerate condition in that city where the 'drunken soldiery' and 'night-walkers' (symbols for the unpurified sexes) are removed from view; where the mind tends always to be fixed on God; where the soul learns that it is master of its own destiny, and can choose rebirth or escape from the time-world at its own discretion; where imperfect souls suffer purification through flame and the sea of time and space is denied ingress. The iconography of the poem is something Yeats had meditated for years and in such cases we have to expect multiplicity of reference; this is why 'Byzantium' can imply such connotations and also be a poem about death. I think Yeats now has primarily in mind the world of purgatorial experience after death, partly because of the special solemnity of the verse (the measured nature of which has made some critics, inexperienced in religious poetry, think his sequel inferior to the first Byzantium poem); and partly because of the several pointed allusions within the text: the allusion to *Motomezuka* and the Buddhist purgatory, first pointed out by Henn, and the allusion in verse two to Dante's netherworld also. 'Qual che tu sii, od ombra od uomo certo' (Inferno I). But I would like to stress my present feeling that both the readings I have suggested co-exist, and indeed correlate; also that critics who throw up their hands before both and call them 'unnecessary to the text', are simply not interested in symbolism, though they may be interested in other kinds of poetry.

I ought also to have noticed the relevance to 'Cuchulain Comforted' of the line from Inferno XV, 'come vecchio sartor fa nella cruna', as perhaps I would have done if I had been better read in past Yeats-Dante scholarship. And I should have acknowledged to Jeffares' valuable essay on Yeats's gyres:[3] his conclusions should be read against my own.

Though I think my reading is right, I accept Blackmur's criticism that I give disproportionate space to the last lines of 'Chosen'; and I accept Helen Gardner's suggestion that I might have expanded my elucidation of the honey-bee symbolism in 'The Stare's Nest At My Window' (to make the bees emblems of patience, assiduity, sweetness and light as well as of justice), though I still think that Porphyry is immediately relevant to my text (p. 212). So of course is the Gaelic bee-symbolism used in *The Celtic Twilight* and 'Baile and Aillinn', where the meaning corresponds with Porphyry's. I do not see that I have misread 'News For The Delphic Oracle' and I still stand by all that I have written of it; Yeats was a very highly sophisticated and subtle poet. I do not, again, accept Donald Pearce's[4] readings either of *The Herne's Egg* or of *Purgatory*, and it seems to be required of me that I should now point this out.

NOTES

NOTES

Part One

CHAPTER ONE

[1] *Cf.* Quaritch *Blake* I, 304; II, 85. But of course (as these references will confirm) my sentence is an oversimplification in that such symbols as those mentioned are likely to have similar meanings in most branches of Yeats's tradition: they do not derive from one branch in isolation.

[2] *v.* the introduction to *The Heritage Of Symbolism.* For 'eclecticism', *v.* p. 3.; but contrast p. 6.

[3] 'W. B. Yeats And The Noh' (Keio University, Japan).

[4] *The Cuchulain Saga In The Works Of W. B. Yeats.* Most of the book bears on *Emer*.

[5] *The Japanese Tradition In British And American Literature*, pp. 261-2.

[6] *v.* Becker: 'Yeats As A Playwright' (Oxford thesis, 1953), pp. 382 ff.

[7] *Plays And Controversies*, p. 213.

[8] *Essays 1931-6*, p. 20. Yeats is discussing a poem by Edith Sitwell, but I think the context makes clear that we are to see this poem as representative of symbolist poetry generally.

[9] This is quoted from Ransom's notice of *Yeats And Tradition*. Of the 'special gravity' of 'The Three Bushes', something is said by Vivienne Koch (p. 129); but this critic makes too much of the merely phallic aspect of the poem. She writes naïvely of its 'terrifying frankness' and tells us that Mrs. Yeats disliked it for this reason, a legend which Mrs. Yeats assures me has no foundation of any sort.

[10] Philip Sherrard: *The Greek East And The Latin West* (London, 1959).

[11] *v.* Frijdhof Schuon: *Gnosis: The Timeless Key* (London, 1959).

[12] *v.* the essay, 'Anima Mundi' in *Per Amica*.

[13] Quoted from Yeats's introduction to *The Aphorisms Of Patanjali*.

[14] It is easy to forget how favourable the 'nineties really were. One might turn up the (unflattering) portrait of the decade in the first part of Joyce Cary's *A Fearful Joy*.

[15] As I remember him, Sherrard saw nothing a Christian need repudiate in the idea of history as a cyclic process: he simply thought Yeats's dates arbitrary.

This criticism Yeats acknowledges, and partly obviates, in the very interesting introduction to *The Resurrection*, in *Wheels And Butterflies*.

[16] *v.* section four of Chapter Three.

[17] Miner, *op. cit.*, pp. 262-3.

[18] Made in his *Kenyon Review* notice of *Yeats And Tradition*. But I am not sure that I use 'iconography' in precisely Blackmur's sense.

Part Two

In writing these studies of Yeats's plays I have been helped by scholars not listed in my text, of whom I should mention Ure (pp. 20-1) for his readings of *At The Hawk's Well* and *Emer* and Henn (pp. 267-70) for his comment on *Calvary*. Ure has previously pointed out the relevance of Wilde to *Calvary*; Saul that of Morris to *At The Hawk's Well*. All that I say of Yeats's attitude to Christianity should be measured against Virginia Moore's rather different conclusions in her valuable chapter on the subject in *The Unicorn*. My central debt in this section, perhaps I should repeat, is to Bjersby's studies of the Cuchulain plays.

CHAPTER TWO

[1] *v. Plays And Controversies*, p. 213.

[2] *ibid.*, pp. 207-13, 458.

[3] *ibid.*, p. 458.

[4] *Essays* (1924), p. 287.

[5] Or perhaps it is at the producer's discretion whether the Saint is a ghost or a living individual.

[6] This and several of the points that follow originate in Hiro Ishibashi's thesis.

[7] Yeats knew this in Waley's translation; Pound also translated part of it. I do not suggest that it was a direct influence on *At The Hawk's Well*; it is rehearsed here to demonstrate the Noh technique.

[8] Plutarch, *Morals*, III, 401-2.

[9] *A Vision*, B, pp. 239-40.

[10] Of course Yeats's Dancer (symbolising Unity of Being) and his Sphinx (possibly symbolising objective religious vision) can also 'overthrow time' in a similar way. In this study I have assumed that Yeats *originally* meant his Buddha to typify subjectivity and his Sphinx to typify objective intellectualism, despite his difficult note in *A Vision*, B, p. 208.

[11] The Noh masks are very fully discussed in Ishibashi, *op. cit.*

[12] Yeats knew *Nishikigi* in Pound's translation and *Motomezuka* in M. C. Stopes's.

[13] *v.* Waley, p. 44.

[14] *Yeats And Tradition*, pp. 43-4.

[15] *v.* Yeats's preface to *The Ten Principal Upanishads*.

[16] Actually Yeats began his study of Avalon's *Principles Of Tantra* soon after it came out in 1914; but the influence came later. *Cf.* (for instance) *Essays 1931-6*, p. 130.

[17] *Visions And Beliefs*, I, pp. 290-1.

[18] The Yeatsian meaning, that is: I have developed this interpretation out of his prose commentary in *Visions And Beliefs*, I, pp. 291 ff.

[19] *v.* Standish Hayes O'Grady: *Silva Gadelica* (London, 1892) pp. 370-2.

[20] *v.* Jeremiah Curtin: *Myths And Folklore Of Ireland* (Boston, 1890), pp. 101-6.

[21] Quite intuitively, I connect Yeats's porter with the beadsman in Keats.

[22] Reprinted in Vol. VII of the 1908 edition of *Collected Works*.

[23] Standish O'Grady, *History of Ireland* (1881 ed.), I, p. 136.

[24] *ibid.*, I, p. 127.

[25] *ibid.*, I, p. 128.

[26] *Cf.* Ellmann, *Yeats: The Man And The Masks*, p. 127.

[27] *Celtic Heathendom*, pp. 557-8.

[28] In *The Irish Theosophist*, Vol. 5, no. 12, p. 221.

[29] Yeats's main source for the Scathach legend was *Cuchulain Of Muirthemne*.

[30] *v. Yeats And Tradition*, pp. 23-4.

[31] *Psychology And Alchemy*, pp. 7-8.

[32] *ibid.*

[33] *Essays 1931-6*, p. 113.

[34] *The Ten Principal Upanishads*, p. 142.

[35] Quoted from Hone, p. 112.

[36] *The Marriage Of Heaven And Hell*, Keynes, p. 150.

[37] Quoted from Fränger: *The Millennium Of Hieronymus Bosch*, p. 65.

[38] *ibid.*, p. 66.

[39] *v.* Moore, *The Unicorn*, pp. 115 ff.

[40] For Yeats's desire to found a grail order, *cf.* Moore, pp. 73 ff. And *v. The Speckled Bird*, II, 96.

[41] For Yeats's knowledge of this book, *cf. Autobiographies*, p. 151; *A Vision*, B, p. 286.

[42] Her commentary (on the informing myth) is *The Legend of Sir Perceval* (1906-9). *From Ritual To Romance* takes up some of the same issues.

[43] *Sir Perceval*, II, pp. 252-3.

[44] *Cf.* A. Nutt: *The Legends Of The Holy Grail* (London, 1902), pp. 56-7.

[45] *v.* the poem 'Summer And Spring'.

[46] Quoted from Joseph Campbell, *The Hero With A Thousand Faces*, p. 51; on which book I lean heavily in what follows.

[47] Eliot, 'East Coker', III.

[48] There are in fact several virgins (each symbolic of the transcendental virgin) in the Rosicrucian story; and the conclusion is not extant; but it seems clear that Christian would have married one of his spiritual guides.

[49] Boehme 'On The Three Principles': *Zwei Gewalten*.
[50] *ibid.*
[51] Quoted from Fränger, *op. cit.*, p. 124.
[52] *Sir Perceval*, II, p. 257; in Campbell, master of *two* worlds (spirit and sense), p. 229.
[53] Campbell, *op. cit.*, p. 280.
[54] *ibid.*, p. 189.
[55] *ibid.*, p. 167.
[56] *ibid.*, p. 386.
[57] 'The Happiest Of The Poets.'
[58] *v.* her *Poems* (London, 1929), pp. 403, 541.
[59] Morris, *Collected Works* (London, 1913), XVIII, p. 11.
[60] *ibid.*, XVIII, p. 168.
[61] *ibid.*, XIX, pp. 65-6.
[62] *ibid.*, XIX, p. 15.
[63] *ibid.*, XIX, p. 73.
[64] *ibid.*, XIX, p. 83.
[65] *ibid.*, XIX, pp. 65-6.
[66] *Essays* (1924), p. 336.
[67] *ibid.*, p. 337.
[68] *Autobiographies*, p. 144.
[69] *ibid.*, pp. 141-2.
[70] *ibid.*, p. 151.
[71] *ibid.*, p. 150.
[72] *Essays* (1924), p. 78.
[73] *ibid.*, p. 77.
[74] *ibid.*, p. 67.
[75] *Autobiographies*, p. 294.
[76] *ibid.*, p. 292.
[77] *Essays* (1924), p. 336.
[78] *Cf. Mythologies*, p. 114.
[79] *v.* (for instance) *Ideals In Ireland*, p. 97. *Cf.* Blake's maxim: 'The ruins of time build mansions in Eternity.'
[80] I cannot countenance Ure's suggestion that the first chorus describes the Old Man: he is not lofty or dissolute. The first chorus shows us Cuchulain climbing the penitential mountain and is a kind of preview of Yeats's central character, who is late in appearing on stage. For another description of Abiegnos, *v. Plays*, p. 382.
[81] From 'The Pathway' (essay on Mohini Chatterjee); not generally collected, but in the Shakespeare Head Press, *Yeats*, Vol. VIII.
[82] *Visions And Beliefs*, II, p. 303. Quoted also in *Per Amica*.
[83] Villiers is in fact himself quoting, from Aquinas.

[84] *Milton*, I, 29, Keynes, pp. 516-17.
[85] *Cf.* note 9 above.
[86] In the Hanrahan Story, the hero is inhibited by a rather engaging nervousness, but presently falls asleep.
[87] *A Vision*, A, p. 61.
[88] *ibid.*
[89] *Ash Wednesday*, I. Contrast the qualified hope of *The Waste Land*, V.
[90] *Ash Wednesday*, III.
[91] *Essays* (1924), p. 69.
[92] *Ash Wednesday*, VI.

Chapter Three

[1] Yeats's ratio of dialogue to choric song is a simplification of the Noh procedure. *Cf.* Hiro Ishibashi's study of the structure of *At The Hawk's Well*.

[2] *Essays* (1924), p. 342.

[3] *ibid.*, pp. 337 ff.

[4] Lady Wilde: Ancient Legends of Ireland (London, 1888), p. 29.

[5] The sub-plot dealing with the relations between Fand and Bricriu is much illuminated from the early versions of *Emer*, where considerable space is given to it.

[6] *Plays And Controversies*, p. 332.

[7] Wade, p. 612.

[8] What I mean is that the last verse of 'The Statues', after the introduction of the Cuchulain image, is emotional (in its hatred and aspiration), formal (in its adherence to the grand style) and static in the sense that it seems a timeless, 'visionary' judgment. *Cf.* p. 290.

[9] *Wheels And Butterflies*, p. 69.

[10] *Iliad*, Book III. E. V. Rieu (Penguin) translation, p. 75.

[11] This is quoted from Yeats's stage directions: *Wheels And Butterflies*, p. 95.

[12] She makes this point in 'W. B. Yeats And The Noh'.

[13] *The Nō Plays Of Japan*, p. 226. I prefer Waley to Pound here simply for immediate lucidity's sake.

[14] Pound is quoting *Paradiso*, XXIII, 25.

[15] Each wave will be a spirit participating in Anima Mundi (*v.* part three of this essay).

[16] Pound, *The Translations*, p. 311.

[17] *Cf. Yeats And Tradition*, pp. 32, 82, 173.

[18] *Visions and Beliefs*, I, p. 291.

[19] *ibid.*

[20] *ibid.*, p. 292.

[21] *ibid.*

[22] *ibid.*, p. 293.

[23] *Cuchulain Of Muirthemne*, p. 290.

[24] *Mythologies*, p. 68.

[25] *ibid.*, pp. 68-9.

[26] In the first edition only of *The Secret Rose*.

[27] Yeats certainly knew Larminie, whose story 'The Red Pony' is referred to in his poem 'The Secret Rose'.

[28] Actually 'a Latin work of Pico' (*A Vision*, B, p. 20). Yeats may also have picked up information about Pico at second-hand, as he did information about Gemistus Pletho (*Wheels And Butterflies*, pp. 78-9).

[29] *Plays And Controversies*, p. 433.

[30] *Milton*, Book I, 15. Keynes, p. 496.

[31] *The Courtier* (trans. Hoby, 1900 ed.), IV, p. 350.

[32] Nesca Robb: *Neoplatonism Of The Italian Renaissance*, p. 122.

[33] Quoted from 'Per ritornar là donde venne fuora'. And *v*. Robb's commentary: pp. 250-2.

[34] *Essays* (1924), p. 517.

[35] *Essays* (1924), p. 454.

[36] Quoted from 'Negli anni molti, e nelle molte prove'. *v*. also Robb's commentary: *loc. cit.*

[37] *v. Essays* (1924), p. 56.

[38] *Essays* (1924), p. 526.

[39] *Autobiographies*, p. 272.

[40] *Cf.* Kathleen Raine's essay on Enitharmon, 'Female Spaces'.

[41] *Vala*, Night The Eighth, Keynes, p. 346.

[42] *Vala*, Night The Seventh, Keynes, p. 323.

[43] *Wheels And Butterflies*, pp. 78-9.

[44] *Mythologies*, p. 352.

[45] *ibid.*, p. 346.

[46] *Works* (1662 ed.), p. 125.

[47] In his preface to *Gitanjali*. Wordsworth's *Ode* is not overtly discussed, but no one could read Tagore's poem 60 (which Yeats is discussing) without being reminded of it.

[48] Wade, p. 768.

[49] *v*. Mathers: *Kabbalah Unveiled*, p. 104 *et passim*.

[50] This point is substantiated in Chapter Seven below.

[51] *Gebir*, I, 170 ff.

[52] *Cf. Essays* (1924), pp. 182, 354.

[53] 'The Circus Animals' Desertion.'

[54] Rhys strangely is not explicit about Vulcan and Manannan, but *cf.* p. 638, pp. 661 ff. And *v*. also *Gods And Fighting Men*, p. 101.

[55] *v*. for instance, *A Vision*, B, p. 105 (where Yeats speaks of the 'old primary' becoming the 'new antithetical').

56 *Essays 1931-6*, pp. 112-13.
57 *ibid.*
58 *v.* 'Franklin's Tale' (Robinson's ed.), F 1129-32.
59 Three Books Of Occult Philosophy, II, XXXIII, pp. 285 ff.
60 'The Crazed Moon.'
61 *op. cit.*, XXXII, pp. 284-5.
62 *Milton*, Book II, 35. Keynes, p. 526.
63 Oliver Edwards suggested this to me.
64 *A Vision*, A, pp. 61-3.
65 'Lacking a day to be complete', Plays, p. 292.
66 *A Vision*, A, pp. 66-9.
67 All this detail comes from *A Vision*, A, pp. 69-71; and *v.* also A, pp. 241 ff.
68 Quoted from 'The Phases Of The Moon'.
69 *A Vision*, A, pp. 91-7.
70 *ibid.*, A, p. 116.
71 *Wheels And Butterflies*, p. 79.
72 Quoted from 'The Double Vision Of Michael Robartes'. The dark and full moon of the poem symbolise the opposites in any of their aspects.
73 More particularly, I think a Jungian of the cast of, say, Joseph Campbell might see the play in the way I suggest.
74 *Romantic Image*, pp. 60 ff. But I should add that Kermode exonerates Yeats from 'obvious pathological interest' in his 'cult of the dead face'.
75 *A Vision*, B, p. 133.
76 *ibid.*, B, p. 286.
77 Quoted from 'The Old Age Of Michelangelo' in *Soldiers Bathing* by F. T. Prince.
78 *A Vision*, B, p. 286. The poem mentioned is 'Under Ben Bulben'.
79 Quoted from *The King Of The Great Clock Tower*: Plays, p. 639.
80 *The Speckled Bird*, typescript, book II, p. 106.
81 *America*, 8, 13. Keynes, p. 199.
82 *v.* Kathleen Raine's essay on 'Visions Of The Daughters Of Albion', where Blake's words are interpreted as I suggest.
83 *v. The Ascent Of Mount Carmel*, trans. D. Lewis, pp. 94-7. Quoted in Von Hügel's *The Mystical Element Of Religion* (which Yeats had read), II, 343.
84 *The Irish Dramatic Movement* (1953 ed.), p. 112.
85 Emer 'made' Cuchulain 'impure': 'Plays', p. 293.
86 In his epigram 'On Those That Hated "The Playboy Of The Western World", 1907'.
87 Quoted from 'Beautiful Lofty Things'.

[88] Keynes, p. 776.
[89] *Autobiographies*, pp. 364-5.
[90] *Wheels And Butterflies*, p. 77.
[91] He uses both for *The Bridegroom* (*v.* Appendix I).
[92] 'When Helen Lived.'

Chapter Four

[1] *The Cat And The Moon And Certain Poems*, p. 36.
[2] Waley, p. 18.
[3] *Wheels And Butterflies*, p. 135.
[4] *ibid.*, p. 138.
[5] *The Cat And The Moon And Certain Poems*, p. 35.
[6] *Autobiographies*, p. 295.
[7] *The Cat And The Moon And Certain Poems*, p. 35.
[8] *The King Of The Great Clock Tower*, p. 19.
[9] For this aspect of the play, *v. Wheels And Butterflies*, p. 141.
[10] Quoted from Campbell, *op. cit.*, p. 169. I am not claiming that Yeats knew this particular story, but that it is representative of stories he knew. I quote it because the doctrine behind it will help later with 'Solomon And The Witch'.
[11] *v. Yeats And Tradition*, p. 134.
[12] *The Cat And The Moon And Certain Poems*, p. 36.
[13] *ibid.*, p. 36.
[14] *ibid.*, 'preface to Lady Gregory'.
[15] *ibid.*
[16] Quoted from Yeats's preface to *Gods And Fighting Men*.
[17] *Essays 1931-6*, p. 80.
[18] *ibid.*
[19] *ibid.*, p. 86.
[20] In *Seven Short Plays*, Dublin, 1910.
[21] Published in *The Yellow Bittern And Other Plays*, Dublin, 1920.
[22] *ibid.*
[23] *Cf. The Lonely Tower*, pp. 74 ff. But Henn makes the point I am after more directly in an unpublished paper on Synge.
[24] At one level, as Henn once pointed out to me, *The Player Queen* celebrates the triumph of 'beauty's cruelty'. For the 'brutality' of *The Herne's Egg*, *cf.* the rape scene: *Plays*, pp. 662 ff.
[25] *Cf.* my *Emer* essay, p. 125 above.
[26] *Essays* (1924), pp. 343 ff.
[27] *Cf. Essays* (1924), pp. 361 ff.

[28] *A Vision*, B, p. 81.

[29] *Isis Unveiled*, I, 5.

[30] v. Campbell, *op. cit.*, pp. 255 ff.

[31] I quote the Mandukya Upanishad as a text much discussed by Yeats: e.g. in *Essays 1931-6*.

[32] v. the last section of the present essay.

[33] 'Meditations In Time Of Civil War', IV: 'My Descendants.'

[34] v. Burnet, *Early Greek Philosophy*, p. 248; for Yeats's idea of Empedocles' theory, *A Vision*, B, p. 67.

[35] v. *Statesman*, 270 ff.

[36] *Wheels And Butterflies*, p. 106.

[37] *Cf.* Campbell, pp. 263 ff. Whatever of this Yeats did not know from Madame Blavatsky, he knew from Hastings's *Encyclopaedia*.

[38] Cornford: *Principium Sapientiae*, p. 183.

[39] *Wheels And Butterflies*, p. 106.

[40] 'Dove Or Swan': *A Vision*, B, p. 267 ff. (Text in A version identical.)

[41] *A Vision*, B, p. 279.

[42] *ibid.*

[43] *ibid.*

[44] *ibid.*, p. 280.

[45] *Cf. A Vision*, B, p. 281, where the pesfectibility of humanity at this time is certainly implied.

[46] *A Vision*, B, p. 284.

[47] *ibid.*, p. 285.

[48] *ibid.*, pp. 292-3.

[49] *Autobiographies*, p. 291.

[50] *Cf. Yeats And Tradition*, pp. 80, 159.

[51] Quaritch *Blake*, II, 85 ff. *Cf.* I, 259.

[52] *Cf.* a book known to Yeats, *The Lost Language Of Symbolism*, by Harold Bayley (London, 1912), I, pp. 84, 288; *cf.* pp. 271-2.

[53] v. Bayley, I, p. 288; *cf. Essays 1931-6*, p. 87.

[54] Quaritch *Blake*, I, 337; *cf.* II, 89-90.

[55] For Yeats's reading of the elemental connotations, *cf.* Wade, p. 286. Earth=body, water=heart, air=mind, fire=soul.

[56] 'Flighty' is also used *by* Septimus of Decima and the Unicorn; but it belongs peculiarly to him, as the favourite commendation in his vocabulary.

[57] *The Cat And The Moon And Certain Poems*, p. 36.

[58] Yeats knew Vico from Croce's *The Philosophy Of Giambattista Vico*, London,

1913. Vico's works had not at the time been translated. For Vico's 'cyclic series', *v*. Croce, pp. 124-5.

[59] *v*. Croce, p. 122.
[60] *Wheels And Butterflies*, p. 138.
[61] Three Books Of Occult Philosophy, I, Cap XXIV, p. 55.
[62] *Essays* (1924), p. 289.

Chapter Five

[1] *Plays And Controversies*, p. 332.

[2] Wade, p. 645.

[3] This preoccupation is discussed in Hiro Ishibashi's thesis.

[4] *Plays And Controversies*, p. 459.

[5] *Arabia Deserta*, II, 190.

[6] *ibid.*, II, 192.

[7] *Cf.* Plutarch, *Morals* II, 413 and *Yeats And Tradition*, pp. 244-5.

[8] *Plays And Controversies*, p. 459.

[9] Mathers: *Kabbalah Unveiled*, p. 104.

[10] *v.* note 10 to Chapter Two. This is perhaps the statement in the present book about which I feel most doubtful; though not doubtful enough to delete it.

[11] *v.* the preface to 'Psychology And Alchemy' and Kathleen Raine's essay 'Jesus The Imagination'.

[12] For a commentary on 'The Moods', *v.* Witt, in *Explicator*, VI. Kathleen Raine and I both suspect an Indian influence on this poem; though I cannot prove one.

[13] I write this; but I would not care to speculate on the logical distinction between them.

[14] *v.* Fränger: *The Millennium Of Hieronymus Bosch*; *passim*.

[15] *v. Autobiographies*, pp. 286-7.

[16] Wilde; *Works* (London, 1948), pp. 843-4.

[17] *Plays And Controversies*, p. 460.

[18] 'Comfort and succour all them, who in this transitory life are in trouble, sorrow, need, sickness, or any other adversity.'

[19] Or perhaps it may simply be that Yeats and Wilde use a similar 'period' style for their prose history plays.

[20] *v. Autobiographies*, pp. 286-7.

[21] *Cf.* Wade, p. 379.

[22] *v.* (for example) Wade, pp. 402, 403.

[23] *The Birth Of Tragedy* (trans. Haussmann, 1909; edition in Yeats's library), p. 34.

[24] *ibid.*, p. 23.

[25] *ibid.*, p. 36.

[26] Vacillation, VIII.

NOTES

27 *The Birth Of Tragedy*, p. 26.

28 *ibid.*

29 For example, in St. Augustine and Tertullian: and see my essay on 'Demon And Beast'.

30 Reproduced in *The Identity Of Yeats*, p. 97.

31 *ibid.*

32 *ibid.*

33 My point of view here has been expressed on p. 168.

34 *Cf. Essays 1931-6*, pp. 112-16 and Burnet, *Early Greek Philosophy* (1892), pp. 156, 173, 176. But whatever Yeats says in his *Essays*, my references in Burnet suggest that he founded on Heraclitus at a time when he still doubted the ultimate efficacy of subjective religion. 'Lunar' souls are immature.

35 Plato: *Sophist*, 242, D, E.

36 *1930 Diary*, p. 18.

37 *ibid.*

38 *Essays 1931-6*, p. 116.

39 *The Secret Rose* (1897 ed.), pp. 212-15.

40 *Antony And Cleopatra*, III, 2.

41 The note ran 'And what is this God, for whom He taught the saints to lacerate their bodies, to starve and exterminate themselves, but the spiritual objective?'

42 *Plays And Controversies*, p. 459.

43 'The White Birds'; 'Upon a Political Prisoner'.

44 Here I interpret the symbol in its strict Platonic sense (the sea of *Hyle*), as opposed to the sense conferred on it in Italian Renaissance Neoplatonism.

45 So Yeats consistently interprets the eagle-symbol in the Quaritch *Blake*.

46 *v.* p. 152 above.

47 *Cf.* the discussion of swan-symbolism in Horrwitz: *The Indian Theatre* (in Yeats's library).

48 *v. Essays* (1924 ed. *only*), p. 440.

49 *Plays And Controversies*, p. 188. Yeats is comparing the audiences who listened to 'old writers' such as Wolfram von Eschenbach, and his ideal modern stage audience, an audience of Platonic 'friends' and 'lovers'.

50 'Where There Is Nothing': in 'The Secret Rose'. There is also of course a play with the same title and theme; and *cf.* Martin's last speeches in *The Unicorn From The Stars*.

51 *Plays And Controversies*, p. 459.

52 The draft also says: 'Perhaps Lazarus and Judas are also among those whose daemons are birds.'

53 *Plays And Controversies*, p. 461.

54 *ibid.*

55 I am thinking of Jung's theory of synchronicity.

[56] First draft version.
[57] *A Vision*, B, p. 224.
[58] Superior and inferior cycles (and thus by analogy those who live in them) are symbolised, in Indian tradition, by high and low throws of the dice. Yeats knew this from Hastings, *Encyclopaedia Of Religion And Ethics*, I, 200.

Chapter Six

[1] *Cf.* Bjersby, p. 63.
[2] *Cf. The Irish Republic* by Dorothy Macardle (Dublin, 1951 ed.), p. 179.
[3] Quoted from the notes to Vol. I of *Irish Folk History Plays* (London, 1912), p. 205.
[4] *ibid.*, p. 206.
[5] *Cf. A Historical Memoir Of The O'Briens* by John O'Donoghue (Dublin, 1860), pp. 124-6.
[6] 'Red Hanrahan's Vision.' My text here is that of *The Secret Rose* (1897 ed.), pp. 181-3.
[7] Hone, p. 304.
[8] *Inferno*, V, 91.
[9] *ibid.*, 139.
[10] *Paradiso*, XXX, 87.
[11] The metre of 'Pardon, Old Fathers' seems to me as close to *terza rima* as, say, 'Little Gidding', II. The bareness and thrustfulness of the verse seem eminently Dantesque.
[12] 'The Pentameron': *Works*, IX, p. 164.
[13] Macardle, *loc. cit.*
[14] *Cf. Yeats And Tradition*, p. 200.
[15] I cannot stress too strongly how important I think *The Courtier* in Yeats's development (*cf.* my *Emer* essay). How deeply he remembered Castiglione can be gauged from such references as *Autobiographies*, pp. 478, 545.
[16] First published in *Certain Noble Plays Of Japan*; reprinted in *Nō, or Accomplishment*, and *The Translations Of Ezra Pound*.
[17] This story is told in *Visions And Beliefs*, I, 122-3.
[18] *Visions And Beliefs*, II, 334 ff.
[19] This and the following quotations are from Pound, *The Translations*, pp. 286 ff.
[20] *Cf. Macbeth*, I, 3: 'What are these . . . /That look not like the inhabitants o' the earth/And yet are on't'; *et seq*.
[21] This seems a very Miltonic construction. *Cf.*, for instance, from *Paradise Lost*, II, 'These passed, *if any pass*, the void profound/of unessential night receives him next'.
[22] *v. Yeats And Tradition*, pp. 140 ff.
[23] *Cf.*, for example, *A Vision*, B, p. 236.
[24] *Visions And Beliefs*, II, 331.

[25] *Three Books Of Occult Philosophy*, III, Cap XLI: pp. 476, 479.
[26] *ibid.*, p. 475.
[27] *Fairy And Folk Tales Of The Irish Peasantry* (London, 1888), p. 311.
[28] Lady Wilde: *Ancient Legends Of Ireland* (London, 1888), p. 29.
[29] *ibid.*, p. 133.
[30] Robert Kirk: *The Secret Commonwealth* (London, 1893 ed.), p. 6. Cf. *Visions And Beliefs*, I, 287.
[31] *The Immortality Of The Soul* (in *Works*, 1662 ed.), pp. 176-7.
[32] *Visions And Beliefs*, II, 332.
[33] More, *op. cit.*, p. 182.
[34] *ibid.*, p. 181.
[35] *ibid.*, p. 182.
[36] *Visions And Beliefs*, II, 167-8.
[37] *v. Yeats And Tradition*, pp. 185, 238.
[38] I should stress that this is one place where I am giving a maximal interpretation, and that we are not *forced* to see symbolism in 'A Last Confession'.
[39] Yeats's theory here is explained in all detail in 'The Great Year Of The Ancients' in *A Vision*.
[40] *Plays*, pp. 428-9. He brays 'as if he were the Voice of God'.
[41] *v. Yeats And Tradition*, pp. 223 ff.

Appendix to Part Two

[1] They are merely handwritten sheets of paper clipped together: rough preliminary notes, a verse draft of scenes one and two, a prose draft which goes on to cover the remainder, and some revisions and amplifications to the climactic scene four.

[2] *v. The Unicorn*, p. 411. I am reducing Virginia Moore's question (which is general) to the special sphere of sexual love.

[3] Pound's translation is so scrappy that Yeats may have taken the play to mean almost anything, but Hiro Ishibashi agrees with me in supposing that he read it as 'about' the 'image'. *Cf.* Waley, p. 179.

[4] Yeats read this poem in Burkitt's *Early Eastern Christianity* and drew on it for 'Cuchulain Comforted'. *Cf. Yeats And Tradition*, p. 250.

[5] Yeats of course knew Symons's translation of 'Songs Of The Soul' and I take it as virtually certain, from his text, that he also knew 'Songs Between The Soul And The Bridegroom'.

[6] *Cf. A Vision*, B, p. 70. Flaubert's story was in fact projected, but never written.

Part Three

In this section of the book again, I ought to acknowledge to scholars not mentioned in my text: especially to Parkinson (pp. 13 ff.) on 'The Two Trees', Ellmann (*The Identity of Yeats*, p. 76) on 'He thinks of his past greatness', Witt (*Explicator*, VII) on 'The Collar-Bone Of A Hare'—Saul also wrote me a helpful letter about this poem—Jeffares (p. 228) on Yeats's shell-symbolism, Witt again (*Explicator*, IV) on 'Mohini Chatterjee', and Ure (*Rev. Eng. Studies*, XXV) on 'The Statues'. While writing these notes I find that Dume (*M.L.N.*, LXVII) has anticipated me in relating 'Sailing To Byzantium' to Gibbon.

CHAPTER SEVEN

[1] *v. Romantic Image*, p. 96; and Keynes, p. 7.

[2] *Vala*, Night The Seventh, Keynes, p. 321.

[3] *v. Celtic Heathendom*, pp. 222, 296, 359, 557-8.

[4] *The History Of Magic* by Joseph Ennemoser, (i), 377-8. Information from Mrs. Yeats.

[5] For these references, see *The Migration Of Symbols*, pp. 127, 130, 155, 161, 162, 166-7, 169.

[6] Mathers: *Kabbalah Unveiled*, pp. 104, 158-60.

[7] *v. Yeats And Tradition*, p. 238.

[8] *Cf. Romantic Image*, p. 94.

[9] *v.* p. 169 above.

[10] *The Identity Of Yeats*, p. 76.

[11] *Cf.* also the distorting mirror in the second verse of Part II of 'A Dialogue Of Self And Soul'.

[12] Yeats's main source for his understanding of the Dionysus myth was probably Thomas Taylor's *A Dissertation*, q.v. for the symbol in question.

[13] *Cf.* Yeats's own name within the Order of the Golden Dawn: 'Demon Est Deus Inversus.'

[14] The detail of 'men's souls bartered and bought' suggests the play.

[15] Lady Charlotte Guest's translation (1906 ed.), p. 273.

[16] *ibid.*

[17] Taken from *The Irish Mythological Cycle* by H. D'Arbois de Jubainville, p. 137.

[18] *ibid.*

[19] Trans. J. M. Crawford, I, p. 126. Yeats often refers to the *Kalevala* in *Ideas Of Good And Evil*.

[20] The relation is of course tangential: the tree is in the poem, the cauldron in the story.

[21] *Cf. Poems*, notes, p. 525.

[22] I should stress that this paragraph is merely 'about' two symbols in Yeats's poem: it is not meant as a commentary on its total meaning. And even the symbol of the 'obscure dark' has further implications: it could be read as standing for Anima Mundi ('true civilisation is tossed up out of Spiritus Mundi, made possible by an influx of grace').

[23] *Visions Of The Daughters Of Albion*, 3, 16, Keynes, p. 191.

[24] *Cf.* Ellmann, *The Identity of Yeats*, p. 254.

[25] *Cf. Yeats And Tradition*, pp. 248-9.

[26] *Cf.* p. 243 above; and *Yeats And Tradition* p. 75. Medieval Christianity also uses these symbols of prince and princess, less reasonably, since its deity has no feminine aspect. For the logic of such symbolism, *cf.* my *Bridegroom* essay.

[27] More: *Works* (1662) pp. 181 ff.

[28] *ibid.*

[29] *Visions And Beliefs*, II, 310.

[30] *ibid.*

[31] It would not be objective if we could read 'tomb' as a synonym for 'the heavenly world', but the correlation of poem and source suggests that 'tomb' represents 'extinction'.

[32] Saul: *Poems*, p. 29.

[33] *Literary Works of da Vinci* (ed. Richter), II, p. 242. Neumann, p. 278.

[34] *The Wheel* was actually written (spontaneously) in 1921, but it is 'reactionary' as the unadorned versification of an idea that had haunted Yeats since the 'nineties. *The Hour Before Dawn* is taken after it, as the embellishment of this germinal idea.

[35] *Cf. The Well At The World's End*, I, 213, 221; and A. J. Wensinck, *Encyclopaedia of Islam*, I, 497-8.

[36] MacNeice, p. 113.

[37] I am quoting 'Tom O'Roughley'.

[38] The *Lausiac History*, trans. W. K. L. Clarke, p. 78.

[39] *ibid.*, p. 65.

[40] *ibid.*, p. 103.

[41] *ibid.*, p. 164.

[42] *v. The Permanence Of Yeats*, p. 338. To be just, he calls *The Spur* 'not very pleasant' but 'impressive'.

[43] For this phrase (used often by Yeats) *v*. the *Lausiac History*, p. 79.

[44] If 'being no more demoniac' modifies 'stupid happy creature' we have a

second, more tangible clue; though I doubt this. But it may be that it is the 'gull' that seemed 'demoniac'.

[45] *Mythologies*, pp. 337-8.
[46] Boehme, 'The Threefold Life Of Man', vi, 43.
[47] *Jerusalem*, I, 13 and *Milton*, 31; Keynes, p. 633 and p. 520.
[48] *Milton*, 35, Keynes, p. 526.
[49] Parkinson, reviewing *Yeats And Tradition*, speaks of 'Stream And Sun At Glendalough' as a poem written in emotion on Lady Gregory's death. Perhaps the fact that it is also a 'mystical' and 'traditional' poem may show how real Yeats's tradition was to him. For my Boehme reference, a scholar might compare *The Speckled Bird*, II, 88.
[50] Henn, p. 57.
[51] Lafcadio Hearn translation, p. 17.
[52] *ibid.*, pp. 48 ff.
[53] *ibid.*
[54] *Plays*, pp. 424 ff.
[55] *Essays 1931-6*, p. 130.
[56] *ibid.*, pp. 130-1.
[57] 'Estrangement', VII.
[58] *v. Gods And Fighting Men*, p. 285.
[59] *The Decline And Fall Of The Roman Empire* (ed. J. B. Bury), VI, 26.
[60] 'Die Nachtigall.'
[61] *v.* Bury, VI, 81.
[62] I owe to Kathleen Raine the suggestion that, at the level of regeneration, the Emperor will symbolise the Demiurge; in Gnostic tradition, the lower function of deity, sunk in the amnesia of generation (*v.* her essay 'Who Made The Tyger?'). Thus 'to keep a drowsy emperor awake' can be given particular significance on this plane.
[63] 'The Four Ages Of Man.'
[64] 'Ribh Considers Christian Love Insufficient.'
[65] *v. Gitanjali*, poem 60; page 54.
[66] *v.* Yeats's introduction to *Gitanjali*, p. xxii.
[67] *Cf.* S. Brodetsky, *Newton* (London, 1927), p. 153.
[68] *v.* Thomas Taylor, *A Dissertation*, *passim*.
[69] Not reproduced in *Collected Poems*.
[70] I take this line as a deliberate ambiguity: Yeats will relive his experience both now, in the process of casting out remorse, and in another incarnation.
[71] *Cf. Yeats And Tradition*, p. 126 (note).
[72] *W. B. Yeats: The Tragic Phase*, pp. 59-75.
[73] *The Permanence Of Yeats*, pp. 202, 213.
[74] It is interesting to recall that Nietzsche influenced this side of Yeats's thought. *v.* p. 183.

[75] *Autobiographies*, p. 150.
[76] *Essays* (1924), p. 278.
[77] *ibid.*, p. 280.
[78] *ibid.*
[79] *A Vision*, A, p. 182.
[80] *ibid.*
[81] *v. Masterpieces of Greek Sculpture, passim*; for Scopas, p. 302.
[82] *ibid.*, pp. 437-50.
[83] *ibid.*
[84] *Autobiographies*, p. 150.
[85] *ibid.*, pp. 364-5.
[86] *On The Boiler*, p. 37.
[87] *Visions Of The Daughters Of Albion*, 7, 3, Keynes, p. 194.
[88] *On The Boiler*, p. 22.
[89] Wade, p. 911.
[90] *Autobiographies*, p. 152.
[91] *ibid.*, pp. 141-2.
[92] *v. Plays And Controversies*, p. 215.
[93] *A Vision*, B, p. 277.
[94] *Wheels And Butterflies*, p. 73.
[95] *Essays 1931-6*, p. 3.
[96] *v. Wade*, p. 911.
[97] *v.* for instance, Standish O'Grady, *History Of Ireland* (1881), I, p. 164.
[98] *op. cit.*, pp. 63-5.

Appendix to Part Three

[1] v. *Yeats And Tradition*, p. 72. I should stress that the *Mabinogion* is only tangentially relevant to Yeats's two sister-plays, and only relevant at all to the first of them.

[2] I mean this simply as a statement of fact and there is of course no implied slur.

[3] 'Gyres In The Poetry Of W. B. Yeats' (*English Studies*, June, 1946), as well as his comments in *W. B. Yeats: Man And Poet*.

[4] In *E.L.H.*, March, 1951.

SELECT BIBLIOGRAPHY

SELECT BIBLIOGRAPHY

(*a*) Texts

Collected Poems Of W. B. Yeats. London, 1950.
Collected Plays Of W. B. Yeats. London, 1952.
Autobiographies. London, 1955.
The Cat And The Moon And Certain Poems. Dublin, 1924.
Essays. London, 1924.
Essays 1931 to 1936. Dublin, 1937.
The King Of The Great Clock Tower. Dublin, 1934.
Letters, ed. Allan Wade. London, 1954.
Letters On Poetry To Dorothy Wellesley. London, 1940.
Letters To The New Island. Cambridge, Mass., 1934.
Mythologies. London, 1958.
On The Boiler. Dublin, 1939.
Pages From A Diary Written In 1930. Dublin, 1944.
Plays And Controversies. London, 1923.
A Vision. London, 1925.
A Vision (revised). London, 1937.
Wheels And Butterflies. London, 1934.
Where There Is Nothing. London, 1903.
W. B. Yeats And T. Sturge Moore: Their Correspondence. London, 1953.

I have also been greatly helped by the Variorum edition by Alspach and Allt and by Saul's *Prolegomena* to Poems and Plays.

(*b*) Works introduced, translated, etc., by Yeats

Blake: *Works*. Edited by E. J. Ellis and W. B. Yeats. Quaritch, London, 1893.
Fairy And Folk Tales Of The Irish Peasantry. Edited by W. B. Yeats. London, 1888.
Ideals In Ireland. With a contribution by W. B. Yeats. Dublin, 1901.
Irish Fairy And Folk Tales. Edited by W. B. Yeats. London, 1893.
A Book Of Irish Verse. Selected by W. B. Yeats. London, 1895.
Gitanjali, by Rabindranath Tagore. Introduction by W. B. Yeats. London, 1913.
The Ten Principal Upanishads. Trans. Shree Purohit Swami and W. B. Yeats. London, 1937.
The Aphorisms Of Patanjali. Introduction by W. B. Yeats. London, 1938.
Visions And Beliefs In The West Of Ireland, by Lady Gregory. With essays by W. B. Yeats. London, 1920.

(c) Criticism, Biography, etc.

Adams, Hazard:	*Blake And Yeats: The Contrary Vision.* New York, 1955.
Bjersby, Birgit:	*The Interpretation Of The Cuchulain Legend In The Works Of W. B. Yeats.* Uppsala, 1950.
Ellmann, Richard:	*Yeats: The Man And The Masks.* London, 1948.
	The Identity Of Yeats. London, 1954.
Henn, T. R.:	*The Lonely Tower.* London, 1950.
Hone, J. M.:	*W. B. Yeats.* London, 1942.
Hough, Graham:	*The Last Romantics.* London, 1949.
Jeffares, A. N.:	*W. B. Yeats: Man and Poet.* London, 1949.
Kermode, Frank:	*Romantic Image.* London, 1957.
Koch, Vivienne:	*W. B. Yeats: The Tragic Phase.* London, 1951.
MacNeice, Louis:	*The Poetry Of W. B. Yeats.* London, 1941.
Moore, Virginia:	*The Unicorn.* New York, 1954.
Parkinson, Thomas:	*W. B. Yeats, Self-Critic.* Berkeley and Los Angeles, 1951.
Rudd, M.:	*Divided Image.* London, 1953.
Ure, Peter:	*Towards A Mythology.* London, 1946.

The Permanence Of Yeats. Selected Criticism. New York, 1950.

(d) General

Agrippa:	*Three Books Of Occult Philosophy* (1651 translation).
d'Alviella, Count Goblet:	*The Migration Of Symbols.* London, 1894.
Avalon, Arthur (Sir John Woodroffe):	*Principles of Tantra.* London, 1914.
Bayley, Harold:	*The Lost Language Of Symbolism.* London, 1912.
Blavatsky, H. P.:	*Isis Unveiled.* London, 1910.
Bowra, Sir C. M.	*The Heritage Of Symbolism.* London, 1947.
Brodetsky, S.:	*Newton.* London, 1927.
Burkitt, F. C.:	*Early Eastern Christianity.* London, 1904.
Burnet, John:	*Early Greek Philosophy.* London, 1892.
Campbell, Joseph:	*The Hero With A Thousand Faces.* New York, 1949.

SELECT BIBLIOGRAPHY

Corkery, D.:	*The Yellow Bittern And Other Plays.* Dublin, 1920.
Cornford, F. M.:	*Principium Sapientiae.* Cambridge, 1952.
Crawford, J. M. (trans.):	*The Kalevala.* London, 1889.
Croce, Benedetto:	*The Philosophy Of Giambattista Vico.* London, 1913.
Curtin, Jeremiah:	*Myths And Folklore Of Ireland.* Boston, 1890.
Doughty, C. M.:	*Travels In Arabia Deserta.* London, 1926 ed.

The Literary Works Of Leonardo Da Vinci. Ed. J. P. Richter. Oxford, 1939.

Ellis-Fermor, Una:	*The Irish Dramatic Movement.* London, 1954 ed.
Ennemoser, Joseph:	*The History Of Magic.* London, 1854 trans.
Flaubert:	*The Temptation Of St. Anthony.* Trans. Lafcadio Hearn. London, 1911.
Fränger, Wilhelm:	*The Millennium Of Hieronymus Bosch.* London, 1942.
Furtwängler, Adolf:	*Masterpieces Of Greek Sculpture.* London, 1895.
	Greek And Roman Sculpture. London, 1914.
Gibbon:	*The Decline And Fall Of The Roman Empire.* Ed. J. B. Bury. London, 1909-14.
Gregory, Lady:	*Cuchulain Of Muirthemne.* London, 1902.
	Gods And Fighting Men. London, 1904.
	Irish Folk-History Plays. London, 1912.
	Seven Short Plays. Dublin, 1910.
Hastings:	*Encyclopaedia Of Religion And Ethics.*
Horrwitz, E. P.:	*The Indian Theatre.* London, 1912.
Von Hügel, Baron:	*The Mystical Element Of Religion.* London, 1908.
Jowett, B.:	*The Translations Of Plato.* Oxford, 1892 ed.
de Jubainville, H. D'Arbois:	*The Irish Mythological Cycle.* Dublin, 1903.
Jung, C. G.:	*Psychology And Alchemy.* Trans. R. F. C. Hull. London, 1955.
Keynes, G.:	*The Complete Writings Of William Blake.* London, 1957.

Kirk, Robert:	*The Secret Commonwealth*. London, 1893 ed.
Landor:	*Works*. Ed. T. Earle Welby. London, 1928.

The Lausiac History of Palladius. Trans. W. K. L. Clarke. London, 1918.

Lewis, David (trans.):	*The Ascent of Mount Carmel*. London, 1889.

The Mabinogion. Trans. Lady Charlotte Guest. 1906, Everyman's ed.

McAnally, T.:	*Irish Wonders*. Boston, 1888.
Macardle, Dorothy:	*The Irish Republic*. Dublin, 1951.
Mathers, Macgregor:	*Kabbalah Unveiled*. London, 1887.
Miner, Earl:	*The Japanese Tradition In British And American Literature*. Princeton, 1958.
More, Henry:	*A Collection Of Several Philosophical Writings Of Dr. Henry More* (1662).
Morris, William:	*Works*. London, 1913.
Neumann, Erich:	*The Origins And History Of Consciousness*. London, 1954.
Nietzsche:	*The Birth Of Tragedy*. Trans. W. Haussmann. London, 1909.
Nutt, A. T.:	*The Legends Of The Holy Grail*. London, 1892.
O'Donoghue, John:	*A Historical Memoir Of The O'Briens*. Dublin, 1860.
O'Grady, Standish:	*History Of Ireland*. Dublin, 1881.
O'Grady, Standish Hayes:	*Silva Gadelica*. London, 1892.
Plutarch:	*Morals*. Trans. several hands. London, 1870.
Pound, Ezra:	*Nō Or Accomplishment*. New York, 1917. *The Translations*. London, 1951.
Prince, F. T.:	*Soldiers Bathing*. London, 1954.
Rhys, Sir J.:	*Lectures On The Origin And Growth Of Religion As Illustrated By Celtic Heathendom*. London, 1888.
Rieu, E. V. (trans.):	*The Iliad*. London, 1950.
Robb, Nesca:	*Neoplatonism Of The Italian Renaissance*. London, 1935.
Schuon, F.:	*Gnosis: The Timeless Key*. London, 1959.

Sherrard, Philip:	*The Greek East And The Latin West.* London, 1959.
Stopes, M. C.:	*Plays Of Old Japan: The No.* London, 1912.
Symons, Arthur:	*Collected Works.* London, 1924.
Taylor, Thomas:	*A Dissertation.* Amsterdam, 1790.
Waley, Arthur:	*The Nō Plays Of Japan.* London, 1921.
Wensinck, A. J.:	*The Encyclopaedia Of Islam.*
Weston, Jessie:	*The Legend Of Sir Perceval.* London, 1906-9.
Wilde, Lady:	*Ancient Legends Of Ireland.* London, 1888.
Wilde:	*Works.* London, 1948.

(e) Theses

Becker, W.:	'Yeats As A Playwright.' Oxford, 1953.
Ishibashi, Hiro:	'W. B. Yeats And The Noh.' Keio University, Japan, 1956.

(f) Articles

Full details of articles mentioned are given in the notes.

INDEX

INDEX

AE, 39-40, 41, 51
Aeschylus, 298
Agrippa, 159, 204, 224, 229, 231, 233; Mansions of Moon, 106-7; on ghost, 223, 227-9
alchemy, 13, 14, 20, 39-40, 44-6, 54, 65, 258-9
d'Alviella, 249, 280, 284
Amadan, 57, 60, 300
Amergin, Song of, 256-7
Andersen, Hans, 284
Aoife, 40-1, 87
Arabian Nights, 165
Aristotle, 147
Arthurian Myth, 259, 304
Awoi No Uye, 84, 243
Axël, 44, 62, 241

Balzac, 125 (and note)
Bardesan, 243
Baudelaire, 261
Becker, W., 15
Bjersby, B., 15, 41, 311
Blackmur, R. P., 23, 306
Blake, 14, 15, 20, 45, 51, 62, 143, 160, 167, 171, 177, 221, 248, 252, 258(n), 264, 269, 291; *Thel*, 15, 100; on soul 'shaping its vehicle', 93-4, 'Enitharmon's Daughters', 96; two 'paths' of soul, 107; on free love, 117-18, 260-1; *Laocoon*, 122; *Tiriel* symbolism, 152-7; on 'Shape-changers', 229-30; on 'centres', 275; on 'moment of desire', 296-7
Blavatsky, 146, 170, 252, 284

Boehme, 13, 47; on 'transcendental virgin', 49-50; on 'centres', 274-6; on divine matrix, 280
Bosch, 162, 171
Botticelli, 14, 100, 103, 153
Bowra, Sir C. M., 14
Browne, Sir Thomas, 223
Buddhism, 17, 30, 33, 37, 43, 57, 62, 66, 129, 146, 147, 170, 203, 249, 305; Buddha myth, 46-52; Buddha-image, 294, 299-300; Zen, 30, 224-5; Tantric Buddhism, 33, 51(n), 130-1, 225, 280
Burne-Jones, 110
Burnet, 194

Calvert, 264
Campbell, Joseph, 50-2, 61, 257(n)
Castiglione, 92, 94-5, 101, 116, 151, 211-12
Catullus, 276
Cavafy, 270 (and note)
Cavalcanti, 213
Chaucer, 106
Chrétien de Troyes, 280
Claude, 264
Cloona, 90, 108, 241, 242
Colum, Padraic, 132, 136-7, 138 (and note), 141
Connla, 34, 38-9
Connolly, Cyril, 282
Coomaraswamy, Ananda, 294(n)
Corkery, D., 132, 135-6, 137, 138
Crookes, Sir William, 122-3
Cudworth, 224
Curtin, J., 36-7

Dante, 27, 28, 44, 84, 150, 151, 156, 210, 211, 212, 213, 224, 241, 305; Paolo and Francesca, 207-8, 210-11
Davie, Donald, 23(n)
Delacroix, 165
Donne, 276, 281, 289
Dostoievsky, 270
Doughty, 164-5, 199
Druidism, 252, 257
Dume, T. L., 328

Egypt, 20, 35, 152, 237; Isis and Osiris, 35; art, 293; Ireland and, 302
elemental symbolism, 153, 166(n), 195-6
Eliot, T. S., 22, 261, 272, 275; *Ash Wednesday*, 69-72, 89(n), 114; *Burnt Norton*, 126-7; *The Cocktail Party*, 243
Ellis-Fermor, Una, 120
Ellmann, Richard, 166(n), 252, 258(n), 328
Empedocles, 147, 184
Ennemoser, Joseph, 249
Eschenbach, Wolfram von, 46
Evans, Sebastian, 46

Fenollosa, 84(n), 213
Ferguson, Sir Samuel, 304
Flaubert, 244, 278-9
de Flora, Joachim, 171, 173, 196
Freud, 54(n), 244
Frobenius, 63
Furtwängler, Adolf, 294

Galatea, 121, 296
Gibbon, 284-5
Gita, 289
Goethe, 45, 167; *Wilhelm Meister*, 251
Golden Dawn, Order of, 38, 46, 59, 169, 170, 236, 280, 305

Gonne, Maud, 30, 102, 121-2, 125, 213, 250, 264, 282, 289, 295, 303
Gore-Booth, Eva, 53
Gregory, Lady, 104(n), 132, 137, 138, 205; *Gaol Gate*, 134-5; *Dervorgilla*, 209

Haggard, Rider, 284
Hagoromo, 84-6, 97, 98, 110
Henn, T. R., 106, 276, 281, 305, 311
Heraclitus, 107, 184
Hinduism, 17, 43, 96, 119, 130, 146, 147, 165, 170, 182, 280
Homer, 97, 147, 178, 179, 180, 182-3, 197 (and note), 260; Aphrodite rescuing Paris, 81-2, 109, 121
Hone, J. M., 207

Ibsen, 74
Ishibashi, Hiro, 15, 84

Jainism, 147
Jeffares, A. N., 305, 328
John of the Cross, St., 119, 244
de Jubainville, 257
Jung, 13, 17, 34, 43, 44, 46, 47, 48, 54, 96, 97, 114, 115, 146, 167, 169, 266

Kabbala, 13, 20, 39-40, 44, 64, 98-9, 166, 168, 250, 251 (and note), 252, 253, 257, 263, 276, 280, 284, 285, 287, 305
Kalevala, 257
Kallimachos, 293, 294
Kant, 146
Keats; *Eve of St. Agnes*, 37
Kermode, Frank, 115, 247, 248
Kirk, Robert, 232
Koch, Vivienne, 122, 290, 296, 299, 302, 309
Koran, 267

INDEX

Landor, 165; *Gebir*, 100; on Paolo and Francesca, 210-11
Larminie, W., 91-2
Lausiac History, 270-2, 274, 278
Lawrence, D. H., 267
Lucretius, 178, 194

Mabinogion, 87, 256, 257(n), 304
MacNeice, Louis, 268, 295
Maeterlinck, 57
magic, 83
Mahler, 263
Mallarmé, 57
Malory, 46, 48, 59
Marlowe, 124, 289
Marvell, 281(n)
Mathers, Macgregor, 20, 250, 251(n)
Mead, G. R. S., 237
Michelangelo, 94, 95, 101, 104, 116
Milarepa, 42(n)
Milton, 20, 223
Miner, E., 15, 23
Moore, George, 80, 130
Moore, Virginia, 15(n), 243, 304-5, 311
More, Henry, 92, 94, 95, 96, 98, 117, 204, 224, 260, 264; body of air, 232; music of the shade, 233-4
Morris, 14, 52-9, 61, 63, 66, 70-2, 73, 149, 267, 300
Motomezuka, 32, 214, 225, 305

Narcissus, 52, 59
Neoplatonism, 13, 14, 17, 20, 83, 168, 170, 179, 224, 225, 253, 261, 266, 296, 302; Italian Renaissance Neoplatonism, 92-104; beggar symbolism in, 152
Neumann, Erich, 266-7
Newton, 287
Niall, 34, 35-6, 41, 46, 49, 53
Nietzsche, 67, 108, 125, 146, 168, 187, 190, 194, 197, 254; on personality, 177-86

Nishikigi, 32, 213-23, 224, 228, 235, 239
Noh, 15, 23, 27-33, 73, 76, 82, 124, 138-9, 162, 163, 201, 204, 209, 213, 224, 242; *Kyogen*, 128-31; ritual of 'making a journey', 215, 217

O'Brien, Donough, 204, 206
Orpheus, 228

Palmer, Samuel, 264
Paracelsus, 96, 224
Parkinson, T., 328
Patmore, 292
Pearce, Donald, 306
Pheidias, 151, 293, 294, 298, 299, 300
Philolaus, 107, 184
Pico, 92
Plato, 47; on reincarnation, 96(n); on physical beauty, 116; on historical cycles, 147, 184; Nietzsche on, 178
Pletho, 83, 92, 98
Plotinus, 117, 149, 155, 260, 289
Plutarch; *Morals*, 29; *Lives*, 274
Porphyry, 306
Pound, Ezra, 84, 213, 219(n)
Pythagoras, 228, 295, 296, 297, 298, 299, 302

Raine, Kathleen, 96, 107(n), 229(n), 330
Ransom, J. C., 19
Rembrandt, 151
Rhys, Sir J., 39, 87, 249, 257
Robb, Nesca, 94, 95(n)
Rodin, 115, 119
Rosicrucianism, 20, 44, 62, 241, 263; *Marriage Of Christian Rosicrux*, 46-52
Rossetti, 57, 58
Rousseau, 155
Rudd, M., 107(n)

Samkara, 83
Saul, G. B., 266, 311, 328
Savage, D. S., 291
Scathach, 40-1
Schopenhauer, 51, 168, 177, 178, 179, 257
Schuon, F., 21
Scopas, 151, 293, 294, 298
Shakespeare, 17, 124, 151, 162, 223; *Antony And Cleopatra*, 189; *Macbeth*, 223; *Hamlet*, 235, 299-300; *Romeo And Juliet*, 242; *Julius Caesar*, 304
Shelley, 14, 57, 58, 71, 97, 269; *Epipsychidion*, 107, 117; and Platonic love, 120; *Prometheus Unbound*, 243
Sherrard, Philip, 21
Shintoism, 30, 182
Slieve Gullian, 34, 38, 39
Socrates, 178, 182-3
Sophocles, 178
Sotoba Komachi, 29, 30-1, 32
Spengler, O., 146
Spenser, 97
Stendhal, 301
Swedenborg, 13, 92(n), 165, 170, 224, 225, 229, 260, 264, 304; on love in heaven, 117; on 'shape-changer', 231(n)
Symons, Arthur, 276-8, 281, 283
Synge, 132, 133-4, 137, 138 (and note), 140, 142

Tagore, 100, 286-7
Taoism, 51, 257
Tennyson, 269
Tibetan folk-lore, 111; theology, 225
Titian, 59, 300
Tolstoy, 270
Toynbee, A., 146
Trismegistus, Hermes, 20, 237

Upanishads, 20, 33, 43, 112, 179, 184, 304; 'fortnights', 105-6; Mandukya-Upanishad, 146
Ure, Peter, 311, 328

Verhaeren, 57
Verlaine, 276
Vico, 146, 157-8
da Vinci, 266-7
Virgil, 185

Wagner, 56, 59, 181
Waley, Arthur, 84(n)
Weston, Jessie, 46-52
Wilde, Lady, 75, 231
Wilde, Oscar, 169, 174-7, 192, 194
Witt, Marion, 328
Wordsworth, 98, 287

Yeats, W. B.,
(i) *Books and Novellen cited*:
Adoration Of The Magi, The, 173, 237
Autobiographies, 59, 122, 129, 300
Celtic Twilight, The, 262, 306
Cutting Of An Agate, The, 28, 249; 'Discoveries', 74
Dhoya, 37-8, 39, 47(n), 66
Essays, 1931-6, 16, 105; 'Parnell', 301
Ideas Of Good And Evil, 52, 56, 166, 240(n)
On The Boiler, 295, 297, 298, 301
Per Amica Silentia Lunae, 159, 274
Rosa Alchemica, 169, 170, 171-3, 200
Secret Rose, The, 186; 'Red Hanrahan', 47-52, 64, 65, 258; 'Hanrahan's Vision', 207, 209
Speckled Bird, The, 46, 117, 253
Tables Of The Law, The, 169, 171, 173-4, 177, 266
Vision, A, 18, 29, 42, 67, 202, 218, 237(n), 244, 265, 271, 272,

INDEX

Yeats, W. B.—(*cont.*)
273, 301; 'Dove Or Swan', 21; Rebirths, 107-13; Woman's beauty, 115-16; history, 145-52; on 'shape-changer', 227, 231

Visions And Beliefs, 84(n), 87, 214, 224, 227, 229, 231, 233, 235, 264, 304

Wheels And Butterflies, 129, 157, 158

Wind Among The Reeds, The, 256

(ii) Plays mentioned:

At The Hawk's Well, 15, 18, 19, 27-72, 73, 74, 75, 83, 86, 88, 90, 108, 114, (and note), 126, 128, 152, 161, 168, 247, 254, 258, 259, 260, 275, 291, 300

Bridegroom, The, 79, 241-4, 260, 263, 303

Calvary, 15, 18, 70, 152, 161, 163-203, 227, 247, 251(n), 252, 265, 276

Cat And The Moon, The, 13, 15, 18, 28, 128-62

Countess Cathleen, The, 254, 262, 280

Death of Cuchulain, The, 152

Deirdre, 243

Dreaming Of The Bones, The, 15, 18, 28, 128, 204-40, 247, 276

Fighting The Waves, 17, 79-83, 97, 241, 301

Full Moon In March, A, 176, 183, 276, 282, 304

Green Helmet, The, 86, 97, 103

Herne's Egg, The, 131, 140, 187, 189, 230, 241, 304, 306

Hourglass, The, 143

King Of The Great Clock Tower, The, 127, 130, 183

King's Threshold, The, 250

On Baile's Strand, 88, 102, 143

Only Jealousy Of Emer, The, 15, 18, 19, 21, 23(n), 35, 70, 73-127, 161, 211, 224, 225, 226, 229, 238, 247, 260, 283, 290, 296, 298, 302

Player Queen, The, 140, 154, 237, 275, 280

Pot Of Broth, The, 137

Purgatory, 220(n), 254, 306

Resurrection, The, 79, 123, 176, 182, 183, 192-5, 268

Shadowy Waters, The, 230, 231

Unicorn From The Stars, The, 137, 177, 243, 275

Where There Is Nothing, 199

Words Upon The Windowpane, The, 23

(iii) Poems referred to:

'Aedh Wishes For The Cloths Of Heaven', 247, 265

'Aedh Pleads With The Elemental Powers', 250

'Among School Children', 47, 83(n), 127, 248, 251, 254, 303

'At Algeciras', 98-9, 100, 166, 247, 283-90

'Baile And Aillinn', 306

'Black Tower, The', 239, 304

'Blessed, The', 269

'Blood And The Moon', 87

'Broken Dreams', 210

'Bronze Head, A', 122, 291

'Byzantium', 22, 166, 214, 235, 248, 251, 280, 286, 289, 305

'Chosen', 306

'Circus Animals' Desertion, The', 102

'Collar Bone Of A Hare, The', 117-18, 247, 260-5

'Conjunctions', 236

'Coole Park And Ballylee, 1931', 197(n)

'Crazy Jane On God', 220(n)

'Cuchulain Comforted', 305

'Curse of Cromwell, The', 220(n)

'Dawn, The', 262

'Demon And Beast', 269-74

Yeats, W. B.—(cont.)
- 'Dialogue Of Self And Soul, A', 22, 70, 119, 220(n), 258(n), 289
- 'Double Vision Of Michael Robartes, The', 30, 66, 112, 300(n)
- 'Easter, 1916', 212
- 'Ego Dominus Tuus', 210
- 'Empty Cup, The', 60
- 'Ephemera', 276
- 'Fergus And The Druid', 255, 256
- 'Gift Of Harun Al-Rashid, The', 277
- 'Gyres, The', 268
- 'Happy Townland, The', 263
- 'He And She', 43
- 'Hosting Of The Sidhe, The', 185
- 'Hour Before Dawn, The', 267-8
- 'Kanva On Himself', 288
- 'Lamentation Of The Old Pensioner, The', 254
- 'Lapis Lazuli', 51, 294
- 'Last Confession, A', 236
- 'Man Who Dreamed Of Faeryland, The', 247
- 'Meditation In Time Of War, A', 62, 254
- 'Meditations In Time Of Civil War', 21, 66(n), 259-60
- 'Men Improve With The Years', 119
- 'Meru', 42(n)
- 'Mohini Chatterjee', 21, 247, 283-90
- 'Mongan Thinks Of His Past Greatness', 255-8
- 'Municipal Gallery Revisited, The', 297
- 'Nativity, A', 165-6
- 'News For The Delphic Oracle', 261, 306
- 'Nineteen Hundred And Nineteen', 21, 112
- 'Old Age Of Queen Maeve, The', 37, 284
- 'On A Picture Of A Black Centaur', 268-9
- 'On A Political Prisoner', 196, 197(n)
- 'On Woman', 276
- 'Pardon, Old Fathers', 210
- 'Parnell's Funeral', 297
- 'Parting', 242
- 'Paudeen', 291
- 'Phases Of The Moon, The', 76, 101, 111
- 'Prayer For My Daughter, A', 42, 103, 297, 302-3
- 'Ribh Denounces Patrick', 280
- 'Rose Tree, The', 212
- 'Running To Paradise', 261
- 'Sailing To Byzantium', 79, 284-5, 297, 305
- 'Saint And The Hunchback, The', 274
- 'Second Coming, The', 195(n), 200
- 'Secret Rose, The', 269
- 'Solomon And Sheba', 276, 277
- 'Solomon And The Witch', 130, 237, 247, 248, 276-83, 284, 303
- 'Song, A', 119
- 'Spur, The', 272
- 'Stare's Nest by My Window, The', 306
- 'Statues, The', 79, 100, 122, 127, 167, 247, 290-303
- 'Stream And Sun At Glendalough', 119, 275-6
- 'Three Beggars, The', 186-7
- 'Three Bushes, The', 19
- 'Three Songs To The One Burden', 103
- 'Three Things', 240
- 'To A Friend Whose Work Has Come To Nothing', 231(n)

Yeats, W. B.—(cont.)
  'Towards Break Of Day', 258
  'Tower, The', 92, 297
  'Two Trees, The', 251-4
  'Under The Moon', 248
  'Vacillation', 40, 165, 197, 248, 251, 254, 276
  'What Magic Drum', 167
  'What Was Lost', 289
  'Wheel, The', 247, 266-7
  'Wild Swans At Coole, The', 195(n), 198
  'Wisdom', 268
  'Withering Of The Boughs, The', 258

Yeats, Mrs. W. B., 243, 309